Facing Reality

Books by Cord Meyer

PEACE OR ANARCHY
FACING REALITY

HARPER & ROW, PUBLISHERS, New York
Cambridge, Hagerstown, Philadelphia, San Francisco,
London, Mexico City, São Paulo, Sydney
1817

FACING REALITY

From World Federalism
to the CIA

CORD MEYER

FIRST EDITION

Designer: Gloria Adelson

Library of Congress Cataloging in Publication Data

Meyer, Cord, 1920–
    Facing reality.
    Includes bibliographical references and index.
    1. United States. Central Intelligence Agency.
2. Meyer, Cord, 1920– 3. Intelligence officers—United
States—Biography. 4. World politics—1945– I. Title.
JK468.I6M49   327.1'2'0924 [B]   79-1677 ISBN 0-06-
013032-6

80 81 82 83 84 10 9 8 7 6 5 4 3 2 1

For my wife,
Starke Patteson Meyer

Contents

x

Acknowledgments

I OWE A PARTICULAR DEBT to those who encouraged me to write this book and who helped me to see it through to completion. Winthrop Knowlton, Chairman of the Board of Harper & Row, and Cass Canfield, Honorary Director, both approached me five years ago with the suggestion that my memoirs might be of general interest, and without their consistent support, I doubt that I would have undertaken the task. Erwin Glikes, when he was publisher at Harper & Row, provided helpful advice on form and content, while Ann Harris, who took over as editor when he left, did much to improve the clarity of presentation.

I am also indebted to Georgetown University for enabling me to complete the necessary research and to teach a course on the role of intelligence, with Professor Roy Godson, that helped me learn much from the questions of eager students. Peter Krogh, Dean of the School of Foreign Service at Georgetown, took an interest in the book from the beginning and was kind enough to make me a Research Associate, which allowed me to take advantage of a small office in the university library.

I also wish to express my appreciation to Richard Helms and Samuel Halpern, who as former colleagues at the CIA took the trouble to read the manuscript and to make useful suggestions correcting errors of fact and interpretation. Camilla Hersh, a Georgetown graduate student, was of great assistance in checking the source notes and putting them in proper order. Angela Steiger, my secretary, proved indispensable in deciphering my handwriting and never complained about long hours. Without her skill, the book could never have been completed in time to meet its deadline.

Finally, I want to thank my wife, Starke, for her generous encouragement and patient forbearance. I dedicate this book to her with love and respect.

Preface

In this book I've attempted to tell enough of the story of my life for the reader to understand a career that almost ended at its beginning in a night battle on a Pacific island. Autobiographical material and historical events are blended to explain how one individual American's search for a peaceful world led from the battlefield to the presidency of the United World Federalists, and finally to twenty-six years of active duty with the Central Intelligence Agency.

In retracing with me thirty years of involvement in the foreign affairs of our country, readers will, I hope, be persuaded to think afresh and to reconsider opinions that may be firmly held. Having played an active part in the unwritten history of our times, I have long felt an obligation to try to set the record straight on many controversial episodes and to explain motivations that have been widely misconstrued in secondhand accounts. Whether I have succeeded in shedding new light into the dark places of our recent past the reader will have to judge for himself.

This is not a book of revelations that seeks to attract a mass readership by making sensational disclosures of information previously kept secret. There has already been enough such material published by others for financial or ideological reasons. At the outset, I wish to make it clear that I submitted this text for security review by the CIA, in accordance with the obligation that Agency employees accept as a condition of their employment. Much as I dislike the idea of any kind of official censorship, I recognized the possibility that I might have inadvertently revealed information that could betray agents or still-secret intelligence methods to our adversaries. I was prepared to make changes in my manuscript only where genuine damage to the national security could be demonstrated and was quite unwilling to soften criticism of official behavior. As it turned out, very few changes proved to be necessary, and the counterintelligence experts of the KGB will be disappointed to find nothing in these pages that will help them to neutralize ongoing American intelligence operations.

Unlike so much of the recent literature on American intelligence, this book attempts to describe the activities of the CIA in their historical context, and not as if they took place in a friendly world where no powerful opponents exist. It has become fashionable for many Americans to believe that the arrogance and folly of their own government are the root cause of the troubles that beset us abroad. The fact that we are confronted with a real and determined opponent in the form of an expansionary Soviet state has often been dismissed as the chimera of unreconstructed cold war warriors. To dispel that illusion, I have drawn on my intelligence background in an effort to explain, in specific detail, just how the secretive machinery of the Soviet state operates and how it has scored major advances in recent years. Only by understanding Soviet purposes and methods can Americans come to agreement on the kind of foreign policy and intelligence organization needed to survive in a highly competitive world.

In my own case, I came only gradually and reluctantly to the conclusion that Americans faced a formidable adversary in the Soviet Union. My personal experience may help bring home to others the real nature of the dangers that we face. What I know now I didn't know to begin with. I had to learn it the hard way.

Chapter 1

War

FOR THE MEMBERS of my generation who spent our childhood and adolescence in the America of the 1930s, the Second World War did not come as an unexpected and unforeseen catastrophe, like an earthquake or tidal wave. Rather, the clouds that announced the approaching storm built up gradually on the horizon and cast shadows back across the landscape of our youth to trouble us from time to time with vague premonitions of impending disaster. For myself, I can remember the first time that the possibility of another world war entered my conscious mind. My twin brother and I were with our parents in a New York apartment in 1936 when we heard a newsboy shouting "Extra, Extra," in the street below. I was sent to buy a copy and can recall the black headlines proclaiming Hitler's invasion of the Rhineland. I listened as my father and mother discussed the bad news and agreed between themselves that war would eventually be unavoidable if the French and British did not act promptly to compel Hitler to withdraw his troops. My father had served in the First World War as a fighter pilot on the Western Front and my mother as a nurse in army hospitals in France, and, after they married, he had served in the diplomatic service abroad for a few years. As a result, I thought they knew what they were talking about

1

and did not forget their mood of somber apprehension.

In the years that followed, my family spent each summer in an old, rambling farmhouse on the New Hampshire coast. There were four boys. In addition to my twin brother and myself, there was another set of twins, four years younger. I cannot say that we worried much or thought deeply about the distant events that were conspiring to transform our lives. We played fiercely competitive tennis on a court that we kept up ourselves and shot crows in the pine woods behind our house. Ritualistically, we rode our bicycles to the beach each morning to lie on the sand and swim briefly in an Atlantic so cold that it numbed the limbs.

One morning in the summer of 1937, I remember leaning my bicycle against the rail outside the bath houses where the cars were parked and noticing that a summer neighbor and good friend of my parents, Ogden Nash, was sitting alone in his car, apparently lost in thought. In the bright sunshine, I walked over to ask why he didn't join us on the beach. He motioned to me to get into the front seat. He had the radio turned up, and the hysterical foreign voice rose in a crescendo. "Hitler?" I ventured. He nodded. "What does it mean?" I asked. After a long pause, he answered slowly, as if he hated to have to say it, "I'm afraid it means war." We sat in silence for a few minutes, contemplating that idea from our different perspectives. Finally, I made my way to the beach, and the sand burned my bare feet. Looking at the gulls wheeling over the glittering sea, I thought to myself that I had better make the most of such days because they were not going to last.

By the time I entered Yale from St. Paul's School in the fall of 1939, war had been declared in Europe, and the march of German armies across that continent reverberated like approaching thunder. To an extraordinary extent, the university preserved its academic calm and usual ways. To me and to many of my classmates, the wide learning and intellectual brilliance of most of our professors was a revelation after the more limited teaching ability we had experienced in our high schools. I felt as if the doors had been thrown open and I had been ushered into a vast and splendid chamber where delicacies had been laid out in such profusion that one hardly knew where to begin.

English verse from the metaphysical poets of the seventeenth century to the modern poetry of Yeats and Eliot was taught by Professor Maynard Mack in such a way that he left with us a permanent respect for the graceful majesty of that achievement and an ambition in some of us to try to write as well. Three times a week, Professor Robert Calhoun lectured without a single note to a packed auditorium on the history of Western philosophy from the ancient Greeks to the present day and challenged all our previous assumptions and lightly held beliefs with his explanation of those citadels of systematic inquiry into the nature of reality and man's place in the world that were erected from Plato's time to Immanuel Kant and Alfred North Whitehead. On a more mundane level, Nicholas Spykman, a veteran of the Dutch colonial service in Indonesia, explained in his thick accent and with a skeptical objectivity the workings of the nation-state system from the time of the Greek city-states to modern times and the inevitability of competition and armed conflict between sovereign nations in the absence of any enforceable supranational law.

The imminence of war heightened our appreciation of what we were being taught so brilliantly. Since the only career that most of us could foresee in the immediate future was that of a soldier, we felt free to take those courses in which we were genuinely interested, and we valued our new knowledge for its own sake and not as a stepping-stone to graduate study in medicine or law. As a concession to practicality, I did, however, take a course in military history and a cram course in the German language on the chance they might be useful in an uncertain future. In retrospect, if I have any criticism of what Yale had to offer, it was the concentration on Western civilization and the fact that we were not required to learn more about the Chinese, Muslim, and Indian cultures. In later days, when trying to comprehend developments in the far-flung corners of the world, I was only too aware of my own lack of knowledge of their rich and complicated past.

Those undergraduate years were not by any means entirely devoted to study. We took our athletics seriously. My twin brother and I both played on the varsity hockey team, he, much the better skater, as a forward and I as goalie. The floodlit arenas with their cheering crowds were an exciting relief from the library and lecture halls, even though in those days a goalie's job was more risky than today, since the face mask had not yet been developed. In another direction, I tried my hand at poetry and published some passable verse in *The Yale Lit* and became one of its editors. Then there were the football weekends and the debutante parties in New York during vacations, each one more lavish than the one before, as if the fathers of those young girls wished to stretch out the waning time of peace by having the music play till dawn.

During my sophomore year in 1940, the debate on campus began in earnest between those who argued for immediate American intervention on the side of beleaguered England and those who favored strict neutrality. In the columns of the *Yale Daily News* and in the debates of the Political Union, the idealistic wing of the America First movement urged that we stay out of the ancient quarrels of the corrupt continent and concentrate instead on building a just society in our own land that could serve as a model and example to the world. The anti-war writing of the thirties and the history we had been taught of the bloody and inconclusive folly of the First World War led many to support this isolationist position. The interventionists stressed the horrors of the Nazi dictatorship and warned that, if we did not come to England's aid, we would be left alone to face Hitler's conquering armies. There were some who felt so strongly that England must be helped in its extremity that they quietly excused themselves from these collegiate debates and volunteered for service with the British and Canadian forces. The university was about as evenly divided on the issue as the country as a whole, where the closeness of the division was indicated by the fact that Congress extended the draft by the margin of a single vote.

I took no public part in this mounting controversy, having decided by that time that we had no choice but to fight if Hitler was to be stopped. I was sure that events would eventually force us into the war and was determined to use the remaining time to complete as much of my education as possible. However, in our dormitory rooms, private arguments flared long into the night between old friends. One of my friends, Arthur Howe, was a Christian pacifist and believed there was nothing that could justify killing another human being. I maintained with Plato that a citizen could not accept the protection of the laws and the education provided by the state and then refuse to obey those laws when they required him to bear arms in the state's justifiable defense. We did not convince each other, but Howe proved the strength of his convictions by departing to join the American Field Service, in which he drove ambulances for the British in the fighting in North Africa.

For all of us, the discussion came to an abrupt end on December 7, 1941. The Japanese attack on Pearl Harbor united the university community as it did the entire country, and the only question left for debate was which branch of the armed forces to join. The long lines of volunteers outside the recruiting stations made us acutely uncomfortable in the refuge of our academic existence. During Christmas vacation, my roommate, Charles Hickox, and I went to Washington and tried to enlist in the training program for Marine Corps officers. The Marine colonel was sympathetic but explained that the training camps were full and that if we went back to finish college, there would be room enough for us on graduation. Yale abolished the summer vacation, and by taking a few extra courses I managed to graduate in September of 1942. By November, I found myself enlisted as a private in the Marine officer training course at Quantico, Virginia.

In twelve weeks of intensive training in everything from close-order drill to weapons familiarization to map reading, the veteran Marine sergeants tried to transform us from undisciplined college boys into reasonably competent second lieutenants. On accepting our commissions, we were only too well aware of our shortcomings as we proceeded under orders to the large Marine staging base in North Carolina. After a few weeks of waiting, I was assigned to a replacement battalion and on the thirtieth of April 1943 was riding westward across the country on a troop train to San Diego. An excerpt of that date from the journal that I kept intermittently during the war gives some idea of how one young soldier felt as the long journey began, although my literary pretensions are all too evident.

I've worked hard all day loading men and equipment and have had no time for thought but, as evening came on, I sat at the train window and enjoyed the lengthening shadows across these meadows and patches of woods. The green is still much variegated and the new, light green of spring in evidence against the lush foliage. In the fields, men and women looked up from their work to wave and call encouragement and our men waved back. I had one of those rare moments when the war is reduced to its simplest and most honorable terms. It seemed that we, the young and the strong, were going out as the champions and defenders of the people in the fields and everywhere in this wide country to fight for our heritage against the inhuman invader. It was a very strong feeling, and one could easily for the sake of one's peace of mind allow oneself to consider it true. But I know too well that the invader is not inhuman and in all probability considers himself as a loyal defender of a great cause. The war is infinitely complex and so are the reasons for which it is fought. How I wish it was all as clear and demonstrably just as it seemed then.

A few days later the battalion was marched aboard a troopship in San Diego harbor, while a small band played the Marine Hymn and a few spectators waved good-by. To mark the occasion, I made the following entry in my journal:

10 May '43—I write this entry in a most awkward position, leaning on my elbow in the lower bunk of three on a troopship. I have just returned from the bridge, where I watched the misty hills of California fade into the horizon of the limitless Pacific. It was with mingled feelings of regret and anticipation that I turned from my last glimpse of my own country and faced westward where my future lies, among the fabulous and dangerous islands. Slowly the sun sank and evening with its clear stars and half a moon came on. The wideness of the placid ocean, the steady light of the moon and the bright star above the masthead seemed to assert a peace that nothing could disturb, beyond and aside from man and all his silly quarrels and pointless ambitions. I let the calm envelop me and from the very fact of nature's indifference to our struggle I derived satisfaction, sure that a thousand years hence the moon will shine with the same resplendent peace on the long Pacific swell. Just at the height of my disinterestedness, glorying in my knowledge of man's insignificance, the sentry passed with rifle slung below me. His watchful figure reminded me that I also was a man, that I was committed to the play in progress, and must act out my part faithfully to the end.

After an uneventful crossing, made longer by the zigzag course we steered in order to evade enemy submarines, we finally sighted our destination, the island of American Samoa, known by its native citizens as Tutuila. Full of literary descriptions of the South Seas derived from Conrad, Stevenson, and Maugham, I tried (too hard) to do our landfall justice in the following entry in my journal:

22 May '43—Yesterday, we stood on the bridge and watched a blue cloud on the horizon gradually resolve itself into definite land, reaching abruptly out of the restless sea that for eleven days had been empty, the horizon limitless. Land seemed a mystery after so much tossing waste, and I could imagine the green cliffs under sea towering up through the iridescent depths to break with final triumph into the light of blue waves and sun. In the long distance, the land was blue. On nearing it became a deep green darkly shadowed like a green satin mantle carelessly flung. Finally we slipped into the harbor bounded on each side by tall cliffs clothed in the thickest green. Through our glasses we could see the natives wearing the skirt-like lava-lava, all in bright colors. Then suddenly darkness fell and it rained. In the wet, we disembarked, happy to find beneath our feet the stability of earth.

At that time, Samoa was being used by the Marine Corps as a training base in which to apply the experience that had been learned the hard way in the bitter fighting in the jungles of Guadalcanal, since its terrain was very similar. Our group of twenty or so newly commissioned second lieutenants quickly discovered that the Marine high command fully shared our own doubts about our ability to lead troops in action. We were abruptly informed that we were to consider ourselves privates again and that as a group we would have to take a four-week course in jungle warfare, taught by officers and sergeants who had survived the Guadalcanal campaign and learned its costly lessons.

Since the Japanese had excelled in conducting ambushes and attacks under the cover of darkness in dense jungle, most of our training maneuvers took place at night. Using the dim light of our compass needles and counting every step, we learned to navigate by dead reckoning in the sea of matted growth. It was not all hard work, as an entry in my journal indicates.

8 June '43—Yesterday evening we finished a patrol by a native village and by the wall of a ruined church we rested our weapons and ate our canned rations in the coolness of the tropic

night. There were many little native children, who gathered about us as we ate, eager for pieces of sugar and G.I. chocolate. They sang songs in English for us, including that song which is inseparable from the Marine Corps everywhere: "You are my sunshine, my only sunshine." It is typical of really popular war songs in that it deals not at all with war or patriotism but with the simple longing of the wandering soldier for his home and his long ago girl. Inside the old church with its mouldering white walls and Spanish type architecture, a little brown-skinned girl chanted cadence that she must have picked up from the marching Marines. While we were singing and laughing with the children, a parent chided severely from a nearby fâle (native hut), and the children cautioned us to be quiet. It was prayer time, and the Catholic prayers rose in a long undertone. It is a strange thing the way these people have adopted that old, demanding religion to their easy ways and pagan lives.

By the time the course was over, we had learned the ways of the jungle and how to use its clinging vines for ambush and camouflage. I summed up our new confidence in our professional ability in the following journal excerpt:

29 June '43—No entry for so long because of the demands of this Jungle Warfare School, which left little enough time for rest and none at all for writing. The time, however, was well spent, and I now look forward with new confidence in my knowledge and ability to whatever the close-mouthed future may offer. If it be the demolition of a railroad bridge, a reconnaissance patrol deep into enemy country, a night assault on entrenched positions, the erection of barbed wire entanglements at night, I know myself to be capable of it. The accident of being born at the particular time I was, a long succession of complex historical causes, which no one can certainly unravel, an individual destiny have forced these arts upon me and I who long to build in hope have learned to destroy.

After a few days rest, my friends and I were assigned as officers to the newly formed 22d Marine Regiment, which was being built up to strength on Samoa by a continuous flow of new troops from the States. I was given command of a machine gun platoon in the First

Battalion. During the following months, we marched and counter-marched across the mountainous spine of that island in a series of field maneuvers growing in size from company to battalion to regimental. Finally, the word came in mid-November that we were being transferred to the Hawaiian Islands for final training in assault landings in the amphibious tractors that had been developed to cope with the coral reefs that surrounded the Japanese-held island citadels in the central Pacific. I tried to describe my feelings on departure in a journal entry.

18 Nov. '43—There is a nostalgic regret attached to any irrevocable leave taking. So it was that, as the truck loaded with troops and sea bags rolled down the dusty familiar road into Leone Village, I looked with particular intentness and some regret upon that scene I knew I should never see again. It impressed me then as a beautiful if primitive view. The two heavily jungled arms of the land stretched out to embrace the glittering blue of Leone Bay, across the mouth of which the reef runs to draw a white line of surf. On the bend of the bay is the native village and the two partially decayed churches standing white against the encompassing green. In the middle of the village, the road forks, one branch running along the coast and the other down to Pago-Pago. We took the latter route for the last time and I watched the jungles and villages of that twelve miles of road disappear behind me forever. As we passed them, I repeated to myself their fascinating names, Malaeeola, Futingu, Ili-Ili, Pavaii, Mopazonga, the Marine Cemetery, Mormon Valley, Utilei and finally as the road parallels the indented coast from which the green hills go back steeply we rounded the last headland and into the beautiful harbor.

Though these last six months have not been the most happy or fruitful of my life by any stretch of the imagination, I looked back at the fading silhouette of Tutuila this morning and reflected. When one takes a final departure from any scene, one knows the meaning of mortality. Leone Village shall never see me more; to that place I am as good as dead. Just as the dying man must devour with his eyes the last of physical reality so I looked back closely and attempted to imprint all that I saw indelibly upon my memory. Thus, in my head, the bay, the churches, the jungled headlands, the open fâles shall enjoy a vicarious existence and have a shadowy part in all my journeyings.

What does that scene mean to me, for according to the nature of one's life in each environment, those surroundings take on a symbolic meaning, a quality equivalent to what one did and thought and felt. Leone is the symbol of a primitive life, the living example of what it means to merely be "natural," to exist without ambition, or ideal or restraint. I learn that what is unusual and unique is not necessarily best, that the longing of the super-civilized for the primitive-natural life is romantic and illusory. In other words, the search for the strange and exceptional is as nothing compared to the quest for what is normal and eternal in human experience. Thus Leone marked the final step in the awakening of him who was once an incurable dreamer, the final decision of a man to put away childish things, to see things as they are, instead of as one wishes them to be.

After completing two months of amphibious training on the island of Maui in the Hawaiian chain, the regiment was combat loaded onto troopships and sailed westward to launch the attack on the Marshall Islands, which the Japanese had transformed into fortresses. Our particular objective turned out to be Eniwetok Atoll, situated 2400 miles west of Pearl Harbor. Its string of low-lying islands and coral reefs surrounded a deep lagoon that provided one of the best anchorages in the whole vast expanse of the Central Pacific. We sailed into the lagoon on February 16, 1944, and watched with satisfaction that evening as the cruisers and battleships raked with naval gunfire Engebi Island with its airstrip in the north of the atoll, which was our battalion's assigned objective. Before dawn the next morning, we climbed into our amphibious tractors with all our weapons and ammunition. As the sun rose, we formed into successive assault waves and headed toward the beach, where we could see our carrier pilots making their last strafing runs. Since mine was a machine gun platoon, we were in the second wave, and I remember passing under the looming bow of a great battleship, from the deck of which the lucky sailors cheered us on. As this was the first battle experience for most of us, the mood was one of excited anticipation, and we could not believe that after such devastating naval gunfire there could be much resistance. We were to learn better, and thirty-six hours later, when the island was declared secure, we knew a great deal more about ourselves, the nature of the enemy, and the tragic reality of war.

Only three days later the battalion was again thrown into the assault, this time against Parry Island at the southern end of the atoll. The fighting here was more intense, since the Japanese seemed more numerous and better prepared, but within forty-eight hours the battle was over. In the two landings, I had lost five of the forty-four men in my platoon and a disproportionately high number among the rifle platoon leaders had been killed or wounded, as was always the case since it was their job to lead each attack.

We were astonished by the behavior of the Japanese, although we had been amply warned. The sensible thing for the Japanese on Eniwetok to have done would have been to run up a flag of surrender when they first saw our armada of battleships, cruisers, and heavily loaded troopships steam into the lagoon. Among most Western armies, it would have been no disgrace to surrender to such an overwhelming show of force. However, they chose to fight to the last man and to take as many of us with them as they could before they died. With their last bullet, they would commit suicide rather than allow themselves to be captured. If they were wounded they would hide a grenade so that those of us who attempted to help would be blown up with them. Only those most seriously wounded or those stunned into unconsciousness by a shell burst could be taken prisoner. We had a grudging respect for their suicidal bravery.

On their bodies and in their shelter trenches, we found letters that, when translated, shed some light on their determination to die fighting. Devoted to their emperor, they believed that to die in battle in his service was their highest duty. To allow oneself to be taken prisoner was to condemn oneself to permanent exile from the close-knit national family and to bring shame and dishonor on one's self and one's relatives. To these compelling motives, there was added the pervasive influence of official propaganda, which, we discovered, wildly misled these isolated garrisons as to the actual course of events and the progress of the war. One Japanese sergeant of the Imperial Marines, who had been captured while unconscious, announced defiantly on being brought aboard our ship that we might succeed in capturing Eniwetok but we would never win back California and

Montana. It was hard to convince him that the Japanese army had not succeeded in conquering and occupying our entire West Coast.

After we had buried our dead, we boarded the transports again and were shipped south to Guadalcanal, where by this time a large Marine base had been established. New recruits from the States arrived to fill the holes in our depleted ranks, and once more we began the arduous training cycle, pushing our way through the sweltering jungle and marching until our clothes were wet beneath the glare of the tropic sun. At night by the dim light of lanterns in our tents, we pored over maps of the Pacific and speculated what new island citadel we would have to storm before we reached the well-defended beaches of Japan. Fully aware now of the fanatical determination of the waiting enemy, we saw the road ahead as infinitely long and perilous. There was not one of us who did not in his own mind realize that the chances of his surviving long enough to see the end of that road were remote. The entries in my journal became less frequent and they reflect a new mood of bleak resignation. The following entry is representative.

21 April '44—It has been a long time since I have made any entry in this journal. Tonight I write by candle light which flares and flickers in a light breeze through the tent from the ocean. I am in another place, another tropical island much like all the rest, camped by the eternal ocean, by whose banks we train, on whose broad back we ride and on whose beaches we live or die as fate decrees. News of new deaths of old friends and a sudden awareness of the hopeless blankness of the future have put me in a foul mood. The remembrance of the battle has dimmed and with it my thankfulness for being merely alive. I am no longer content with merely breathing but begin to wish for what makes life full and rich, love, friendship, work that one believes in and hope in the future. Instead, I face the prospect of another desperate adventure but this time not with innocent eagerness but with resigned determination.

Finally, the word came that our next objective was the Mariana Islands, a new giant step of a thousand miles across the Pacific and within bombing range of Japan. The Second Marine Division, with the assistance of an army division, was assigned the task of capturing

Saipan and Tinian. Our regiment joined with the Fourth Marines was to become the First Provisional Marine Brigade. We were to stand by in floating reserve off Saipan and Tinian until victory was assured and then together with the Third Marine Division and an army division move southward to attack Guam, an American possession that had been captured by the Japanese in the early days of the war.

The plan made strategic sense to us, and there was a certain relief in knowing that the long days of uncertain waiting were at an end. We were combat loaded onto LSTs, landing ships whose bows opened to allow the amphibious tractors in the hold to go down a ramp into the sea. There were only enough bunks for the officers and a few of the men, and the rest of the battalion had to sleep on the open deck, taking refuge under tarpaulins when it rained. For anxious days, our convoy circled lazily at sea, while just over the horizon the Marines of the Second Division fought and paid dearly for every foot of ground on Saipan, where the Japanese were heavily entrenched. The ship's signal center could intercept the radios of our tank commanders on the island as they attempted to coordinate their supporting fire for the advancing infantry, and those excited and sometimes desperate voices gave us dramatic evidence of how intense the fighting was.

One evening, flying low over the water out of the setting sun, three Japanese torpedo bombers attacked our convoy, and the alarm for battle stations sounded. One plane came directly for us but was hit by antiaircraft fire and veered off. I could see the sun glistening on the pilot's goggles just before he crashed into the sea and watched the torpedo's harmless wake as it missed our bow by a few feet. Finally, the powers that be decided that we would not be needed to reinforce the troops ashore. Because of the long delay, we had to double back to Eniwetok to replenish our supplies before proceeding to Guam.

On this leg of our voyage, a strange incident occurred that I was reminded of later when reading *The Caine Mutiny.* The only clothes our men had were the dungarees they wore, and in view of the scarcity of fresh water the only way to wash them was to tie the clothes to ropes over the ship's rail and let them drag in the sea. Our ship's captain was a navy lieutenant, recently promoted from being a third mate in the merchant marine. His newfound authority over a battalion of Marines had obviously gone to his head, and he enjoyed giving peremptory and unreasonable orders. On this occasion, he decided that there was a danger that the clothes over the side might be torn loose and form a kind of trail, like Hansel and Gretel's crumbs, by which a Japanese submarine might locate and destroy us. He, therefore, ordered that the practice of dragging clothes over the side should cease and desist.

We passed these orders on reluctantly to our men and were not surprised to find them ignored. The next morning before dawn the captain arose to find the clothes still dragging in the sea. In a rage, he ordered two of his unfortunate sailors to take fire axes and to cut the lines. They had cut no more than two when the outraged Marines seized both sailors and threw them overboard. Lights flashed and emergency signals passed throughout the convoy. Our destroyer escort circled back, picked up the two sailors, and deposited them safely back aboard our ship, wet and bedraggled. The captain retired to his stateroom where he remained until we arrived in Eniwetok. The ship's doctor certified him as having a bad case of malaria, and he returned to the States. His executive officer, an eminently reasonable and competent man, took over command; the ropes with the clothing attached continued to drag over the side and harmony reigned throughout the rest of our voyage. If it was a mutiny, it was quickly over, and nobody talked about it.

Freshly provisioned, we sailed from Eniwetok and a few days later, on July 20, joined the armada that lay poised for attack off the beaches of Guam. As dawn broke the next day, we climbed again into our amphibious tractors and in successive waves made toward the shore, which was almost entirely obscured by the smoke from exploding shells and rockets. What happened next I tried to convey in a short story entitled "Waves of Darkness," which I wrote immediately after the war and which was first published in the *Atlantic Monthly*. I chose the fictional form as opposed to a chronological narrative in the first person in order to achieve dramatic intensity and an objective universality beyond what a personal memoir could suggest. However, the events described in the story are a faithful description of what actually happened to me during my twenty-four-hour participation in the battle. The lieutenant in the story is obviously me, and his thoughts are mine as best I could reconstruct them. The story has appeared in a number of anthologies, but I include it here because it sums up my experience of war, which had much to do with what followed.

Chapter 2

Waves of Darkness

"WAVES OF DARKNESS"[1]

THEY LAY IN A HOLE just wide enough to lie in side by side, and not more than a foot deep. They had arranged that one should keep guard while the other rested. Every two hours they changed.

Lying on his stomach, the lieutenant was able to prop himself up with his elbows to see over the mound of dirt. He held the Thompson gun in his arms and kept two grenades in readiness by his right hand. The even breathing of his friend comforted him with the knowledge that he was not alone. During the day, physical action and the necessity for decision occupied his mind. Now he had nothing to do but wait and watch. Each minute of waiting made the next more difficult.

He tried to remember the surrounding terrain as it had looked before the light failed. He looked for the broken stump of a coconut tree and the large boulder whose relative position he had deliberately impressed on his memory as he dug his hole. He had memorized the harmless shadows so that he might know the shadows of the real enemy for whom he waited. A heavy layer of clouds obscured the tropic stars and he could see nothing but the formless night, isolating in worlds apart each small hole with its occupants.

He continued to stare into the blackness with wide-open, unblinking eyes, and found fear crouched menacingly at the end of every

15

corridor of thought. He deliberately attempted to lose his fear, and the hysteria that mounted in his heart, in another emotion, and strove to awaken lust by summoning up pornographic memories. It proved a poor substitute, and he could find hardly a passing interest in the indecent scenes that he paraded before his mind's eye.

Then he attempted to rationalize his fear. What was he afraid of, he asked himself. Death, was the simple answer. He knew that it might come at any moment out of the dark, carried on the bayonets of a banzai charge or dealt skillfully by the well-placed hand grenade of an infiltrating scout. He could not deny this fact on which his fear nourished and grew. It was inevitable that the enemy would attack during the night. They must know how thinly the line was held and that they would never again have such an opportunity. It was merely a question of time.

Most of his companions had a superstitious faith in their own luck. No matter how great the odds, the vast majority of his men always preferred to believe that though others might fall, they would not. It was only on the basis of this conviction that they found the courage for the risks they had to take. He preferred to think death inevitable. By absolving himself of all hope prior to each battle, he had found himself prepared for the most desperate eventualities. Now, with an effort of the will, he urged his mind down this accustomed path of reasoning. He stripped the night of its hideous pretensions to find only death, an old familiar companion. Though his fear remained, it became controllable, and this was all that he asked.

He turned his head sharply toward the sound of a gun fired off-shore. An illuminating shell burst overhead with a soft popping sound, like the breaking of a Fourth of July rocket. For fear of being silhouetted against the light, he allowed only his eyes and the top of his helmet to project above the rim of dirt. He knew the shell was fired from a friendly destroyer lying off the beach, but it must have been ordered because of the suspicion of enemy movement. With a scarcely audible hissing the flare settled slowly down.

The blasted coconut trees cast deceptive shadows that danced in slow rhythm as the flare swayed to and fro in its descent. The unearthly, pallid light accentuated rather than dispelled the threat of horror that the night held. It was impossible to distinguish shadow from substance. Every small depression in the ground was filled with darkness, and the line of thick jungle growth some sixty yards ahead presented an impenetrable question. He could make out nothing for certain. Each natural object assumed enormous and malevolent proportions in the shadows that lengthened toward him. He felt as if he were lost in the evil witch forest of some ancient folk tale and he shivered involuntarily.

With his finger on the trigger, he longed to let go a burst of fire in defiance, but restrained the impulse. In the game he played, the one who first revealed his position became the hunted and was lucky to escape with his life. The flare settled on the ground and burned up brightly for a moment. Then the night surged back. It was as if he sat in a theater where the scenes are silently shifted in the dark. Even more than before, the darkness seemed a curtain behind which some fantastic tragedy waited. Again the destroyer fired and a shell burst.

He glanced behind him and saw the village they had paid for so dearly during the day. It sprawled desolately beneath the uncertain light. No roof remained, and only a few of the walls stood upright, like the remnants of a decaying skeleton. It seemed an archaeological curiosity from the long-vanished past instead of a place where men had lived forty-eight hours ago. When the naval bombardment began, the natives had fled to the hills and left their town to the foreigners who fought in a war the inhabitants could not understand and the outcome of which could leave them no different than before. He guessed that there were many who had fought bravely, on both sides, who understood it all no better than the natives and had as little stake in eventual victory. The flare sank to the earth behind the village. Ghastly, still as the dead that lay among its wreckage, he saw it in the flare's sick light as the symbol of all war.

The ship fired three more shells at irregular intervals. He waited for the fourth in vain. Each silent minute seemed a tiny weight added on a scale that slowly tipped toward destruction. He allowed himself to think of the dawn and looked hopefully for the long, thin streak of gray in the east, as if by some special dispensation the sun might rise six hours early. The day appeared infinitely remote, and he thought of it as one dreams of some distant and charming country which one has no real hope of ever seeing.

The small sound of a stick broken near-by focused all his senses. He twisted his body quickly and brought the Thompson gun to bear in the direction from which the sound came. He held his breath and the blood drummed in his ears. His friend felt the movement and inched over onto his stomach. Together they stared fruitlessly into the blackness. Gradually the tension left his limbs, and he allowed his breath to escape softly.

"Guess it was nothing."

"Sand crabs probably. What time is it?"

Cupping his watch in his hands, as if the slightest wind might blow out the light, he made out the tiny green figures. It was four minutes past one.

"Past time. Your turn," he said.

He felt for the two grenades and put them into the hands of his friend. Without words they traded weapons.

He rolled over on his back. Unbuckling his chin strap, he rested his head in the leather harness of the helmet and stretched out his legs. There was hardly room for them, and he pushed his feet into the soft dirt at the end of the shelter trench. His breathing came easier. He was aware that there was just as much danger as ever, but he liked the feeling that he was no longer directly responsible. There was nothing now that he could do to prevent their being surprised, and his eyes closed. He did not attempt to sleep. Perhaps after two or three nights like this one, he thought, he would be tired enough. But not yet.

A cold, thin rain began to fall. He buttoned his dungaree jacket to the throat and hugged his body. There was nothing to do but lie there under the open sky. The earth in the narrow hole turned slowly to a sticky mud, and his clothes clung to him. A long spasm of shivering shook him. He wondered whether it was caused by cold or fear. The rain seemed a wanton addition to his misery. Slanting down, it pinned him to the earth.

For a moment he was overwhelmed by self-pity.

But gradually the rain no longer seemed directed especially against him. He felt its huge indifference and imagined how the tiny drops fell on all that lay without shelter beneath the night. The rain merged with the saltier oblivion of the sea, each drop leaving a transient ripple on its broad impassive face. It seeped down to the roots of the tropic plants and nourished that abundant life. With an equal carelessness it streaked the dirt on the faces of the living and washed the blood from the bodies of the friends he'd lost. He imagined the rain falling through the dark on their upturned, quiet faces.

2

Slowly he went over in his mind the names of the men of his command. Of the platoon of forty-four who had climbed up the steep beach in the morning, thirty remained to dig their holes in the evening. The bodies of the others lay behind to mark the path of the advance.

The lieutenant could form no continuous picture of what had happened. With terrible clarity a particular scene would present itself, only to be replaced by another equally sharp but unrelated vision. It was as if he watched magic-lantern slides whose logical order had been completely disarranged.

He saw himself crossing a rice paddy and signaling his first squad to follow. There was the familiar whistle of an approaching shell and he flattened himself. When he looked up, the three men who had been carrying the machine gun lay sprawled in the open field. He ran back but they were past help. In the awkward attitudes of death, they looked like small boys who had flung themselves down to cry over some little sorrow. He wondered at the brute chance that chose them and left him alive.

He saw again the still body of one of the enemy collapsed against the wall of a trench with his head thrown back. The man was obviously dead, but in a moment of childish bravado he lifted his carbine and fired a bullet through the throat. The body did not move, and the high-cheekboned Oriental face continued lost in its impenetrable dream. A thin fountain of dark blood sprang from the hole in the throat and spilled down over the wrinkled uniform.

He stood staring and ashamed, feeling that he had wantonly violated the defenseless dead. One of his men walked past him and stood over the corpse. Casually and with a half smile he swung his rifle butt against the head, which wobbled from side to side under the impact. Jocularly, as if death were an intimate joke they shared together, his man addressed the corpse. "You old son of a bitch," he said, and there was a note of admiration in the remark.

He remembered standing behind a tank trying to direct its fire. A great bull whip seemed to crack by his ears and he fell to the ground as if some enormous hand had jerked him roughly by the shirt front. Scrambling to cover, he ripped open his dungaree jacket and found only a small welt. With resignation, for he understood that he could not continue to escape, he climbed to his feet. The bullet had torn through his breast pocket and cut the tip of the cigar he carried there. Though his fingers trembled, he lit the cigar with a melodramatic gesture and pretended a courage that he did not feel.

The day came crowding back. Again he was lying beside Everett, the youngest man in his platoon, under the remorseless sun. The boy had been shot through the abdomen and chest. A medical corpsman joined him and together they attempted to stop the flow of blood. Because of the continuous enemy fire, they had to keep close to the ground while they wound the bandage around the body. The flies gathered. The boy's head arched backward. His mouth was wide open, gasping for air. Both the lieutenant and the corpsman knew in their hearts that there was no hope for the wounded man, but they tightened the bandages mechanically, as one might shut a house at evening to keep the night out.

"I've got to leave," he said to the corpsman, who kept waving the flies away with one hand while he felt the failing pulse in the boy's wrist. "Has he got any chance?"

"Always a chance, Lieutenant," was the cheerful reply. "Now if we had him on a good clean operating table we'd bring him round in no time." The corpsman smoothed the hair back from the wet forehead with a tender gesture. Then, realizing there was no operating table and no need for professional optimism, he shook his head wordlessly and finally added, "I'll keep the flies away. They bother him."

When some time later the lieutenant returned, the corpsman had gone to other duties and Everett lay dead and alone, the bandages dark with his blood. He had liked Everett best of all his men, and because of the boy's youthfulness felt particularly responsible for him. He remembered a letter he'd had to censor, which Everett had written to his mother just before the landing. It was full of hope and assurances that there was no need to worry. Now the body was covered with flies and already he thought he could detect the odor of decay. He caught the slight form under the armpits and dragged it to where a low bush cast a dark pool of shade. The feet, dragging limply, left two furrows in the sandy soil. Opening the pack, he took out the poncho and wrapped it carefully around the body, and stuck the rifle, bayonet first, into the earth as a marker for the burial detail.

Out on the oil-smooth sea the battleships and transports stood silhouetted against the burning sky. As he stared at them, he was surprised to find his vision blurred with tears. An unreasoning indignation shook him against all who had placed Everett where he lay. For the frightened enemy that shot Everett and was probably already dead he had pity. "But I wish," he thought, "that all those in power, countrymen and enemy alike, who decided for war, all those who profit by it lay dead with their wealth and their honors and that Everett stood upright again with his life before him."

3

Then the present claimed him. His friend was shaking him gently by the shoulder and whispering, "Listen." The rain had stopped but the earth still smelled of it. Then he heard. Overhead there was the beating of tremendous wings. He twisted quickly onto his belly and pressed his face into the dirt as the night's stillness exploded. The shell landed well to their rear. Then, like pond water gradually rearranging itself after it has been disturbed, the fragments of silence fell back into place.

Quickly he buckled on his helmet. He listened. Sharp and distinct came the sound for which he waited. It was the crack of a gun, but the pitch was higher than that of the destroyer's and the sound came from inland. Slowly he counted the seconds before the shell reached them. Then again the great wings beat overhead, only this time louder and more insistently. "The angel of death passing," he thought. The shell crashed to their rear still, but closer.

"Goddamn them, George. They're walking the stuff in on us."

"Must have somebody spotting for them right near," was the almost inaudible reply.

Because the unknown and imagined were more terrible than the known, he found relief in the certainty that the enemy's plans were no longer a total mystery. After adjusting their artillery fire onto the thinly defended line with a single gun, they obviously intended to open a barrage with all their batteries and probably follow it closely with a banzai charge.

The distant gun fired once again. The enforced inaction became almost intolerable. They must cower in their holes while the invisible enemy deliberately found the mathematical formula for their destruction. Each explosion closer than the last was like the footfalls of some enormous beast. The shell crashed in front of them this time instead of behind. The trap was set. In order to spring it the enemy gunners had only to split the difference between the range settings on the last two shots.

"Bracketed," George said.

It did not enter his head to pray. His mind was washed vacant by fear, and long fits of trembling ran through his body as he clutched the wet earth. The enemy batteries opened fire simultaneously and sent their shells curving through the night. Enough presence of mind remained for him to raise himself just off the ground with his elbows and toes in order to avoid the dangerous shock of a near miss.

The barrage fell on them. It ripped and plowed the earth into smoking craters and lit the night with the hot flash of the explosions. The deep roar of the shell bursts mingled with the high, despairing wail of jagged splinters of steel flung at random against the night. Indiscriminately the shells dropped.

A near miss erupted in a geyser of flame and sound close to their hole. His head rang with the concussion, and the fine earth sifted down over their bodies. The stinging smell of the high explosives lingered in his nostrils for a moment to remind him how tenuous was his hold on life. The casual purposelessness of the destruction appalled him. One moment you lived and the next you were snuffed out like an insect—no courage, no skill, no strength could make one iota of difference. He pinned his faith on the narrowness of their small hole and endured, helpless and insignificant.

As suddenly as it had begun the barrage lifted. Softly, he worked the bolt of his weapon back and forth to assure himself it was ready. "If they're going to come, they'll come now," he thought. By contrast the silence was more profound than ever and stretched like a precarious bridge from minute to minute, until the beating of his heart seemed to fill the world. The darkness pressed down on him, and the air itself seemed too thick to breathe. Tightening his grip on the weapon, he noticed that his hand was wet and slipped along the smooth wood of the stock.

"What in hell are they waiting for?" his friend murmured.

He did not answer. With a detachment that astonished him, he found himself suddenly able to look down on the spectacle as if he were no longer involved in it. On the one side, he saw his countrymen lying in their scooped-out holes with their backs to the sea, each one shivering with fright yet determined to die bravely. On the other, the poor peasantry from which the enemy recruited his soldiers were being herded into position like cattle, to be driven in a headlong charge against the guns. For a moment it appeared impossible to him that what was about to take place could actually occur. Adult human beings of the civilized world did not slaughter one another. There must be some mistake which could be corrected before it was too late.

What if he should get out of his hole and explain the matter reasonably to both sides? "Fellow human beings," he would begin. "There are very few of us here who in private life would kill a man for any reason whatever. The fact that guns have been placed in our hands and some of us wear one uniform and some another is no excuse for the mass murder we are about to commit. There are differences between us, I know, but none of them worth the death of one man. Most of us are not here by our own choice. We were taken from our peaceful lives and told to fight for reasons we cannot understand. Surely we have far more in common than that which temporarily separates us. Fathers, go back to your children, who are in need of you. Husbands, go back to your young wives, who cry in the night and count the anxious days. Farmers, return to your fields, where the grain rots and the house slides into ruin. The only certain fruit of this insanity will be the rotting bodies upon which the sun will impartially shine tomorrow. Let us throw down these guns that we hate. With the morning, we shall go on together and in charity and hope build a new life and a new world."

4

A single rifle shot interrupted his imaginary eloquence. "What a fool I am!" he thought. Suspended in that last moment when the whole black wall of the night seemed a dam about to break and engulf him, he felt utterly helpless. All the events of the past seemed to have marched inevitably toward this point in time and space, where he lay shivering between an implacable enemy and the indifferent sea. To object or to struggle was like shouting into a big wind that tears the words from the corners of one's mouth before even oneself can hear them. He, his friend, his countrymen, the enemy, were all dying leaves cast on the black waters of some mysterious river. Even now the current ran faster and the leaves whirled toward the dark lip of destruction.

The echoes of the rifle shot were lost now, and the wave of silence mounted and hung poised. Catching his tongue between his teeth, he held himself rigid to prevent the trembling. Then, at last the night was fulfilled, and the listeners had their reward. A long-drawn-out cry of furious exultation rose from the line of jungle growth, wavered, then rose higher in barbaric triumph.

"Now," his friend breathed.

A crescendo of rifle fire swept down the line in answer. The steady rattle of machine guns sounded in his ears. Rocked by conflicting emotions, hoping all, fearing all, confused by the roar of sound, he knew nothing but that he must defend himself. An illuminating shell burst. In its brief light he could make out figures stooped and running. Smoke swirled from his machine guns and obscured the scene with monstrous shapes. Flame from the muzzles leaped against the dark. Holding his weapon ready, he could find nothing to shoot at. The strange foreign voices, high with excitement, seemed all about him.

A bullet snapped overhead. He ducked instinctively. Nearby, a man screamed in the universal language of pain and he could not tell if it was friend or enemy. All human thought and emotion withered and died. Animal-like, he crouched, panting. Like a cornered beast run to earth at last, he awaited the fierce hunters. He could hear them at their savage work, uttering harsh, short cries of triumph, and he imagined them plunging the long bayonets through the twisting bodies of his companions. He could see nothing.

Then a voice began shouting, running the words together in an incomprehensible stream of speech. The firing faded to sporadic rifle shots.

"They're falling back," whispered his friend incredulously.

It was true. The high tide of the attack had rolled to the edge of the foxholes, wavered while a few grappled hand to hand, and then drifted back into the dark. In the battalion combat report long afterward it would read, "In the Battalion's first night ashore, C Company repelled a local counterattack in its sector and suffered minor casualties." For him, there had been such noise, confusion, and terror that he knew nothing for certain except that by some miracle he survived. He had not fired a shot. Gradually the tension left his limbs and he was aware again, almost gratefully, of physical discomforts, the wet clothes and the mud. He would have been willing to believe the attack a fevered nightmare if it had not left behind it appalling evidence. The cries of the wounded rose in supplication or diminished to low continuous moans of incoherent agony.

His watch showed half past one, and his friend shook his head in disbelief. Settling himself on his back again, he could feel his heart still pounding. It seemed longer than ever to the dawn. The enemy might well attempt another mass attack, and the danger of infiltration was continuous. Looking up into the apex of the night, he noticed that the clouds were thinning and that a few stars shone with a cold, implacable brilliance. Full of a sweet regret, gentler times came back to him when in another land the stars had seemed close and warm. Now it appeared as far to that land as it was to the stars, and as improbable a journey.

5

Abruptly, a heavy object bounced in the hole and rested against his right leg. It lay there and gave off a soft hissing sound. Though he moved with all the speed in his body, he felt in a dreamlike trance and seemed to stretch out his hand as a sleepwalker toward the object. His fingers closed around the corrugated iron surface of a grenade, and he knew that it was his own death that he held in his hand. His conscious mind seemed to be watching his body from a great distance as with tantalizing slowness his arm raised and threw the grenade into the dark. In mid-flight it exploded and the fragments whispered overhead. Another bounced on the edge of the hole and rolled in. He reached for it tentatively, as a child reaches out to touch an unfamiliar object.

A great club smashed him in the face. A light grew in his brain to agonizing brightness and then exploded in a roar of sound that was itself like a physical blow. He fell backward and an iron door clashed shut against his eyes.

He cried aloud once, as if through the sound the pain that filled him might find an outlet to overflow and diminish. Once more a long, rising moan was drawn from him and he lifted his hands in a futile gesture as though to rip away the mask of agony that clung to his face. Then, even in that extremity, the will to survive asserted itself. Through the fire that seemed to consume him, the knowledge that the enemy must be near-by made him stifle the scream that rose in his throat. If he kept quiet they might leave him for dead, and that was his only hope.

There was no time yet to wonder how badly he had been hurt. Like a poor swimmer, he struggled through the successive waves of pain that crashed over him. There would be a respite and then, again, he would be engulfed, until the dim light of consciousness almost went out. He pressed his hands to his temples, as if to hold his disintegrating being together by mere physical effort. His breath came chokingly. He allowed his head to fall to one side and felt the warm blood stream down his neck. There were fragments of teeth in his mouth and he let the blood wash them away.

It did not seem possible that anyone could have done this to him without reason. In a world on the edge of consciousness, he forgot the war and kept thinking that there must be some personal, individual explanation for what had happened. Over and over he repeated to himself, "Why have they done this to me? Why have they done this to me? What have I done? What have I done?" Like an innocent man convicted of some crime, he went on incoherently protesting his innocence, as if hoping that heaven itself might intervene to right so deep a wrong.

At last he became calmer. Hesitantly, he set out to assess the damage done his body. The pain was worst in his face, but to investigate it was more than he yet dared. His right arm moved with difficulty, and blood slipped down his shoulder. It seemed that his ears were stuffed with cotton or that he stood at the end of a long corridor to which the sounds of the outside world barely penetrated.

From a great distance he heard a heavy thud on the ground, as of a fist pounded into the earth. There was another even heavier, followed by silence. He attempted to form the name of his friend with his lips. "George," he tried to whisper, but no sound came. He could see nothing, but in the loneliness of his pain reached out his hand. It seemed that a gradually widening expanse of darkness separated him from everything in the world, but that if he could only make contact with his friend it would be easy to find the way back. His fingers touched a dungaree jacket and felt the warm body beneath it. His hand moved upward, until suddenly he withdrew it. There was no need to search further.

A flood of the kindest memories obliterated momentarily the knowledge of his own misfortune. The empty body beside him had housed the bravest and the simplest heart. Between them there had been an unspoken trust and the complete confidence that comes only after many dangers shared together. If he had met him years later he would have had to say simply, "George." They would have shaken hands and the years between would have been nothing at all. Now, cold and impassable, stronger than time, stood death, and a hopeless, irremediable sense of loss flowed through him. The noise that at first had attracted his attention must have been the last despairing movement of his friend. Gently, he wiped the blood from his hand on his trouser leg. A long spasm of pain recalled him to his own condition.

Gratefully, he noticed that the edge of the pain was dulled. It continued to flow through his body, but his conscious self seemed to be slightly removed from it. The occasional rifle shots appeared to come from further and further away. His right arm had lost almost all power of movement. With care, he rested it across his stomach. While sufficient strength remained, he determined to know the extent of the damage done his face. Truth was never more terrible than at that moment when, fearfully, he raised his left hand to trace the contours of his personal disaster. As delicately as a blind man touches the features of one he loves, he ran his fingers over the lineaments of the face he did not know. Though there was considerable blood, the bones of his chin and nose seemed intact.

Then at last there was no choice. The fear whose existence he had refused to admit grew monstrous and possessed his mind. Tightly he cupped his hand, without touching the eye itself, over his left eye and suddenly withdrew it. He repeated the process with the other eye. There was no change in the even texture of the dark. It remained impenetrable, unrelieved by the slightest glimmer of starlight. One hope remained and he clung to it as the condemned believe to the last in the hope of pardon. It might be that the clouds had returned and that the complete blackness was not his alone, but shared by all. There was a way of finding out. For a moment he hesitated, and then with cold fingers touched his left eye. There was no eye there, only a jelly-like substance peculiarly sensitive to the touch.

A long sigh escaped his lips. The evidence was undeniable and the sentence pronounced. He did not care to investigate the other eye. Even the idea of touching again that useless jelly revolted him. With slow reluctance his mind accepted the full meaning of his loss. The emotional portion of his being continually revolted against the real event and kept asserting the reality of a world where such things do not happen. It was an almost irresistible temptation to reject the whole experience as an illusion. He felt that he would almost welcome madness if it could save him from his empty tomorrows. But little by little his reason forced him to understand.

"Blind," he whispered at last. "Oh, my God, my God." It was not a prayer so much as the expression of the bitterest despair. In all its poverty his life as it would be appeared before him. All other things, he felt—the mutilation of his face, the loss of his limbs—would have been endurable, but not this: the dark dragging hours, the mocking blackness of his nights, the loneliness of a world where people are only voices which if beautiful are more bitter to hear, the unassuageable regret provoked by every memory of the lighted past, the cheerful self-sacrifice of kind relations to goad the sense of his own parasitic uselessness, and always the mind growing more deformed in its crippling attempts to escape the dark prison.

6

The memory returned of how as a boy he had almost drowned. It seemed that again he struggled upward through the black water. An illusory hope filled him that he could break the confines of the dark that pressed down on him as the ocean had so long before, but the excitement passed quickly. Above this ocean no sunlight flashed on white waves. It was infinite, and extended in black perspective from that moment to the day of his death, when, he thought, one form of eternal night would be exchanged for another devoid of anguish and regret. Behind the sightless eyes, his mind would burn down like a fire in a room the guests have left until, mercifully, darkness was all.

There was nothing in those weary years that he wished to have, nothing for which he cared to wait. He felt a strange and brotherly companionship with the dead. The fact that such friends as he had known were gone seemed a warm assurance that death could be no terrible disaster. Their presence in that other world into which he drifted lent it a familiarity that the world of the living lacked, and took all fear from the journey he was about to make. Deliberately, he felt for his weapon.

He could not find the gun. Perhaps the explosion had blown it out of reach. The difficulty he had finding it allowed him a moment of indecision. What a spectacle he would make in the morning! The others who had died had done so bravely in the performance of what they had considered to be their duty. Death crowned their boyish honor, but would remain his shame, for he perceived well enough that he wished to die because he could not endure the pain and feared the dark years to come. He guessed that many during the long war had endured a life more unbearable than his. If they had not been happy, they had been admirable by the courage that they brought to their misfortune, and the knowledge of his own weakness was bitter.

A solitary, stubborn pride refused him the oblivion for which he longed, just as so often before, far more than any fear of social disgrace, it had forced upon him the consistent series of decisions that led inevitably to where he lay. Why did he enlist in so dangerous a service? Why did he refuse the job with the artillery or with the regimental staff, where one could afford to hope? Asking himself these questions, he knew there was no logical answer.

Certainly he had always expected this, or something like it. Not because he believed the war was fought for any cause worth dying for. Rather, he saw war clearly as the finished product of universal ignorance, avarice, and brutality. A little out of adolescent vanity, but more because he had failed to become a conscientious objector, as he ought to have done, he chose to accept the consequences in an effort to redeem by personal valor a lost consistency of purpose. From the monotony and occasional violence, he had saved only his courage intact, and now he stood to lose it in a final ignominious act. Giving up his search for the weapon, he accepted his dark fate.

7

There was no way to tell the passage of time. It might have been hours or minutes since he had been hit. Whenever he tried to move his right arm the blood would start running again. Body and mind seemed to be drifting further apart. It was not the pleasant sensation of slipping gradually off to sleep. He seemed to fight the slow effect of a drug that paralyzed his limbs but left his mind active.

Occasionally he would test himself by raising his left arm. It became heavier, and the translation of wish into action grew more difficult. All sounds reached him from very far away, as if he were listening on a faulty telephone connection. Like one dying of cold, he abandoned himself to the slow change that was taking place, and hoped that death would not be too long in coming. He was sure now that he was dying, and was grateful that nature would accomplish what he had hesitated to do himself.

In the certainty that he would soon leave the world, he looked down from a great height and was glad that he was done with it. With a new severity, he contemplated the few short years of his life to discover some strand of meaning running through the trivial sequence of days and nights stretching back to the earliest memory. There was nothing in those transient joys to interest him, and even the moments of love or insight that he had once valued seemed entirely inconsequential when weighed against the vast extent of the descending night. Life seemed so poor a thing that he smiled to himself at having feared to lose it.

There was no hatred in his heart against anyone, but rather pity. He considered the shortness of man's days, the pointlessness of his best hopes in comparison with the certainty and conclusiveness of death, and could see him only as a poor creature struggling for a moment above a forever escaping stream of time that seemed to run nowhere. It would have been better for man, he felt, if he had been given no trace of gentleness, no desire for goodness, no capacity for love. Those qualities were all he valued, but he could see they were the pleasant illusions of children. With them men hoped, struggled pitifully, and were totally defeated by an alien universe in which they wandered as unwanted strangers. Without them, an animal, man might happily eat, reproduce, and die, one with what is.

Above him he imagined the imperturbable stars swinging on their infinite wanderings to God knows what final destination, and the knowledge of how slight a ripple there would be when he slipped beneath the surface of reality reconciled him easily to oblivion. Part of a prayer from his schooldays returned: "When the shadows lengthen and the evening comes and the busy world is hushed, and the fever of life is over, and our work is done, then in thy great mercy, O Lord, grant us a safe lodging and peace at the last." A safe lodging he would have as his body decayed to feed the rich jungle growth, and his mind the peace of nothingness as its precarious balance dissolved like a soap bubble into air.

Without hope or fear, he waited for death. It was a long time later, he guessed, when he felt a tear run down his cheek. Where his right eye should be there was a smarting itch that made him wish to rub it.

Surprise wakened him from the dreamy state into which he had fallen. There must be more of his right eye left intact than he thought. In the depths of his consciousness stirred an indefinite hope. He tried to work the lid but there was no movement. The beating of his heart echoed the expectation he hardly dared admit. Starting to raise his arm he let it drop. What difference could it make? Bereft of all desire and convinced of the futility of existence, he had no cause now to disturb that profound indifference. It was his strength. Hope was weakness and could bring only a vain regret and the despair he had renounced. Reasonably he knew all this, but it did not stem the rising flow of excitement.

With gentle, inquiring fingers he touched the tissues of the right eye. It was swollen shut, but beneath the dried blood on the lid he could feel the rounded form of the eyeball. Hardly aware of the pain, he forced the lid open roughly and searched the blackness above him for a sign. Gone was all indifference. Light was life, and the possibility of hope both intoxicated and appalled. All that he was hung poised in dreadful suspense on the frail miracle he awaited.

Then down the long corridor of the night it swam into his vision. Out of focus, it trembled for a moment hazily, and then burned steady and unwinking. Fearing that he might have created it out of the intensity of his wish, he let his lid close and then forced it open again. The star still lay in the now soft and friendly dark. It flooded his being like the summer sun. He saw it as the window to Hope. Another appeared, and another, until the whole tropic sky seemed ablaze with an unbearable glory. Joyful tears rose in his heart. Gently, he permitted the torn lid to shut. Warm on his cheek and salty in his mouth were the tears of his salvation.

The End

When morning came, I could not move at all, but was still conscious and could feel the warmth of the sun on my face. Soon I heard friendly voices, speaking in hushed tones. Someone leaned down and felt my pulse. I heard him say in surprise, "This one's alive." An amphibious tractor was brought up and I could feel myself being loaded into it. My right eye was swollen shut and I could see nothing. The tractor took me and other seriously wounded back to the battalion command post on the beach. I could feel the battalion doctor checking my pulse and hear him say, "He's got about twenty minutes to live." Unfortunately, he believed it and he proceeded to list me as dead on the battalion roster, with the result that my parents received a telegram from the Marine Corps regretting that I had been killed in action. It took a few days for the authorities to correct the error resulting from a prematurely pessimistic diagnosis.

As it happened, I was taken by amphibious tractor to an LST on the coral reef, which had been converted into an advance first-aid station. There the doctors were able to transfuse enough blood plasma in time to save my life. I could feel them softly sponging the dried blood off my face. When they had cleaned my right eye, they forced open the lids and I could follow the flashlight that they slowly waved in front of me. With satisfaction, they assured each other that my sight had been saved, and I tried to murmur my approval of their belated discovery.

From there, the many other badly wounded and I were loaded on board a hospital ship which sailed us back to Eniwetok, where a plane was waiting to fly the worst cases to the naval hospital near Pearl Harbor. There an expert eye surgeon removed piece by piece the fragments of metal and coral that had lodged in the cornea of my right eye, and, as my sight improved, so did my spirits and general health. Soon I was well enough to start thinking about the future, as the following entry in my journal indicates.

10 September '44—These are the first words I have written since that last evening on the ship before battle, since the evening of July twentieth. I wrote then in the expectation of death. I preferred to believe it almost inevitable and thereby thought to prepare myself for it. I had no wish for any foolish hopes that might lead me to avoid the duty then before me. My scale of values was simple. First and most to be preferred was life with honor. Secondly, death with honor. And what I hoped for least was life without honor. I find myself now with the first, and therefore in spite of the loss of an eye consider myself fortunate. If not my body, my integrity remains intact and I can truthfully say that as a soldier I have nothing to be ashamed of.

So then I have discharged my duty in that capacity, but the whole center and axis of my world has changed. I did not realize before how much I had completely discounted the future. If I thought of "after the war" at all, I thought of it as a man might think of a distant country which he was quite content to admit as beyond the possibility of his ever seeing. So if my life was not fruitful or pleasing, it was simple. I lived in the present and to a certain extent in the past and was assured in my own mind that there was no alternative to the life I led and the decision I had made. Now my duty is not so obvious, and the future full of conflicting alternatives. In the hospital convalescing as I am now, there is not yet the necessity for action. I inhabit temporarily a Lotus Eater's land of eating and sleeping but soon I must start again on that expanding adventure that is every man's life and before me are the most important decisions.

In many ways, I am not prepared to make that step. My future to a frightening extent is in my own hands, and there is no external circumstance and no man that can really sway my decision. To have so wide a choice is an enviable privilege I realize well enough, but it is also a large responsibility. The general notion of what I have to do is clear. I owe to those who fell beside me, and to those many others who will die before it's done, the assurance that I will do all that is in my small power to make the future for which they died an improvement upon the past. The question is how? In what field of endeavor? Where to begin? Education? Politics? Writing? Continue my education or not?

Chapter 3

Peacemaking

FROM HAWAII, I was flown to a hospital in the San Francisco area and finally back to New York City in September of 1944. I lived with my parents and commuted to the Brooklyn Naval Hospital, where I was fitted with a reasonably convincing glass eye. After some minor plastic surgery, I was ready to face the world and began seeing a lot of Mary Pinchot, whom I'd known slightly before the war and who was working in New York as a free-lance magazine writer. Knowing the suicidal determination of the Japanese, I thought the war would last at least for another year and went down to Washington to see if I could make any useful contribution as a civilian. I saw Dean Acheson, who had a high-ranking position in the State Department and whose son had been a friend of mine at college. He offered me a job at an appropriately low salary with an official mission going to Vienna. I would have taken it but by that time was so much in love with Mary Pinchot that trying to persuade her to marry me seemed far more important than a diplomatic assignment. As a result, I enrolled in the Yale Law School in January with the help of the G.I. Bill, and we saw each other on weekends.

I found it difficult to concentrate on the technicalities of the law, as my good eye had not yet sufficiently recovered to cope with the small print. Therefore, it was with enthusiasm that I accepted an invitation from Harold Stassen to become one of his two veteran assistants in his newly appointed capacity as an official U.S. delegate to the San Francisco conference convened by the Allied powers to establish the structure of the new United Nations Organization. I'd never met Stassen previously but knew that he had made a reputation as an able young governor in Minnesota, had distinguished himself as a naval officer in the Pacific, and had built a record as a liberal Republican internationalist. In a brief meeting in Washington, he explained that he had read excerpts from my war letters to my family, which had been published in the *Atlantic,* and that the Yale Law School had recommended me. The other veteran he had chosen, John Thompson, and I would be responsible for running his office and for briefing him on meetings that he was not personally able to attend. Both Thompson and I realized that Stassen would do himself no harm politically by having two young veterans on his staff, but even if our jobs were more symbolic than substantive, we looked forward eagerly to the chance to participate in the making of the peace.

In April of 1945 Mary and I were married in her mother's New York apartment by Reinhold Niebuhr. He was more familiar with the intricacies of theological argument than with the marriage ceremony, and he stumbled a bit over the text in the Book of Common Prayer. A few days later, I boarded the official train in Washington that was taking the lower-ranking members of the national delegations to San Francisco, and Mary flew out to join me with press credentials from the North American Newspaper Alliance. As the train rolled westward, I could not help comparing this trip with the voyage across the country by troop train in that innocent springtime of two years before. I felt myself a much wiser man, but I must have seemed incredibly naive to a legal adviser to the Soviet delegation named Golunsky, whose acquaintance I made in the course of the trip. As I explained my hopes for international cooperation, he listened with a detached air and limited himself to extolling the virtues of big-power unanimity—without a hint, of course, of the Byzantine terror of Stalin's regime of which he was very much a part.

As the official train moved through the railroad stations along the route, we were astonished by the huge crowds that were waiting to see us pass. They were curious, watchful, and quiet, with only an occasional wave and no cheers. In their mood of restrained expectation we could sense their hope that this time the peace might be built on a sure foundation and simultaneously their suspended doubts about the eventual outcome. Their patient, questioning stares brought home to many of us for the first time the enormity of the responsibility that the world's leaders faced in San Francisco.

As the conference got under way, I watched with growing concern the construction of the foundations and scaffolding of the new international organization that was to replace the defunct League of Nations. In the drafting committee meetings that often lasted late into the night, the delegates attempted to define the powers and authority to be granted to the Security Council, the General Assembly, and the other organs of the United Nations. Step by step, it became increasingly apparent that the voting provisions agreed to by Roosevelt, Churchill, and Stalin at Yalta would have to be incorporated into the United Nations Charter if there was to be any new international organization. At the insistence of the Big Three, this was accomplished by providing that the Security Council could take no enforcement action against aggression without the concurring votes of the five permanent members, the United States, the United Kingdom, the Union of Soviet Socialist Republics, France, and China.

To me, this veto power was incontrovertible evidence that the major nations intended to retain intact their complete sovereign independence within the new structure. Every other provision of the emerging charter served to emphasize the original implications of this voting rule. The General Assembly was given no authority to enact binding law but only the power to make recommendations to the Security Council. The International Court of Justice was to sit in judgment on a case only if both parties to the dispute agreed to allow it to do so. Indeed, in certain respects, the new structure seemed to me even more impotent than the old League of Nations, whose defects Professor Spykman at Yale used to describe with mordant wit.

When I expressed my fears and reservations to Stassen, he quite realistically pointed out that the U.S. delegation was bound by the previous commitments made at Yalta and Dumbarton Oaks, and that ratification of the charter by the U.S. Senate would be endangered by any effective limitation on our sovereign independence. Although I disagreed with Stassen's pragmatic approach, I found him easy to work with and admired his deft handling of the press. He overlooked the mistakes that I made through inexperience, even when I kept a furious Arthur Krock of *The New York Times* waiting in the outer office for half an hour because I did not realize who he was. Cool and intelligent, Stassen was, however, driven by consuming ambition, and I was sorry to see him later in his search for the presidency so compromise his liberal position that he lost the support of moderates, without ever winning over the conservatives.

In a luncheon conversation with Alger Hiss, who was the secretary general of the conference, I remember mentioning my fear that in the official publicity the State Department was putting out about the progress we were making, we might be misleading our own people as to the limits of what was actually being accomplished. In a heated argument, Hiss insisted that the veto power was a realistic recognition that big-power unanimity and the continuation into peace of the voluntary cooperation between the wartime allies were the only sure foundations for the future. Hiss struck me at the time as a disciplined if somewhat arrogant State Department official, and nothing about him gave the remotest indication that there would later be allegations that seemed persuasive to me that he could once have been one of the Soviets' most important agents of influence within the American government.[1] In those days, of course, I hardly knew the Russian secret police existed.

Not all the delegates shared the prevailing optimism. Prime Minister Fraser of New Zealand in a courageous speech warned that the veto power forced the new organization to depend for its success on unanimity among the Big Five and that such unanimity was already conspicuous by its absence. He called the charter "a series of platitudes—and petrified platitudes at that" if it could be amended only with the consent of all the large nations. On the fringes of the conference, where the international press gathered to exchange news, I became friends with two men whose views confirmed my deepening skepticism. One was Emery Reves. A Hungarian by birth, he had become a British citizen, had run an international press syndicate before the war, and was also Churchill's literary agent. He had with him at all times galley proofs of a book he had written entitled *The Anatomy of Peace*, which he attempted to bring to the attention of any delegate who would listen. It was a logical and forceful argument that peace required some surrender of national sovereignty and the creation of an enforceable world legal order. My other new friend was E. B. White, who was covering the conference for *The New Yorker.* In his articles, he enjoyed poking gentle fun at some of the more preposterous claims of the official propagandists. The three of us would meet weekly to review events and to identify new structural weaknesses in the edifice that was being built before our eyes to such general and uncritical applause.

Also on the fringes of the conference were lobbyists of every conceivable description, representing untold millions whose fate might be affected in one way or another by the terms of the charter. Some of them, like the supporters of Ukrainian independence and the anti-Communist Polish exiles, were courageous defenders of lost causes. Others, like J. J. Singh, who led the public campaign in the United States for India's independence from Britain, were to live to see their efforts crowned with success. They all wanted to see Stassen, who during the conference had distinguished himself as one of the most able members of the American delegation. Since his time was limited, they had to settle in many cases for a meeting with me, in the hope that, however indirectly or inadequately, their pleadings might filter back and have some influence on the American delegates. These importunate lobbyists, who crowded the corridors outside the sterile and formal committee meetings, provided a generous education in the problems of the real world that existed beyond the glittering facade of the conference. From them, I learned far more than I had known before concerning the nature of Stalin's rule, not only within Eastern Europe but inside the Soviet Union. The depth and intensity of the demand for independence from Western colonial rule was also brought home to me, and the inadequacy of the provisions in the charter for coping with this problem was dramatized by the unofficial representatives of the subject peoples of Asia and Africa.

Suddenly, in the middle of May, reality crowded in upon me in a much more personal way. I was awakened one morning by a telephone call from my parents in New York, who told me through their tears that they had just been informed that my twin brother had been killed in action. He was a lieutenant with the First Marine Division, which I knew was engaged in the desperate fighting against the entrenched Japanese on Okinawa. For a brief time, I hoped that as in my own case the news might be false. However, official confirmation was quick in coming. Although we were not identical twins, we were very close and had shared together all the days of our childhood and youth. Stassen was kind enough to excuse me from my regular duties, and my wife tried to comfort me. I could do nothing for a time but sit in my hotel room, trying gradually to come to terms with the reality that my loss was final and irretrievable. For some reason, the last lines from E. E. Cummings' poem on Buffalo Bill kept repeating themselves endlessly in my mind:

> and what i want to know is
> how do you like your blue-eyed boy
> Mister Death?

As with all of us, sorrow slowly lost its edge, and I went back to work. However, I was more determined than ever to do what I could to see to it that the victory these sacrifices made possible was used to build a more just and peaceful world. Therefore, as the conference ended, I accepted eagerly a proposal by Edward Weeks, editor of the *Atlantic*, that I write an analysis of what had been achieved at San Francisco from the perspective of someone who had been in the war. My wife and I took a long-delayed honeymoon at a ranch in Montana. A trout stream ran through the property, and in the mornings we both enjoyed casting our flies close to the banks, where the big and elusive browns could sometimes be coaxed to strike. In the long afternoons, I worked on my manuscript in an effort to meet the deadline for the September edition of the magazine.

In my article, I tried to define the strict limits of what had been accomplished at San Francisco, in contrast to the extravagant claims of the official press releases that a major step had been taken toward ensuring a peaceful future. My basic point was that the veto power combined with certain other provisions of the Charter doomed the United Nations to impotence and made it impossible for the organization to protect national states against armed aggression. I was not optimistic about the possibility that the Big Three could preserve the peace through the so-called principle of unanimity, since it was evident that deep conflicts of interest lay just below the surface of the conference, and I mentioned the growing threat of civil war in China as an example. I warned that the Soviets had adamantly opposed every attempt to give the United Nations any grant of power that would infringe upon their complete freedom of action, and that the necessity of Senate ratification drew an invisible boundary line over which the American delegation dared not advance. I concluded that international laws, courts, and police were the price of peace, and that, since this price had not been paid, every nation, including the United States, would have to continue to rely on the strength of its own armed forces.

I advocated support for the United Nations as the best that could be accomplished at the time but warned that by radical amendment it would have to be given law-making and law-enforcing powers in the near future if there was to be any chance of avoiding a new arms race. Ending on a note of resignation, I recognized that workable constitutions grow from a community of belief and there was no such unifying supranational belief. In view of the strength of nationalistic feeling and the deep-going ideological differences in the world, I accepted the possibility that despite our best efforts "the death agony of nationalism will be prolonged beyond our lifetime."[2]

On the way back east from Montana I corrected the galley proofs of my article on the train. In Chicago, where we had to change trains, the newspapers carried in black headlines the news of the destruction of Hiroshima by a single atomic bomb, the first evidence that most of us had that such a weapon even existed. I had room in my proofs for only one additional sentence referring to the destructive power of the new weapon but, as its significance sank in, this development began to have a profound effect on me as on many others.

Why, I wondered, had the people at the top of our government and other leaders who were informed allowed the delegates at San Francisco to go through the elaborate charade of creating a peace-keeping structure for a world that no longer existed and that was about to be radically and permanently transformed in ways beyond their wildest imaginings? It seemed to me then, as it does now, that it would have been wiser to have postponed the San Francisco conference on whatever pretext, until the new facts of life and death were evident for all to see and until some effort had been made to work out in advance with the Soviets and the British the broad outline of the international controls that would be necessary to contain the new force. At least then, the assembled delegates would have been compelled to deal with the reality of man's new destructive power, and the justifiable fears of an aroused public opinion would have demanded stronger safeguards.

I was to learn later that Henry Stimson as secretary of war in 1945 had in fact urged the postponement of the San Francisco meeting and, on the day that it convened, April 25, briefed President Truman for the first time on our imminent capacity to explode an atomic bomb. He left with Truman a prophetic memorandum warning that our nuclear monopoly would not last for long, including the following paragraph:

> To approach any world peace organization of any pattern now likely to be considered, without an appreciation by the leaders of our country of the power of this new weapon, would seem to be unrealistic. No system of control heretofore considered would be adequate to control this menace. Both inside any particular country and between the nations of the world, the control of this weapon will undoubtedly be a matter of the greatest difficulty and would involve such thorough-going rights of inspection and internal controls as we have never heretofore contemplated.[3]

By then, it was too late to turn back. The sheer momentum of advance planning, the difficulty of explaining a decision to postpone, the confusion surrounding the transfer of power and knowledge to Truman after Roosevelt's death just thirteen days earlier, and the widely held belief that the American atomic monopoly would last for a generation all combined to allow the San Francisco meeting to proceed in general ignorance of the enormous force that was soon to be set loose in the world—a force that would dramatize the pitiful inadequacy of the international machinery available to control it. Moreover, it should be remembered that the top Soviet leaders were by that time secretly aware of the progress our nuclear program was making through their effective espionage apparatus, but for obvious reasons chose not to raise the issue.

My own reaction was to feel that although a great opportunity had been missed, the very destructiveness of the new weapon put a new and powerful argument in the hands of those who were prepared to use it. In a sense, I welcomed the advent of the atomic bomb as "the good news of damnation" and began to believe that, faced with its vivid threat, it might be possible to overcome the ideological differences and narrow nationalism that had previously seemed to raise such insuperable obstacles in the way of any progress toward world federation.

A few days later, in my family's home in New Hampshire, we heard on the radio the news of the Japanese surrender. We were deeply grateful that the war was over, but there was no joy in that house as there would have been had the war ended three months sooner and left my brother still alive. While regretting the civilian casualties in Hiroshima and Nagasaki, we shared the general feeling in the country that the shock effect of the new weapon had been necessary to avoid the need for invading the Japanese home islands at the cost of millions of casualties on both sides. Only later, when I heard how some of the scientists in the atomic project had urged an initial demonstration under a flag of truce on an uninhabited island, did I think that this step might well have been taken before unleashing the weapon against the Japanese urban population.

Meanwhile, I had to decide what to do next. After some thought, I finally made the decision not to return to law school but to enter the Harvard Graduate School in order to qualify for a professional career that I intended to spend partly in academic life and partly in government service. We moved to Cambridge, and my wife worked as an editorial assistant at the *Atlantic Monthly,* while I took courses toward a graduate degree in government. At the end of the first term, Edward Weeks persuaded me to write a book on the political and military consequences of the atomic bomb. He proposed me to the Society of Fellows, and I was lucky enough to be elected a Junior Fellow with a generous three-year grant and wide freedom to do my own research and writing. Not the least of the advantages of that arrangement was the fact that we twenty-four Junior Fellows dined every Monday night with the Harvard professors who were the Senior Fellows and who invited a variety of guests to join us. I remember sitting next to Vladimir Nabokov ten years before *Lolita* made him famous and hearing him discourse urbanely about the pleasure of collecting butterflies. T. S. Eliot joined us on one occasion and Alfred North Whitehead on another; they were fascinating evenings. Among my colleagues who became good friends were Richard Wilbur, whose war poetry was among the best that any American produced, and Pierre Schneider, who later became a well-known art and literary critic in Paris.

As a result of the publication of my article in the *Atlantic,* I was invited in October of 1945 to participate in a meeting in Dublin, New Hampshire, to discuss the problems posed by the new weapon. The meeting was called at the instance of Grenville Clark, a senior partner in one of the big New York law firms, and of Owen Roberts, a Supreme Court justice. Those who attended included a prominent New York banker, Frank Altschul; Thomas K. Finletter, lawyer and later secretary of the air force; and among many others, Henry Smyth, the atomic physicist who had been authorized by the government to write the unclassified account of the processes by which our atomic bombs had been constructed. A large majority of those who attended, including myself, ended the meeting by agreeing to a declaration that was published in its entirety in *The New York Times* on October 17, 1945. This declaration warned of the consequences of atomic warfare and of the damaging effect that a nuclear arms race would have on traditional American freedoms; it spelled out the inadequacy of the existing United Nations and called for our government to take the lead in proposing drastic amendments to the U.N. Charter sufficient to give the organization closely defined and limited supranational authority to enforce prohibitions against large-scale national armament. The fact that older men of stature and wide practical experience shared my concern and my belief that something could be done to avert a worldwide arms race persuaded me to take an active part in the growing national debate. While writing my book in Cambridge, I accepted speaking engagements before a variety of public groups and was encouraged by the favorable reaction.

In February of 1947, again as the result of the *Atlantic* article, I was invited to a meeting, in Asheville, North Carolina, of the various world federalist groups that had sprung up. The objective was to merge these groups into a single national organization capable of making a sustained appeal to the country at large and of bringing effective political influence to bear on the Congress. There was considerable debate on the question of the extent of the authority that should be advocated for a revised United Nations. In this discussion, I took the view that the U.N. should be granted no more authority than was absolutely indispensable for the effective control and limitation of national armaments, while the "maximalists" argued for a broad grant of authority sufficient to enable the U.N. to control national trade and tariff policies. The Asheville meeting finally reached agreement on a compromise policy statement and established a national organization, the United World Federalists, to whose Executive Council I was elected.

That spring I took part in the effort to find someone to serve as president of the new organization. I was finally persuaded by Grenville Clark, T. K. Finletter, and W. T. Holiday, president of Standard Oil of Ohio, to take the job myself, with the understanding that they would serve as vice-presidents and help me raise the necessary funds. Having been elected president by the Executive Council, I moved my family to New York and in June took up my duties.

My reason for making such an abrupt change in my career was a conviction that the United States, through its atomic monopoly, had for a brief period the opportunity to lead the world toward effective international control of the bomb. I was not optimistic, but it seemed to me that if there was one chance in a hundred it was worth taking in view of the consequences of an unrestricted competition between national states for more and bigger nuclear weapons. To turn down this chance to lead the fight for supranational and legally enforceable control of nuclear energy was something I could not do, in view of my stated convictions and a private sense of obligation to those who had died in the long war. It was a move that was to cause me much trouble later but I have never regretted it.

For the next two years, I became a full-time organizer, fund raiser, lobbyist, and itinerant lecturer. Our specific political purpose was to obtain passage by both houses of Congress of resolutions that would put the legislature clearly on record as favoring radical amendment of the U.N. Charter and so encourage the administration to act. To that end, we built up a national headquarters in New York with more than forty paid and volunteer staffers and a legislative office in Washington. From that base, we attempted to build a network of local UWF chapters across the country in every city, town, and university in an effort to bring direct popular pressure to bear on senators and congressmen. The membership consisted of those who were prepared to pay the minimal dues and to attend meetings. The local chapters were manned almost entirely by volunteers and were extremely diversified in the nature of their leadership, varying from liberal Democrat to quite conservative Republican. I never knew, when traveling to address a new chapter, what manner of people I would be dealing with. In a wealthy Chicago suburb, the leaders would be prominent businessmen and their wives. In El Paso, a local chapter leader turned out to be the owner of a photography shop who had been a Trotskyist in his youth and claimed to be the man who had brought Trotsky across the Mexican border in a fake coffin to address the San Francisco dock strikers. I was particularly impressed by the energy and organizational competence of the many women volunteers and came to have a healthy respect for their role and influence in a community once they had convinced themselves that UWF offered some hope for a peaceful future.

Money was always a problem, made more difficult by the fact that our political purpose disqualified us from receiving tax-deductible gifts. It got to the point where my few rich friends would turn and walk hurriedly in the opposite direction when they saw me coming down the street. There were months when I didn't know up to the last moment how we were going to pay the salaries of our professional staff. But thanks to the fund-raising efforts of Cass Canfield, the New York publisher, and the generous help of many others, we were able to stay in business and keep growing until our paid-up membership exceeded fifty thousand.

One organizational technique that we used was to encourage those of our members who had influential positions in professional organizations, trade associations, or labor unions to lobby for passage at their annual conventions of resolutions favorable to our cause. This had a multiplier effect on our influence because the lobbyists of these organizations in Washington were then committed to bringing pressure on the members of Congress to whom they had access. At the high tide of our campaign in June of 1949, sixty-four Democrats and twenty-seven Republicans in the House of Representatives joined in sponsoring a concurrent resolution which declared that "it should be a fundamental objective of the foreign policy of the U.S. to support and strengthen the U.N. and to seek its development into a world federation open to all nations with defined and limited powers adequate to preserve peace and prevent aggression through the enactment, interpretation and enforcement of world law."

We did not confine our efforts to the Congress. We also tried to influence the executive, and a group of us met with President Truman in the White House to put our case. He listened attentively, with his head cocked to one side, and then asked a few questions that showed considerable skepticism. Secretary of State Marshall was

later to testify before the House Committee on Foreign Affairs that
the administration did not oppose amendment of the U.N. Charter
in principle but believed an attempt to do so to be premature on the
ground that there was not sufficient support for such a move either
in the U.S. Congress or in the United Nations itself. We also met in
the spring of 1948 with General Eisenhower in his office at Columbia
University. He was cordial and clearly interested. While we were
talking, he took a phone call from a prominent Democratic politician, and from what we could hear of the conversation it was obvious
that the General was being urged to run on the Democratic ticket
for the presidency, which showed how little confidence there was in
Truman's chances for reelection even in his own party at that time.
Eisenhower turned the offer politely aside and then returned to our
topic with a number of pertinent questions. Our explanations had
some temporary effect as evidenced in a speech that Eisenhower
gave at Columbia University in March 1950, in which he stated, "In
a disarmed world—should it be attained—there must be an effective
United Nations, with a police power universally recognized and
strong enough to earn universal respect."

That summer, I attended the Democratic and Republican conventions in Philadelphia and testified before their platform committees.
The Democratic platform committee meeting was a lively affair,
with many of the party leaders in attendance and the representatives
of many private organizations waiting to testify. I received a fair
hearing, and there were intelligent questions. When I testified a few
weeks later before the Republican platform committee, I was struck
by the difference. Most of the committee members were dozing in
their chairs and there were few public witnesses. This startling contrast did not so much reflect a difference in the nature of the two
parties as it did a gap in their expectations. The Republican leaders
obviously believed the polls, took it for granted that they would
defeat Truman in November, and saw the platform hearings as a
necessary but boring formality. If I had been an acute political observer, I might have generalized from this experience and concluded
that Republican overconfidence was so great that they might well
lose the election. However, I was as surprised as everyone else—
except Truman—when Truman won.

In trying to put our case to the public, we consistently ran into
opposition from those who were convinced that the American mo-

nopoly on nuclear weapons would last for at least a generation and therefore saw no urgent need for the radical and risky institutional reforms we were advocating. With this uniquely powerful weapon in our sole possession for the next twenty years, they believed that we were in an unassailable position and could discourage any aggressor by threatening to use our decisive advantage. Unfortunately, this popular illusion was reinforced by the expert testimony of two men who had played important roles in the development of our nuclear weaponry. General Leslie Groves, who had directed the Manhattan Project, the wartime code name of our nuclear program, and Vannevar Bush, who had been a key adviser, were both convinced that Russian science and technology were so backward in comparison to our own that it would take the Soviets at least a generation to duplicate our feat.

On the other side of this argument were ranged many of the theoretical physicists whose contribution had made possible the development of the bomb. They were convinced that the Soviets had the scientific talent and the technical ability to produce their own bombs within five years. They warned that, once two or more nations began stockpiling nuclear material, such proliferation would severely complicate the establishment of effective international control. They formed themselves into a group called the Emergency Committee of Atomic Scientists, with the purpose of trying to get these convictions across to a complacent public. I was invited to attend one of the early meetings of their organization in Princeton, New Jersey, and there for the first time met Einstein, Leo Szilard, and many of the other leading nuclear physicists. They discussed the theoretical possibility of producing a hydrogen bomb with many times the destructive power of the fission process and agreed that it might be feasible. The logic of their impassioned argument I found irrefutable, and their desperate sense of urgency reinforced my own conviction that we had little time left.

Of all the extraordinary men at that meeting, the most remarkable, Albert Einstein, was the one who attached himself most actively to our cause. He allowed us to use his name on our letterhead and, during our periodic financial crises, he would personally undertake to send telegrams soliciting funds from our wealthiest potential donors. He wrote an enthusiastic endorsement for my book, which was used on the dust jacket when the book was published in the fall of

1947 under the title *Peace or Anarchy*. When one of the networks proposed a nationwide broadcast, he agreed to join me, with Raymond Swing as moderator, in broadcasting from his little house in Princeton. At first he was hesitant, claiming that the American public might resent a recent émigré's presuming to give advice. Such reluctance was typical of his genuine humility. Many of the great and famous one encounters in this world display an egocentric arrogance. Yet this man, who had more reason to be proud than any of them, always showed a humble gentleness that made their arrogance seem to me even more pretentious and less excusable.

As with most organizations that have an idealistic purpose and presume to promote the general welfare, factional quarrels within UWF over strategy and tactics were frequent. These policy disputes were resolved by democratic debate and decision at our annual conventions of the delegates elected by the UWF chapters throughout the country. One such issue was whether the organization should oppose unilateral disarmament and support U.S. defense expenditures in the absence of any effective system of world security. There were a number of Quakers in the organization, and they tended to oppose a policy that was inconsistent with their pacifist convictions. I insisted that the organization must go on record as favoring an adequate U.S. military defense system and was supported by a large majority of the membership.

In my speeches around the country to every conceivable variety of audience, from the Oklahoma State Legislature to the annual convention of the Junior Chamber of Commerce, I would try to leave time for a question period. There were two lines of questioning that consistently emerged and to which we had no really satisfactory answers. Quite understandably, many people wanted to know what the reaction of the Soviet government would be toward our proposals and how such a one-party state would fit into a federal structure. Our standard reply was to stress that no system of internationally enforced disarmament could work without the Soviets as participants, in view of their size and military strength. Whether they would agree to the necessary controls, we argued, could be determined only when and if the U.S. government put the proposition squarely to them. As the first nation to develop and use the atomic bomb, it was our responsibility to take the initiative in proposing the means by which it could be controlled. Only then would the Russians have a chance to react. We acknowledged that Marxist ideology and the totalitarian structure of the Soviet state would make it enormously difficult for the Soviet leaders to accept international inspection and control, but we argued that, faced with the alternative of a nuclear arms race and universally destructive war, they might accept. I would end my answer to this question by quoting Bertrand Russell: "Men are sufficiently rational to acquiesce in their own survival."

To queries regarding the Baruch Plan, which our government had proposed and the Soviets had rejected, I would explain that this plan as finally presented to the United Nations called for an international system of inspection and control that was confined to nuclear weapons, while allowing the competition to continue for all other types of weaponry and providing no effective means of enforcement in the event of evasion. In effect, I maintained that we were lucky that the Soviets had not accepted this proposal, since it would have left them in control of their huge conventional army, while we would have given up the one weapons system in which we had a decisive advantage.

A second major category of persistent questions related to the problem of representation in a revised United Nations. If lawmaking authority were transferred to the U.N. General Assembly, where each nation had one vote, would this not give disproportionate voting strength to the increasing number of small nations? In reply, we would stress the limited grant of authority that we were advocating and admit that some system of "weighted" voting would have to be worked out, which would take into account size of population, industrial strength, and other factors. Grenville Clark and Professor Louis Sohn at the Harvard Law School did in fact come up with a specific and carefully calculated system of weighted voting, but the questioning on this point was persistent. It would be even more troublesome today if such an issue were being debated. The number of nations that are members of the U.N. has nearly tripled, and we have learned that the less developed countries can act together as an influential voting bloc.

Despite the undercurrent of skepticism that these legitimate questions reflected, the size and influence of the UWF grew steadily in the 1947–48 period, as did the number of our supporters in the Congress. With increasing influence came the growth of organized opposition on the left and on the right. The American Communist Party staked out its position early in a theoretical article that appeared in the July 1946 issue of *New Masses*. It condemned "the reactionary utopianism of the world state project" and stated that, "by seeking solutions in abstract reason and justice rather than in the actual class forces in society, it [world government] weakens the struggle for progress and strengthens the hand of reaction."

Obviously disturbed by the progress that our cause was making not only at home but in Western Europe and elsewhere, the Soviet regime launched a vitriolic propaganda campaign against us. In an address, delivered in Warsaw in September 1947, to the leaders of the European Communist parties, Zhdanov, then a leading member of the Soviet Politburo, coupled his attack on the Marshall Plan with the following assault on world federalists and all our works:

> One of the lines taken by the ideological campaign that goes hand in hand with the plans for the enslavement of Europe is attack on the principle of national sovereignty, an appeal for the renouncement of the sovereign rights of nations, to which is opposed the idea of a "world government." The purpose of this campaign is to mask the unbridled expansion of American imperialism, which is ruthlessly violating the sovereign rights of nations, to represent the U.S. as a champion of universal laws, and those who resist American penetration as believers in an obsolete and "selfish" nationalism. The idea of a "world government" has been taken up by bourgeois intellectual cranks and pacifists. . . .

This invective against the general idea of world federalism was combined with venomous attacks on me personally. Moscow radio ransacked its knapsack of well-worn clichés and came up with the accusation that I was "the fig leaf of American imperialism." One beneficial by-product of this doctrinaire opposition was the fact that our organization was never troubled by attempts of American Communists to infiltrate our ranks.

However, this clear evidence of Communist antipathy did not deter our critics on the far right from charging that we were part of a Communist conspiracy. These extreme nationalists and right-wing isolationists believed that any proposal to limit American sovereignty was virtually synonymous with treason. In language that equaled the violence of Communist rhetoric, Joseph P. Kamp charged, in a pamphlet entitled "We Must Abolish the United States," that "crafty subversive schemers—Socialists, Communist-fronters, Left-wing Liberals and One World Firsters—control the World Government movement." Similarly, Myron C. Fagan in a pamphlet distributed by the Cinema Educational Guild charged that in comparison to me, "Benedict Arnold was a small-timer." I was not the first and will not be the last to learn that any proposal for the radical reform of society, no matter how well intentioned, brings down on the reformer's head a heavy weight of emotional hatred and personal invective. Xenophobic nationalism was thriving in those days.

During this period, in addition to my work with the UWF, I took an active part in the formation of the American Veterans Committee (AVC). Through my acquaintance with Charles Bolte at the San Francisco conference, I became interested in the new organization and was impressed both by its refusal to become a lobby for veterans' bonuses and by what appeared to me to be its intelligent commitment to the idea that America would have to continue its active participation in world affairs and avoid the retreat to isolation of the 1920s. I believed that an articulate organization of World War II veterans of this persuasion might have an important political role to play.

In the spring of 1946, I learned from Bolte that the American Communist Party was attempting to infiltrate and gain control of the American Veterans Committee. The Communists had previously directed their veteran members to infiltrate American Legion posts, but seeing the growth of the new organization, they switched their strategy and attempted to take over the leadership of the AVC in the formative stage. This large influx of hard-core party members with their disciplined tactics would have been a serious threat to even the most mature and skillful anti-Communist leadership. In spite of our lack of experience in this type of infighting, we determined to meet the threat and to attempt to save the organization rather than withdraw. I went to the first national convention of the AVC in June 1946 in Des Moines, uncertain whether we had the votes and the organizational discipline to defeat our determined opponents.

At Des Moines, most of the time was devoted to the political struggle. In order to ensure as much unity of action as possible, both on policy and in the election of the twenty-four member National Planning Committee, which was to run the organization between annual conventions, a caucus was formed under the leadership of Bolte. We later called it the Independent Progressive Caucus. Its leadership included, among others, Oren Root, who had run Wendell Willkie's campaign for the presidency; G. Mennen Williams, later governor of Michigan; Franklin D. Roosevelt, Jr.; Robert Nathan; Gus Tyler, one of David Dubinsky's trusted lieutenants in the International Ladies' Garment Workers Union; and me. Tyler provided invaluable assistance because of his experience in the struggles against the Communists in the labor movement.

Our strategy at Des Moines was threefold. First, we were determined to prevent the inclusion of party-line policy statements in our national and foreign policy platforms. This we succeeded in doing, but it required night-long committee sessions in which the Communists attempted to postpone the decisive voting in the hope that our supporters would leave through sheer fatigue. I remember that in the foreign policy platform committee the sun was streaming through the hotel windows when we finally finished our work. Secondly, we attempted to inform the innocent and uninformed in all the state delegations that the opposition was composed in fact of genuine Communists and not of well-intentioned liberals. Finally, our caucus agreed on a slate of twenty-four candidates for the National Planning Committee and attempted to avoid dissipating our voting strength by ensuring that all those who agreed with us voted for the entire slate and did not exercise independence of judgment. In some ways, our strategy was a departure from the democratic ideal of free and open debate. But it was forced upon us by the disciplined political machine the Communists employed against us. Our only hope was to meet their disciplined unity of action with a self-imposed singleness of purpose of our own.

The Communist organization called itself the Unity Caucus and was led by extremely able men. We discovered that day-to-day strategy at the convention was decided in the party headquarters in New York and relayed to the faithful by John Gates, then editor of the *Daily Worker*, on whose hotel room we maintained a twenty-four-hour watch in order to identify as many as possible of the individual Communist leaders. Communist tactics were aimed at confusing the real issue by charges that our caucus was weakening, and splitting the organization at a time when unity was needed in the fight for the rights of returning veterans. Unity to the Communists meant agreement with their position.

The Communists also refused to admit their true allegiance and called us red-baiters, thus playing on the doubts of many who had only too often seen honest liberals accused of Communist sympathies by fanatics on the extreme right. I saw at first hand how genuine Communists can profit by the fact that innocent people have been falsely accused. Ill-informed or maliciously false accusations of communism enable the covert party members to seek sympathy and support from those who erroneously believe them to be among the innocent victims of slander and libel. The Communists also were aided by the right-wing press, which gave wide publicity to the attempted Communist infiltration but no coverage to the successful fight our caucus waged against that attempt. This one-sided publicity persuaded many whose votes we needed to resign from the organization in fear of repercussions in their home communities.

The Des Moines convention ended with the election of a solid majority of our caucus to the National Planning Committee and a strong minority we suspected of being Communists or consistent fellow travelers. Together with Root, Williams, and Roosevelt, I was among those elected from our slate. This proportion was somewhat of an exaggeration of the voting strength of the suspected Communist sympathizers, since they engaged in "bullet voting." They concentrated all their votes on eight selected candidates and left the rest of their ballots blank, which under the proportional system of election worked to their considerable advantage. I first became aware of this technique when I picked up a packet of matches on the convention floor during the election and asked Gus Tyler why there were only eight names written on the flap. He laughed and commented, "When are you Ivy League liberals ever going to learn?" Needless to say, we closed this loophole at the next convention by requiring that all ballots carry twenty-four names to be valid.

In addition to our majority on the National Planning Committee, we succeeded in reelecting Charles Bolte to the chairmanship and another member of our caucus, Gilbert Harrison, as vice-chairman. In this way, we ensured our control of the national office and of the funds collected on a national basis.[4]

The National Planning Committee met four times during the year, and these sessions were largely spent in jockeying for position in preparation for the next convention. The left-wing element attempted to build a record of militant activity. It came out in favor of bigger veteran bonuses to corral votes and to embarrass our caucus, which opposed bonuses and favored instead the integration of the veteran into a generally prosperous economy under the slogan "Citizens first, veterans second." It resorted to slanderous charges of misuse of funds by the national office.

By the time of the second national convention in Milwaukee in June of 1947, we had built a disciplined organization and were prepared for the fight. The balance of political power in Milwaukee was complicated by the emergence of a third grouping, which called itself the Build AVC caucus. This group was separate from the left-wing element; it was composed of those who felt it was time to call a truce in the bitter factional fighting and to concentrate on the objectives of the organization. I had some friends in this third caucus and tried to convince them that their compromise position could only work to the advantage of the Communists by splitting the anti-Communist vote. I was to learn only years later that a vocal member of this third force had been a controlled secret agent of the KGB, at that time, and that his strategy of splitting our ranks had been devised in Moscow.

At Milwaukee, I was one of the leaders in the struggle to write a foreign policy platform, and here as usual the left-wing group opposed the idea of world federalism and offered in opposition resolutions in favor of Big Three unanimity. In spite of the confusing effect of the Build AVC group, our caucus succeeded in reducing left-wing representation on the National Planning Committee, and together with most of the other leaders of our caucus I was reelected. One revealing incident occurred on the convention floor when I was presenting the foreign policy resolutions. In the confusion of last-minute drafting, we had forgotten to include a ritual denunciation of the Franco dictatorship. The left-wing leaders seized upon this omission as proof that we harbored secret Fascist sympathies. A number of their veterans who had been wounded in the Spanish Civil War rose to denounce me. To repair the damage, I could only argue that the omission had been inadvertent and offered a suitable resolution condemning Franco, which passed by a large majority.

Subsequent meetings of the National Planning Committee were riven by bitter disputes over such issues as the Marshall Plan and the Soviet coup in Czechoslovakia in February 1948. With our majority, we committed the organization to full support of the Marshall Plan against the last-ditch opposition of the left wing. Similarly, we condemned the Soviet role in the brutal liquidation of Czech freedoms. When one of the leftist leaders attempted to argue that what had happened in Czechoslovakia was merely a routine change of cabinets, he was greeted with derisive laughter.

By the time of the third convention at Cleveland in November 1948, we were ready for the showdown. Those who supported the Soviet position on the increasing number of issues that divided the Russians and the West had revealed their true identity and made their motivation suspect to the innocent and the gullible. In a long and highly emotional session, we proceeded to amend the bylaws so as to deny membership in the organization to members of the Communist Party. The battle for control had been won, and our victory proved that Communists and Communist sympathizers can be outorganized and outvoted without the necessity of dismantling the democratic freedoms and rights of our society in order to defeat them.

My participation in this struggle provided a unique opportunity to learn at first hand the strengths and weaknesses of Communist organizational strategy. As nothing else could, it gave me an understanding of how formidable is that dedicated man, the Communist true believer, and it taught me never to underestimate the potential strength of a disciplined Communist minority. It revealed the techniques of covert infiltration and control, through which Communists have too often captured organizations from those who awoke too late to these dangers. In microcosm, our struggle was an extension of the political battle being waged then in Western Europe between the democratic left and the mass Communist parties of Italy and France. My role in this small skirmish made me realize how much was at stake on the larger stage.

During 1949, I became convinced that our attempts to transform the United Nations had been overtaken by events that could no longer be ignored or explained away. Stalin's drive to impose his rule through satellite Communist parties on the nations of Eastern Europe dramatized the impossibility of believing that he would allow any kind of international inspection or control within his monolithic empire. I came to feel that we would be deceiving the American public with illusory hopes if we continued to promise that there was any chance of Stalin's accepting a supranational structure of enforceable law. In the fall of 1949, I resigned as president of the United World Federalists, to be succeeded by Alan Cranston, who later was elected to the Senate from California, and I returned to Harvard to take up the remaining two years of my fellowship.

In that same year, the Soviets exploded their own atomic bomb. In four brief years, our atomic monopoly had been broken, and we and our friends in the Emergency Committee of Atomic Scientists had been proved correct in our prediction that the Russians could accomplish the feat within a five-year period. A secret international competition in the construction of more and bigger nuclear weapons now loomed as inevitable on the darkening horizon. The secreting of increasing amounts of fissionable material in national arsenals would make more and more difficult the acceptance of international controls that could be relied upon to account for all that had been produced. The bargaining power that the United States had gained from its sole possession of the new weapon was lost.

Finally, my first-hand exposure to Communist organizational strategy in the AVC struggle had made me realize how dangerous it could be to give substantial power to a United Nations that might in time come to be heavily influenced by a Communist voting bloc. Minimal standards of protection for individual rights and personal liberty against the police power of the state came to seem more and more essential to a restructured United Nations as the flickering lights of such freedom were snuffed out one by one by the Communist leaders of Eastern Europe.

These rational doubts about the continued relevance of the world federalist solution to the real problems of our time would have been enough to persuade me to retire from the arena, but there were also personal reasons. After two years of itinerant speaking and organizing, I had ceased to enjoy my role as Cassandra. My repetitive warnings of approaching nuclear doom echoed hollowly in my head, and I came to dislike the sound of my own voice as I promised a federalist salvation in which I no longer had real confidence. I took no pleasure in being looked upon as a remote and dedicated person, and I resented the distance that public notoriety had put between me and my wife and two sons. I felt that I had fulfilled my obligation to my friends who had been killed in the war by trying to make the most of the brief opportunity that our nuclear monopoly had offered. I was sure by then that we faced a protracted struggle with the Soviets and looked forward to returning to Harvard to improve my understanding of the nature of that rivalry and to repair the obvious gaps in my comprehension of the complex play of economic and political forces behind the flow of international events.

An excerpt from the journal that I kept intermittently after the war conveys my feelings on retiring from active leadership of the world federalist movement.

3 Jan. '50—To be always talking and thinking about an imminent catastrophe is unbecoming and in a certain sense rude and barbaric. I read somewhere that during the years of the plague in London the subject was by common consent avoided in conversation. But there is a difference in this case. The plague was like fate itself; there was nothing that one could do about it, so why discuss it. This war is not yet inevitable and predestined, so that one does in fact have the right to warn and exhort.

But there are limits. It is a mistake to become totally engrossed in this matter to the exclusion of everything else. And that is what I have done, forgetting that love between individuals, that small acts of kindness and respect, that the pleasures of artistic enjoyment and creation, that all these things and more are an essential part of one's life to be omitted only at the cost of that feeling of barren sterility that I feel now.

The difficulty is to avoid on the one hand the unproductive and inhuman fanaticism of which I have perhaps been guilty and on the other the amused and contemptuous objectivity of some of the Harvard professors, who are able to be disinterested only because they lack sympathy for their fellow men. To be able to admit the probability of one's defeat and yet to be able to fight on without bitterness or fanaticism is the real accomplishment.

Looking back, I ask myself where we were right and where we were wrong in our understanding of the choices faced by the United States in those times. Certainly, we were correct in predicting that

our atomic monopoly would be short-lived and that the newly
created structure of the United Nations was completely incapable of
controlling the resulting nuclear arms race that we foresaw as inevitable. The Security Council and General Assembly have too often
degenerated into propaganda forums for the exchange of charge and
countercharge for anyone to claim that the United Nations in its own
right has been able to contribute much to the solution of disputes
between the United States and the Soviet Union.

Where the big powers have been able to agree on the need for the
peaceful settlement of disputes between third parties, the United
Nations has played a useful role. It has demonstrated its ability to
organize peace-keeping forces from the contributions of the smaller
countries to police the agreed terms of settlement. The specialized
functional organizations of the United Nations such as the World
Health Organization and the Food and Agricultural Organization
have improved international cooperation and understanding in their
respective fields. However, the United Nations has proved as impotent as we predicted in dealing with the rivalry between its most
powerful members.

As for the arms race between the Soviet Union and the United
States, it has followed much the course that we anticipated, with
some significant exceptions. The balance of terror that rests on the
ability of each side to wreak enormous retaliatory damage has proved
more stable than we feared it might be. The damage within the
United States to democratic institutions, and the limitations on personal liberties that we predicted as the inevitable result of the armaments competition, has not yet occurred, although the McCarthy era
was a warning that this danger is real.

Finally, we underestimated the pace of technological innovation
and could not anticipate the development by both the United States
and the Soviet Union of orbital surveillance satellites capable of high-
resolution photography. This technological breakthrough made the
SALT agreements possible by giving each side the ability to verify
independently the limits accepted on the number of certain types of
weapons. We had always thought that close and continuous on-site
inspection by international authorities was an essential requirement
if there was to be any acceptance of arms control. In fact, such on-site
inspection is eventually going to be necessary, if the SALT agreements are to be broadened to cover a wide range of weaponry that

cannot be accurately counted or identified by cameras in the sky.

Our most serious miscalculation was the assumption that the danger of devastating nuclear war could be used to bridge the gap between differing institutions and ideologies. It would have been difficult enough, though not impossible, to persuade the American body politic to accept the necessary limitations on national sovereignty if the Russians had been willing to make similar concessions. However, it was impossible for Stalin's regime to accept the enforceable legal order that we proposed, and still survive. International inspection would have exposed the horrors of Stalin's concentration camps and destroyed the carefully constructed illusion of Russia as a progressive society. Nor was the Soviet regime prepared to give up its own version of an eventual world government as a union of Communist-dominated nations, under the leading influence of the Russian Communist Party.

The early pessimism expressed in my *Atlantic* article of 1945 proved to be realistic and prophetic. There was not a sufficient foundation of shared belief and democratic institutions on which to build the federal structure that was required to contain the nuclear threat. It did not follow from the fact that we could split the atom that we could unite a world divided by deep ideological differences and conflicting national ambitions. Contrary to our hopes, the advent of the atomic age did not bring with it "the good news of damnation." Rational fear of nuclear destruction could not substitute for the absence of common purpose.

Were the time and effort that we spent in the cause of world federalism then entirely wasted? Not in my opinion. Our specific criticism of the weaknesses and deficiencies of the United Nations was realistic and borne out by subsequent events. To the extent that we contributed to public understanding of how little had been accomplished at San Francisco, and how brief our atomic monopoly would be, we helped remove some prevalent illusions, and defined the price that will eventually have to be paid if there is to be a peaceful conclusion to the arms race. We were premature in the sense that we proposed more than the world was yet ready or able to accept. We were too late because the basic structure of the postwar world had been frozen into place by the decisions of the major allies before the guns fell silent.

Chapter 4

Secret Trial

ON RETURNING TO HARVARD in the fall of 1949 to complete my fellowship, my wife and I rented a small house on the outskirts of Cambridge. With the birth of a third son, it came to seem even smaller, but the quiet life we led was a welcome relief from the constant turmoil of our previous existence. My wife took courses in painting at the Cambridge School of Design and began to discover that she had talent as well as interest in the work. I had more time to spend with our boys.

In my academic work, my objective was to equip myself with as thorough an understanding as possible of the complex diplomatic, political, and economic problems that American policy would have to confront on the world stage. I sought to prepare myself for active participation in what I foresaw would be a protracted competition between the United States and the Soviet Union.

With this end in view, I plunged into an intensive study of economic theory and fiscal policy. My mentor was a Harvard professor named Arthur Smithies, who combined theoretical brilliance with the practical experience derived from his previous position in Washington as chief of the fiscal policy division of the Bureau of the Budget. He transformed economics, which Churchill once called "that dismal science," into a fascinating exploration of the practical consequences of the revolution in economic thinking brought about by John Maynard Keynes and his followers. Smithies was committed to the principles of the free market economy but believed in the necessity for compensatory governmental action to moderate the periodic swings of the business cycle. He exposed the simplified and doctrinaire assumptions of current Marxist economic thinking and satisfied me that, given intelligent management, there was no inherent necessity for the market economy to suffer sequential and ever more disastrous depressions, as the Marxists predicted.

In the field of international trade, taught by Gottfried von Haberler and Seymour Harris, my work convinced me of the need for maintaining a high level of American production and employment and for reducing American tariff barriers and trade restrictions if a struggle for protected world markets was not to destroy the unity of the West. I also became convinced of the need for a much larger flow of both governmental and private investment into the under-developed world if these countries were to have a chance of making a democratic transition to an industrialized economy.

Exposure to the grim arithmetic of exploding population growth in the poorer countries made me an early true believer in the need for effective national and international programs designed to limit the increase. Otherwise, I could see in the unappeasable hunger of starving millions a threat to future peace and to democratic institutions almost as great as the atomic bomb itself. With a few exceptions, population trends in the third world since that time have served to dramatize and increase the size of the problem.

While engaged in these explorations, I also began work on a new book, in which I tried to document chronologically the events that led to the deterioration of relations between the U.S. and the U.S.S.R. By studying the documents and memoirs that were available to the public at that time, I attempted to come to an objective conclusion as to where the responsibility lay for starting the cold war. By the fall of 1950, my research was sufficiently advanced for me to give a series of public lectures under the auspices of the Lowell Institute.

My study of the sequence of action and reaction by the Soviet Union and the United States led me step by step to the conclusion that Stalin had never had any intention of honoring his wartime pledge at Yalta to permit free elections in Eastern Europe. His plans to install Communist regimes under Moscow's control in that area were far advanced long before the fighting stopped; the Red armies halted at the gates of Warsaw in a deliberate attempt to ensure the liquidation of the anti-Communist Polish underground which had risen in premature revolt against the Germans.

Nor did the record seem to me to show that Stalin was prepared to settle for a stable and well-defined sphere of influence. The increased territorial demands at Potsdam, the Soviet pressures against Iran, Turkey, and Greece, and the manipulation of the disciplined Communist parties and front groups in Western Europe all appeared to be part of an expansionary drive that assumed an American postwar unwillingness to become engaged in international power politics. The rapid demobilization of the U.S. Army must have confirmed Stalin in his perception of risks and opportunities.

It struck me as significant that an internal propaganda campaign to condition Soviet minds against the capitalist West and the United States in particular began as early as the beginning of 1945, and that Stalin, in a major speech on February 9, 1946, denied the possibility of genuine cooperation with the non-Communist world long before American opinion had given up hope of such cooperation. It seemed to me then, as it does now, that American policy and public opinion moved only slowly and reluctantly to the belief that the Soviets posed an expansionary threat. Through much of this period, I was engaged in trying to persuade American opinion of the possibility that the Russians might cooperate in controlling the new weapons, and I know how much goodwill there was to begin with.

The revisionist historians have since tried to paint a very different picture of this era and to demonstrate that American policymakers bear a large share of the responsibility for the deterioration of the alliance into cold war competition. Having lived through the period and reviewed the chronological sequence of decision making, I cannot accept their version of events. In fact, the most important new evidence that has appeared since those days has given us a much more complete understanding of the internal dynamics of Stalin's regime.

Solzhenitsyn's *Gulag Archipelago*, Robert Conquest's *The Great Terror*, and the publication of Khrushchev's secret speech in 1956, taken together, have added a new dimension to our grasp of why and how Stalin made the decisions that he did. A regime based so completely on the murderous ambition of one man and ruled so thoroughly by an arbitrary and brutal secret police could not afford to allow in any of the foreign territories that it occupied the existence of an organized political opposition. By the nature of his regime at home and the ideological doctrine needed to justify it, Stalin had no choice but to duplicate on a smaller scale in Eastern Europe and in North Korea the same police state and systematic use of terror that were the foundations of his rule.

In the spring of 1951, I suspended work on my half-finished book in order to take the Ph.D. exams. By this time, American involvement in the Korean War had convinced me against the pursuit of an academic career, and I decided to go to Washington to see if there was a place for me in that part of the bureaucracy that dealt with foreign policy. For the time being, I had had enough of scholarly research and felt again the need to be actively involved in a cause that I believed in. After the Berlin blockade and the attack on South Korea, the challenge that Stalin's policy presented seemed very real, and I was anxious to make whatever contribution I could to the worldwide effort to contain the outward thrust of Soviet power.

Looking far ahead, I was convinced that by confining the Soviet empire within the boundaries that emerged from World War II, we had our best chance of assisting developments that might eventually lead to basic internal changes in the Soviet system itself. In the triumphant extension of Soviet-directed Communist rule into new national territories, I could see only a strengthening of the Soviet system at home and the gradual enforced isolation of the United States in an increasingly hostile world. The best chance for the development of a more open society in the Soviet Union seemed to me to lie in demonstrating with patient firmness that Stalin's police state was not exportable and that the tides of history did not inevitably flow in the direction of a Communist-dominated world. I believed then, as I do now, that the talented and long-suffering Russian people would eventually demand a greater voice in the management of their own affairs and a wider scope for the expression of individual talent and opinion. When that day came, I believed we would have a new opportunity to build together a supranational structure of enforceable law.

That hope, however, was far in the future as I went down to Washington in the spring of 1951 to enlist in a struggle that was less violent but more complex and ambiguous than the war I had volunteered to join ten years before. I had some friends in the State Department, and they listened with polite attention as I offered my services and described my qualifications. However, they were not encouraging. They explained quite frankly that my prominent association with the world federalist movement had made me so controversial that the department could not risk the public criticism that my appointment might cause.

My next interview was with Allen Dulles, who was at that time deputy director for plans of the Central Intelligence Agency. We had met as participants on radio and TV talk shows in New York, and we had a number of friends in common at whose houses we had played tennis together on Long Island weekends. However, I did not know him well and knew little about his wartime career in the OSS. He was kind enough to give me more than an hour of his time, and we had a fascinating discussion. In a serious and careful way, he spelled out the nature of the world situation as he saw it and the complex challenge with which we were confronted by Stalin's regime. He was well-informed concerning my active role in the struggle for control within the American Veterans Committee, and we discussed at some length the strength and influence of the Communist parties of Western Europe. At the end of the meeting, he made me a firm offer of a job with the Agency at a middle level of executive responsibility and assured me that the work would be suited to my abilities and past experience, although for security reasons he could not describe the job in any detail. I took with me the voluminous personal history forms that had to be filled out and said I would let him know within a week.

While I was in Washington, I looked up an old college friend who had joined the CIA a year before. I needed some reassurance about what life was like inside a large secret bureaucracy. He turned out to be enthusiastic about his work and high in his praise of the ability and quality of his colleagues. He mentioned the names of a few other old friends who had recently joined the Agency and assured me that they also found the work rewarding. I still had some reservations about the general nature of the intelligence business and was only too well aware of my own ignorance as to what was actually involved.

Therefore, before leaving Washington, I asked Walter Lippmann for his advice on whether to take the job. I had met him during the time I was active in the federalist movement and, although we did not always agree, I admired his breadth of mind and respected his knowledge of the Washington scene. Lippmann's reaction was cautiously positive. From his experience in World War I, he had had some exposure to the role that intelligence can play and he was convinced that we were going to need a competent intelligence service in the difficult years ahead. He had a high regard for Allen Dulles, and I came away from my talk with him reassured in my own mind that I would not be making a mistake in accepting Dulles' offer.

Looking back, I think that the impression Allen Dulles made on me was the decisive factor in my final decision. Behind his jovial and bluff exterior, he struck me as having a searching and undogmatic mind and a cosmopolitan and sophisticated knowledge of the world. My talk with him convinced me that we shared a common perception of the dangers that our country faced, and it seemed to me that an organization that had such a man in one of its top positions was one well worth working for. In the years that followed, I was to learn that in addition to his other qualities, he was a loyal and courageous friend in time of trouble.

On my return to Cambridge, I found that my wife was all in favor of the move to Washington. Her sister and other good friends lived there and she looked forward to a change of scene. After mailing my acceptance and personal history statement to Washington, I had to wait for the long process of security clearance to be completed, and we used the time to find an old house in McLean, Virginia. By early October 1951, I was at work with the Central Intelligence Agency in one of the dilapidated buildings along the reflecting pool that lies below the Lincoln Memorial.

After a brief period of training, I was assigned to what was then called the Office of Policy Coordination, headed by Frank Wisner, which was responsible for the conduct of covert operations abroad. By chance, I arrived just as a new presidential directive called for an intensification of covert action operations to cope with what was seen as a worldwide Communist political and propaganda offensive. This directive, NSC 10/5, was issued on October 21, 1951, and clearly assigned to the CIA the responsibility for mounting an expanded covert action program with policy guidance to be supplied by an NSC subcommittee. In fact, I happened to join the Agency at a time

when its responsibilities, its budget, and its manpower were all expanding rapidly as the result of presidential decisions that had the
full support of the relevant committees of the Congress.[1]

It was an exhilarating atmosphere in which to work. Policy direction from the top levels of the government was clear and unambiguous, and reflected a broad consensus in the country as a whole. The
opposition in the form of Stalin's regime obviously threatened the
survival of democratic freedoms in Western Europe and elsewhere
through its control of disciplined indigenous Communist parties and
front groups. The massive and secret subsidies that the Soviets channeled to their chosen political instruments gave them a dangerous
advantage over the poorly financed and disunited democratic forces.
The progress achieved by the Marshall Plan and the efforts to bolster
Western European defense could all be undermined by a successful
Communist takeover organized from within. American assistance to
democratic political parties and institutions seemed essential if a free
and pluralistic society was to survive in Western Europe.

The fact that our assistance had to be kept secret did not disturb
me. The European political and cultural leaders who solicited our aid
in their unequal struggle with the Soviet-subsidized apparatus made
it a condition that there be no publicity, since the Communist propaganda machine could exploit any overt evidence of official American
support as proof that they were puppets of the American imperialists. Discretion and secrecy were required if our assistance was not
to be self-defeating. We could take no public credit for our timely
rescue of democratic institutions, since such publicity could have
destroyed the very people we were trying to help. Even today, when
a recovered and prosperous Europe no longer needs this type of
American assistance, it would serve no useful purpose to identify all
the individuals and groups we were able to help in those days, since
they are still vulnerable to Communist propaganda attack.

I have no intention of adding to the many exposés of past secret
Agency activity that are already in the public domain as the result
of leaks and congressional investigations. But where such disclosures
have already occurred, I do intend to explain the motivation behind
these actions and to place them in a historical context that has often
been missing in the sensational press coverage. It violates no confidence to point out that in the case of the covert action program in
Western Europe, the bulk of our support went to left-of-center dem-

ocratic parties. The right wing and conservative forces had their own sources of financial support, and the real competition with the Communists for votes and influence was focused on the left side of the political spectrum, where the struggle for the allegiance of the European working class and the liberal intelligentsia would be decided.

As the Church committee was later to conclude, this particular program enjoyed all the advantages that are likely to make covert action a successful instrument of national policy.[2] Our assistance was in close tactical support of a national objective, the rebuilding of Western Europe, which had the approval of the Congress after being thoroughly debated. Moreover, those whom we were trying to help shared a common purpose with us and had the will and organizational ability, if given the means, to achieve their objective.

Engaged in work that I believed in and enjoying the company of able and congenial colleagues, I had no reason to be concerned when on August 31, 1953, I was summoned to a meeting with Richard Helms. At that time, Helms was chief of operations and second in command under Frank Wisner of what had become the Directorate for Plans.[3] Although we later became close friends, I did not know him well at the time but I respected his competence as a manager. The beginning of what then transpired I recorded a week later in some notes that I kept on these events.

7 Sept. '53—Suddenly and unexpectedly, I have been plunged into the treacherous rip tides that have gone so far recently toward undermining the confidence of Americans in one another and have eroded the liberties and rights we once took so easily for granted. What the outcome will be, I cannot foresee, but I remember the opening scene with especial vividness.

At 4 P.M. August 31st, I was in my office discussing with a Branch Chief certain lines of action we planned to follow when the phone rang and I was requested to go to the office of Dick Helms. He seemed uncomfortable as I sat down opposite his desk. Offering me a cigarette, he said, "I've got a rough one." He went on to remind me that an FBI investigation into my past had been going on for the last three months. I'd been told about this at the time, my name having come up in the course of an

FBI investigation of someone else. I had not been worried, since I could remember nothing in my past that could cast any doubt on my loyalty.

Helms then said, "Well, they've apparently found something in your past that looks serious."

There my journal entry ends, but I recall that Helms went on to explain that under the terms of the new Executive Order No. 10450, issued in April by President Eisenhower to tighten security standards for federal employees, I was subject to suspension if the charges against me were sufficiently grave. He added that the CIA regulation that had been issued to conform to the new Executive Order was very strict.[4] It gave the deputy director of administration the authority to suspend with or without pay any Agency employee whose continued retention was not "clearly consistent with the interests of the national security." In my case, it had been decided that the allegations against me in the FBI report were so serious that I was to be suspended immediately without pay. Helms explained that in the absence of Allen Dulles, who by that time had become Director of Central Intelligence (DCI) but who was on a trip abroad, his deputy, General Charles P. Cabell, had approved the decision.

I listened to this in stunned silence, and Helms seemed almost as disturbed as I was myself by what he had to tell me. Finally, I asked to see a copy of the charges, but Helms told me that a final version of the FBI's allegations was not yet ready for my review because the bureau was still trying to find language that would protect its confidential sources. He went on to advise me that in three or four days the Agency's general counsel, Lawrence Houston, would be able to give me a full description of the allegations and that I would then have a thirty-day period in which to respond. In the meanwhile, I was instructed to leave my office that evening and told that I would not be able to return to work until I had satisfactorily disposed of the charges against me.

A cover story, Helms said, would be devised to explain my absence. He promised that the Agency would do everything possible to restrict the number of people aware of my trouble and to prevent leaks to the press. He assured me that I would receive a fair hearing if I chose to fight for reinstatement. I made it clear that I intended to defend my record and reputation, and we both agreed that I would need a good lawyer.

Numb and bewildered, I shook hands and, walking down the corridor, began the endlessly repetitive and futile process of searching my memory for any conceivable explanation of what the FBI might have discovered or misconstrued. During this entire unhappy affair, the worst period for me emotionally was the four-day delay between the time I stood accused of disloyal acts so grave that my suspension without pay was required and the time I was finally informed of what my anonymous accusers had to say against me. These shadowy and mysteriously malevolent allegations hung poised above my head, filling every waking moment with threatening suspense. When sleep deserted me in the hours before dawn, I read for the second time Kafka's *The Trial* and understood as I never had before the plight of his bewildered hero, who could never discover why or by whom he had been accused.

My wife was inclined to treat the whole affair lightly and encouraged me to think that it must be the result of some misunderstanding or mistaken identity that could easily be explained. I was not so sure. In those days when the high tide of Senator McCarthy's power in the land was still rising, I knew that suspicion was in the eyes of many synonymous with guilt and that publicity was tantamount to conviction.

I was from the first moment determined to fight my case through to the end, because I knew that the least I could lose was my right to a government job. Far more significant was the fact that if I resigned, I would by implication be admitting the truth of the charges against me. My entire reputation, the possibility of being of any future service to my country, and the chance of enjoying any position of responsibility in our society were at stake, and I knew it. I realized also that the cards were stacked against me. Under the terms of Eisenhower's new Executive Order, the burden of proof was on the accused, and the government did not have to prove that any specifically disloyal act had been committed; it only had to find that my continued employment was not "clearly consistent with the interests of the national security."

I tried to explain these unpleasant facts of life to my wife and also warned her that the period of my suspension without pay might be protracted and that legal advice would be expensive. With three children to feed and clothe and little in the way of private income, the loss of my government pay was a serious blow, as we discovered when we sat down to work out a skeleton budget and to figure out how long our savings would last.

On September 4, after four days of steadily mounting suspense, I was called into Larry Houston's office and handed a memorandum that contained a summary of the charges contained in the FBI report, with the language carefully phrased so as to protect the anonymity of my accusers and the nature of the surveillance techniques that might have been employed. This is the complete document as it was given to me:

4 September 1953

Memorandum for: Mr. Cord Meyer, Jr.

In accordance with the provisions of Executive Order 10450 (Security Requirements for Government Employment) and CIA Regulation No. 20-730 (Regulations Under Executive Order 10450 Relating to Security Requirements for Employment in the Central Intelligence Agency), this Agency is in receipt of information indicating that your retention as an employee of the Government may not be clearly consistent with the interests of the national security.

In view of the information received, and in accordance with Section 5(c) of CIA Regulation No. 20-730, you have been suspended without pay, as you were notified, effective as of the close of business on 31 August 1953, in the interests of the national security.

In accordance with Section 5(e) of CIA Regulation No. 20-730, the reasons requiring consideration of your case under Executive Order 10450 are stated to be as follows:

1. You are reported to have been in agreement with the concept that the international situation in 1947 was based upon a struggle between "American Fascism" and "Russian Democracy";

2. An individual in contact with you in 1948 is reported to have said that he had concluded, on the basis of that contact, that you must be in the Communist Party;

3. You are reported to have stated that in 1947 the United States was attempting to press the USSR into an incident in order to take advantage of the atom bomb and destroy Russia;

4. It is reported that you attended, and were one of the speakers at, a meeting of the Massachusetts Citizens Political Action Committee in Boston on 22 January 1946. It is reported in the January 28, 1946 issue of the Boston *Globe*, that you presented a resolution to the meeting, signed by Angus Cameron, calling upon the United States Government to implement the Moscow declaration with respect to the governing of

China and the opposing of military and undemocratic intervention in the internal affairs of Far Eastern countries;

5. You are reported to have expressed yourself as in agreement with certain political convictions of Professor Harlow Shapley of Harvard, who is alleged to have engaged in Communist front activities, and to have associated yourself with Professor Shapley on political matters in which he is reported to be pro-Communist.

6. Under the provisions of Section 8(a)(1)(v) of Executive Order 10450, you are reported to have associated with the following persons who have allegedly supported pro-Communist policies or have been associated with Communist front organizations or organizations pro-Communist in their sympathies:

> a. James Aldridge
> b. Cass Canfield
> c. Angus Cameron
> d. Hugh DeLacy
> e. Philip Jaffe
> f. Walter Orr Roberts
> g. Andrew Roth
> h. Prof. Harlow Shapley
> i. Miss Helen Shuford
> j. Theodore White
> k. Mr. & Mrs. Richard Wilbur

7. Under the provisions of Section 8(a)(5) of Executive Order 10450, there is evidence that you have appeared before or have been otherwise associated with the following organizations:

   a. The National Council of the Arts, Sciences and Professions (cited as a Communist front by the House Committee on Un-American Activities),

   b. Massachusetts Citizens Political Action Committee, which at the time was reportedly infiltrated and possibly dominated by Communists or Communist sympathizers,

   c. National Council Against Conscription (cited as a Communist front by the California Committee on Un-American Activities).

8. Under the provisions of Section 8(a)(1)(v) of Executive Order 10450, there is evidence that:

   a. Your wife, Mrs. Mary Pinchot Meyer, is alleged to have registered as a member of the American Labor Party of New York in 1944, at which time it was reportedly under extreme left-wing or Communist domination.

   b. Your wife, Mrs. Mary P. Meyer, is acquainted with James Aldridge.

Under the provisions of Section 5(h)(2) of CIA Regulation No. 20-730 you are afforded an opportunity to reply to these charges within thirty (30) days of their receipt by you. This will make such an answer due on the morning of 5 October, or sooner if you so desire. Any reply which you make in refutation of these charges, together with any supporting documents, should be transmitted to the CIA General Counsel. Following receipt of such reply, the matter will be handled in accordance with the procedures set forth in Regulation No. 20 730.

Your reply to the charges outlined above should be extremely complete and detailed. In particular, all elements of association with the persons and organizations listed should be given, including dates and places of such association and pertinent conversations or correspondence with the individuals listed, where it is felt that such connections bear upon this case.

You are authorized to be represented by counsel at your own expense, but your work in CIA may not be discussed with counsel or others consulted by you in this matter.

These charges may be amended within thirty days after delivery to you.

[signed]
L. K. WHITE
Acting Deputy Director/Administration
Central Intelligence Agency

As one by one I read the eight separate allegations in Houston's presence, my first reaction was incredulity, followed by relief and then by indignation. It seemed to me beyond belief that a document containing such loose, anonymous, and irrelevant accusations could be used to question the loyalty of someone like myself, whose political views and ideological position were available on the public record. I was relieved as I read on because, although I did not recognize the names of some of those with whom I was supposed to have associated, it was clear to me from what I did remember that I could easily demonstrate that there was no subversive intent in any of the associations charged against me. No old friend turned out to have been a secret Soviet agent, which was one of the fears I had conjured up while waiting to see the charges.

As I finished reading, a wave of indignation swept over me, and I angrily asked Houston why it had been necessary to suspend me without pay before I had even been given a chance to explain my version of the associations and incidents charged against me. He explained that the FBI and the Agency's own security people took the allegations very seriously, and that in Dulles' absence General Cabell, as acting director, had decided to follow the strict letter of the regulations so as to protect the Agency in the event of publicity.

He assured me that I would have thirty days to prepare my reply, and that a thirty-day extension would be granted if necessary. He suggested that I obtain competent legal advice to help me answer each allegation in specific detail with as much supporting evidence as possible. Although sympathetic to my initial reaction, which was to dismiss the document as a monstrous absurdity, he warned that a general denunciation of the allegations would not help my case and that in the current climate of suspicion I would have to try to explain the facts behind each incident.

Houston went on to point out that, once my written response had been submitted, he and the director of security would have to review it and then submit a joint recommendation to the DCI. If the initial decision went against me, I would be entitled to a hearing before a three-man board and on the basis of the board's recommendation the DCI would have to make a final decision. As I listened to this procedural guidance, I realized that it might be months before I could hope to be back at work, and my savings account seemed even smaller than it had before.

Before parting, Houston and I agreed on a cover story to the effect that I had been assigned to work on a highly sensitive project that would require my absence from the office for a number of weeks. Such assignments were not unusual in the Agency, and my colleagues were disciplined in not asking questions about operations when they had no "need to know." We reviewed the list of those who already had had to be informed of my suspension, including my immediate superior, Tom Braden, now a Washington columnist, and a few others up the line. We both agreed that publicity would be fatal to my chances of emerging unscathed from this affair. Feeling that I now knew what had to be done and encouraged by Houston's assurances that I would receive a fair hearing, I took my leave and said I would be back as soon as I could complete my response.

Driving home, I wondered who it was in the FBI who had spent so much time and effort in researching every corner of my past to weave together this tapestry of unrelated incidents designed to prove my disloyalty. I speculated what his motives might have been and guessed that probably he was an ambitious bureaucrat who, sensing the climate of the times, believed he could make a name for himself by forcing the resignation of a ranking CIA official. Senator McCarthy and Allen Dulles had already crossed swords over a number of cases where Dulles had refused to bow to McCarthy's pressure to fire certain Agency employees, and my forced resignation as potentially disloyal would have strengthened McCarthy's hand. However, this was all speculation, and I never did discover the identity and motivation of those in the FBI who prepared the charges against me. In later years, I worked closely with FBI officials on a number of occasions and came to respect and like most of them. They never raised with me the subject of my suspension, and I never asked them about it, content to leave the matter in the past as part of a McCarthy era that was over and done with.

My next step was to fly to New York to give my parents the bad news. Not knowing whether my phone was tapped but suspecting that it might be, I hesitated to say anything specific to my family until I had a chance to meet them in their New York apartment. They read the memorandum and their first reaction was incredulity. My father then exploded in anger and insisted that my only course was to resign from the Agency and to call a press conference to denounce the methods that had been used against me. It took me some time to explain that publicity could only ruin me in the prevailing climate, and I extracted a promise that they not tell anyone but my two brothers about the trouble I was in. Describing how I proposed to answer the charges, I expressed confidence that I would get much fairer treatment before the Agency's hearing board than I would being browbeaten by McCarthy before the TV cameras. We discussed finances, and I was much relieved by my father's offer to pay the legal fees. I couldn't help thinking that there must be many as innocent as I was myself who had been forced to resign by the loss of their government salary and the absence of any outside help. It was a Catch 22 situation in which the anonymous accuser could force his victim's suspension without pay and then use the fact of his resignation under financial pressure as proof of self-admitted guilt.

While I was in New York, I began my search for a lawyer. The father of one of my college friends was a senior partner in one of the big New York law firms, and my friend took me to see him. I had thought that a conservative and established New York lawyer would help my case by the very fact that he was willing to undertake to defend me. However, the interview did not go well. In his imposing office, the corporate lawyer was polite but pleaded unfamiliarity with the procedures of the loyalty review process. Beneath the surface of his cordiality, I thought I could detect some doubt as to whether there might not be an element of truth in such serious allegations and a feeling on his part that the government must have had some justification for proceeding as it had against me. I was becoming an acute observer of the way people reacted when first told of my predicament and felt I had learned to detect the least flicker of suspicion behind their polite expressions of concern.

The meeting ended inconclusively, and on my return to Washington, I asked for advice from my then brother-in-law Steuart Pittman, an old friend and a practicing lawyer. He introduced me to Walter Surrey, a young Washington attorney who had successfully handled a number of security cases before loyalty review boards. Surrey turned out to be exactly what I needed, and I remain eternally grateful to him for his advice and support during that strangely menacing period of my life. He was bright, witty, courageous, and, best of all, refreshingly disrespectful of the new loyalty standards and the way they were being administered by the government. He exuded a self-confident and buoyant optimism that helped to change the mood of self-doubt and depression into which I had fallen. I remember our first conversation very well. He started with a question.

"First, I've got to ask you a question that I ask all my clients in this kind of case. Are you or have you ever been a member of the Communist Party?"

"No," I said, "not now nor in the past."

"Good, another innocent victim," he commented. "Don't think you're alone in your misery. There are hundreds in the same position you're in, walking the streets of Washington. Now let's see the charges."

After reading the memorandum, he leaned back in his chair reflectively and advised, "There's no way of responding specifically to the first three charges. Your accusers are anonymous and will choose to remain so. We can't compel the government to produce them as witnesses so that we can cross-examine. We don't know the exact date, the circumstances, the context, the nature of their political views, what motives they might have had for accusing you. There's only one way of defending against this kind of anonymous allegation. You've got to write your political autobiography."

"What do you mean?" I asked.

"Just what I said," Surrey replied. "You've got to write the story of your life. What manner of people your parents were, the circumstances of your early upbringing, what schools and colleges you attended, which professors influenced your thinking, your war experience, and, most important, any active political involvement. You'll have to summarize any books or articles that you've written and we'll file them as attachments."

"How is this going to help?" I queried.

"We've got to show them," Surrey responded, "that in the total context of your life, in the light of all that you've been taught, experienced, thought, and written, it's just plain impossible to believe that you are a Communist or sympathetic to their views, notwithstanding these anonymous allegations to the contrary. I've handled a lot of cases like this and I can assure you there's no other way of dealing with these goddamn confidential informants."

"It will take time to pull all this together," I ventured.

"We'll ask for another thirty days, if we need it," Surrey stated briskly. "While you're writing the autobiography, you'll have to contact a number of your most reliable and influential friends. We'll need sworn affidavits from them testifying to their knowledge of your political views and to the nature of your association with the individuals and organizations that have been cited against you. In addition to the autobiography, we're going to have to prepare a detailed sworn statement by you replying to each of the separate charges as best we can, and we'll need a statement from your wife on the charges that involve her. But this can come later. The first thing is to get started on the autobiographical part of it. By the way, I've got an extra office you can use to do your writing."

Encouraged by Surrey's brisk confidence, for the next month I drove each morning from Virginia into Washington, to all outward appearances a dutiful member of the army of government workers who daily commuted to their appointed tasks. Once at my desk, my work, however, was far different from theirs. Step by step, I reconstructed my past, drawing on family records, scrapbooks, old newspaper clippings, and publications in which my articles had appeared. Within thirty days, I had completed a political autobiography, eighty-five pages in length, with voluminous footnotes and attachments. On the basis of this record, Surrey felt that we had sufficient evidence to dispose of the anonymous allegations contained in the first three charges, but the remaining five charges required detailed explanations. We requested and obtained a thirty-day extension.

In trying to answer the allegations that I had been associated with organizations that were claimed to have been controlled or infiltrated by the Communists, my research into the facts in each case led me to adopt three distinct lines of defense. In the case of the Massachusetts Citizens Political Action Committee, there was, in retrospect, evidence, based on the positions the organization took, of Communist influence; but I was able to prove that my only association with the group was as an invited speaker at a single public meeting, that I had in fact spoken in support of U.S. policy, and that there was no way of my knowing at the time that the organization had been secretly infiltrated.

In the case of the National Council of the Arts, Sciences and Professions, I was able to demonstrate from newspaper accounts that I had actually joined with Sidney Hook, Arthur Schlesinger, Jr., Norman Thomas, and other anti-Communist liberals in criticizing the organization and in warning of the extent of Communist infiltration within it. Genuinely bewildered by the charge that I had been "associated" with this front group, I was later to find out that a penetration of the FBI within the organization had reported that the leaders of this group had at one time thought it would be to their advantage to persuade me to join. No approach was ever made to me, but the very fact that they had considered trying to win me over was taken as evidence of my political disloyalty. Here was an instance where it was not what you did or thought that was held against you but rather what others thought you might be persuaded to think that became evidence of political unreliability.

Finally, in the case of the National Council Against Conscription, I admitted to signing a statement issued under their auspices warning of excessive military influence, but then went on to demonstrate that the California Committee on Un-American Activities had been completely irresponsible in labeling this group as a Communist front. In fact, the leadership consisted of prominent Protestant, Catholic, and Jewish religious leaders, and there was no evidence of Communist influence or control.

As for the list of individuals with whom I was accused of associating, most of them I could prove I had met only once or twice in my life in a casual way, nor did I know any reason why their names should have appeared on this list. Two were good friends of mine, Cass Canfield and Richard Wilbur. The fact that my friendship with them could have been cited as somehow reflecting on my loyalty shows to what extremes the guilt by association technique can be taken. Canfield was at that time chairman of the board of Harper and Brothers, the New York publishing firm. He had been chairman of the executive committee of the UWF while I served as president, and I knew him as a moderate Democrat in his political opinions with no sympathy whatsoever for the Communist cause. In speculating as to why his name had appeared on the list, he could only remember that he had once during the war given a contribution to Yugoslav relief.

Richard Wilbur, one of our finest poets, had been a colleague in the Society of Fellows at Harvard. During the 1948 elections, he had supported the candidacy of Henry Wallace on the Progressive Party ticket. I had disagreed with him at the time, but it had never been an issue between us since he was much more interested in literature than in politics. I made it quite clear in my response that I had no intention of giving up my friendship with these two men and requested some explanation as to why my association with them was considered dangerous.

During this time, I came to know who my friends were and to realize the value of personal loyalty. I had no difficulty in obtaining affidavits from those who could testify concerning my past political beliefs and activities. Oren Root was quick to provide a sworn statement describing in detail my active role in the fight against Communist infiltration of the American Veterans Committee. Edward Weeks, the editor of the *Atlantic*, described my political views as he had come to know them in the course of editing my book and the articles I had written for his magazine. Thomas K. Finletter, who had served as secretary of the air force in the Truman administration, was able to describe my role and motivation during the time I served as president of UWF.

In fact, Finletter as a trained lawyer went further, and courageously took exception to the looseness of the charges made against me. He singled out for particular attack the anonymous allegation contained in the second charge which read as follows: "An individual in contact with you in 1948 is reported to have said that he had concluded, on the basis of that contact, that you must be in the Communist Party."

Regarding this language, Finletter commented: "I find it difficult to believe that this is the correct text of the CIA Memorandum; that a charge would be made in the United States on the basis of a *report* of an unidentified person as to what the unidentified person had *said* he had *concluded* as to the *beliefs* of another person. No one could possibly answer such a charge; for it is not a charge but only the repetition of a rumor of a state of mind of an unidentified third party. If though this is the correct text of the CIA Memorandum, I will say only that I consider it an advanced case of taking on the coloration of our enemies and their notion of justice and 'due process of law.' "

Most of my new friends within the Agency proved to be as loyal in their support as those on the outside. A colleague and friend, John Bross, was generous enough to offer financial assistance while I was deprived of my government salary, and although I didn't have to ask for such help, I was deeply grateful for the confidence the gesture showed. My immediate boss, Tom Braden, was consistently support-ive and encouraged me to believe that there was never any doubt that I would be able to clear myself. And Allen Dulles called to assure me that I would have a fair hearing once my response was submitted. Inevitably, there were a few whom I had thought of as friends who went out of their way to avoid me and to make it clear that they were suspending judgment pending demonstration of my ability to rebut the accusations. In the poisonous atmosphere of those times, it took genuine courage to associate with someone suspected of being a security risk.

When my autobiography and all the attachments and affidavits had been typed and notarized, Surrey and I took the foot-thick bundle of documents to Houston's CIA office on October 20. I dumped the bundle on his desk with the remark, "Here's an elephant gun with which to shoot a mouse." Houston promised that the evidence would be reviewed as rapidly as possible but, in view of the weight of documentation, warned that it might be another month before I heard from them.

Having nothing to occupy myself with, I jumped at the chance to continue using a desk in Surrey's office suite when he offered it, and I decided to try to write a play about someone in a position similar to mine as a way of easing the suspense of waiting. I found the invention of plot and character a demanding but absorbing task and learned how difficult it is to introduce and identify one's characters in a way that seems credible to the audience. On rereading, the dialogue is laced with too many long speeches and the characters are too transparently mouthpieces for different political points of view. But it was good therapy, and in Surrey I had an appreciative audience of one. He rather enjoyed the part played by the lawyer in the play, which I had modeled on him. For obvious reasons, I never attempted to have the play produced and doubt if it would have had much success.

Finally, on Thanksgiving Day, I received a call from Allen Dulles with the good news that my secret trial had ended in acquittal. On the basis of a joint recommendation from the general counsel and the director of security, he had found my continued employment with the Agency "clearly consistent with the national security." He congratulated me on the outcome and assured me that there were no lingering doubts that might impair my future career and no need for a hearing board to review the case. Reminding me that my suspended salary would now be paid back for the period of my absence, he wished me a happy Thanksgiving and hoped to see me in the office the next day. He sounded as relieved as I was. Our Thanksgiving dinner that day was a more joyful occasion than our family had seen in a long time. Although I knew I was innocent, I was never sure until the end that I would be able to win my case.

I emerged from this ordeal with increased respect for Allen Dulles and for most of the Agency officials with whom I had had to deal. The allegations against me were not invented by the CIA but rather contained in an official FBI report to which the Agency had been compelled to react. In Allen Dulles' absence, that reaction had in my opinion been hasty and excessive in not allowing me time to give an explanation of the allegations before suspending me, but the Agency had been as good as its word in protecting me from damaging publicity. There were no leaks, and the number of those familiar with my case had been held to a disciplined few. Insofar as the Executive Order permitted it, I had been dealt with fairly. There was never any pressure on me to resign, and in fact I was encouraged to defend myself. I received an objective review of the evidence that I was able to present, and the decision to restore me to duty was taken by Allen Dulles on the basis of that review. He could have sought to protect himself by convening a hearing board as a way of sharing the responsibility of decision, but he spared me the prolonged agony and expense of such a procedure.

In my case and in other cases more publicized than mine, Allen

Dulles proved to be a pillar of courageous strength inside the Eisenhower administration during the McCarthy era. Once he had determined the facts and satisfied himself as to the loyalty of a CIA official, he was prepared to defend him and he refused to give in to the pressures that McCarthy was able to bring to bear. As a result, morale within the Agency was high during this period, in contrast to morale in the State Department, where Secretary of State John Foster Dulles was less willing to defend the innocent victims of McCarthy's campaign. This difference in approach was evident to the outside world, and the Agency was strengthened over the long term by the very high quality of recruits from American universities that it was able to attract to its ranks, whereas the caliber of State Department recruiting deteriorated and the effect was to be felt for years to come.

I often wondered why McCarthy had chosen not to drag me before the TV cameras during my suspension. It was just possible that he never discovered that I was under suspicion, but his network of informants within the government was so wide that it is much more likely that he was well aware of my case. Perhaps he decided that he didn't want to confront a Marine officer who had seen more action than he had, or that the allegations against me were too flimsy for effective exploitation. At any rate, I was spared the ordeal of public inquisition.

In the light of hindsight, McCarthy appears to me to have been a highly opportunistic and unscrupulous politician who stumbled on the issue of Communist penetration of our institutions and then in an undiscriminating and reckless manner used the public's genuine concern to advance his own personal power. He was significantly assisted by an uncritical press that gave him far more coverage than he deserved, but he would never have vaulted to national prominence unless there had in fact been serious Communist penetrations and evidence available to the public of the government's failure to cope with it.

In retrospect, the sequence of cause and effect that pushed the pendulum of American opinion on the issue of Communist infiltration from one extreme to the other, and then back again, is clearly discernible. In the first phase, during World War II and its immediate aftermath, our alliance with the Soviets against the Nazis seemed so important to final victory that evidence of Soviet espionage against us was discounted or deliberately ignored. For example, Whittaker

Chambers' story of his futile efforts to alert the U.S. government to the existence of a Soviet network including Alger Hiss is told in well-documented detail by Allen Weinstein in his book on the Hiss case.[5] Far from being the remorseless hunter of Communist spies, the FBI emerges as being remarkably uninterested in pursuing the leads that Chambers initially supplied, perhaps out of fear of rocking the boat of the wartime alliance. After a casual interview with Chambers in 1942, the FBI's lack of interest caused Weinstein to comment: "It is extraordinary that the FBI deemed Chambers unworthy of a followup interview for the next three years, or that among those whom he had named, only J. Peters received even a cursory investigation by the New York field office."

The next wild swing of American opinion was given its initial push by a key defection from the Soviet espionage apparatus. In 1945, Igor Gouzenko, a code clerk, defected from the Soviet Embassy in Canada with more than one hundred documents. In the revelations and trials that followed, it became quite obvious to the general public that the Soviets during the war had succeeded in stealing many of our atomic secrets and that the laxity of both British and American security precautions had been a contributing cause.

The Hiss trial gave the pendulum an additional shove and set the stage for McCarthy. When the jury found Hiss guilty of perjury on evidence that was more than sufficient, as Weinstein has shown in his book, Pandora's box was opened. If a man of such impeccable credentials and with so many character references from the Eastern liberal establishment was found guilty of lying, where did suspicion end? By persuading his many highly placed friends and acquaintances of his innocence, Hiss compounded the damage by involving their reputations and credibility in his downfall. If the FBI had moved aggressively with the evidence they had in 1945, McCarthy would have been denied the ammunition that he used so effectively in charging that Communist infiltration had been condoned and Communist agents befriended by the high and mighty.

However, McCarthy overplayed his hand. His wild charges and reckless accusations caught up with him. The whole shaky edifice of hysterical suspicion that he created began to collapse as it became evident that most of those whom he accused were not Communists at all but innocent victims. Reacting to the excesses of the McCarthy era, the pendulum of American opinion swung back to the other extreme, and it became fashionable to believe that there never had been any real threat of Communist infiltration.

In the short run, the damage that McCarthy did to individuals whom he falsely accused was serious and in some cases irreparable. But the cases that were brought to public trial before the TV cameras with McCarthy sitting as judge and jury were only the tip of the iceberg. The hidden damage included the unnumbered thousands of innocent individuals who were caught up in the loyalty review procedures that were established by Eisenhower's Executive Order and with which I had had to contend. As we have seen, these regulations were ostensibly designed to tighten security standards in response to McCarthy's allegation of laxity and to prevent Communist infiltration of government agencies. In fact, the standards of guilt were so loosely drawn and the anonymous informant granted such complete protection that in actual operation these regulations created a hunting ground for secret informers who out of envy or ambition wished to destroy those against whom they leveled their anonymous charges. My own experience with these regulations and with the injustice they invited led me to bring the situation to the attention of friends of mine in the New York Bar Association in the hope that remedial action might result.

Although not a lawyer myself, I wrote a memorandum on the basis of my experience that defined the main problem areas, and gave it to Finletter and to other lawyers whom I knew in New York. As the tide of McCarthy's influence ebbed, changes were made in these regulations and in their interpretation by the courts.[6] What happened to me and to many others could not happen today.

In addition to the serious damage that McCarthy did to innocent individuals and the temporary restraints his activity placed on the exercise of traditional American freedoms, his more lasting and significant legacy was the incalculably valuable contribution that he inadvertently made to the Soviet Union and to the success of its disciplined Communist operations throughout the world. By falsely accusing so many of being Communists who were not, he gave real Communists the protective coloration of injured innocence. His excesses made it appear to a whole generation of American liberals that anticommunism was synonymous with paranoid hysteria and that those accused of Communist subversion or espionage must by definition be innocent. Government agencies such as the FBI and CIA, whose task it is to cope with the continuing reality of Soviet-directed espionage at home and abroad, came in many minds to be associated with Fascist repression. In fact, opinion swung so far that the press itself became infected with the hysteria it had had—on the other side of the issue—in McCarthy's time. Exaggerated headlines fanned the fears of an incipient police state presided over by intrusive intelligence agencies. McCarthy's legacy lives in the continuing conviction of many people that any attempt to uncover evidence of Communist spying or political manipulation must be part of an attempt to rekindle the hysteria of the McCarthy era.

There are signs that American liberal opinion is beginning to swing back toward a more balanced and realistic appreciation of the fact that Communist espionage is a continuing threat and that effective intelligence agencies are necessary to cope with it. Learning from the past, we must guard against an overreaction that could again endanger the innocent and undermine our liberties. Hiss, the suspected Communist agent, and McCarthy, the reckless political gambler, between them succeeded in disorienting and confusing the intellectual community. Perhaps this account of my own experiences can help to bring the pendulum to rest on a point of balance, where a clear-eyed recognition of the danger is combined with a scrupulous regard for individual rights.

Chapter 5

Cold War

LESS THAN A YEAR AFTER the charges against me had been dropped, Allen Dulles proved that he had meant what he said when he assured me that my career in the Agency would not be damaged. When Tom Braden decided to resign from CIA in order to publish a newspaper in California, Dulles approved my appointment as Braden's successor as chief of the International Organizations Division in September of 1954. In that capacity, I became head of one of the major operating divisions of the Directorate of Plans, with a growing budget and a wide policy mandate under a new National Security Council directive to counter with covert action the political and propaganda offensive that the Soviets had launched through their control of a battery of international front organizations.[1]

In March of 1962, the International Organizations Division was merged with the Covert Action Staff. As the new head of an expanded Covert Action Staff, I became responsible not only for international operations but also for reviewing and providing policy guidance to the geographical area divisions in their conduct of covert activity authorized by NSC directives.

This bureaucratic history is relevant because it explains why my name inevitably came to figure prominently in the wave of publicity that crashed over the Agency in 1967. Up to that time, there had been very few leaks, and over a period of fifteen years many American citizens and private voluntary organizations had cooperated discreetly with the CIA in joint efforts to cope with the Soviet political offensive.

The immediate cause of the rash of publicity concerning Agency involvement with American voluntary organizations that broke out in the spring of 1967 was the publication of three articles in *Ramparts* magazine in February of that year.[2] They revealed that the National Student Association (NSA), the organization representing American college students, had for several years secretly been receiving funds from the CIA to help finance its international activities, and that its senior officials had cooperated with the CIA in this program. Contrary to the findings of the Church committee[3] and the generally accepted mythology, these *Ramparts* revelations were not the work of an elected officer of the NSA who, after having agreed to accept Agency funding, became disillusioned and decided to expose the connection. The source was rather a young radical NSA staffer who never had met with CIA officials and had no direct experience of how the relationship between the two organizations functioned. Having learned about the secret funding as the result of a conversation with an excessively loquacious NSA officer who did know the facts, this young man, Michael Wood, decided that it was his duty to expose the whole relationship.

A last-ditch attempt was made by the president and international vice-president of the NSA to persuade him not to go public. Although the strains of the Vietnam war had begun to create policy differences between the NSA and the Agency, these elected officers had no desire to terminate the relationship in a blaze of publicity and were thinking of a quiet parting of the ways if the policy conflicts could not be resolved by mutual agreement. They respected the CIA officials with whom they dealt as liberal and enlightened men and in fact argued with Wood that his revelations could only damage and impair the influence of those within the Agency who understood the importance of supporting the non-Communist left. They also tried to explain to Wood how his disclosures would damage the reputation of the NSA and provide the Soviets with a powerful propaganda card to play in the continuing worldwide struggle for the allegiance of the younger generation.

None of these arguments moved Wood. He proceeded to take his story to the editors of *Ramparts* magazine, who were at that time riding the rising tide of New Left opposition to the Vietnam war. Their published version of the CIA's role in supporting the NSA cast the relationship in the worst possible light and accused the Agency of having seduced, bribed, and manipulated a generation of American college students for its nefarious purposes. The James Bond image of the Agency in the public mind as being exclusively associated with the shadowy world of espionage gave credibility to these charges. As the first public exposure of the CIA role, the *Ramparts* coverage set the tone and colored the content of the massive press and media publicity that followed.

The challenge of the Soviet front apparatus and the serious political purpose of the CIA assistance were explained by a few respected journalists like James Reston of *The New York Times*,[4] but their voices were drowned in the general clamor for termination of a program that was widely identified as malevolently manipulative.

Prior to the actual publication of the *Ramparts* articles, we in the Agency had advance knowledge of the general content from our contacts with the NSA leadership, and steps were taken to alert the White House and the State Department to the storm that was about to break. It fell to my lot to brief Senator J. William Fulbright (D., Ark.), as chairman of the Senate Foreign Relations Committee. He was not a regular member of our congressional oversight committees, but in his key role his reaction to the disclosures would be critical in determining congressional response. I found him alone in his office on a Saturday afternoon and reviewed for him the history of the program and the sequential policy approvals by successive administrations. He listened courteously as I described why we had found it useful to give assistance to democratic groups in their rivalry with the Communist fronts. He did not entirely accept my explanation and clearly thought that a decision to terminate should have been made at an earlier date. However, he did accept that the program had been duly authorized at the appropriate policy levels, and he understood that our purpose had been not to subvert the students but to help them achieve their own objectives. When the publicity finally broke, he was restrained in his comment and his attitude was important in moderating the congressional reaction. Unless key members of Congress are given a timely and factually accurate description of the nature and purpose of major covert operations, they cannot be expected to react responsibly when exposures occur that force them to take a public stance concerning events of which they are ignorant.

As the result of advance coordination, when the March issue of *Ramparts* hit the newsstands, the State Department issued a statement to the press, on February 14, 1967, confirming an admission by the NSA leaders that they had been receiving covert assistance from the Agency since the early 1950s. Nor was that all. The editors of *Ramparts* had done an ingeniously speculative job of research on the sources of the NSA funding. In the course of a congressional investigation into the tax-exempt status of private American foundations by Representative Wright Patman (D., Tex.) in August 1964, an inadvertent leak had occurred which identified a number of foundations as having received CIA funds. The story was carried on a back page of *The New York Times*[5] and caused little stir at the time, although within the Agency it caused us anxiously to review and attempt to improve the security of funding mechanisms. However, working from the public identification of these foundations as having been previously associated with Agency funding, the *Ramparts* editors went on to speculate about the size and purpose of the grants the Agency had contributed to the international program of the NSA.

Stung by the feeling that they had been scooped by the young upstarts who edited *Ramparts*, the *Washington Post*, *The New York Times*, other newspapers, and the wire services went to work on trying to unravel the traces of Agency funding that might lead from the foundations identified by Patman to a large number of private voluntary American organizations and institutions. Under the pressure of the media, the confidentiality of records that had been submitted to the government by many private foundations for tax-exemption purposes was breached, and a competition ensued between elements of the press to identify all those organizations that might possibly have been recipients of the Agency's beneficence. In the event, some of this speculation was correct and some was not, but the net effect was to create the impression of a national scandal in which the CIA stood accused of subverting and manipulating for its sinister purposes many of the most respected and liberal private institutions functioning on the American scene. The condemnatory tone of the initial *Ramparts* coverage was echoed and amplified in a drumfire of editorial denunciation and cartoon excoriation that swept across the country.

One of the most damning lines of attack on which some newspapers focused was the charge that the Agency had initiated this program of alleged subversion on its own initiative and without policy approval by the executive branch or authorization by Congress. It was only when Senator Robert Kennedy stepped forward to state clearly that the Agency should not be forced "to take the rap" for programs that had been approved by high officials of three successive administrations that this charge was dropped.[6] I was grateful to Kennedy for his timely intervention but not surprised, since I had personally briefed him when he was attorney general on these programs on a number of occasions and received his enthusiastic encouragement to expand our activity in this field. Similarly, after I had reviewed with our congressional oversight committees the record of previous briefings and funding authorizations, the two chairmen, Senator Richard Russell (D., Ga.) and Representative Mendel Rivers (D., S.C.), made it clear on the record that the Congress had been kept properly informed. I should add that throughout this difficult time Richard Helms, who had by then become CIA director, was consistently supportive. His coolness under fire and the strength of the support he enjoyed in the Congress made it possible for the Agency to survive the publicity with its morale intact and its essential capabilities unimpaired.

However, Kennedy's intervention and the statement of the congressional leaders did not stop the torrent of condemnation but merely channeled it in new directions. Just as I had been the object of attack from both ends of the political spectrum in my UWF days, so now both left and right joined in the assault on the Agency for contradictory reasons. The Soviets predictably jumped on the bandwagon and excoriated the imperialistic subversion of innocent youth by the monstrous CIA, and the theme was replayed around the world by the Communist propaganda apparatus.

The non-Communist left in the United States was almost as harsh in its denunciation, although its reaction was somewhat tempered by the dawning realization that most of the groups accused of receiving Agency funds were on the left of the political spectrum and were liberal and internationalist in their outlook. A CIA that could be condemned for consistently supporting right-wing dictatorships was an easier and more inviting target than the kind of Agency that emerged from these revelations. The dilemma was resolved for the liberals in the Americans for Democratic Action by a statement charging that Agency funding of voluntary organizations "indicated a serious perversion of the democratic process" and then going on to explain, "It matters little that the activities were in many cases positive advances over the declared foreign policy of the U.S."[7]

The thunder on the right was caused by the fact that the NSA in its foreign policy resolutions had been taking an increasingly critical attitude toward the Vietnam war. Two Republican congressmen demanded an investigation by the House of "how much CIA money has been channeled to private organizations which was used for leftist purposes having nothing to do with the conduct of the cold war."[8] A leader of the conservative Young Americans for Freedom announced, "There can be no justification for the use of American taxpayers' money to support this kind of radical left-wing group. The Congress has a duty to see that those responsible for this policy in the CIA are removed and that such subsidies are ended."[9] The implication was that the Agency had not sufficiently used its influence to correct the errors of the NSA's policy, while from the left the charge was that the Agency in some undisclosed way had subverted that policy.

These ideologically motivated assaults were made more personal when *The New York Times* published a biographical profile of me, identifying me as the CIA official responsible for the Agency's covert funding program and speculating about the motives that could have led me to change from an idealistic world federalist into a member of the CIA's secretive bureaucracy.[10] The article attributed to an anonymous acquaintance speculation to the effect that I had been corrupted by the pressures of the cold war, and other anonymous sources were quoted as believing that my former humane and liberal attitudes had been transformed into a fanatical and doctrinaire loyalty to the CIA. Here began the assiduously cultivated myth that my career and personality represented a kind of Jekyll and Hyde development. According to this stereotype, I had begun as a liberal crusader for world federalism and then, seduced by the lure of power into joining the Agency, had become transmogrified into a heartless manipulator of the young and innocent. This simplistic demonology had a certain dramatic appeal for some literary journalists who specialized in amateur psychology. Quoting from anonymous sources, Merle Miller tried his hand at the game in a long biographical sketch of me that later appeared in *The New York Times Magazine*[11] and, while I was in London, the *Sunday Times* exposed its British readers to a similar version of my life and career.[12]

Employed as I was during this time by the CIA, I could make no public reply and had no choice but to remind myself of Harry Truman's advice, "If you can't stand the heat, stay out of the kitchen." It was hard to resist the impression that these highly personal attacks on me served a political purpose. As a secret and powerful component of the government establishment, the CIA was an inviting target for the New Left. It was important to them not to allow their preferred image of the Agency as a conspiratorial group of right-wing fanatics to become blurred by the intrusion of embarrassing evidence that many of its policies were enlightened and its leaders intelligently liberal. The public having been given an indication that this might be the case, my reputation had to be damaged, and the instrument at hand was the convenient theory that from a humane Dr. Jekyll I had been transformed by exposure to the Agency's influence into an evil Mr. Hyde.

The most obvious example of this motivation in action was a scurrilous article that was published in New York in *The Village Voice* during my stay in London.[13] It was written by a well-known British leftist who arranged for its publication in the States. It probably could not have been published in England where the libel laws are stiff. In his article, he charged that in addition to my political sins, I was in the habit of forcibly seducing secretaries in my office. Feeling that this bit of character assassination was going too far, I wrote my friend Steuart Pittman to inquire whether I could sue for libel. He advised me that so long as I was employed by the Agency there was no real point to it because Supreme Court rulings had made it virtually impossible for a public official to successfully bring a libel action. I contented myself with assuring my amused wife, my troubled mother, and my startled secretary that secretarial rape was not one of my character deficiencies.

When the *Ramparts* story broke, President Johnson moved rapidly to contain the damage. To head off a wide-ranging congressional investigation of all clandestine financing by CIA demanded by Senator Mike Mansfield (D., Mont.) the President appointed a special three-man committee, composed of Under Secretary of State Nicholas Katzenbach, as chairman; Secretary of HEW John Gardner; and CIA Director Richard Helms. As Katzenbach later testified, Johnson "wanted John Gardner on it because he thought that would help politically in getting acceptance of whatever the recommendations turned out to be because he thought Helms would defend everything and wanted to continue everything. Gardner would want to stop everything. It was my job to come out with something in the middle."[14]

Established on February 15, 1967, the committee was given two mandates by the President. It was required to review relationships between the CIA and American educational and private voluntary organizations operating abroad. It was also asked to recommend ways through which open governmental assistance could be given to these organizations to allow them to continue "their proper and vital role abroad."

I worked closely with the committee as Helms's principal staff assistant as it labored to complete its report to the President. It quickly became obvious to us all that what had been done could not be undone. Once the curtain of secrecy had been torn and many of the funding channels exposed, there was no way through which the Agency could reconstruct a secure method of providing discreet assistance to the overseas activity of the organizations we had previously assisted. If these groups were to receive governmental assistance in the future, it would have to be supplied through open government grants and be subject to annual public review and authorization by the Congress.

Most of the elected leaders of the voluntary organizations with whom we had cooperated were reluctant to accept this conclusion, because over the years a relationship of mutual trust and confidence had grown up between us, and they did not know what type of official bureaucracy they might have to deal with in the future. Some organizations took the position that they would prefer to do without any government funds if grants would have to be made a matter of public record. The political sensitivity of their relations with foreign groups was such that they would be severely damaged by a public admission of dependence on U.S. government funding.

The committee resolved the dilemma with an unambiguous and definitive policy recommendation in its final report, which was ac-

cepted by the President and announced as official policy.[15] The pertinent language read as follows: "It should be the policy of the United
States Government that no federal agency shall provide any covert
financial assistance or support, direct or indirect, to any of the nation's educational or private voluntary organizations." The committee explained the Agency's past program of covert assistance to
American private groups as a necessary reaction to the Communist
front apparatus, and laid out the record of high-level policy review
and approval. However, the report concluded that in the light of all
the publicity, it was necessary to terminate such secret grants "to
avoid any implication that governmental assistance, because it is
given covertly, is used to affect the policies of private voluntary
organizations" and "to make it plain in all foreign countries that the
activities of private American groups abroad are, in fact, private."

In order to allow some time for the affected organizations to find
alternative sources of support, the Katzenbach report set December
31, 1967, as a target date for the termination of covert Agency funding. As the Church committee report subsequently explained, this
time limit was in effect extended by a congressionally approved
process whereby a number of substantial terminal grants were made
prior to the December deadline.[16] This process, called surge funding,
ensured the survival of politically vital organizational activity and
enabled the leaders of the groups to keep their professional staffs on
the payroll while they sought open funding from other government
agencies and from private foundations. As we shall see later, this
surge funding was critical in allowing Radio Free Europe and Radio
Liberty to survive while the Congress debated whether they should
be publicly supported.

Once the recommendations of the Katzenbach committee had
been promulgated by the President as official policy in March of
1967, within the Agency we went to work to identify all the projects
and programs that fell within the new restrictions. Although this
process of disengagement meant the weakening, reduction, and, in
some cases, the destruction of organizational activity that had for
many years successfully contained the Communist front apparatus
around the world, the leaders of the affected organizations regret-
fully accepted that we had no choice but to implement the new
policy. They cooperated closely with us in working out termination
plans that would limit the damage as much as possible, and by the

end of December we were able to report to our policy masters on the senior interdepartmental review committee, then called the 303 Committee, that the disengagement was complete.

In its subsequent review of how the Agency complied with the Katzenbach restrictions, the Church committee made an intensive study of the classified documents and took testimony from many of the officials involved, including myself. The Church committee concluded that "the actual investigation of the Katzenbach Committee was vigorous and thorough."[17] While suggesting that Katzenbach should have gone further to restrict Agency relationships with individual academics as well as with educational institutions, the Church committee "found no violations of the policy the report sets forth."[18] In this case as in so many other instances, the specific findings of the Church committee were in glaring and direct contrast to the ominous warning of its chairman, Senator Frank Church (D., Ida.), who in the course of the inquiry observed that the Agency might have been rampaging out of policy control like "a rogue elephant." This sensational allegation drew newspaper headlines that implanted dark suspicions in the public mind, while the more judicious and reassuring conclusions of the committee's Final Report received very little publicity. How many people, one wonders, struggled through the report to find on p. 427 its general conclusion, based on all the evidence, that "the Central Intelligence Agency, in broad terms, is not 'out of control.' "

The above explanation of how the Agency's involvement with the NSA came to be exposed, and the consequences of that exposure, do not deal with the more fundamental questions of why the Agency chose to provide covert assistance to the NSA's international program in the first place, nor with the rules accepted by both parties in their dealings with each other. Before addressing those questions, it is necessary to review briefly the nature of Communist organizational strategy. This topic was only very superficially touched upon in a few paragraphs of the Church committee's report, but without an understanding of the threat posed by Communist "front" tactics our reactions to that danger cannot be understood.

To summarize and oversimplify an extraordinarily complicated historical record, the Soviet Communist Party under Stalin and the obedient Communist parties abroad made a basic shift in international strategy in the period after the Nazis came to power in Germany. Prior to that time, the Soviets had followed a line laid down at the Sixth World Congress of the Communist International (the Comintern) in 1928. This strategy called for the establishment wherever possible abroad of disciplined Communist parties that accepted the guidance and direction of Moscow both in the interpretation of Marxist doctrine and in day-to-day implementation of political tactics. Since the main opponents during this ultraleft period were identified as the capitalistic and bourgeois democracies of the West, it was the task of the combat parties to win the allegiance of the Western industrial proletariat and to increase Communist Party strength by recruiting and training ideologically reliable cadres. In Western Europe, the main obstacles to the growth of Communist influence among the workers were the older social democratic parties, and their affiliated trade unions, with their belief in civil rights, parliamentary democracy, and the need for gradual reform, not revolution. Spurning any effective cooperation with social democrats and liberal reformers, the Communists condemned them as "social fascists" and in Germany even cooperated with the Nazis in the parliament in the early thirties and in the Berlin transportation strike of 1932. Underestimating Hitler's ability to appeal across class lines with his brand of militaristic nationalism, the Communists split the opposition to the Nazis by their attacks on the Socialists as the main enemy and actually facilitated Hitler's rise to power.

Belatedly realizing the magnitude of their miscalculation, the Communists adjusted their tactics at the Seventh Congress of the Comintern in 1935, and the new flexible policy line was laid down in Georgi Dimitrov's famous speech on that occasion.[19] He declared "an end all along the line to what frequently occurs in our practical work—the ignoring of or contemptuous attitude towards the various organizations and parties of the peasants, artisans, and urban petty-bourgeois masses." The hardened cadres of the combat parties that had been forged during the sectarian isolation of the ultraleft period were now ready for deployment on a much wider political stage, and were given as targets for their infiltration and control every type of organization that might be useful to the Soviet state. Retaining their internal discipline through the practice of democratic centralism and slavishly obedient to Moscow, the Western Communist parties were able to use their cadres to penetrate and covertly manipulate Western democratic organizations and institutions ranging from labor unions to student groups to political parties.

The tactics employed were infinitely various, but the objective was always the same: to extend Communist influence beyond the limited circle of those who could be fully converted to Stalin's brand of communism.[20] For example, in the American student field, the Socialist Student League for Industrial Democracy and the Communist National Student League merged in 1935 to form the American Student Union (ASU). Naively attracted by the slogan of student unity, the Socialists found themselves outmaneuvered by the more disciplined Communists, who gained control of local chapters and eventually of the national office. The Communists did not win by preaching Marxist-Leninism but by secretly deploying their trained members into key positions while allowing the Socialists to occupy posts of more prestige but less power. As a result, the Communists ended up by controlling a major American student organization which attracted thousands of innocent and apolitical members, while the policy resolutions of the organization represented a subtle orchestration of the party line and received wide publicity.

The Stalin-Hitler pact was a serious blow to foreign Communist parties and their front organizations, but they recovered quickly once Hitler's attack brought the Soviet Union into the war. The sympathy in the West for the heroic sacrifices of the Russian people transferred itself to the regime, and the need for preserving the wartime alliance muted criticism of Stalin's totalitarian rule. In France and Italy, Communist partisans won fame and respect for their guerrilla exploits. When the war ended in 1945, the Soviets and their local Communist parties were in an extraordinarily favorable position to exploit the flexible strategy that Dimitrov had defined ten years before. The Soviets moved quickly to take full advantage of the opportunity.

Even before the guns fell silent, the Soviets took the initiative in the trade union field by proposing, at a conference in London in February 1945, the formation of an international labor confederation that united in a single organization national labor federations in both Communist and democratic states. Attracted by the appeal of labor unity and wishing to preserve the spirit of cooperation engendered by the wartime alliance, the British Trade Union Confederation (TUC) and the American Congress of Industrial Organizations (CIO) agreed to join, although the leadership of both groups was firmly in the hands of a non-Communist majority. As a result, the World Federation of Trade Unions (WFTU) was founded in Paris in October 1945, with a claimed membership of 66 million in 65 national centers representing 44 countries and 12 colonies. Of the organizations refusing to join, the most prominent and powerful was the American Federation of Labor (AFL), which was then separate from the CIO. The AFL leaders claimed that there was a basic difference between democratic trade unions that enjoyed the right to strike and to elect their leadership freely and unions in the Communist bloc, which the AFL contended were controlled, official organs of the state. On this basic issue of principle, the AFL has been entirely consistent, while U.S. government policy has wavered. State Department officials have periodically tried to persuade the AFL to be more accommodating, but the AFL has hewed to its independent and principled position.

Even without the participation of the AFL, the WFTU, with its substantial non-Communist membership, was a considerable achievement for the Soviets. It could rightfully claim to be the only international organization representing the interests of workers throughout the world. It enjoyed official status as a nongovernmental organization at the United Nations. Its policy pronouncements carried weight and credibility as the voice of its mass membership and could not easily be dismissed as the propaganda of any government. Its traveling delegations and investigating commissions successfully claimed the right to intervene actively in the birth pangs of labor unions in the colonial areas, and complaints that this intervention was always to the advantage of local Communist labor leaders could be brushed aside. Its budget seemed inexhaustible, and its publications in many languages enjoyed a worldwide readership. So long as it could legitimately claim to be representative of both Communist and non-Communist workers, it was an enormously valuable organizational weapon in the hands of the Soviets, a successful front whose representative facade concealed its true character and purpose.

There was never any doubt concerning the ability of the Soviets to control the levers of power within the WFTU. The mass membership of the government-controlled unions in the U.S.S.R. and Eastern Europe, combined with Communist control of the largest labor federations in France and Italy, gave the Soviets a decisive numerical majority. In addition, the secretariat of the WFTU headquarters was lodged in Paris, firmly in the hands of Louis Saillant, who was also secretary of the Communist-dominated French Confederation of Labor (CGT). As a result, day-to-day administrative and editorial decisions were made by trusted cadres, and most of the purse strings were in Russia's hands.

Initially, the Soviets leaned over backward not to offend the British TUC and American CIO with a too open and obvious exercise of their controlling authority, and genuine concessions appear to have been made to the Anglo-American viewpoint in order to obtain and secure their valuable participation. However, as the issues dividing the West and the Soviet Union in the postwar period proliferated, culminating in the Czech coup in 1948, it became increasingly difficult for the British and American labor leaders to accept the WFTU policy line, and eventually impossible. The TUC and the CIO finally withdrew and joined with the AFL and most of the democratic labor movements in founding in 1949 a rival organization, the International Confederation of Free Trade Unions. The facade of the WFTU was badly cracked by these democratic defections, but the WFTU continues in existence to this day, heavily subsidized by the Soviets and with its international headquarters now located in Prague. Its policy pronouncements no longer ring with the authenticity they once enjoyed, but ample funds and indefatigable organizing and propaganda activity in the less sophisticated reaches of the third world still make the WFTU a formidable organizational weapon in the Soviet political arsenal. Even after the right-wing dictatorship was overthrown in Portugal, WFTU subsidies and trained organizers gave crucial assistance to the successful effort of the Portuguese Communists to gain control of the majority of the newly formed trade unions.

This struggle within the labor movement is only one example of the broad strategy that the Soviets developed after the war. Using covert subsidies and disciplined party members, the Soviets moved rapidly to establish a controlling influence within a series of mass and specialized organizations at both the national and international level. Their purpose was to reach beyond the limited number of committed Communists to large functional groups within society which could be appealed to by offering them membership in organizations that appeared to serve their social and economic needs and to offer a hope of redress for their grievances. The fact of Communist control was hidden behind the facade of generous social purpose. As these "front" groups proliferated, they opened up new avenues for propaganda and political action that would have been closed to Communists identified for what they were.

In the university student field, the Soviets and their Communist allies abroad began the struggle holding nearly all the cards. In Russia and in Eastern Europe, the student population was already organized in tightly disciplined student federations, controlled from the top down by mature party activists, who saw in student political work one of the most promising career ladders for advancing to the top levels of the party bureaucracy. In addition, the Soviets could count on substantial Communist penetration of the French and Italian student populations, and they had pockets of strength in the third world. Finally, the Soviets were prepared to commit large amounts of money to the organizing effort. Secret state subsidies, camouflaged as dues and contributions from their controlled organizations, gave their student delegations freedom to travel and assured the attendance at international meetings of their hand-picked delegates from around the world.

By comparison, the non-Communist students in the West were badly organized, perennially broke, ill-prepared ideologically for the coming struggle, and naively innocent in comparison to the professional party activists they had to confront. And the American student leadership was among the least well prepared. In fact, when the first World Student Congress convened in Prague in August 1946, there did not exist in the United States a national student organization representative of the American student community. As a result, the twenty-four U.S. delegates to the Prague conference were an ad hoc group paying their own way and representing several American colleges. Inevitably, the Communists were in the majority at the congress and some of their party-line rhetoric generated disputes. However, the meeting ended with an agreement to cooperate in building a genuinely international student organization, and thereafter the International Union of Students (IUS) was established with the Communists in firm control of the headquarters staff in Prague and of a majority of the member organizations. Indicative of the extent of Soviet control is the fact that the first Soviet vice-president of the IUS was Alexander Shelepin, who later became chief of the KGB.[21]

Exposed to Communist tactics and beginning to realize how much was at stake in allowing the Soviets a free hand, the American delegation returned with the conviction that it was essential to construct a representative national student organization, which could speak with authority at international meetings in the name of the American student community. They formed an organizing committee, and at a constitutional convention in Madison, Wisconsin, in the summer of 1947, the U.S. National Student Association (NSA) was formally established to represent the student governments of all universities and colleges that chose to participate on a democratic basis. As can be seen, it was the need for a representative organization that could speak for the American student on the world stage rather than domestic considerations that primarily motivated the founding of the NSA.

Just as in the labor field, it was the Czech coup in 1948 that caused the NSA to break with the IUS for its failure to condemn the coup or to protest against the police brutality used against the Czech students. A period of informal discussion between NSA representatives and the non-Communist national student unions in Western Europe followed, and led to a meeting in Stockholm in 1950, at which agreement was reached on establishing a new international student organization on a democratic basis, which later became known as the International Student Conference (ISC). Subsequently, a small permanent staff was set up as a coordinating secretariat in Leiden, Holland, to carry out organizational and editorial work between the annual meetings of the ISC. Through these steps, the representative and democratically run national student unions in the West created a structure to serve the common interests and needs of university students in free societies, to speak for them on international issues, and to assist in the development of representative student unions in the third world. Formed to escape the excessive politicization of student issues by the IUS, the ISC was inevitably compelled to defend itself against Communist attacks and to compete with the Communists for the allegiance of the emerging student populations of the less developed countries.

At the beginning, the struggle was decidedly unequal. The Soviet national student union and the international operations of the IUS headquarters in Prague were backed by virtually unlimited funds from the state treasury of the Soviet Union. Owing a supranational allegiance to the Soviet Communist Party, disciplined young party activists throughout the world provided an interlocking directorate through which to influence the decisions of national student federations on matters ranging from policy positions to the selection of delegates, to the orchestration of propaganda campaigns. The combination of inexhaustible funds and the indefatigable organizing activity of a conspiratorial supranational apparat presented a formidable challenge to the fledgling efforts of the democratic student groups to cooperate with one another.

Having established a representative national organization and joined in creating the beginning of an international structure, the elected leaders of the NSA found themselves almost entirely dependent for funds on the minimal dues that its student members could afford, and the Western European student groups were in even worse shape. In the United States at that time, the fund-raising climate was not propitious for an organization that on most issues took a line that was definitely on the left in the political spectrum. The private foundations were intimidated by the hysteria that Senator McCarthy was generating, and few of them were willing to make even small grants to NSA's international activities, which could be attacked as controversial and excessively liberal. The State Department was equally reluctant to provide grants from its limited budget for cultural affairs, and the open receipt of official government funds would have damaged the reputation for independence that the NSA had found valuable in dealing with foreign students.

One of the American students who had taken part in the international negotiations that led to the Stockholm meeting in 1950 subsequently joined the CIA. From his position within the Agency, he was able to alert his superiors to the size and scope of the Communist effort in the student field on the basis of his own direct experience, and to explain the financial limitations on effective NSA international participation. He succeeded in obtaining policy approval for a limited number of travel grants, and the NSA leaders who knew him well and trusted him saw this discreet assistance from an old colleague as a satisfactory solution to their most pressing financial problem. The signing of a secrecy agreement with one's own government seemed a reasonable price to pay for timely assistance in a common cause.

By the time I joined the Agency in the fall of 1951, there was therefore already in existence a limited program of covert assistance to the NSA leadership for their international activities. The World Youth Festival in Berlin in the summer of 1951 dramatically demonstrated to the policy levels in the State Department and in the Agency the extent of the growing Communist ability to organize and orchestrate vast international meetings of youth and students from around the world. These meetings served as sounding boards for the transmission of Communist propaganda themes and as social occasions to celebrate the progressive cause as the wave of the future. Prodded by the National Security Council directive 10/5, Agency officials were under pressure to compete more effectively with this obviously successful Communist apparatus. One of my first assignments on joining the Agency was to take responsibility for the small but very able group of young officers who were already working on this problem and knew far more about it than I did, although I did find my AVC experience relevant and helpful. Working in cooperation with the NSA leaders as coequal partners, we agreed to expand our financial support through private foundations, and the student leadership undertook to build up the international staff of the NSA and to strengthen the International Student Conference and its coordinating secretariat in Leiden.

To a considerable extent, the NSA leaders were successful in this effort, and by 1955 the ISC claimed the membership of national student unions from fifty-five countries, including more than half from the less developed states. Under ISC auspices, the Leiden secretariat edited student publications in many languages and managed travel and exchange services suited to student needs. At home, the NSA international staff conducted summer seminars in international affairs to ensure the availability of competent leadership to take over from those who were graduating. Grants were made by the NSA for foreign student leaders to come to this country, and in this way the first American contacts were established with young nationalists in the colonial areas who were later to play a prominent role in the struggle for independence from colonial rule. As members of traveling ISC delegations or as NSA representatives to the annual conventions of foreign student unions, the NSA leaders accumulated a wealth of detailed knowledge concerning foreign student politics and personalities, which in many countries play a critical role on the national scene. They were willing to share that knowledge with us in the Agency, and their perceptions served to sharpen and make more accurate the American official assessment of many foreign developments.

When the Soviets attempted to stage massive propaganda circuses in the form of world youth festivals in Vienna in 1959 and Helsinki in 1961, they found the American student community much better organized to challenge their control over these events and to engage in effective ideological debate. The NSA and the other national unions in the ISC boycotted these meetings and condemned them for being extensions of official Soviet propaganda. But the NSA leadership encouraged selected American students to attend as an informal group of activists, and through foundation grants the Agency helped to pay the costs of their participation. Working with democratic representatives from other countries, during the course of the festivals this group even managed to put out, in five languages, a daily newspaper that challenged the party-line interpretation of events.

The intervention of this group in policy discussions broke the facade of ideological unanimity the Communists were trying to construct. So successful was this American effort that since the Helsinki festival the Soviets have never again tried to organize a similar propaganda circus in the West.

As attorney general, Robert Kennedy took a personal interest in the CIA's support of this democratic challenge and, before the Helsinki festival, I was required to review with him in detail the plans we had worked out with the American student leaders. At the conclusion of the Helsinki festival, he was so impressed by the results that he asked to meet with the four or five student activists who had been the principal organizers. We met in his office, and he congratulated them on their effective performance and assured them that the Kennedy administration would continue to support such programs.

The CIA relationship with the NSA during a fifteen-year period of discreet cooperation is worth describing in some detail because essentially the same ground rules were observed in the many similar programs that the Agency conducted in support of the international activities of many of the most influential and respected private American voluntary organizations.

First, the relationship was based on a shared commitment to a common purpose. The NSA leadership wanted to cooperate with democratic and representative university student groups abroad and to oppose the attempt of the Communists to dominate the international student community. The Agency shared that objective and was prepared to help them achieve what they had already decided to do.

Second, both sides accepted that Agency funds would be used exclusively for international activity and that such funds would not be used to support NSA's domestic program.

Third, the new president and vice-president for international affairs, elected at annual conventions by democratic vote of the membership, would decide each year whether they wished to continue the secret cooperation with the Agency.

Fourth, Agency funds would be used to supplement what the NSA was able to raise from private foundations for its international program, and these funds would be channeled through private foundations for mutually agreed-upon objectives.

Finally, the policy of the NSA on both domestic and foreign affairs would be set by democratic vote in annual convention, and the Agency accepted that this policy might differ in substantial respects from official U.S. policy. In the event of fundamental disagreement, both sides reserved the right with due notice to withdraw from the arrangement.

Under these ground rules, which clearly respected and preserved the democratic integrity of the NSA, cooperation between the Agency and the annually elected leadership of the NSA continued for many years without any major disagreement or any security breach. The elected leaders of the NSA proved consistently to be extremely competent and politically astute young men and women. What they lacked in experience they made up for in intelligence and energy. In addition to the funds they needed, the Agency was able to help with detailed briefings on the Soviet strategy in the student field and occasionally was able to identify secret Soviet agents with whom they had to cope. With this assistance, they more than held their own in debate and organizational competition with the aging professional student cadres on which the Soviets relied.

However, the entire relationship depended on a broad consensus as to what the course of American foreign policy should be. As we have seen, that essential consensus began to erode before the *Ramparts* revelations as the result of rising student opposition to the Vietnam War. Under the circumstances, there is no doubt in my mind that the NSA and the CIA would have had to part company even if the revelations had never occurred. In fact, both sides were thinking of a quiet divorce before the outbreak of publicity. If we in the Agency had assessed more realistically and promptly the shift in student opinion that was taking place, we could have moved in time to arrange for an amicable and quiet severance of relations and avoided being overtaken by publicity that proved so damaging not only in the student field but in many other fields as well. I blame myself for that mistake in judgment.

After President Johnson announced the Katzenbach restrictions, not only was all Agency support withdrawn from the NSA's international program but the NSA leadership decided to terminate most of its international activity and to concentrate on domestic affairs. The leaders of the numerous other American voluntary organizations that the Agency had been assisting were determined to continue their international programs and made a strong case to the Katzenbach committee that some way be found to replace the secret Agency funding with open government support that would allow them to continue to compete effectively against the still powerful Soviet international fronts. The Katzenbach committee responded to the need to fill this gap by recommending to the President in the second of its two basic recommendations "that the Government should promptly develop and establish a public-private mechanism to provide public funds openly for overseas activities of organizations which are adjudged deserving, in the national interest, of public support." The committee did not attempt to spell out how such a structure might work but proposed instead to the President that he appoint a larger group, including individuals in private life, to attack the problem. The committee concluded with a warning: "To be effective, such a new institution would have to be . . . and be recognized as . . . an independent body, not controlled by the government."

President Johnson accepted this recommendation and in April 1967 appointed an eighteen-member committee to address the problem under the chairmanship of Secretary of State Rusk. The membership was drawn from the executive branch, the Congress, and the private sector. After wrestling with the complex issues involved, the Rusk committee confessed itself unable to reach agreement and in effect the political vacuum left by the withdrawal of

Agency support from the international activities of many effective private voluntary American organizations continues to the present day. These private institutions have attempted to compete on the world stage with the massively financed Soviet front apparatus by relying on an unstable and inadequate mix of membership dues, private foundation grants, and occasional grants from government agencies.

In retrospect, the decision taken by default not to replace the termination of secret CIA funding by some reliable method of open government support was an act of unilateral political disarmament in the face of a continuing Soviet challenge. The international network of Soviet front organizations has become less strident but more sophisticated in its orchestration of propaganda themes. While these organizations are invariably controlled by Communists, they have expanded into the third world and won over many non-Communists as members. Steady infusions of Soviet funds and new leadership have helped them to recover from the setback caused by the Soviet invasion of Czechoslovakia in 1968. A good example of their continuing effectiveness even in Western Europe was their orchestration in the summer of 1977 of the successful propaganda campaign against U.S. development of the neutron bomb. A torrent of mass petitions, demonstrations, and declarations was let loose and had its undeniable effect on public opinion. Equally effective and perhaps more dangerous was the critical role played by the funds, organizers, and propagandists of these organizations that were deployed into Portugal to assist the Communist Party there in its nearly successful bid for power in 1975.

To give some idea of the scope and variety of this international apparat, here is a partial list of the organizations now funded and controlled by the Soviets.

> *The International Union of Students*—Headquarters in Prague. Claims 10 million members.
> *The World Federation of Democratic Youth*—Headquarters in Budapest. Claims 150 million members but most are in Communist countries.
> *The World Federation of Trade Unions*—Headquarters in Prague. Claims 150 million members.
> *The World Peace Council*—Headquarters in Helsinki.

Claims affiliates in 120 countries and propagates the party line on such issues as peaceful coexistence, disarmament, and anticolonialism.

The Women's International Democratic Federation—Headquarters in East Berlin.

The International Association of Democratic Lawyers—Headquarters in Brussels.

The World Federation of Scientific Workers—Headquarters in London and Paris. Claims 300,000 members in twenty-eight countries.

The International Organization of Journalists—Headquarters in Prague. Claims 150,000 members from 110 countries.

The International Federation of Resistance Fighters—Headquarters in Vienna.

The International Institute for Peace—Headquarters in Vienna. Purports to provide a forum for East-West scientific exchange but consistently supports Soviet policies.

Central direction by the Secretariat of the Central Committee of the Soviet Communist Party, heavy and continuous funding, and consistency of purpose have combined to make this international apparat a formidable source of Soviet strength in the continuing struggle for influence and political advantage in the third world during the last decade. With the termination of the CIA's financial and advisory role in 1967, private American organizations and their democratic counterparts abroad have tried to compete as best they can, relying on their own limited resources and spasmodic open grants from government agencies.

Among the democratic states, only the West Germans have organized themselves effectively to deal with this problem. The West German Social Democratic Party has for many years supported with party funds the Friedrich Ebert Foundation, and the Christian Democratic Party has similarly supported the Adenauer Foundation. With supplemental assistance from the foreign aid budget of the West German government, these two foundations have proved to be flexible instruments through which to channel training and logistic and financial support to democratic groups abroad competing with the Communists for control of key sectors of society. Their grants are not secret but they are given discreetly and they make no attempt to claim credit for their work through publicity. They played a crucial role in providing support to the indigenous democratic forces in Portugal in their rivalry with the Communists after the right-wing dictatorship was overthrown. Whether our political parties have sufficient ideological coherence and organizational discipline to conduct a similar effort is doubtful, but at the least the possibilities are worth serious exploration in view of the size and urgency of the need.

Although some of the leaders of those private American groups that the Agency supported prior to 1967 have urged me to describe our cooperation in the same detail as I have done in the case of the National Student Association, I see little advantage in doing this and many disadvantages. After the *Ramparts* revelations, the State Department specifically and publicly acknowledged that the NSA had been receiving Agency support. The history of the relationship was subsequently spelled out in a somewhat tendentious manner in the Church committee report. However, in the case of the other organizations, there are only individual allegations and press speculations on the record, and these have not been officially confirmed by the government. For me to try at this late stage to straighten out the record by identifying the organizations that the Agency did support in their international activity could only damage their continuing effectiveness and give the Soviets ammunition to use against them.

When I was called back from London to testify before the Church committee in 1975, I was told by the staff that some senators were pressing for open and televised hearings on the past history of Agency support to private American institutions. I argued then that the important point for the committee to establish was whether or not the Agency had strictly adhered to the Katzenbach policy restrictions after they had been issued. If full compliance with the Katzenbach guidelines could be demonstrated, as I thought it could be, I urged that plans for televised hearings be dropped. The one certain effect would be to damage the reputations of individual citizens whose only fault had been their willingness to cooperate with their government against what had then been perceived as the real and present danger posed by the Soviet political offensive. As we have seen, the Church committee did in fact after exhaustive investigation conclude that the Katzenbach guidelines had been faithfully followed by the Agency. The televised hearings on this topic were never held, and the committee's report was careful not to reveal more than had already been officially confirmed. It would hardly be appropriate for me to do now what I urged the committee not to do for good and sufficient reasons.

Suffice it to state that the relationship between the Agency and these private institutions during the years of our cooperation was governed by the same ground rules that I have described in the NSA case. The elected leaders of these institutions jealously guarded their independence and organizational integrity. As a result, secret funds did not become a corrupting influence. In all the years of our cooperation in attempting to promote the democratic cause abroad, I cannot remember a single incident in which the Agency was accused of attempting to manipulate or unfairly influence the policies or activities of those with whom we dealt. The democratically selected leadership of this private sector had won its position by proven competence, and it demonstrated more initiative, imagination, and dedication in its conduct of the struggle abroad against the Soviet fronts than could have been expected of the slower-moving government bureaucracy. When the time came to part company by presidential decision, it was with genuine regret on both sides and with mutual respect.

Chapter 6

The Radios

WHEN I SUCCEEDED THOMAS BRADEN as chief of the International Organizations Division in September of 1954, I also inherited from him responsibility for the Agency relationship with two unique organizations, Radio Free Europe and Radio Liberty. In 1971, the widely held belief that these two radios received most of their funds from the CIA was officially confirmed by Republican Senator Clifford Case of New Jersey.[1] As a result of that disclosure, the Congress took action to terminate all CIA funding and connection to them and to provide for their continued existence by open appropriations. The radios survived the difficult transition period and again proved their effectiveness in keeping their mass audience in the Soviet Union and Eastern Europe currently informed concerning the dissident activity in support of human rights that swept these countries in the wake of the Helsinki Declaration in 1975. Much has been written about this unique effort to communicate across the Iron Curtain, but nowhere has the nature of the twenty-year Agency relationship to the radios been described accurately. Perhaps a description of that long cooperation, presented from my vantage point, can help to dispel some popular myths and widespread misconceptions.

The origins of Radio Free Europe (RFE) are to be found in the

110

step-by-step consolidation of Communist regimes in Eastern Europe in the years following World War II. Many of the most prominent democratic leaders and cultural figures in these countries were forced to flee into exile. Having extended diplomatic recognition to the Eastern European Communist regimes, the State Department could not resort to the device used during the war of recognizing these leadership elements as governments in exile. On the other hand, the promise of democratic freedoms for the Eastern European peoples had been explicit at Yalta, and the United States was not prepared to accept as permanent the imposition of Communist rule in that area. It was thought important to keep intact the cadre of democratic leaders who had escaped and to provide them with some way of communicating with their own people in order to keep alive the hope of eventual freedom.

As a result, in early 1949, George Kennan in his role as chief policy planner in the State Department, after clearing with Secretary of State Dean Acheson, approached a veteran retired diplomat, Joseph C. Grew, with the proposition that he head up a private group of prominent American citizens to find useful employment for the distinguished exiles and to help them communicate with their people.[2] Grew accepted the assignment and on June 1, 1949, he announced the incorporation of the National Committee for a Free Europe, later to become known as the Free Europe Committee. The original membership of the committee included, among others, Dwight D. Eisenhower, Adolph Berle, Mark Ethridge, Allen Dulles, and representative leaders of business and labor. Returning from his proconsul role in Germany, General Lucius Clay joined the committee and agreed to head up an organization called the Crusade for Freedom to raise funds for the endeavor from business corporations and the general public.

From the beginning, it was accepted that private fund raising would not be sufficient to sustain the large effort that was required, while open State Department funding would compromise the department's attempt to put some distance between itself and the political exiles. The solution to the dilemma was the decision by the Truman administration to direct the CIA to provide confidential funds and to exercise policy control on the basis of State Department guidance. In view of the large amounts involved, this arrangement was reviewed with the responsible congressional committees and approved by them. In this way, the State Department relieved itself of the complex and time-consuming job of negotiating with the often quarrelsome exile groups while at the same time ensuring that their activities would not exceed the limits of official policy.

At the start, the somewhat naive notion existed that all that was necessary was to build some radio transmitters and to hand the microphones to the exiles to say what they wished. As Joseph Grew put it, "Our second purpose will be to put the voices of these exiled leaders on the air, addressed to their own peoples back in Europe, in their own languages, in the familiar tones."[3] It quickly became evident that the exile leaders were so divided among themselves on ideological lines, and the different political groups were so prone to infighting, that a tower of Babel would be erected if they were left to their own devices.

By 1951, the American management of the RFE office in Munich, Germany, where most of the programming was done, had devised a delicate and ingenious compromise to give the exile broadcasters wide autonomy while preserving enough policy control to ensure objectivity and coherence. The exile political groups were excluded both from propagating their views, except in policy statements specifically attributed to them, and from nominating their representatives to the broadcast desks. Instead, the American management reserved the right to appoint the chiefs of the five desks broadcasting to Poland, Hungary, Czechoslovakia, Rumania, and Bulgaria. In cooperation with the desk chiefs, the scriptwriters and broadcasters were to be hired on the basis of individual talent and ability. Policy control over content was obtained by the formulation of general guidelines, supplemented by daily meetings with the American policy adviser to determine the handling of specific news items. Out of this compromise arrangement emerged the fruitful partnership between exile talent and American policy advisers that has made RFE broadcasts so widely popular and so well-respected to this day throughout its mass audience in Eastern Europe. Crucial to this success was the early decision to make the news reports as objective and as accurate as possible and to concentrate coverage on those internal developments within the bloc which neither the Voice of America nor BBC was able to cover in any depth. A high reputation for credibility earned by performance over a long period of time was seen to be RFE's most valuable asset.

On the technical side, the apparently simple task of siting and building transmitters turned out to be almost as complex as the policy control problem. The heavy jamming by the Communist regimes in Eastern Europe against the RFE medium- and short-wave transmitters in West Germany was a tribute to the effectiveness of the broadcasts but badly impaired their intelligibility in the target area. In an ingenious but costly move to beat the jamming, RFE took advantage of the best propagation conditions for short-wave broadcasting into the target area by building a massive array of high-powered transmitters north of Lisbon through an agreement reached with the Portuguese government, considerably improving signal strength and audibility.

While RFE was expanding in this way in the early fifties, another somewhat similar but separate organization was established with CIA confidential funds to focus on the Soviet Union. Formed in 1951 by a group of private American citizens at government instigation, this organization, which later became known as the Radio Liberty Committee, had as its objective broadcasting into the Soviet Union by exiles using the Russian and national minority languages. Its main programming base was also located in Munich, but in its early stages it lacked the transmitter power to break through the heavy and continuous Soviet jamming.

From this brief history, it can be seen that in 1954, when I took over responsibility within the Agency for the conduct of relations with the two radios, the foundations had already been laid, and they were well advanced toward becoming a powerful means of communicating with the peoples behind the Curtain. I was delighted to take on this additional duty. During my world federalist days, I had become increasingly aware of the serious danger posed by the determination of the Soviet regime to control completely the access to information of its own people and of the captive populations in Eastern Europe. Strict travel restrictions, effective censorship of all incoming mail, and total control of all internal media gave the Communist regimes a monopoly on what their peoples were told about events in the outside world and within the bloc itself. I had seen how this monopoly had been used by Stalin to distort and misrepresent our federalist proposals, and it seemed to me that to break through this curtain of censorship was an essential step toward reducing the threat of a managed and monolithic public opinion.

In his eloquent support of Western efforts to communicate across the Curtain, Solzhenitsyn described the extent of the danger in dramatic terms in his Nobel Prize speech in 1970:

> Suppression of information renders international signatures and agreements illusory; within a muffled zone it costs nothing to reinterpret any agreement; even simpler, to forget it as though it had never really existed. A muffled zone is, as it were, populated not by inhabitants of the Earth, but an expedition corps from Mars; the people know nothing intelligent about the rest of the Earth and are prepared to go and trample it down in the holy conviction that they come as "liberators."

I had no naive belief that the broadcasts of RFE and Radio Liberty (RL) could quickly bring the walls of the dictatorship tumbling down like those of Jericho. But I did strongly believe and remain convinced that persistent efforts to expose those within the bloc to both external and internal reality make aggressive foreign adventures more difficult for the regimes and incrementally over time improve the chances for gradual change toward more open societies. On taking over the function of providing policy guidance, I was also relieved to find that there was broad agreement between the State Department, the Agency, and the American management of the two committees on a basic issue. Whatever domestic advantage might have accrued to the Eisenhower administration from its electoral use of slogans like "liberation" or "roll back" as applied to Eastern Europe, it did not affect the standing injunction that the radios were not to provoke premature and suicidal internal revolt by any implied promise of external assistance. When it came to the tone and content of what was to be said on a daily basis to the people behind the Curtain, the Eisenhower administration was far more cautious and responsible than its campaign oratory would have led one to expect.

In carrying out my Agency role of providing support and guidance to the radios, I had the indispensable help of a small but competent staff in CIA headquarters. When controversial issues arose, I reported directly to Allen Dulles as long as he was director of the Agency. As a private citizen, he had been an original founding member of the Free Europe Committee, and he had many personal acquaintances on the boards of trustees of both organizations. He was deeply committed to the objectives of the radios and kept himself currently informed not only on conditions within the bloc but on the state of play in the complex world of exile politics. I quickly learned to consult with him first before making any controversial decisions, since his acquaintances among the trustees were quite capable of going over my head to appeal to him for a reversal. When he was informed ahead of time about a pending issue, he would usually back me up, and there is no doubt that his determined personal support of the work of the radios played a decisive role over the years in the Congress and in the executive branch in ensuring their survival and expansion.

In dealing with these two organizations, our basic principle was to give the top American management the widest possible autonomy and to delegate to them the responsibility for day-to-day decision making. The trustees of each committee would consult with us before choosing a new president, and most of the time they chose well. In my experience, the most effective president of the Free Europe Committee was John Richardson, who left a lucrative investment banking practice to take on the job and who later served as an assistant secretary of state. I believe the most able leader of Radio Liberty was Howland Sargent, who had known the Washington jungle from the inside as an assistant secretary of state in the Truman administration. Although we did not always agree, they were both extremely able and dedicated men, and the frictions inevitable in so complex a relationship were kept to a minimum during their tenures.

Wide as the grant of autonomy was to these two institutions, there were certain matters that could not be delegated. The first of these was the annual budget. The process began with the submission by the two radios to my staff of their proposed financial requirements for the next fiscal year. After detailed review, which usually resulted in substantial reductions, we then had the task of defending these budget requests within the Agency against the urgent and competing demands of other Agency elements for what they considered to be their fair share of the total budget. As the need for increased transmitter strength and the effects of inflation forced the financial requirements of the radios steadily upward, this internal competition for funds became more intense each year, and there were understandable complaints that the radios were devouring too large a portion of the resources of an organization that was supposed to be concerned primarily with intelligence collection and analysis. There was an obvious case to be made for breaking the radios out of the Agency and providing for open funding by Congress. However, neither the executive branch nor the congressional committees were willing to consider this alternative until events finally forced a decision. The existing arrangement worked tolerably well, and no one at the policy level wanted to face the high risk of exposing prior Agency involvement that was inevitable in any shift to public financing.

On occasion, these budget battles raised basic and momentous policy issues. When Howland Sargent took over as president of Radio Liberty, he realized quickly that its weak transmitters in West Germany had no chance of being heard by any large audience inside the Soviet Union because of massive Soviet jamming. Taking a leaf from RFE's book, he proposed the construction of a powerful short-wave transmitter base on the Spanish coast north of Barcelona. Engineering studies showed that this location would give Radio Liberty its best chance of being heard over the Soviet "sky-wave" jamming, and preliminary negotiations with the Spanish government indicated that it would grant a license to broadcast.

When I first broached this proposal to Allen Dulles, he was hesitant. The capital cost of building the transmitter site was heavy, over $5 million, and at that time there was little evidence of any substantial body of dissident opinion behind the monolithic facade of the regime's control. Fortunately, Dulles had recently finished reading an Agency study which demonstrated that the Soviets had made enormous strides toward eliminating illiteracy and in improving the technical education available to their citizens. I remember his remarking that we were no longer dealing with an uneducated peasantry. He went on to speculate that, however narrow and ideologically controlled was the education being offered, it was bound to stimulate the imagination and curiosity of millions of Soviet citizens. As they learned to read and to reason, he concluded that they would inevitably begin to ask questions and then to listen to foreign broadcasts when the dusty answers of the regime left them unsatisfied. If we could override the jamming with consistently accurate reports as to what was really going on inside their country and in the outside world, we could look forward to the day when a mass audience would dare to eat the forbidden fruit of foreign broadcasting. In those days, this gamble was like trying to shoot birds in the dark in a country where there were very few birds, as Einstein once described the early possibilities of nuclear fission. But Dulles was prepared to accept the long odds and managed to convince the skeptical congressional committees that this bet on the innate human thirst for knowledge was worth making.

To this day the heavy Soviet jamming continues against Radio Liberty, and it is particularly effective in the larger cities where ground wave jammers are able to lay down a steady barrage of interfering noise. But in the smaller towns and in the wide stretches of the countryside reaching into central Russia, the voice of the radio is audible. The proliferation of short-wave radio sets and of tape recorders has widened the listening audience until now it is conservatively estimated at 3–4 million regular listeners, greatly magnified by tape-recorded replays.

Broadcasting not only in Russian but in most of the national minority languages, Radio Liberty found a unique role for itself in the mid-sixties that has become increasingly important with time. The growth of the dissident movement, beginning with the trial of Sinyavsky and Daniel in 1966, and the proliferation of *samizdat* publications reaching the West have given the radio an opportunity to broadcast back into the U.S.S.R. the creative work and courageous protests of the dissidents. For reasons of policy, there are strict limits on the amount of such rebroadcasting that official radios like VOA or BBC can do, and Radio Liberty has filled the gap.

The significance of the role that it has come to perform has been indicated by Solzhenitsyn. When he was asked in 1972 what he thought of Radio Liberty, he replied, "If we learn anything about events in our own country, it's from there."[4]

In addition to budget decisions, another function that we could not delegate to the American management of the radios was our responsibility for providing policy guidance and control. We finally worked out an arrangement with the Department of State under which we cooperated in drafting an annual guidance directive for each country to which the radios broadcast and then we hammered out agreement with the radios on its provisions. In times of crisis, this general collection of do's and don'ts was supplemented by daily advice. In the main, we relied on the American management to ensure implementation, but as a check each month my staff reviewed one day's taped broadcasts, chosen on a random basis, to identify mistakes in tone and content. Journalists and historians in the past have commented on the dangerous degree of freedom that these private radios seemed to exercise in influencing U.S. relations with the Soviet bloc. In fact, this missing link did not exist, and our control function, although not publicly evident, served to keep the broadcasts responsive to official policy.

My staff and I saw our job as one of protecting the integrity and credibility of the radios within the broad guidelines laid down. Pressures to distort that objective occasionally came from American ambassadors in Eastern Europe. They sometimes felt that their diplomatic negotiations with their host governments were being hampered by the publicity given to regime failings by RFE. Subjected to daily complaints from Communist officials, an American ambassador would infrequently bend under the pressure and demand that RFE moderate its criticism on a particular issue. If the radio had its facts straight and was not exceeding agreed policy, we would defend its role, and these bureaucratic battles would be fought up the line to the secretary of state's office for decision.

Pressure to distort the purpose of the radios also came occasionally from within the Agency. Ingenious schemes to use the radios in disinformation campaigns against particular Communist leaders were raised with us from time to time, and my answer to all such proposals was negative. Compromise of the reputation for reliable accuracy that the broadcasts had come to enjoy was not worth the ephemeral and dubious advantage that might be gained by the use of false information. Similarly, we did not attempt to mix apples and oranges by allowing the American and exile staffs to be used for secret agent operations. Contrary to the persistent Soviet allegations that exiles working for the radios were being used by the CIA as espionage agents, this was not the case. It would have been foolishly shortsighted to expose the broadcasts to the kind of regime attack that the apprehension of a single spy behind the Curtain would have made possible. This self-restraint did not prevent the Soviets from running into the exile staffs controlled double agents, who would then pretend to defect with loud accusations that they had been hired as CIA spies while working for the radios.

Both radios did, however, collect openly a vast amount of information on conditions and developments within the Soviet Union and

Eastern Europe which was essential to the timely production of accurate news broadcasts and commentaries. Monitoring stations in West Germany recorded and translated the broadcasts of all the government radios behind the Curtain, so that there could be an up-to-date record of what the Communist regimes were telling their own people. The daily newspapers and publications put out by these regimes were assembled in cross-indexed files by competent research staffs. Both radios maintained news bureaus in the major Western European capitals to interview travelers and escapees and to report on developments affecting the target audience. Munich headquarters became a magnet for a continuous flow of information smuggled out to the West with the request that it be aired.

In time, Munich became a repository for so much information and analytical expertise that Western journalists, scholars, and diplomats made it a regular practice to stop there for briefings before visiting the bloc, and they would review their findings on their return with the American policy advisers. Part of my responsibility was to ensure that the cream was skimmed from this avalanche of open information and analytical expertise and relayed promptly to Washington from the field.

Immersed in this information flow and working close to each day's breaking news, RFE's American policy advisers during the 1950s became acutely aware of the changing mood in Eastern Europe. I remember their warning to me in the early summer of 1956 that events were moving toward a confrontation with the Soviets in Poland and Hungary. When I tried to convey this impression of approaching crisis to the State Department and intelligence analysts in Washington, they were inclined to be skeptical and tended to assume on the basis of past experience that the Communists would remain firmly in control. Allen Dulles was later to criticize me for not having brought RFE's advice more forcefully to his personal attention and that of senior policymakers. I admit to not having been sufficiently sure of my case to challenge the prevailing consensus directly. It was a salutary lesson in the reality that not all wisdom resides in Washington and that access to even the most secret intelligence is no guarantee against human error.

Although the CIA did not use radio personnel as agents to collect secret intelligence, we sometimes were able to provide the radios with significant information that they would not otherwise have had access to. It was part of our job to cull the intelligence flowing in from defectors for factually accurate items that could be used by the radios in their daily reporting on internal developments. For example, in December of 1953 a colonel in the Polish secret police, Josef Swiatlo, defected to the CIA in Berlin. After months of debriefing to establish his bona fides and for intelligence purposes, we made him available for interviews to the Polish exile editors of RFE. He turned out to be a gold mine of detailed and accurate information on the corruption and personal rivalries that flourished among the leadership of the Polish Communist Party. In a series of more than one hundred tape-recorded interviews from September to December 1954, Swiatlo's testimony was broadcast back into Poland by RFE, and hundreds of thousands of copies of leaflets based on his evidence were ballooned into Poland on the prevailing winds. By December 23, these dramatic revelations had forced the resignation of the dreaded chief of the Polish secret police, General Stanislaw Radkiewicz, from his job as minister of security. Subsequently, three of his top officials were also fired and the structure of the secret police was hastily reorganized and its powers restricted. It was a startling demonstration of the effective influence of RFE within Poland and was an important step in the sequence of events that finally led to the establishment of the more moderate Gomulka regime in the autumn of 1956.

Finally, there was the problem posed for the radios by the continuing attempts of the Soviet and Eastern European secret police to intimidate the exile staffs, to sabotage the installations, and to exacerbate frictions between the radios and the West German host government. This campaign of harassment ranged from the macabre to the ridiculous. Two Radio Liberty exiles were murdered in mysterious circumstances, and suspicion focused on Soviet agents who had disappeared behind the Curtain. Colonel Swiatlo confessed that part of his assignment had been to "silence" Wanda Bronska, a former Communist broadcasting for RFE. Through double agents infiltrated into the staffs, the KGB and the satellite services were able to identify exile personnel and then to take reprisal action against members of their families remaining behind the Curtain. An attempt was made to poison the salt in the RFE cafeteria and to blow up its balloon sites. An effort was made to introduce a doctored tape into the tape library in order to convince the West German government that an anti-German policy was being pursued.[5]

It was part of my staff's responsibility, working with other Agency elements, to try to provide the radios with counterintelligence protection against this continuing intimidation. The first line of defense was to prevent the initial hiring of double agents, and job applicants were checked against our central files to reduce this danger. Defectors were regularly debriefed on their knowledge of penetration operations, and security officers were trained to ensure prompt investigation of every incident or allegation. It was a never ending task, but we managed to keep the level of intimidation within tolerable limits.

The events in Poland and Hungary during 1956 provided a severe test of RFE's ability to perform under pressure and to remain responsive to policy controls in the face of extreme temptation. In the case of Poland, RFE passed the test with flying colors. Here again the pace of events was influenced by a successful CIA espionage operation. The Agency obtained the full text of Khrushchev's February speech denouncing Stalin at the 20th Congress of the party. When this was published in *The New York Times,* both radios replayed the explosive revelations to their target audiences. New fuel was added to the smoldering fires of discontent with Poland's Stalinist regime. Critics both within and outside the party took the Soviet admission of Stalin's crimes as a license to launch a broad attack on Stalinist policies and personalities. Fortuitously, Boleslaw Bierut, Stalin's henchman in Poland, died in Moscow in March of 1956. The more moderate Communist leader, Gomulka, was released from prison in April, and in May the Stalinist deputy premier, Jakob Berman, was forced to resign.

Then in Poznan on June 28, the workers rose in sudden and spontaneous revolt in protest against a reduction in wages. The uprising was put down by the tanks of the regime's Internal Security Corps at the cost of fifty-three dead and three hundred wounded. This revolt caught both the Polish government and RFE by surprise. In its news reports, the radio broadcast factual accounts of the uprising to the rest of Poland and to the other Eastern European countries. In its commentaries, the Polish desk of RFE advised great caution and warned against a suicidal insurrection, while urging the regime to avoid harsh reprisals against the rebellious workers. In so doing, the radio adhered closely to its policy guidelines and helped to contain the incipient violence.

After a few days' hesitation, Premier Cyrankiewicz assured the country that the wrongs against which the workers struck would be investigated, and the regime promised improvements in the living standards of both workers and peasants. Trials of the striking workers held in September were hastily abandoned after a few light sentences had been handed down. Meanwhile, demands increased for the return of the more moderate Gomulka to the leadership of the party. On October 19, the Central Committee of the Polish party elected Gomulka and three of his closest associates to full membership and simultaneously dismissed a Russian officer, Marshal Konstantin Rokossovsky, from his posts as defense minister and commander-in-chief of the Polish Army. In a secret arrangement with the surviving Polish Stalinists, Khrushchev flew into the Warsaw airport on this same day, with Molotov, Mikoyan, and Kaganovich. In his meeting with Gomulka and other Polish leaders, Khrushchev threatened to bring in the Red Army if Marshal Rokossovsky was not reinstated. The Poles refused and warned that the Warsaw workers had been armed and were prepared to fight. Poland teetered on the edge of war. In this showdown, Khrushchev gave in and accepted the Polish demands for increased autonomy. On October 21, Gomulka was elected First Secretary and appealed for calm and discipline throughout the country. The reformist Communist faction had won out over the Stalinists and established a new degree of autonomy in their relations with the Soviets.

During this crisis and its uncertain aftermath when full revolt against Soviet rule flared in Hungary, RFE consistently warned the Polish people not to demand the immediate withdrawal of Soviet troops and the holding of free elections, which would certainly have provoked armed Soviet intervention. RFE made it clear that it fully shared the people's hope for eventual independence, but in this tactical situation it supported Gomulka's compromise as the only responsible course. As evidence of Gomulka's realization that RFE was playing a crucially important moderating role, internal jamming against RFE was lifted during the crisis so that its calming voice could be more widely heard.

In Washington, we were well satisfied with RFE's performance during this extraordinarily dangerous period. The radio had followed and even anticipated our cautionary advice, and as a result the Polish people had won a significant if not decisive improvement in their condition. Much of the credit must go to the exile chief of the RFE Polish desk, Jan Nowak. He had served in the Polish Home Army during its premature revolt against the Germans in Warsaw in 1944, and in fact had been one of the last to escape from the city on a courier mission to take a final desperate appeal to Winston Churchill. He was determined to make sure that this time the Polish people kept their heads and avoided the suicidal romanticism that had characterized previous Polish revolts.

During the spring and summer of 1956, many of the same pressures that finally brought about the "bloodless revolution" in Poland were also at work in Hungary, but there were significant differences. The widespread resentment against the Stalinist rule of Matyas Rakosi, First Secretary of the Hungarian Communist Party, flared into open demands for his removal with the publication of Khrushchev's secret speech. Rakosi tried to ride out the storm by dissociating himself from Stalin. He announced that fabricated charges had been used in condemning to death as a Titoist the former Hungarian foreign minister, Laszlo Rajk, in 1949. Rakosi was remembered as the man who had taken the credit for exposing Rajk at the time of the trials, and his attempt to shift the blame was not accepted. The young intellectuals and journalists who belonged to the Communist youth organization formed a new group of their own called the Petoefi club, in memory of the Hungarian poet who died in the 1848 revolt against czarist Russia. The meetings of this group, established ostensibly to discuss the lessons to be learned from Stalin's crimes, became open forums for attacks on the Rakosi regime. Demands were made for the return of Imre Nagy, who had been ousted from the premiership a year before after attempting to introduce moderate reforms.

Alerted by the Poznan riots in Poland to the revolutionary potential of the situation the Soviets faced in Eastern Europe, and under prodding from Tito to get rid of the old Stalinists, a senior member of the Soviet Politburo, Anastas Mikoyan, flew into Budapest to meet with the Central Committee of the Hungarian Communist Party. Instead of following Tito's advice to replace the hated Rakosi with the respected Nagy, a compromise was reached under which one of Rakosi's colorless lieutenants, Erno Geroe, was selected to replace him as First Secretary. It was too little and too late. In spite of a decade of rigid Communist indoctrination, university students held a series of increasingly well attended public meetings to demand far-reaching democratic reforms, and they were backed by a majority of the faculty and the members of the Petoefi club.

Geroe tried to appease these mounting demands with modest concessions. On October 13, Nagy was accepted back into membership in the party, and the compulsory study of the Russian language was dropped. But the effect of these palliatives was washed away by the news from Poland that Gomulka had come to power and that the Soviets had backed down. On the night of October 22, mass meetings of students, workers, and intellectuals were held to draft new demands for the return of Nagy, the withdrawal of Soviet troops, and the holding of free elections. When the government radio refused to broadcast these demands, the students and workers posted copies on the walls of buildings throughout Budapest. Spontaneously, on October 23, a huge crowd formed at the statue of General Benn, who as a Polish officer had led Hungarian troops in the revolt of 1848 against the czar. Like a great river gathering strength as it flowed, the crowd surged toward the parliament building and, now nearly 300,000 strong, chanted for the return of Imre Nagy. Having just returned from a futile attempt to win Tito's support in Belgrade, Geroe broadcast a reply condemning the demonstration and offering no concessions.

Student crowds then toppled Stalin's statue in Budapest and marched again that evening on the government radio building to request that their demands be broadcast. When the state security police opened fire, the demonstrators charged the building. Hungarian regular police were rushed to the scene, but instead of restoring order, they joined in the attack on the hated security police. Alerted by telephone, workers collected arms from their factories and launched a series of attacks on security police command posts throughout the city. Early in the morning of October 24, the first Soviet tanks rolled into Budapest. The Hungarian revolution had begun. Throughout the country, Hungarian Army elements joined the young students and workers, and one by one the provincial radios came on the air to announce that revolutionary councils had seized control. Their broadcast demands for reform steadily escalated the objectives of the revolution, including abolition of the one-party system and the security police, restoration of multiparty democracy and civil liberties, immediate withdrawal of Soviet troops, and proclamation of Hungary's neutrality and withdrawal from the Warsaw Pact.

The regime broke and ran. Premier Hegedus and First Secretary Geroe fled from Budapest. Nagy as premier announced a new coalition government, including János Kádár as First Secretary and some non-Communists. By October 30, Nagy was able to proclaim a cease-fire, and the Soviet troops began an apparent withdrawal. In effect, Nagy now joined the revolution by broadening his coalition government and pledging free elections. On November 1, he went one step further. He proclaimed Hungary's neutrality and then appealed to the U.N. Security Council in New York for protection.[6]

The rest is history. Stalling for time in the U.N. on the grounds that negotiations for withdrawal were progressing, the Soviets secretly brought in more reliable troops who had not been contaminated by exposure to popular feelings. In a massive betrayal, First Secretary Kádár and three former members of Nagy's brief coalition announced a new government on November 4, and formally requested the assistance of Soviet troops in putting down the forces of "fascism and reaction." The Soviet Army then proceeded methodically to crush the rebellion, although in some districts the fighting lasted for more than a month. As a revealing commentary on the Soviet claim to leadership of the working class, it was the workers in their factories who put up the most prolonged and determined resistance. On November 22, Nagy was captured by the Soviets through a ruse and later secretly tried and executed in Russia.

I have included this brief chronological summary of the Hungarian revolution because it is only by understanding the sequence of events that one can evaluate the role of RFE in the unfolding drama. That role was and remains controversial. The first and most serious charge against RFE was that it had deliberately incited and provoked the Hungarian uprising and that it would not have occurred without the inflammatory broadcasts of RFE. This allegation was initially launched by the Rumanian Communist Party newspaper on November 3, 1956, followed up by Vasily Kuznetsov in his position as chief Soviet delegate to the U.N. during the Security Council debate, and finally sanctified as part of the official Communist version of history by inclusion in the Kádár regime's publication "The Counter-Revolutionary Forces in the October Events in Hungary." This official document concluded: "The subversive broadcasts of RFE—backed by dollars, directed from America, and functioning on the territory of West Germany—played an essential role in the ideological preparation and practical direction of the counterrevolution, in provoking the armed struggle. . . ."[7] This charge was subsequently repeated in the West German and American press. In fact, it became an article of faith in certain liberal circles to believe that RFE had irresponsibly caused the Hungarian revolt and had innocent blood on its hands. When President Kennedy took office in Washington, I found that some of his key advisers were initially hostile to the radios for this reason.

After the Hungarian revolt was crushed, my office in the Agency, with the help of two Hungarian-speaking analysts, did a careful review of the taped broadcasts that had been made in the weeks before the revolution. We could not find evidence that in this period RFE had violated the standing instructions against inciting to violence or promising external assistance. It did give full news coverage to internal developments and cross-reported into Hungary in depth on the Polish drama, which undoubtedly raised hopes for liberalizing change. But the clear lesson of the Polish experience was that the possibilities for change were limited and that the dominant position of the Communist Party and membership in the Warsaw Pact were not policies that could or should be challenged in the context of existing East-West relations. In that sense, exposure to the Polish reality and to the careful strategy of Gomulka should have functioned as a cautionary warning to the Hungarian audience.

In retrospect, the real mistake in Hungary was the failure of the Soviet and Hungarian party leaders to understand in time the depth of the opposition to years of Stalinist misrule by the Rakosi regime. If the Soviets had moved in the summer to replace Rakosi with Nagy instead of the ineffective and compromised Geroe, there might well have been an opportunity for the kind of modest reform that Gomulka was able to keep under control in Poland and that the Soviets were just barely willing to tolerate. As it was, by the time Nagy did come to power, a spontaneous national uprising had already swept past the limits observed in Poland and carried him along with it. The genuine spontaneity of a massive popular revolt was both the glory and the downfall of the Hungarian revolution. Within a few brief days the secret police was destroyed and the Hungarian Communist

Party had disintegrated, so there remained no organized internal political power capable of keeping the demands for change within the bounds acceptable to the Kremlin, in contrast to what had happened in Poland.

Far from having planned or directed the Hungarian uprising, both RFE and officials in Washington were taken very much by surprise when the fighting broke out. In the early morning of October 24, I was awakened by a telephone call from Allen Dulles. "All hell has broken loose in Budapest," he said. "You had better get in to the office as soon as you can." Arriving at the CIA's watch office, I found a few senior officials already there, and we spent the rest of the night trying to piece together a coherent picture of what was happening from fragmentary news reports, RFE monitoring, and U.S. Embassy cable traffic. The actual sequence of events described above was not at all clear to us, and could only be reconstructed later from interviews with the many Hungarian freedom fighters who had managed to escape across the border into Austria. At the time, all we could be sure of was that there was confused fighting and that Soviet tanks appeared to have rolled into Budapest. In fact, so widespread and deeply held was the Washington belief in the stability of Communist rule that realistic contingency plans did not exist for dealing with this unforeseen revolt.

From my own exposure to these events and from the findings of the working group within the Agency that reviewed the taped RFE broadcasts, I am satisfied that RFE did not plan, direct, or attempt to provoke the Hungarian rebellion. The spontaneous combustion of a popular revolution does not fit easily into the conspiratorial theory of history, but in this case it is the best explanation of what occurred. Two independent and objective reviews of RFE's taped broadcasts were later undertaken and reached the same conclusion. Chancellor Konrad Adenauer directed that a study of the tapes be made by the West German government in response to press criticism, and on January 25, 1957, he announced that there was no evidence that RFE had incited the revolt by promises of Western assistance. A similar review by a special committee of the Council of Europe also found RFE not guilty.

In the period immediately following the outbreak of fighting in Budapest, RFE became the best source of information available to the United States on what was actually happening throughout Hungary. As the low-powered provincial radio stations were seized by local revolutionary councils to announce their demands, the sensitive monitoring equipment of RFE in West Germany was able to pick up these weak signals and get translations promptly back to the Washington analysts and policymakers. From these broadcasts, it became quickly apparent that the revolution was on a national scale and not simply confined to street fighting in Budapest.

Since these local radio stations, fourteen in all, could be heard only in their immediate provincial areas, they soon began making direct requests to RFE to replay their revolutionary demands on its powerful transmitters so that the whole country could be informed of the speed and depth of the revolt. From the beginning, an extraordinary unanimity was revealed in these provincial broadcasts on the basic goals of the revolution. They all agreed in calling for the immediate withdrawal of Soviet troops and for the dissolution of the secret police. They unanimously demanded the holding of free elections and the withdrawal of Hungary from the Warsaw Pact. The American management of RFE recognized immediately that the decision to rebroadcast back into Hungary such far-reaching demands involved policy considerations beyond their competence and they asked me for guidance on how to react.

I took the problem up with Allen Dulles. He asked me to discuss it with Robert Murphy, then the number three man in the State Department. By the end of the day, we had our policy guidance from the top level of the Eisenhower administration. RFE was given authority to rebroadcast local programs when specifically requested as a communication service, but with attribution to the local station making the request and with identification of the program as a verbatim repeat of the original broadcast.

To the extent that RFE then served as a transmission belt for communications between provincial revolutionary councils it played a significant role in spreading throughout Hungary the news of what was happening not only in Budapest but in the outlying towns. In so doing, the radio did not act irresponsibly but as the disciplined instrument of a conscious policy decision by the Eisenhower administration. To have refused to replay these internal broadcasts would not have altered the course of events because by the time this rebroadcasting began the revolution had already achieved an irresistible momentum. Such a denial of RFE's technical facilities would have been read at that time by the large majority of the Hungarian population as an act of abandonment and betrayal in their hour of greatest need. On the other hand, this rebroadcasting by RFE did serve to identify the radio with the fundamental goals of the revolution, and in the wisdom of hindsight RFE was later blamed for what was in fact a high-level policy decision of the administration.

Another line of criticism of RFE's role developed after the revolt was crushed. While not attempting to blame the radio for provoking the revolt, these critics charged that the exiles on the Hungarian desk of RFE were so carried away by the euphoria of the revolution that they tended to exaggerate its chances of success and to raise false expectations of assistance from the West and the United Nations. In so doing, the charge was that the radio had helped to prolong the fighting needlessly and thereby increased the number of casualties. This view was not widely shared among the Hungarian freedom fighters who managed to escape to Austria and who were later interviewed in depth.[8] Their particular resentment was directed against the British and French governments for their decision to join with Israel in launching the Suez invasion against Nasser's regime in Egypt at the very moment that Nagy's plea for U.N. protection was under debate in the Security Council. They felt correctly that any possibility of effective U.N. action to deter Soviet intervention was destroyed by the Anglo-French invasion of Suez, which divided the West and removed any hesitation the Soviets may have had about launching their second armed invasion on November 4. The diplomatic confusion caused by the Suez attack provided the Soviets with the perfect cover and excuse for their own assault.

However, our own review of RFE broadcast tapes did reveal that their tone was more exuberant and optimistic than the situation warranted. In contrast to the cautious and sober restraint maintained by RFE's Polish desk, the Hungarian exiles reported the debates in the U.N. Security Council as if the international organization could provide real protection to Hungary's fragile and newly declared neutrality. Little stress was placed on the inherent limitations of the United Nations and on the veto power through which the Soviets could prevent the Security Council from taking any effective action. Similarly, in reporting on the widespread demonstrations of support for the Hungarian cause in the United States and Western Europe, RFE failed to emphasize that this emotional outpouring of sympathy could not be translated into effective intervention without inviting an unacceptable risk of nuclear war.

In addition to this excessively optimistic tone, one particular script in its content clearly violated the basic policy guidelines and should never have been broadcast. On the morning of the second Soviet attack of November 4, the Hungarian desk broadcast a review of an article in the London *Observer* which implied that if the Hungarians could keep fighting until the results of the American presidential election were known, the U.S. Congress might approve armed intervention. To this misleading speculation, the RFE broadcaster added the gratuitous comment that "a practical manifestation of Western sympathy is expected at any hour."

Although clearly innocent of the major charge of having provoked the revolution, the conclusion is inescapable that the Hungarian desk of RFE did not demonstrate the same disciplined restraint under pressure that had distinguished the performance of the Polish desk. The American management of the radio needed no urging from me to make personnel changes in the leadership of the desk and to bring into its staff a number of the most talented members of the new emigration who had escaped when the revolt was crushed. In the years that followed, RFE's Hungarian broadcasts have played a responsible and effective role in helping the Hungarian people to win step by cautious step some improvement in their living conditions and a limited degree of cultural autonomy. Having demonstrated their capacity for revolt, the Hungarians have compelled the Russians to treat them with a grudging respect, and ironically, the Kádár regime has become one of the comparatively more liberal governments in Eastern Europe.

The lessons learned in the crucible of the Hungarian revolution were later put to good use during the "Prague spring" of 1968 when the Dubcek regime attempted gradually to introduce liberalizing reforms in Czechoslovakia. Knowing how delicate was Dubcek's position as he tried to achieve internal reform while remaining within the Warsaw Pact, both the American management of RFE and we in Washington exercised very tight policy control over the broadcasts of the Czech desk. By daily policy guidance and strict monitoring, RFE was restricted to a calm and scrupulously accurate account of the extraordinary effort of the reformist Communist leaders to achieve "Marxism with a human face." As the weeks went by, the

lifting of censorship controls over the Czech media allowed diverse
opinions to be ever more freely expressed and permitted the internal
coverage of the news to become more accurate and complete. In this
relaxing atmosphere, RFE became less important as a source of information for the Czech and Slovak peoples; in fact, RFE's audience
dropped off appreciably during this period. The more optimistic
observers even began giving serious consideration to discontinuing
RFE broadcasts to Czechoslovakia on the ground that the expanding
area of press freedom within the country might no longer justify the
need for RFE's type of coverage from outside.

To a surprising extent, this sense of optimism was shared at the top
levels of the Johnson administration. Attention was focused on the
preparation of position papers for the anticipated discussions with
the Soviets on arms control. The speculation was that the Soviets
would not be tempted into a military intervention in Czechoslovakia
that would destroy the promising opportunity for arms negotiations
so long as Dubcek maintained his firm commitment in support of
Soviet foreign policy, continued membership in the Warsaw Pact,
and the leading role within Czechoslovakia of the Communist Party.
At a weekly meeting of the State Department policy planning staff,
which I regularly attended as a CIA representative, I ventured to
express my own doubts about the validity of such optimism. I tried
to point out that the independent policy of internal liberalization
pursued by Dubcek and particularly the freedoms of speech and
press being permitted in Czechoslovakia would inevitably be construed by the Soviets as a direct threat to the hard-line Ulbricht
regime in East Germany and to the increasingly harsh rule of Gomulka in Poland. It seemed to me that the Soviets were not likely to
tolerate for long this infectious growth of liberty within the borders
of their empire. At the meeting, I found myself in a small minority;
in fact, I can remember that only Charles "Chip" Bohlen, who held
a top position in the State Department at that time, spoke up to say
that he shared these fears. He went further on the basis of his experience as American ambassador in Moscow and predicted that the
Soviets would not put up with the continuance of the Dubcek experiment.

On August 20, 1968, the Soviets settled this argument for all of us
by invading Czechoslovakia, together with the forces of four obedient Eastern European satellites. After Dubcek and his allies were

forced from office, the repressive regime of Gustav Husak was put in place; and in neo-Stalinist style, the Czechoslovak Communist Party was systematically purged of all those who were found guilty of following the Dubcek deviation. The invasion was justified by invoking the Brezhnev Doctrine, under which the Soviets declared their right to intervene to preserve the ideological orthodoxy of any ruling Communist party.[9]

Throughout the flowering of the "Prague Spring," RFE broadcasts had played so restrained and so responsible a role that after the Soviet invasion not one complaint was heard against its objective coverage of events. In the aftermath of the intervention, as the freedom of internal expression was silenced by the reimposition of pervasive censorship, RFE won back its audience and was able to keep the population informed of the widening consequences for the Soviets of their aggression. Unprecedented public protests by courageous Russian dissidents in Moscow against the intervention had their echoes in Rome, where the Italian Communist Party denounced the invasion; and all this was cross-reported throughout the Soviet bloc by both RFE and Radio Liberty.

In retrospect, the brutal suppression of the Prague experiment was even more costly for the Soviets than the Hungarian rebellion. It widened the divisions in the world Communist movement. It profoundly alienated leftist and liberal opinion in the West and it planted the seeds of Euro-Communist deviation and indiscipline. It set the stage for the interrelated dissident movements that sprang up in the U.S.S.R. and Eastern Europe after the signing of the Helsinki Declaration in 1975, demanding compliance with the Helsinki promise of wider human rights and freer movement for peoples and ideas. Far from having been abjectly defeated in a lost cause, the Czechoslovakians made a major contribution to the complex and continuing struggle for increased freedom within the bloc, and the two radios, with their concentration on reporting and cross-reporting of internal developments, have played an indispensable supporting role in ensuring that this historical event with all its consequences was not obliterated by censorship or distorted by propaganda.

Obviously, these future developments were not clearly foreseeable in 1968. There remained the question of whether and how to support RFE and Radio Liberty when the surge funding provided for at the end of 1967 under the terms of the Katzenbach guidelines was exhausted. The problem was further complicated by the fact that President Johnson was not familiar in any detail with the work the radios were doing and not fully convinced of their effectiveness. The Johnson administration finally decided to continue CIA funding on the ground that the two radios were not private and voluntary organizations as defined by the Katzenbach report but rather government proprietaries established by government initiative and functioning under official policy direction. As such, they continued to be eligible for covert CIA funding. The responsible congressional committees accepted this compromise arrangement but not without a struggle. Richard Helms, as director of CIA, proved to be as able and persuasive an advocate before Congress on the subject of the radios as Allen Dulles had been, but the going was not always easy.

I remember appearing with him to testify before the subcommittee of the Senate Appropriations Committee that was responsible for reviewing the CIA budget. Senator Allen Ellender (D., La.) was chairman at the time, and he had some very definite ideas about the Soviet regime and the attitudes of the Russian people. In years past, he had visited Moscow in an attempt to increase the sale of American agricultural products to the Soviets. When he asked our ambassador in Moscow, then Chip Bohlen, to arrange a meeting for him with Mikoyan, he was told that Mikoyan was one of the top three in the Kremlin and rarely if ever met with even the most distinguished foreign visitors. Not accepting this for an answer, Ellender returned to his hotel and placed a direct call to Mikoyan's office. Within ten minutes, Mikoyan had sent a limousine to pick him up, and he spent a long session with Mikoyan that left him with a lasting and very favorable impression of the Russian leadership, an impression reinforced by a red-carpet conducted tour of the country arranged by Mikoyan. After that Ellender remained convinced that our diplomats were isolated from reality and that the Soviet regime enjoyed the wholehearted support of the Russian people. It was very difficult to convince him that foreign broadcasts could have any purpose or effect.

When the Nixon administration came to power, both the new President and Henry Kissinger made it clear early on that they fully supported continued CIA funding of the radios. Whatever their hopes may have been for détente, they clearly accepted the fact that ideological competition would continue, and were not prepared to make it easier for the Soviets to seal off their peoples from exposure to internal and external realities. Through 1969 and 1970, the radios enjoyed a brief period of stable existence during which their budgets were not under attack nor their roles open to fundamental questioning. This reprieve ended in January 1971, when Senator Case revealed publicly the fact that the radios had been covertly funded by the CIA and announced that he planned to introduce legislation to fund them by direct appropriation and thereby bring them under open congressional oversight.

This unwelcome publicity had the beneficial effect of forcing an open fight on the question of whether the radios should continue. The relevance of their role and their effectiveness in performing it could no longer be decided under the shroud of secret debate within the congressional committees responsible for reviewing the CIA budget. Both RFE and Radio Liberty now had to stand or fall on their own merits in the full glare of publicity by open vote in the Congress. The attack on the radios was led by Senator Fulbright from his influential position as chairman of the Senate Foreign Relations Committee. He opened the battle by declaring that the radios were "an instrument to keep alive animosities of World War II."[10] He went on to argue that the Nixon administration's détente policy of attempting to improve relations with the Soviets required the dismantling of these obsolete relics of the cold war. He stated in May of 1971, "if there is any expectation of improving relations with Russia, it seems to me that this kind of activity, to continue to stir up trouble in Eastern Europe and Russia, is contrary to the President's own policy."[11] The fact that the secret funding of the radios had now become public was used as an argument to prove that their credibility had been irretrievably destroyed.

The Nixon administration did not waver in its firm support of the radios as an essential means of continuing to communicate with the peoples living behind the curtain of censorship; and crucial to the final outcome was Solzhenitsyn's testimony on the indispensable role of Radio Liberty, quoted previously. For almost a year, the radios continued in a kind of limbo, supported by continuing resolutions in the House and Senate with just enough funds to maintain operations and to preserve their staffs. Finally, on March 30, 1972, a bill was passed by the Congress appropriating $36 million for RFE and Radio Liberty for fiscal year 1972. All CIA connections to the radios were completely severed, and the bill provided that the funds were to be administered by the secretary of state.[12] In a further and improved refinement on this procedure, the Congress established in December of 1973 the Board for International Broadcasting, consisting of seven members, five of whom arc appointed by the President with the advice and consent of the Senate for three-year terms, with the further provision that no more than three of these may be of the same party.[13] The chief executives of RFE and Radio Liberty were given nonvoting status as ex officio members of the board. This sensible arrangement for the support of the radios continues to the present day and has been accepted with minor changes by the Carter administration. In effect, the board now performs the budgetary control and policy guidance functions that the Agency used to perform but without the element of secrecy that CIA funding necessarily involved. Needless to say, all CIA connections to the radios have long since been completely and definitively terminated in spite of continuing Soviet propaganda to the contrary, and the board receives its policy direction from the Department of State for implementation by the radios.

In the 1971–72 period, when the radios led a tenuous existence and their survival was in doubt, the brunt of the battle in their defense in Congress was borne by spokesmen for the administration, particularly by David Abshire, who had the job of handling congressional liaison for the State Department and who later became the first chairman of the Board for International Broadcasting. Occasionally, he would ask me to join him in dealing with key congressional figures such as the Speaker of the House, Carl Albert (D., Okla.), and Senator Case. I was able to provide detailed information on the steps we had taken to sever the Agency relationship and also to answer questions on past performance. In the course of these conversations, I became convinced that Senator Case genuinely wished to see the radios survive under public funding and had chosen to publicize the CIA connection only as a way of compelling the administration to face the issue. However, one of his principal aides was John Marks, who did not seem to me to have much interest in whether the radios survived or not. Marks resigned from his Senate staff job, and worked for a time with Philip Agee, the CIA defector, in the effort to expose and harass CIA personnel serving under cover overseas.

The hazardous but successful transfer of RFE and Radio Liberty to open and public funding by the Congress ended a twenty-year period during most of which I had been the official within the Agency directly responsible for providing guidance and support. From being an involved participant in their troubles and triumphs, I had become no more than a concerned bystander, able only to watch and hope, as President Carter assumed the powers of office in January 1977. Carter's stress in his campaign on the need for a new American commitment to the cause of human rights both at home and abroad led me to hope that his administration would look favorably on the essential role the radios were playing in that struggle. One of his campaign statements seemed to point specifically in that direction when he said, "If détente with the Soviet Union and the countries of Eastern Europe is to have real meaning, we must work towards a freer flow of information."

This implied promise was given substance very early in the life of the new administration. On March 22, 1977, Carter submitted to the Congress a "Report on International Broadcasting." In it, he not only confirmed the importance of the role of RFE and Radio Liberty together with the Voice of America (VOA) in broadcasting to the Soviet Union and Eastern Europe, but he called for the installation of additional transmitters to break through the heavy jamming that continues in the Soviet Union, Czechoslovakia, Bulgaria, and Poland. He specifically recommended to Congress the addition of sixteen new 250 kw transmitters (five for VOA and eleven for RFE/RL) at an estimated cost of $22–25 million. In so doing, he took one of the few practical steps within our power that can assist the democratic movement within the Soviet bloc in its courageous efforts to achieve the wider freedoms promised by the Helsinki Declaration in 1975.

One of the clear lessons of the continuing and determined struggle of the people in Eastern Europe to achieve more open societies is that their progress is inextricably linked to what is happening within the Soviet Union itself. In 1968, as we have seen, the Prague Spring and its ruthless suppression inspired an open demonstration of protest in Moscow and a proliferation of *samizdat* literature reaching the West. Conversely, the heroic examples of Solzhenitsyn and Sakharov in daring to criticize the Soviet regime publicly in the early 1970s were a source of encouragement to the intelligentsia in Eastern Europe. When the physicist Yuri Orlov and his courageous friends in Moscow openly formed a monitoring group to report on

the violations by the Soviet regime of the human rights it had promised to observe at Helsinki, his example was followed by the formation of similar public monitoring groups in the Ukraine, Armenia,
Georgia, and Lithuania. Just as significant was the influence of his
example in encouraging the formation of the Workers Defense Committees in Poland, the Charter '77 movement in Czechoslovakia, and
the outspoken dissent of some of the leading cultural figures in East
Germany. Similarly, expressions of specific support for these protest
movements from Spanish and Italian Communists have helped those
inside to realize that the world Communist movement is no longer
an ideologically monolithic entity unified against them but that they
have real friends within its divided ranks.

Within this yeasty ferment of proliferating dissent, RFE and Radio
Liberty have a more important catalytic role to play than ever before. Their function is to serve as an indispensable communication
link between the disparate and isolated dissident groups and individuals by cross-reporting calmly, accurately, and in depth on what
each one of them has been doing and saying. A piece of *samizdat*
literature, written secretly in Russia and circulated among a small
group of trusted friends, is smuggled to the West. Suddenly it is
rebroadcast back throughout the Soviet bloc to millions of listeners
who otherwise would never have heard of it. Recorded on tape, it is
replayed again and again and becomes part of the conscious knowledge of the whole society. Or the tragic plight of an entire ethnic
group like the Meskhetians, who were forcibly exiled from their
ancestral home in Georgia, is exfiltrated in a report to the West and
then rebroadcast back to trouble the conscience of millions with the
knowledge of crimes by their government they had never dreamed of.

In the spring and summer of 1978, a year after their arrests, the
Soviet regime moved in one of its periodic fits of judicial repression
to convict and condemn with harsh sentences Orlov, Shcharansky,
Ginzburg, and many others. Some voices were raised in the West to
question whether publicity for the cause of human rights in the
Soviet bloc could have any effect except to increase the repression
against a few rash young dissidents and to damage the fragile structure of détente. Those directly involved, the dissidents themselves,
overwhelmingly reject this line of argument. With very rare exceptions, the leaders of the human rights movement—those inside the
bloc, those who have a chance to speak at their public trials, and

those who are forced into exile in the West—are firmly agreed that publicity is their best defense and that rebroadcasting of their protests strengthens their chances for eventual success. They intend to continue their protests whatever the West may think, and they believe that if the West stands silent the regime's repression will be more severe. Those openly tried and convicted, like Orlov and Shcharansky, proclaim their innocence, refuse to recant, and accept their draconian punishment with stoic courage as a price they are prepared to pay in the enduring struggle for a more open society.

From the time of the trial of Sinyavsky and Daniel in 1966 to the trials of 1978, the Soviet regime has attempted periodically to suppress dissent by the intimidation of show trials and harsh sentences. Since the Soviet regime remains unwilling to grant the civic and cultural freedoms the dissidents demand, it is compelled to pursue a repressive policy. But victims become martyrs, and the contagion spreads. And all this takes place not in the sealed and airless prison that was Stalin's empire but before a wide internal audience which, through the radios, is able to learn accurately and currently what causes the activists are attempting to defend and to judge for themselves whether the stiff sentences they receive are just.

The final chapter of this book offers a more extended discussion of what the growth of democratic dissent portends for the future of the Soviet Union and Eastern Europe and what consequences it has for the conduct of American foreign policy. I am grateful to have had the opportunity, together with many others, to play some part in establishing and defending the radios as unique instruments of free communication. RFE and Radio Liberty have succeeded in their purpose far beyond our original expectations. Cut loose from secret funding, they are in a better position now to prove themselves even more effective in the future.

One of the most articulate of the Russian activists who was forced into exile, Andrei Amalrik, has defined the future possibilities: "Foreign broadcasts in Russian play an enormous role. It is the only alternative information available to millions of Soviet citizens. The role of the radio is continually growing for two reasons. One is simply physical; the number of transistor radios in the Soviet Union keeps on growing. And second, the activity of the Soviet dissidents is itself continually growing, and the growth of that activity is communicated and becomes widely known."[14]

Chapter 7

Private Sorrow

BENEATH THE CLAMOR OF PUBLIC EVENTS, the stream of one's personal life flows like a subterranean river and has more to do with one's joy or grief than all the actions that take place on the world's stage. At least so it was with my wife, Mary, and our three boys, Quentin, Michael, and Mark, after we moved to Washington. Our first years there were happy ones, except for the brief ordeal of my secret trial. Mary studied painting at American University with increasing seriousness and mounting evidence in her work of real talent. The big house with its wide veranda, an old drovers' inn before the Civil War, was shaded by huge oak trees where the boys built tree houses in the leafy branches. Mary's sister, Tony, and her then husband, Steuart Pittman, lived nearby, and we had many old friends and some good new ones.

Like plants in rich soil, the boys prospered, and it was fascinating to watch the varied growth of imagination and curiosity as their minds were challenged by teachers who were mostly sympathetic and intelligent. During vacations, we either visited my family on the New Hampshire shore or stayed with Mary's mother on the Pinchot estate in Milford, Pennsylvania, where deer and bear roamed in the pine woods and three miles of river gave the boys a chance to learn early how to cast for the spotted trout. The stream descended in a series of small cascades and deep pools to a dramatic waterfall, where the mist from the crashing water filled a dark gorge. The pools that the water had carved smoothly out of black basalt were natural swimming holes filled with froth and bubbles by the swift current.

So the seasons went, and we had no warning that the good times were coming to an end. Then one late afternoon in December of 1956, I received a call at my office from one of the neighbors' children that Michael had been hit by a car while running across the road in front of our house. She could not tell me how badly he had been hurt, only that my wife had taken him in an ambulance to the hospital and wanted me to join her. I drove there hoping against hope, but when I saw Mary in tears in the hospital corridor, I knew that he was dead.

Rather than attempting to reconstruct that remembered grief, let me submit a few excerpts from my personal journal, which I still kept intermittently, as a more truthful way of describing the impact of that premature and unnecessary death.

> 30 December '56—Mikey died two weeks ago, December 18th, just nine years old, hit by a car. We buried him in the overgrown cemetery that lies on the ridge, overlooking Milford. It was a gray morning, with the mist so thick that it isolated the little group around the grave, the nearest trees painted black like stage scenery on the gray walls. The minister, high church Episcopalian, wore a strange black hat with a tasseled button on top, and there was a bit of a Scotch accent as he said the brief prayers. Mark was there with Mary and me and a few family, quiet and absorbed. He couldn't quite believe that his brother lay in that narrow hole in the ground and neither could I. Quentin didn't come.

> 6 January '57—The other night Quentin said, if there was one thing in the world he wanted, it was that his wish might come true and that Mikey would come back from wherever he was and that things would be again as they were before.

> 14 January—Went yesterday afternoon to hear [John Crowe] Ransom and [Allen] Tate read their poems and then discuss the Fugitive movement in which they had both begun. By chance,

they both chose to read poems about the death of little children, Tate the one that starts "When little boys grow patient, at last weary/Surrender their eyes immeasurably to the night." And Ransom one about a boy who was the son of an ancient, dying family and the "Bells for John Whiteside's Daughter." Particularly Tate's is very moving and it was hard for me to sit, calm and interested with the rest, while they talked politely and coolly about their verse, the occasion for which was dulled by the long years between for them. I sat between Robie Macauley and his wife, Anne, who turned her face away so that our eyes would not meet by chance until it was over and I had collected myself.

30 October—A friend of Mikey's at school wrote an essay that is his best epitaph.

> One day my mother took me to be registered at Georgetown Day School. Then the next day I came to school. That same day a boy started to teasing me about my leg. So the teacher was out of class. I got up and hit him and knocked him down. He and another kid got up and hit me. So I was a new guy in school and Mike Meyer thought that he could help. He hit one and that made him stop and then the other. From then on we were good Friends and whenever he was in trouble I helped him or if I got in it he'd help me.
>
> Had lots of fights. Had some fun and best of all moved to a new school. Mike and I had stayed for three years. Then at Christmas Holidays Mike was run down while crossing the street. He was killed. Everybody was sad because he was the heart of the class and my best friend.
>
> Ricky Sowell, Oct. 29, 1957

18 December '60

For Michael

Four years have passed since Michael
left behind his family and friends.
His leaving was so sudden there was no time
for warm goodbyes and wishes.
We thought he was too young to take
so long a journey all alone.
We remember his blue eyes.
His little bones lie lightly on the turning earth
and we see him only now through tears.

Joined by our shared sorrow, Mary and I were closer after this loss than we had been for some time, but then we grew apart. Caught up in my work in the Agency, I took too little care of her interests and concerns. Too many of the domestic burdens were allowed to fall on her shoulders, and I took too much for granted. As a modern and independent woman, she eventually rebelled and asked for a separation. By this time, it was too late to repair the damage. To my arguments that we should stay together for the sake of the boys, she replied that our increasingly frequent quarrels were not good for any of us and that we would be happier apart. I had no wish to become a part-time father and feared the effect of separation and divorce on the two boys after the loss of their brother. But I came to feel more and more like a jailer, imprisoning Mary in the formal institution of a marriage that had lost all meaning for her. Finally I agreed not to contest her decision to seek a divorce, under the terms of which the boys would stay with her and I would be responsible for providing for their education and support. We sold the old house in Virginia and moved into a more manageable house in Georgetown, from which I took my sad departure in September of 1957. Mary and I worked out a schedule whereby I could spend some time with the children each week, but it was not the same.

Every divorce is different, and the chain of cause and effect that leads to the breakdown of a marriage is infinitely various. But one thing is usually true and that is that the burden falls most heavily on the younger children, who lose the fundamental source of emotional security that only a united family can give. An excerpt from my journal indicates that our case was no exception.

22 June '58—Went by the house tonight and found Mark with a slight earache. He seemed sad so I read him three fairy stories, two Irish and one Norwegian which he loves. Afterwards, I put him to bed and was running my fingers through his hair when he suddenly turned his face from the pillow and asked, "Why did you get divorced?"

So I gave the explanation we'd agreed on nine months ago when the boys were first told. Weren't happy together, more so apart, better for all of us, etc. He said, "I know but you shouldn't have done it."

"But you understand?"

"Yes, I understand."

Youth is resilient, and Quentin and Mark recovered from the double shock of accidental death and divorce. But the fates had not yet finished with our now divided family. In October of 1964, I was in New York City attending a meeting when I received a call from an old friend, Wistar Janney. As gently as he could, he broke the news that Mary had been found dead on the tow path along the canal that borders the Potomac, apparently murdered that afternoon by an unknown assailant. To my incredulous questions, he assured me that there could be no mistake. I flew back to Washington immediately to learn all that there was to know. A passing truck driver on the Canal Road had heard screams and a shot. Running to peer over the wall along the road, he had seen a man with a pistol bending over the prostrate body of a woman. He called the police, and by the time they arrived the victim was dead and the murderer had disappeared. Mary's friends had identified her body.

My first thought was that I had to tell the boys before they read about it in the newspapers. By this time, both of them were away at separate boarding schools in New England. Quentin was now eighteen and, when I reached him by phone, he took it with stoic resignation. Mark was only fourteen, and I didn't want to break such news to him over the telephone. I called Milton Academy, where he was boarding, and told them I would fly up that night to see Mark the first thing in the morning, and to make sure that he didn't see any newspapers. When we met in the housemaster's study, he greeted me with cheerful surprise and was eager to know what had brought me up on such short notice. I had no choice but to give him the terrible news, and sat with my arm around him as he wept the inconsolable tears that flow from so irredeemable a loss. On the plane back to Washington, he sat stunned and silent; and then we managed to get through the ordeal of a large funeral service in the Washington Cathedral.

A man was found by the police in the area where Mary's death had occurred. He was later tried for her murder but the evidence against him was circumstantial. No weapon was found, and he was acquitted. Nevertheless, I was satisfied by the conclusions of the police investigation that Mary had been the victim of a sexually motivated assault by a single individual and that she had been killed in her struggle to escape. Later on, some journalistic speculation was published to the effect that I was convinced that Mary's death was the result of some complicated Communist plot. There was no truth whatever to these stories, and I never suspected the tragedy of having any other explanation than the one the metropolitan police reached after careful investigation of all the evidence.

The boys invited me to rejoin them in the Georgetown house, and we gradually put back together again the pieces of a family life in spite of the enormous gap that Mary's death left behind. A cheerful maid named Eloise cooked and cleaned up for us and made up in good humor for what she lacked in efficiency. Little by little the boys came to terms with the reality of their loss and, while mourning the past, began again to enjoy the present and to look forward to the future.

In January of 1966, I married Starke Patteson Anderson. We had met and fallen in love some months before. She herself had been divorced and had two children younger than mine, a daughter, Alexis, and a son, Nicholas. She had come to Washington from Memphis, Tennessee, and had found an interesting job working for Roger Stevens in his capacity as chairman of the newly established National Foundation for the Arts. She brought a harmonious order into our uncivilized masculine lives, and the two sets of children got on well together and became good friends. As if to compensate for the past severity of its treatment, fate went out of its way to be kind to us. In the difficult days ahead, our private life together remained a rock of stability beneath the waves of public controversy, and her calm good judgment and humor kept all things in proportion.

Chapter 8

The Agency Under Fire

As THE RESULT OF the untimely death of Deputy Director for Plans Desmond FitzGerald, in July of 1967, his deputy, Thomas H. Karamessines, was appointed to succeed him by Helms, who had by then become Director of Central Intelligence. I was appointed assistant deputy director for plans, and for the next six years served as Karamessines' number two in the management of the Agency's overseas operations. The Directorate for Plans, as it was then called, was a euphemism to describe the section of the Agency responsible for the collection of secret intelligence abroad, for the provision of counterintelligence protection against foreign agents, and for the conduct of covert action operations abroad, whether political, paramilitary, or propagandistic in nature. Within the Agency, this directorate was commonly referred to as "the clandestine service" and in the press it was later saddled with the title of "the department of dirty tricks."

Now officially rechristened the Directorate for Operations, it is organized today much as it was when Karamessines and I were in charge, although its budget and personnel have been reduced. The basic components of the organization were the geographical area divisions, and the division chiefs were responsible to Karamessines and to me for the management of their headquarters component and for the overseas CIA stations and bases in their respective areas. There was a supporting structure of specialized staffs to assist us in the running of this large and complex undertaking, including the Covert Action Staff, which I had previously headed. In effect, Tom K., as we called him, and I were responsible to Helms for carrying out whatever programs and missions abroad were assigned to us by the National Security Council. In this task, our main opponent and competitor was the Soviet KGB, together with its sister military intelligence service, the GRU. Since the KGB exercised effective control over the Eastern European intelligence services and also had at its disposal loyal Communist cadres throughout the world, the struggle was always an unequal one in terms of resources and numbers of people. We estimated that the KGB alone outnumbered us by more than four to one in the size of their staffs assigned to Soviet embassies abroad. To hold our own, we had the indispensable assistance of the intelligence services of our democratic allies, who were for the most part eager to cooperate with us against the common threat posed by the Soviets.

In many ways, Tom K. was the perfect man to work for as a deputy. He was always ready to assume full responsibility and when things went wrong never tried to blame anyone else. On rare occasions, in extremely sensitive operations when he was doubtful of the outcome, he would keep me in the dark on the theory that, not having been involved, I would be in a position to replace him. But 99 percent of the time we functioned as a team and met every evening to review the day's decisions and agree on how we would handle the next day's workload. He was decisive and able to delegate authority clearly and definitively. A veteran of twenty years' work in the clandestine service, he knew the strengths and weaknesses of all the senior people and was an extremely astute judge of human character, so he made few mistakes in personnel assignments. Recognizing that deadwood had accumulated over the years, he put into effect a system of review panels for each grade and steadily reduced the size of the directorate during his tenure by a careful and just process of early retirement. Generous in his praise, he could be a stern judge of incompetence and could tolerate least of all those who tried to blame subordinates for their own mistakes. Sure of his own abilities, he was not overawed by rank or reputation and was able to differ respectfully but firmly when he thought cabinet officers were talking nonsense. Cheerful by nature, he exuded a humane warmth that endeared him to secretaries and station chiefs alike.

He had earned these admirable qualities the hard way. His father had been a Greek immigrant who had been wiped out by the Depression and died prematurely. Tom K. worked his own way through Columbia University and its law school and became one of Tom Dewey's bright young deputy assistant attorney generals in New York in those racket-busting days. When World War II broke out, he entered the army as a private but later was assigned to the OSS because of his knowledge of Greek language and history, and rose to the rank of major. After the war, he joined the CIA at its inception and devoted his entire life to government service at far less monetary reward than he could have earned in private practice. He retired from the Agency after Helms was fired by Nixon, and died prematurely in the fall of 1978 of a heart attack. At his funeral in Washington, the church was crowded with his friends. His wife had chosen his favorite hymns, "The Battle Hymn of the Republic" and "America the Beautiful," and as we sang those familiar words they were lent such new meaning by the steadfast loyalty of his life and work that there were few dry eyes among us. There was no flamboyance in him, and he shunned publicity, so that few of the American people realized when he died what a true guardian of their interests they had lost.

After Nixon's election as President in 1968, Richard Helms was reconfirmed as CIA director, and he asked Tom K. and me to continue serving in our respective jobs. In late January 1969, the new President requested a briefing on the Agency's overseas operations, and Helms took both of us with him to the White House. A brief entry in my journal after that occasion indicates how hopeful we were that Nixon would rise to the challenge of the presidency, and how anxious we were to see him succeed in leading the country through what we knew were going to be difficult times abroad.

1 February '69—The day before yesterday Dick Helms, Tom Karamessines and I met with Nixon, his new Secretary of State, Rogers, and Henry Kissinger, his aide for National Security Affairs, in the cabinet room of the White House. Nixon was very self-assured, quick to ask the relevant questions and put us at our ease in talking to him. The taut and withdrawn young man

whom I first met at the Junior Chamber of Commerce awards dinner in Chattanooga, Tenn., more than twenty years ago was replaced by a man who struck me as confidently in possession of the enormous power of that office. We shall see what successive crises do to him, but I suspect he will be a far better President than I or my liberal friends ever expected. We shall see.

At the end of our session in which we described some of our more daring and successful operations, I remember that Nixon called out to us jokingly as we left the room, "Don't get caught." Those words were to echo with sad irony in my memory in later times when the complex sequence of events known as Watergate eventually led to Nixon's downfall. Although the CIA was later to be completely exonerated of any institutional involvement in the Watergate break-in and subsequent cover-up, the suspicions and reactions generated by those events played a crucial role in doing lasting damage to the Agency from which it has not yet recovered. There is no need to rehearse the well-known tale of Watergate in any detail, but by isolating a few key episodes it is possible to demonstrate a chain of cause and effect that led like a string of exploding Chinese firecrackers to the public revelations and allegations that did such harm to the effectiveness and reputation of American intelligence. Also in the process of untangling this skein, some light is shed on the motivations and behavior of the principal actors in this strange drama. In all fairness, it is necessary to keep continually in mind the fact that many of the players had no certain knowledge of the full extent of White House involvement until the final act.

The Break-In

On the evening of Saturday, June 17, 1972, CIA Director Richard Helms received a phone call at his home from his chief of security, Howard Osborn, a call whose consequences were to have a drastic effect on his career and on the Agency he headed, although at the time he had no way of foreseeing what was in store. Osborn reported that the men involved in the Watergate burglary of the Democratic National Headquarters the night before had been identified. Two of them, Howard Hunt and James McCord, proved to be ex-CIA staff employees, and the Cuban Americans had had past associations with the Agency related to the Bay of Pigs. As Helms stated in his interview with David Frost in May 1978, and as he has since reiterated to me, his first reaction was to call Patrick Gray, the acting director of the FBI. With the help of the White House operator, Helms reached Gray in Los Angeles and advised him that he had had no prior knowledge of what the Agency's ex-employees were up to. He remembers telling Gray, "You'd better watch out because these fellows may have some connection with Ehrlichman."[1] Helms had no knowledge of White House involvement in the break-in until later, but he did remember that the year before, Ehrlichman had called General Robert Cushman, then Helms's deputy, to announce that the White House was hiring Howard Hunt in a consultant capacity to deal with unidentified matters. Helms had been surprised that Ehrlichman did not ask for any fitness report or judgment by the Agency on Hunt's past performance or qualifications. Helms was later subjected to some criticism for having delayed in informing investigating authorities of White House involvement, but it is evident from this phone call to Gray that he did in fact alert the FBI to a possible Ehrlichman connection on the day of the break-in.

On the Monday after the burglary, in Tom K.'s absence I attended the regular 9 A.M. staff meeting that Helms held with his principal deputies. My recollection of this meeting is much the same as the account given by William Colby in his memoirs.[2] Helms polled each one of us as to whether we had any knowledge of what these ex-Agency employees were doing. There was a unanimous expression of total ignorance and surprise, but there was also general concern that the public and press would suspect some Agency involvement because of Hunt's and McCord's past connection to the Agency. Helms announced that his general strategy would be to stay as far away as possible from this purely domestic crime, which lay outside the Agency's charter, and to protect the Agency against any attempt to involve it in such a sensitive internal political issue. In the harrowing days to come, he did succeed in doing just that to the extent of his considerable ability.

One problem was raised at this morning meeting that was later to add to the general suspicion that the Agency must have had some prior awareness of Watergate. A file check showed that Eugenio Martinez, one of the five who broke into the Watergate, had been employed in a contract capacity with the Agency in the mid 1960s

in Cuban operations and was still employed on a part-time basis by
the CIA station in Miami on a $100-a-month retainer as an informant
on Cuban exile activities. There was no evidence that he had reported to his case officer anything whatever about the nature of his
work with Hunt on the Watergate caper, and the decision was taken
to terminate his services immediately.

The suspicions generated by Martinez' current part-time employment with the Agency at the time of Watergate were later given a
new lease on life by Nixon's aide H. R. Haldeman, in his book *The
Ends of Power.* Haldeman concludes from the fact that Martinez was
on the Agency payroll that he "almost certainly was reporting to his
CIA case officer about the proposed break-in *even before it happened.*"[3] Using this false assumption, Haldeman goes on to spin out
an elaborate theory that the CIA followed the Watergate break-in
from its planning stage through to its execution and then deliberately
sabotaged it in order to prevent Nixon from reorganizing the Agency
and limiting its power. As Haldeman puts it, "I believe that the CIA
monitored the Watergate burglars throughout. And that the overwhelming evidence leads to the conclusion that the break-in was
deliberately sabotaged."[4]

This elaborate conspiracy theory of Haldeman's has not been given
much credence in the press in the light of the total record, but I
would like to put one final nail in its coffin. It happens that, because
of a particular incident, I was in a position to know with absolute
certainty that Martinez did not tell his CIA case officer in advance
about the Watergate planning. In March 1972, before the break-in,
we received in headquarters a cable from the CIA station chief in
Miami stating that Martinez had reported that he was in contact with
Howard Hunt on the White House staff on some unidentified business in the Miami area. The cable reported that Martinez seemed
uneasy about what he was doing, and the station chief suggested that
the Agency should look into what the nature of Hunt's White House
employment might be. The matter came to my desk for decision, and
I authorized a cabled reply making clear that Hunt had retired from
the Agency and that he was working for the White House on domestic affairs in which the Agency had no business being involved. It
seemed clear to me that it was outside the Agency's charter and a
violation of our legal authority to use one of our part-time paid
informants to report secretly to us on what the White House might

be doing in the field of domestic politics. I remember thinking at the time that Hunt was probably engaged in rounding up Cuban American votes for Nixon in the Miami area. We found out what he was up to only when Martinez was arrested in the Watergate that famous night.

In February of 1974 I was called back to Washington from my post as station chief in London to testify in executive session before the Senate subcommittee that had been established under the chairmanship of Senator Howard Baker (R., Tenn.) to investigate the extent of CIA involvement in Watergate. Senator Baker had voiced his suspicions to the press that the Agency was far more deeply implicated than had yet been revealed and he had described the progress of his investigation in such terms as "there are animals crashing around in the forest. I can hear them but I can't see them."[5] In testifying before Senator Baker and his staff on February 23, I realized that I was suspected of being one of those animals. In answer to insistent questioning, I tried to explain that I had not had any prior knowledge of Watergate and that the cable to Miami I had authorized was not an attempt on my part to protect the Watergate planning from compromise. I maintained that the Agency had no legal authority or moral right to report through its confidential informants on domestic political activity and wondered what we would have done with Martinez' information if we had been foolish enough to solicit it. To have provided the information to the White House would have involved the Agency in an admission that we were secretly spying on the President, and to have filed it away in a vault would have exposed the Agency subsequently to the charge of complicity in the whole Watergate affair.[6]

After three hours of close questioning, Senator Baker's staff seemed satisfied that I was telling the truth and the investigation turned to other matters. The incident is worth relating only because it demonstrates conclusively that Haldeman is absolutely wrong in his assumption that Martinez must have told the Agency in advance of the plans for Watergate. He might have, but he wasn't asked and he didn't.

It is to Senator Baker's considerable credit that after exhaustively exploring every shred of evidence and questioning every conceivable witness he finally announced that he had been mistaken in his original suspicions that the Agency was somehow implicated. After serving on the Ervin committee, Senator Baker also was a member of the Church committee and continued his inquiry in that capacity. In a letter appended to the Final Report of the Church committee, Senator Baker takes up the question of CIA complicity in his concluding paragraph and sums up his judgment in the last sentence: "An impartial evaluation of that record compels the conclusion that the CIA, as an institution, was not involved in the Watergate break-in."[7] Unless and until new evidence is produced to the contrary, that judgment by the most persistent and skeptical of the senatorial investigators should stand as the final answer to those who still have doubts about the Agency's role.

The Cover-up

The severest test of Helms's determination not to allow the Agency to become involved in Watergate began on June 23, 1972, in the meeting with Haldeman and Ehrlichman, and lasted for the next few days. I was not privy to the discussions that took place during this time between the White House, the CIA, and the FBI and therefore have nothing to add to the now voluminous public record based on the Nixon tapes, the congressional investigations, the public trials, and personal memoirs. Based on that record, it seems to me quite clear that Helms and his new deputy, Lieutenant General Vernon A. Walters, successfully resisted a deliberate attempt by Nixon and his principal staff assistants, Haldeman, Ehrlichman and Dean, to cover up their own involvement by grossly trying to misuse the CIA's powers and funding authority. Acting under clear instructions from Helms, Walters turned down Dean's persistent effort to get the Agency to pay with its covert funds for the salaries and bail of the jailed Watergate burglars.[8] After a brief hesitation, the Agency also refused to obstruct the FBI's investigation of the "laundered" Nixon campaign funds that had passed through a Mexican bank and, in defiance of the White House demands, informed the FBI on July 6, 1972, that there was no CIA operational interest that could be damaged by a full FBI investigation of the Mexican funding arrangements.

It is evident in retrospect that if Helms had not had the moral courage and strength of character to stand up against these importunate and illegal demands of the Nixon White House, the Agency would have been inextricably involved in Nixon's subsequent downfall and the whole structure of American intelligence done irreparable harm. Not only were the careers and reputations of individuals at stake in this tragic business, but also the existence of institutions vital to the survival of the country.

The fact that this direct confrontation with the White House had taken place was held very closely by Helms to the limited number of his associates in the Agency who had to deal with the problem. Certainly I was given no clue that this clash had occurred, and thereafter Helms made every effort to continue providing the White House with the best available intelligence on a business-as-usual basis. At that time, neither he nor anyone else outside the closed circle of Nixon's immediate entourage had any clear knowledge of the full extent of White House involvement. Events in the great world did not wait for the riddle of Watergate to be resolved, and Nixon's reelection campaign against Senator George McGovern was driving toward a triumphal conclusion.

Helms was later to be criticized for not having come forward earlier with the full story of the White House pressures that were brought to bear on him. In the perspective of the time, he felt that he had done what had to be done in resisting those pressures and that his continuing obligation was then to give the President all the foreign intelligence support he requested and to repair as soon as possible the damage done by the confrontation to the Agency's relations with a man who was obviously going to be reelected. To have volunteered to the press or to the Justice Department attorneys prosecuting the five Watergate burglars the story of his clash with the White House would have involved the Agency directly in the presidential campaign, and convinced Nixon and his supporters that the CIA was attempting to secure McGovern's election. The delay in surfacing McCord's anonymous letters to the Agency regarding White House involvement was similarly motivated.

In his interview with David Frost in 1978, Helms was subsequently to explain his dilemma in the following dialogue:

> HELMS: And I recognize that I have been accused of not having suddenly turned out my pockets and made everything that is possible available to the prosecutors, but the fact remains

their office and the FBI and so forth were leaking about this matter in a way that made it look very dangerous to me.

But, if I said talk to this man, here is publicly a fellow who did such and such, the next thing you know we would never be able to unsnarl the Agency from the Watergate thing, and I wanted to preserve the Agency.

If I was wrong, I was wrong. But, you know, we are a nation of Monday morning quarterbacks, and Monday morning quarterbacks always have a better way to play the game.

I did the best I knew how. I don't have any regrets about it, and if I should have regrets in the eyes of the liberals I am sorry.

FROST: Now I think that makes it very clear that your priority was that you felt the whole future of the Agency might be at stake here, in fact.

HELMS: I did indeed.[9]

Given the extraordinary circumstances that Helms confronted, the reader will have to judge whether he deserves praise or blame for the way he chose to play his role. My own belief is that he showed courage and skill in fending off the White House demands and that, if he had been less discreet about Nixon's attempts to misuse the Agency, he would have been accused of trying to rig the 1972 election. However, that was not the way the White House saw it. Among the Nixon entourage, there was no ambiguity of attitude or hesitation in reaching a judgment as to what should be done with a man who had refused to go along with the cover-up and had displayed such independence of character that he could no longer be trusted as a loyal member of the team. The full extent of Haldeman's venomous resentment against Helms and the Agency permeates the pages of his book, and even in the wisdom of hindsight there is hardly a hint of regret for his role in attempting crudely to misuse the institutional authority of the Agency. Instead, he goes to absurd lengths in trying to demonstrate that the Agency knew in advance about the break-in and deliberately sabotaged it.

The Schlesinger Memorandum—9 May '73

By refusing to participate in the Watergate cover-up, Helms preserved the institutional integrity of the CIA, but he also ensured the end of his career as director. Nixon waited until after his overwhelming election victory to deliver the coup de grace. Then, on November 20, he summoned Helms to Camp David. There were some serious budgetary issues to be resolved and, thinking these would be the subject of the meeting, Helms prepared himself to discuss these fiscal problems. Although, after the election, Nixon had asked his top officials to submit their resignations in order to start his new term with a clean slate, Helms had not offered his own resignation in the belief that the CIA directorship, in accordance with past tradition and precedent, should be kept separate from the election results and not become a political plum.[10] He was therefore surprised when Nixon demanded his resignation at Camp David but subsequently accepted Nixon's offer of an ambassadorship, and chose Iran as a country where his past association with the Agency would not be likely to cause problems.

A few days later, James Schlesinger, then head of the Atomic Energy Commission, was called to Camp David and was offered the job of CIA director by Nixon. In an interview with me in 1978, Schlesinger stated that he tried to persuade Nixon not to fire Helms so soon after the election and argued that Helms's sixtieth birthday the following spring would be a more appropriate time and would raise fewer questions in view of the fact that Agency policy required automatic retirement at age sixty. Schlesinger left Camp David thinking that he had persuaded Nixon to postpone Helms's departure, but he proved to be wrong.

In firing Helms so abruptly, Nixon was taking a chance that he might choose to retire from public life and use his newfound freedom to reveal the White House role in attempting to obstruct the FBI investigation of the Watergate affair and to bribe the participants. However, Nixon probably figured that Helms was too much the loyal public servant to damage the American presidency and its relation to the intelligence community by revealing this information. After Helms's return from Camp David, I began to hear rumors from journalist friends that his departure was imminent. I dismissed these stories as typically ill-founded Washington gossip but nevertheless reported them to Helms. He turned my questions aside but, as the rumors began to be reported in the press, he took me to lunch on December 12 and explained that in fact he had been fired and that he was going to Iran. Since I still had no inkling of the White House role in Watergate or the attempt to involve the Agency, I expressed my astonishment and asked for an explanation. Helms remained the good soldier and only remarked that his relations with the White House staff had deteriorated and that he was lucky to have lasted as long as he had. On December 21, 1972, Nixon officially announced that he was nominating Schlesinger to be CIA director and appointing Helms ambassador to Iran.[11]

The Schlesinger appointment had a traumatic effect on the Agency. Since 99.9 percent of the Agency personnel had no knowledge of the Watergate explanation of Helms's firing, and since Helms himself was not talking, speculation was rife, and the most farfetched theories were invented to explain the sudden departure of so highly respected a leader. To most of us, Schlesinger himself was an unknown quantity, although both in the Atomic Energy Commission and in his previous service under Nixon in the Office of Management and Budget he had earned himself a reputation as a hard-driving and intellectually brilliant manager. Although mystified by the turn of events, the vast majority of us were prepared to give him the benefit of the doubt and to offer him full cooperation in the belief that as a director who was so obviously the President's personal choice, he would be able to give new weight to the Agency's intelligence findings in the highest policy councils.

In the period between Schlesinger's nomination as director and his confirmation by the Senate in early February of 1973, Helms arranged for William Colby, who was then the Agency's executive director, to organize briefings for Schlesinger in his AEC offices. From these sessions came many of the ideas that Schlesinger tried to put into effect in his brief tenure as director, as Colby describes in his memoirs.[12] It was during this period that Colby gained Schlesinger's confidence, which later proved critical in Nixon's decision four months later to appoint Colby as CIA director when Schlesinger was appointed secretary of defense. Strangely enough, Schlesinger spent very little time with Helms during the transition period, and his coolness toward Helms may have reflected the antipathy that he felt existed in the White House domestic staff toward the outgoing director.

In fairness to Schlesinger, it should be pointed out that there is no evidence that at this stage he knew any more than the rest of us about the full extent of White House involvement in Watergate. Shortly after his confirmation he was briefed by General Walters, who continued as deputy director of Central Intelligence after Helms's departure, concerning the White House attempt back in June of 1972 to involve the Agency. It was lucky that Walters did so, because on February 9, 1973, John Dean phoned Schlesinger to request his help in extricating from the FBI certain files on Howard Hunt that had previously been sent to the bureau by the Agency. Acting on Walters' advice, Schlesinger refused the request, and one more attempt by the White House to implicate the Agency was turned aside.[13]

My own relations with Schlesinger during his short tenure were closer than they might otherwise have been because Tom Karamessines chose to retire shortly after Helms's departure, and I served as acting deputy director for plans during the weeks that intervened before Schlesinger finally decided to appoint Colby to Karamessines' job. Tom K. suffered from a serious back ailment, but the real reason for his decision to retire was his conviction that Helms had been treated most unfairly, and he had little sympathy for the abrasive manner with which Schlesinger tended to treat subordinates.

In my dealings with Schlesinger, I quickly came to respect his capacity for sustained hard work and to realize that he was widely read and extremely intelligent. I never had any reason to complain in my own case of the personal rudeness that many others had cause to resent. However, I did quickly discover that he carried with him into his new job a firm conviction that the clandestine service which I temporarily headed exercised too dominant a role within the Agency, was out of phase with the intelligence requirements of the modern age, and was heavily overstaffed with aging veterans of past cold wars. Just where he had obtained these views I am not clear to this day, but Colby explains in his memoirs that he shared Schlesinger's convictions on this point and Colby's early briefings obviously must have had an influence.[14] The resentment within the White House domestic staff against Helms and his close friends and associates may have also played some role. Whatever the reason, Schlesinger did not hide his distrust and dissatisfaction with the clandestine service, and reports reached me on a daily basis of derogatory remarks he had made—I'm sure some exaggerated in the telling and others purely apocryphal. For example, I received two separate accounts of a social occasion at which Schlesinger was reported to have stated, "The clandestine service was Helms's Praetorian Guard. It had too much influence in the Agency and was too powerful within the government. I am going to cut it down to size." Whether true or not, these stories were widely believed, and they did not make my job any easier in trying simultaneously to win the confidence of the new director and to sustain the morale of the people down the line.

One of Schlesinger's early decisions was to order a cut of about 7 percent in the number of Agency employees, and a disproportionate share of that cut fell on the clandestine service. I tried to explain that Karamessines and I had established an annual system of personnel review panels under which those identified in the lowest 3 percent in each grade were separated from the service. Through this process, which was generally perceived to be fair and just, we were steadily paring down the size of the clandestine service while holding to a minimum the number of disaffected ex-employees who might feel they had been dealt with arbitrarily. I argued that we should be allowed to continue this gradual selecting-out procedure in order to bring our size down to Schlesinger's target figure, rather than having to fire a large number suddenly and arbitrarily. The high morale of an intelligence service was, I argued, its most precious commodity and its most lasting and sure protection against penetration by the KGB. We also had to worry about what those who were fired might do with the knowledge of secret operations that they carried in their memories if they became sufficiently disaffected. These arguments did not carry much weight, and the abrupt terminations of that era began a slow deterioration of morale that has had effects that are real, if difficult to measure. Some of those who were peremptorily fired took their grievances to the press, and others later wrote books that revealed more than they should about classified intelligence sources and methods. The fabric of mutual trust that had held the clandestine service together as a disciplined organization over many years began slowly to unravel.

Then in early May of 1973, Watergate with its associated imbecilities cast its shadow again across our professional lives. In testimony before a federal grand jury, Howard Hunt revealed for the first time his role in breaking into the office of Daniel Ellsberg's psychiatrist in Los Angeles in 1971 in an effort to get derogatory information on Ellsberg, who had leaked the Pentagon Papers. Hired as a White House consultant, Hunt testified that he had used a camera and disguises supplied by the CIA in accomplishing the break-in. Almost simultaneously Schlesinger discovered that on White House orders the Agency in 1971 had reluctantly prepared a psychiatric profile on Ellsberg and submitted it to the White House staff. Congressional investigations were later to prove that the Agency assistance to Hunt had been provided as the result of a phone call on July 8, 1971, from Ehrlichman to General Robert Cushman, who was then deputy director of Central Intelligence. When Hunt subsequently escalated his demands by requesting false credit cards, the Agency technicians who were dealing with Hunt expressed alarm, and on August 27 General Cushman called Ehrlichman to inform him that the Agency was terminating its cooperation with Hunt. Most important, the subsequent congressional investigations concluded that the Agency had had no knowledge of the purpose for which Hunt was using the materials given him other than Hunt's own explanation that they were needed for a sensitive one-time interview. Subsequently, after an exhaustive inquiry, the Special Subcommittee on Intelligence of the House Armed Services Committee summed up its findings by stating that "we are convinced that the CIA did not know of the improper purposes for which the technical materials provided were to be used and resisted later efforts to involve the Agency."[15] Once again the Nixon White House had grossly misused the Agency by involving it in a domestic burglary of which it knew nothing.

As Hunt's testimony flowed in over the news tickers, I was summoned to the director's office to face an understandably furious and suspicious Schlesinger. Like the press and public, he found it very hard to believe that the Agency had supplied technical assistance to Hunt without knowing the purpose. Protesting my genuine ignorance, I undertook to review Hunt's file, and we found there photographs of a building with the nameplate of a Dr. Lewis Fielding, who we now learned from Hunt's testimony had been Ellsberg's psychiatrist. The photographs had been developed for Hunt during the period of our cooperation with him back in 1971, but they had meant nothing to us at the time, and copies had been sent to the FBI after Hunt's involvement in the Watergate break-in. Now that we had from Hunt's testimony the missing link of the break-in of Fielding's office, the pieces of the puzzle fell quickly into place, and I reported our findings to an incredulous Schlesinger, who terminated my report with a question that was to haunt the Agency for years to come: "What else have you people been hiding from me?"

Quite rightly, Schlesinger was determined to track down and identify every possible piece of evidence that might bear on the Watergate affair. Only by being completely forthcoming with the congressional committees on Watergate could the Agency hope to put to rest the suspicions that it was deeply implicated, and any new discovery of unrevealed involvement would only confirm the general belief that we must somehow have been party to the cover-up. For this reason, Schlesinger issued a directive to all CIA employees on May 9, 1973, in which he stressed his determination to "do everything in my power to confine CIA activities to those which fall within a strict interpretation of its legislative charter."

To accomplish this objective, Schlesinger included in his memorandum instructions that read as follows:

> I have ordered all senior operating officials of this Agency to report to me immediately on any activities now going on, or that have gone on in the past, which might be construed to be outside the legislative charter of this Agency.
>
> I hereby direct every person presently employed by CIA to report to me on any such activities of which he has knowledge. I invite all ex-employees to do the same. Anyone who has such information should call my secretary and say that he wishes to talk to me about "activities outside the CIA's charter."[16]

This remarkable document, the full text of which is given in the Appendix, is certainly unique in the annals of intelligence since nation-states first began conducting espionage operations against each other. It required a retrospective confession of any perceived guilt by all current and past Agency employees going back to the inception of the CIA in 1947. It was not limited to activities directly or indirectly connected with the Watergate affair. Since the legislative charter of the Agency laid down in the language of the National Security Act of 1947 had been deliberately made general and ambiguous, the directive invited the penitential employee to come forward with his own definition of what might be construed as outside that vague charter. We were required to sit in judgment on all past activities as to which one of them might conceivably have been illegal, improper, or unjustified under the broad language of the 1947 Act. It was a hunting license for the resentful subordinate to dig back into the records of the past in order to come up with evidence that might destroy the career of a superior whom he had long hated. It was an invitation to the self-righteous and the moralistically inclined to resurrect "old unhappy, far-off things, And battles long ago" in an effort to prove in the perspective of the present that they had been right in the dimly remembered past. There are very few human institutions in this world, from the American Civil Liberties Union to the Boy Scouts, that could survive in good working order so broad an injunction to confess all past improprieties or mistakes in judgment, least of all an intelligence agency whose job it is to operate outside the law in foreign countries.

In his interview with me in October 1978, Schlesinger admitted that he had made a serious mistake in issuing a directive so sweeping in scope and so open-ended in time, and in retrospect he wished he had not done so. Schlesinger asserted that he had been primarily concerned with identifying any hidden involvement in Watergate and that he should have restricted his order to that subject. However, he explained that Colby had drafted the directive for his signature and that he had signed it as drafted without giving sufficient thought to its far-reaching implications. In fairness to both Schlesinger and Colby, it should be added that neither of them foresaw that the results of this confessional enterprise would eventually leak to the press; they believed instead that the findings could be used within the Agency to reform past practices and improve existing regulations. They were also motivated by an understandable desire to be fully informed on anything that might rise from the past in the course of the congressional investigations and to be in a position to assure the Congress that remedial action had already been taken.

In the event, the compilation of all possible past misdeeds that flowed from Schlesinger's directive was accomplished with less internal damage than might have been the case in a less disciplined organization. Colby was designated by Schlesinger to oversee the preparation of a report based on all available records and the testimony of those who came forward to confess. Employing the staff of the CIA inspector general, Colby pursued the project with penitential zeal and by May 21, 1973, had collected 693 pages describing all past instances in which the Agency's legislative charter might conceivably have been violated.[17] Individual officers racked their memories for any activity they could recall that might be questionable, and dutifully submitted their reports. The process was certainly thorough, but the results were necessarily skewed by a number of factors. With the passage of time, memories had dulled, crucial witnesses had died or could not be found, and the written record was not always complete. The chain of approval up the line to the policymakers was sometimes deliberately obscure in order to protect the President. Most significant, activity undertaken at the height of the cold war and in a period of direct confrontation with the Soviets had a different aspect in the milder climate of détente. A retrospective severity of judgment tended to color the findings.

For example, Colby's early determination that the opening by the Agency of mail between American citizens and correspondents in the Soviet Union in the period between 1953 and 1973 was clearly illegal was later called into question by the Department of Justice. In his book, Colby makes the point that "opening first-class mail was a direct violation of a criminal statute; I looked it up in the law library to make sure."[18] On the basis of this superficial finding, the mail opening program was cited by Colby as a particularly egregious example of an illegal violation of the Agency's legislative charter. When the story of the Agency's past misdeeds finally broke in the press in December 1974, this mail opening operation figured as a prime example of how the Agency had illegally violated the rights of American citizens, and with scare headlines across the country the American people were made to feel that the CIA had functioned as a domestic Gestapo in operating beyond the law.

However, a very different conclusion was reached by the Department of Justice in 1977 after its lawyers had reviewed all the evidence and the applicable laws in an effort to determine whether to prosecute the CIA officials who had been responsible for the mail opening. Colby's research turned out to have been seriously deficient and his legal findings erroneous. The Justice Department set forth the reasons for its refusal to prosecute in an unusual fifty-seven page document released to the press on January 14, 1977, and entitled "Report of the Department of Justice concerning Its Investigation and Prosecutorial Decisions with Respect to Central Intelligence Agency Mail Opening Activities in the United States."[19] Two paragraphs from this report are worth quoting:

Although the Department is of the firm view that activities similar in scope and authorization to those conducted by the CIA between 1953 and 1973 would be unlawful if undertaken today, the Department has concluded that a prosecution of the potential defendants for these activities would be unlikely to succeed because of the unavailability of important evidence and because of the state of the law that prevailed during the course of the mail openings program.

It would be mistaken to suppose that it was always clearly perceived that the particular mail opening programs of the CIA were obviously illegal. The Department believes that this opinion is a serious misperception of our Nation's recent history of the way the law has evolved and the factors to which it responded . . . a substitution of what we now believe is and must be the case for what was.[20]

The Justice report goes on to state: "There is, however, evidence suggesting that President Eisenhower had knowledge of and had approved the CIA's East Coast [mail opening] operation."[21] And the report cites circumstantial evidence and oral testimony that subsequent Presidents were also informed, although the written record had been deliberately kept clear of specific presidential involvement. None of this is meant to suggest that Schlesinger and Colby were wrong in terminating the mail opening project in the spring of 1973. Times were changing, and from what little I myself knew about this highly compartmented project, it had proved only marginally useful in identifying Soviet agents operating in this country. Nor can it be denied that, in putting together its collective confession of past sins, which later became known as the family jewels, the Agency did identify some serious and inexcusable cases of past misuse of authority. However, as the mail opening case dramatically demonstrates, the hasty rush to judgment caused the Agency to draw up against itself an indictment more severe than the laws and differing circumstances of a previous time could justify. This carelessness in jumping to false conclusions was compounded by subsequent publicity in the press, and the Agency had only itself to blame when it later stood accused of actions that it had itself mistakenly branded as illegal. Most ironically, this confessional exercise uncovered no new and previously unrevealed involvement in Watergate, which had been Schlesinger's primary purpose in initially issuing his directive. Once again the folly of Watergate had widening consequences and reached out to affect in strange ways men and institutions that were trying to avoid its entangling embrace.

One salutary effect of this confessional enterprise was that it did serve to identify some areas of activity where the Agency's own internal regulations had been ambiguous. When Colby was appointed CIA director to succeed Schlesinger in July 1973, he issued a new set of internal regulations that ruled out any involvement in assassination planning or drug testing on unwitting subjects, and set stricter and clearer limits on the amount and type of information that the Agency was authorized to collect on U.S. citizens abroad suspected of cooperating with the Communists. He also reported to the chairmen of the congressional oversight committees on what the collection of "family jewels" had revealed about past activity and won their agreement to maintain secrecy with the assurance that he would see to it that the new regulations were strictly enforced.[22] In a real sense, the highly publicized Church committee investigation of the Agency two years later was redundant. Senator Church and his colleagues did not succeed in unearthing anything substantial that the Agency had not already identified as of doubtful legality, moved to correct by revision of internal regulations, and reported to the chairmen of its oversight committees.

It was naive ever to have hoped to avoid eventual publicity. So many past and present Agency employees had participated in contributing to the family jewels that the knowledge was widespread that such a collection existed. The typing, editing, and copying of the final documents widened the circle of knowledgeability. The congressional chairmen were discreet, but on a subject so explosive one unguarded remark was enough to start a chain of speculation. A time bomb had been set ticking beneath the foundations of the Agency by Schlesinger's directive, and it was only a question of when it would eventually explode in a blaze of publicity.

Chapter 9

London Assignment: Coping with Watergate and Chile

THE CHANGES AT THE TOP in the Agency in the spring of 1973 had their inevitable effect on my own career. With Helms's firing and Tom Karamessines' resignation, I realized that my temporary status as acting deputy director for plans would not last for long. Both Schlesinger and Colby were anxious to bring into the leadership of the clandestine service men of their own choice to replace those who had been appointed by Helms. I had no basis on which to oppose that decision. I thought briefly of retirement but at age fifty-two felt that I had some useful years remaining to spend in active service. The CIA station chief in London was due for replacement in June, and I proposed myself for this position. I had worked closely with British officials over the years and had come to have a high regard for their competence and to value the mutual advantages that both countries gained from the close cooperation between our respective intelligence services. In addition, the fact of our cooperation was well-known, so that my widely publicized connection with the Agency was not the kind of handicap that it would have been in an environment requiring deep cover and complete anonymity. Schlesinger agreed to the assignment and, after clearance with the British government and with the U.S. ambassador in London, Colby confirmed the arrangement when he succeeded Schlesinger as CIA director.

By July, my wife and I found ourselves ensconced in a comfortable London house not far from the U.S. Embassy. After a brief flurry of publicity concerning my arrival in the London papers, the British public and the press accepted my presence as a functioning part of the "special relationship" that existed between our two countries. The overwhelming reaction was one of approval for the continuing cooperation of our respective intelligence services, and my designation as a political officer on the staff of the U.S. Embassy initially raised few questions. I found many old friends and acquaintances in key positions in the Foreign Office, the Defense Ministry, and the intelligence community, and we shared a common objective in exchanging information on the growing military power of the Soviet Union and the worldwide operations of the ubiquitous KGB.

By the time I arrived in London, British intelligence had fully recovered from the deep damage done by the penetration of its secrets by two KGB agents, Kim Philby and George Blake, who had risen to high positions within its ranks in years past. During my stay, I never had reason to question the integrity of British intelligence officers or the security with which they guarded classified information. Our cooperation was governed by strict ground rules that forbade the recruitment of each other's nationals as agents, and ruled out any kind of covert intervention in the democratic political processes of our respective countries. During the entire three years of my tour in London, I never encountered in the course of my official duties a single incident in which either party had any reason to complain of bad faith in carrying out our agreements. There were diplomatic differences and conflicts at the policy level, but these rarely affected the valuable cooperative relationship in the field of intelligence. Even in the most difficult days of my tour, when voices were raised in Parliament calling for my ouster, I was always treated by my British official colleagues with such unfailing courtesy and supportive encouragement that it was easy to endure with equanimity the public attacks of what was in fact a small and unrepresentative minority of British opinion.

Initially my wife, Starke, was none too happy to find herself uprooted from her life in Washington and deposited abruptly in a foreign city far from her two children and her friends. In order to come with me, she had had to resign from her promising career in the National Endowment for the Arts and, although I had been sent abroad under government orders, she had no assurance that she would be able to regain her previous job when we returned to the States. She did, however, gradually come to enjoy the city of London in all its ancient charm and infinite variety and to learn far more about its art, architecture, and history than I was able to do. In time, she obtained a job as a consultant with the public affairs section of the embassy to assist in the planning and observance of the American Bicentennial, which occurred while we were there. Early on, the British decided to join wholeheartedly in the celebration of two hundred years of American independence rather than to mourn the long-ago loss of colonial rule. As a result, the British government and private agencies became involved in a wide variety of special exhibitions and commemorative events that required much coordination between the U.S. Embassy, private and official organizations in the States, and their British counterparts. My wife ended up having her hands full with work that was interesting and that introduced her to talented people in many fields whom she otherwise would not have had a chance to meet.

As time passed, I also learned how indispensable she was as an official hostess and how impossible it would have been to do my job without her. London was not only a center of diplomatic activity in its own right but a stopping-off point for official American delegations of every description traveling to the European continent, to the Middle East, and to Africa. As a result, we had a continuous flow of official visitors, many of whom had to be entertained at social occasions with their British counterparts and others who would stay overnight with us while waiting for their plane connections. My wife handled this stream of official guests with tactful good humor and unobtrusive efficiency and rarely complained of the invasions of our privacy that so many transient dignitaries sometimes created. For myself, these visits were a chance to catch up on what was going on behind the scenes in Washington.

During the Watergate trials and investigations, serving as an American official in London was like living on the distant slopes of an active volcano. One could never anticipate what new and explosive revelation the morning papers would announce. The British public followed the unfolding of the Watergate drama with rapt attention, and coverage in the media was detailed and extensive. In London, it was possible for an American to understand in a way not possible in Washington that the trauma of Watergate was not a private drama played out before an exclusively American audience but an international event having worldwide repercussions. Dependent on the United States for protection against the growing military power of the Soviets and relying on a consistent and coherent American foreign policy, the British people watched, fascinated and appalled, as the damage that Nixon had done to the American presidency unfolded on their television screens. All the suspicions and allegations regarding CIA involvement were paraded before their eyes, and the Agency became a topic of interest and concern that it had never been before.

None of this had any direct effect on my own role until I sat down to breakfast on the morning of January 18, 1974, and opened the most reliable and respected of London newspapers, *The Times.* I was brought bolt upright by a story by a *Times* correspondent on the front page under bold headlines charging that the CIA had just secretly imported into Britain "between 30 and 40 extra intelligence men."[1] *The Times* went on to allege that the primary purpose of these additional American agents was to infiltrate and conduct surveillance against the British trade union movement in an effort to identify "subversive elements" that might be behind the wave of strikes then troubling the United Kingdom. My coffee grew cold as I read on with mounting dismay and astonishment. The story was given dramatic additional credibility by the inclusion of extensive quotes from an ex-Agency official then living in London, Mr. Miles Copeland. His statements seemed to confirm the accuracy of the story, and he went on to explain why this invasion of an army of American spies had proved necessary. He was quoted as saying, "In addition to superior technical competence with all forms of surveillance equipment, it is widely recognized that our agents have a freedom to operate in this country which your own intelligence services do not possess. . . . You are restricted and squeamish on your own territory from doing the type of things that really have to be done to track down terrorists and subversives."[2]

It was hard for me to imagine a more damaging piece of publicity. At a time of high political tension and a three-day workweek caused by the coal miners' slowdown, the Agency stood accused by a responsible newspaper of secret intervention within the labor unions which were the backbone of the opposition Labour Party's strength. To add insult to injury, there was the added implication that the British security services were incompetent to handle their own subversive problem and that American strong-arm methods and surveillance techniques were needed to save the day. There was only one consolation. The story was totally false. As I drove to the embassy, I realized that our problem was how to convince the British government and public of that fact as rapidly as possible.

My first move was to contact the British intelligence community to assure them there was no truth to the story and to offer again to review with them the roster of our personnel so that they would have current proof that no increase had in fact occurred. Next I met with the American Minister and his staff, and we quickly concluded that the usual practice of making a reply of "no comment" to allegations regarding intelligence matters would clearly not be adequate in this case. We agreed on the brief text of a flat public denial and, with Ambassador Annenberg's approval, cabled it to Washington for urgent clearance. It was lucky that we did so, because shortly thereafter I received a call from a high-ranking Foreign Office official who conveyed the request of Prime Minister Edward Heath that the U.S. Embassy issue a public denial, if, as he had been informed, there was no substance to the story. I was able to assure the British that we were waiting for Washington approval of just such a course of action. Washington concurrence was quick in coming, and the embassy denial caught up with the story before it had gathered momentum. Although most of the London press then dropped the story, this was unfortunately not the end of the matter. Under persistent questioning from journalists, Miles Copeland finally clarified his role in the affair with a letter to the *International Herald Tribune*.[3] He explained that the *Times* reporter had come to him with what appeared to be hard facts from official sources concerning the influx of American agents and that he had simply speculated about what their purpose might be without having any facts of his own. He concluded that he was now convinced that "the Embassy's denial is the truth." However, *The Times* was not so willing to back down. It ran an equivocal editorial suggesting that the embassy denial could not be taken at face value and stating that its readers would have to make up their own minds "according to the inherent probabilities of the contradictory accounts and the credit and motives of those giving them."[4] In addition, *The Times* ran a series of letters on its editorial page from understandably irate British citizens protesting bitterly against clandestine American intervention in their domestic political affairs, all based on the assumption that *The Times*'s story was accurate. In Parliament, a few Labour MPs clamored for a full-scale public inquiry into the scandal and demanded that any CIA employees in Britain be deported. Prime Minister Heath brought the debate to an end by citing the U.S. Embassy's denial and by assuring Parliament that there was absolutely no truth in the allegations.[5]

However, a good deal of damage had been done. By refusing to admit its error, *The Times* left lingering doubts in the minds of its influential readership about the sinister potential of CIA activity in Britain. Not to be outdone, the *Guardian* put its investigative reporters on my trail and succeeded in publicly identifying my address and phone number, which by common consent had never previously been revealed.[6] The result was a series of harassing phone calls and the sobering realization on my part that terrorists of whatever type or description now knew where to find me. My driver and I began a practice that we followed throughout my stay in London of continuously changing the routes we used to reach the embassy. In leaving my house, I would dart out the kitchen door and leap into the slowly moving car in order to reduce my exposure to terrorist attack. The car itself was heavily armored and fitted with new bulletproof glass.

More serious, this incident served to establish a link in the public mind between the alleged connection of the CIA to the Watergate plumbers and the suspicion that the Agency might be secretly attempting to intervene in domestic British politics. Representative of this rising concern on the left of the British political spectrum was a poem that appeared in the *New Statesman* shortly after *The Times* story broke. Its first verse read as follows:

O Copeland! my Copeland!
What things must now be done?
What dirty tricks must we employ
Before the prize is won?
O show us, please, your expertise
In tracking down the virus,
With Washington to spur us on
And plumbers to inspire us!
But O Miles! Miles! Miles!
O the rising tide of red!
Teach us the ways of Watergate,
Or see subversion spread![7]

I was learning from personal experience that the suspicions generated by Nixon's unsuccessful attempt to involve the Agency in Watergate were spreading far beyond the borders of the United States. They were beginning to affect the climate of opinion in foreign countries in ways that were deleterious not only to the narrow parochial interests of the Agency but to the broader American national interest. To add to my problems, simultaneously with the false story in *The Times* a spate of articles appeared in the London press containing interviews conducted in America with an ex-Agency employee, Victor Marchetti, who together with a former State Department officer, John Marks, had written a critical book on the Agency entitled *The CIA and the Cult of Intelligence*. Marchetti was at that time engaged in a legal fight with the Agency in an attempt to prevent the deletion from his book of material that the Agency claimed was classified and not publishable under the terms of his security oath. Some of these articles cast Marchetti as something of a hero in attempting to resist official censorship, and quoted Marchetti's allegations that the British government had been "quite content to allow the CIA to construct a headquarters in central London for no other purpose than the steady subversion of the African Commonwealth countries."[8] No such subversive headquarters in fact existed, but investigative reporters from the London papers spent a good deal of time in a fruitless search for its location.

Coming on top of the *Times* story, these allegations left the suspicion not only that the CIA was engaged in subverting the British labor movement, but that it was also using secret bases in England in order to mount covert operations designed to overthrow the newly independent governments of Britain's former African colonies. It was not surprising that many individuals on the non-Communist left in England became convinced that the CIA presence in London constituted a nefarious subversive threat both to internal democracy and to enlightened foreign policy. These corrosive suspicions were not shared by officials in Whitehall or by the leadership of the political parties who had full access to the facts, but their reassurances were not enough to dissuade many from believing that where there was so much smoke there must be some fire. The small British Communist Party and Trotskyist splinter groups, through their publications, leaped on this unique opportunity to discredit the whole idea of cooperation in the intelligence field between the United States and the United Kingdom. Their obvious purpose was not to protect democratic institutions but to drive a wedge between the two countries and to weaken defense cooperation in a crucial area.

Just as these misleading charges were beginning to be forgotten and the drumfire of unfavorable publicity was starting to subside, a new revelation exploded in the American press in early September of 1974. It did not directly affect British interests or my status in London, but it put the Agency back on the front pages and raised fundamental questions regarding the CIA's role as an instrument of American policy. In early September 1974, *The New York Times* broke a story written by Seymour Hersh revealing that the Agency had been involved in a large-scale program of covert action directed against Salvador Allende, the past president of Chile, who had been deposed and killed in a military coup the year before.[9] Hersh gave as his source a confidential letter to the chairman of the House Foreign Affairs Committee written by a radical Democrat, Representative Michael J. Harrington of Massachusetts.

Hersh explained that Harrington had been given access to the text of a secret briefing provided the House Armed Services Subcommittee on Intelligence by CIA Director William Colby the previous April. According to Hersh, Harrington had been so outraged by what he had learned concerning the CIA's covert activities in Chile that he described them at length in his letter and demanded public hearings, giving as one of his principal reasons "CIA activities related to Watergate." Once again the suspicion of Agency involvement in the

Watergate affair had so poisoned the air that Harrington felt he was justified in writing his letter as a way of forcing the exposure of the Agency's role.

Drawing on the Harrington letter, Hersh claimed that Colby's testimony stated that the purpose of the Agency's covert action in Chile was "to destabilize" the Allende regime, and he described in detail the secret financial support given to Allende's political opponents over a protracted period of time. Although Colby wrote a letter to *The New York Times* denying that he had ever used the word "destabilize," the phrase became part of the mythology surrounding the Agency's role in Chile, and the fine print in Hersh's story that seemed to indicate that the Agency had not been involved in the final coup that overthrew Allende was lost in the general outrage.

As *The New York Times'* story flowed into London, a substantial part of the British press erupted with blazing indignation. *The Times* ran a bitterly critical editorial holding the Agency responsible for Allende's downfall. It became an article of faith in British liberal circles to believe that the CIA had masterminded a murderous coup against Allende, who was widely viewed as a social democrat, and replaced his reformist government with a savage right-wing dictatorship. This Manichaean view of the events in Chile was satisfying to those who hold a conspiratorial theory of history with the CIA cast in the role of devil, but in the world of reality things were much more complicated. Although I had never served in the Western Hemisphere Division of the CIA's clandestine service, my positions as chief of the covert action staff and subsequently as assistant deputy director for plans had given me over the years a considerable exposure to the policies pursued by successive U.S. Presidents toward Chile. I tried to give my British friends as balanced and accurate an account of this past history as I could recall in order to reduce at least at the official level the effect of the damaging publicity. It is possible now to write openly about these matters since the Senate Select Committee under Senator Church's chairmanship released in 1975 a staff report entitled "Covert Action in Chile 1963–1973."[10]

This report was incomplete in important respects, as Senator Goldwater pointed out in his statement of individual views appended to the Final Report of the Select Committee.[11] I would not myself agree with many of the subjective conclusions and judgments reached by the committee staff, but the report was accurate in its chronology of the official decision-making process and in its description of specific covert activities and the amounts of money involved. The explanation in summary form that I put before our British cousins may be of some continuing interest, since there is still so much confusion surrounding the Chilean episode. Perhaps the best way of proceeding is to describe the major elements of the still prevailing mythology regarding these events, and to explain as best I can what actually happened and what the motivations were behind the American policy decisions. In the interest of brevity, oversimplification of extremely complex events is inevitable, and the reader will have to judge whether objective truth has been lost in the process.

In the first place, both British and American opinion were confused by the fact that journalists and reading public alike had only limited knowledge of recent Chilean political history. Party labels that meant one thing in Europe were construed to mean the same thing in Chile, and so it came about that many people to this day believe that the Chilean Socialist Party was a democratic reformist party like the Labour Party in Britain or the Social Democrats in Germany. Similarly, Allende, who had led the Socialist Party in successive Chilean election campaigns, was looked upon as a social democratic reformer, fully committed to the preservation of parliamentary democracy and civil liberties.

In actual fact, Chile's Socialist Party was heavily influenced by Marxist-Leninist ideology from its inception in 1933, when Allende joined it as a young Trotskyist. It was troubled throughout its history by factional infighting and by disputes over electoral tactics, and it condemned the Chilean Communist Party in 1939 when the Communists dutifully followed Moscow's orders to support the Stalin-Hitler pact. But at no point was majority control within its ranks exercised by genuine social democrats who believed in gradual reform within a multiparty system. Rather, it was consistently a Marxist revolutionary party committed to the destruction of the bourgeois order. It had within it an extreme radical faction that was in fact to the left of the Communists and believed in revolutionary violence as the only way to achieve power, in contrast to the careful popular front strategy of the Chilean Communists. The strength of this ultraleft faction within the party was indicated by the election of its leader, Carlos Altamirano, as secretary general after Allende was elected to the Chilean presidency in 1970.

Allende himself never tried to hide his Marxist convictions, although he did try to assure the electorate in his campaign rhetoric that he would preserve democratic pluralism in the transition to socialism. In an unguarded moment, he admitted that these assurances were only a "tactical necessity."[12] Certainly, once he had the extensive powers of the Chilean presidency at his disposal, he used them beyond their outermost limits in his attempt to force through the nationalization of the private sector and to control the media. His performance in office justified the worst fears of those who had suspected as fraudulent his campaign promise to respect constitutional democracy. By extralegal expropriations and requisitions, he tried to transfer to state ownership all private corporations whose capital reserves exceeded $500,000 and to break up land holdings that exceeded eighty hectares.

Allende attempted to silence the opposition press and radio that opposed these measures by the manipulation of government control of bank credit and by fomenting labor strikes that proved unsuccessful. In May of 1973, the Chilean Supreme Court declared many of these actions illegal, and on August 22 the Chilean Chamber of Deputies, by a vote of 81 to 47, passed a resolution cataloging the government's illegal acts and declaring, "It is a fact that the present government, from the beginning, has attempted to seize total power, with the evident purpose of subjecting everyone to the most rigorous economic and political controls, and of achieving by this means the installation of a totalitarian order absolutely opposed to the system of representative democracy that the constitution upholds."[13]

In the field of foreign policy, the direction of Allende's sympathies was evident long before he came to power. He was an active member of many Communist-front organizations and was serving as the vice-president of the World Peace Council when he made his first visit to Russia in 1954. After Castro's revolution succeeded in Cuba, the Chilean Socialist Party sent many of its young activists there for training and indoctrination. Allende led the Chilean delegation to the 1966 Tricontinental Conference in Havana, and he played a key role in the creation of the Cuban-sponsored Latin American Solidarity Organization. During his 1970 presidential campaign, Allende declared, "Cuba in the Caribbean and a Socialist Chile in the Southern Cone will make the revolution in Latin America."[14] Once in office, Allende followed through on this promise by reestablishing

diplomatic relations with Cuba and by welcoming an influx of Cuban
intelligence (DGI) officers, including a senior officer, Luis Fernandez
Ona, who became his son-in-law. Cubans were employed to train and
arm the presidential security guard and to help establish a new intelligence organization outside the regular services. With Allende's support, Chile became a base for Cuban efforts to train revolutionary
cadres for action in neighboring Bolivia and Argentina. Political exiles and activists flooded into Chile, where they were given training,
false documentation, and funding by Cuban experts. In November
1971, Allende allowed a group of Bolivian exiles to announce the
formation of the Anti-Imperialist Revolutionary Front, and the
Bolivian government officially protested these preparations to overthrow it.

One final crucial distinction between the Chilean Socialist Party
and the European social democrats was its continuing electoral alliance with the Chilean Communists. Exploiting the real grievances of
the workers in the Chilean nitrate and coal mines, the Chilean Communist Party was from its inception a genuinely proletarian organization and was accepted by Moscow as a disciplined member of the
Third International in 1928. Internally, the party practiced a strictly
enforced policy of democratic centralism, and those individuals who
disagreed with the prevailing party line were promptly expelled
rather than being allowed to form dissident factions within the party
as was the case with the Chilean Socialists.

In both national and international affairs, the Communist Party
dutifully followed the line laid down for it by the Politburo in Moscow. In 1956, at its tenth party conference, when the party was still
illegal under Chilean law, it accepted Moscow's dictum that a popular front strategy was its best way of achieving power rather than
the road of violent revolution. In 1958, Luis Corvalan was elected
the party's secretary general, and he served in that capacity until
Allende's downfall in 1973. An extremely able organizer, Corvalan
was a dedicated Marxist and owed undeviating allegiance throughout his career to Moscow. Even when the Soviets invaded Czechoslovakia in 1968, Corvalan supported the Brezhnev Doctrine and
rallied the party behind the Soviet aggression. He announced in the
party newspaper, *El Siglo,* that the countries of Eastern Europe
"as examples to the Communist movement, have a duty to intervene in or assist any Socialist country that finds itself threatened

by reactionary forces." In the Chilean Communist Party, with Corvalan at its head, Moscow had one of the best disciplined and most obedient organizational instruments available to it anywhere in the world, and it was willing to pay for this support by heavy and continuing secret subsidies for the party's organizational and propaganda activity.

In the 1958 presidential election campaign in Chile, Corvalan followed the basic strategy laid down by Moscow by taking the Communists into an electoral alliance with the Socialists. Their combined forces were called the Popular Action Front (FRAP), and Allende was selected as the presidential candidate of this coalition. It was not by any stretch of the imagination a reformist social democratic alliance but rather a popular front of Marxist parties, secretly subsidized and directed by the Kremlin in an astute attempt to exploit the democratic process as a way of seizing the levers of governmental power in a country strategically located in an area long regarded by the United States as being within its sphere of influence. Also competing in this election for the six-year presidency were the conservatives under Jorge Alessandri, the newly formed and reformist Christian Democratic Party under the leadership of Eduardo Frei, and the centrist Radical Party. The election turned out to be much closer than expected, with Allende losing to Alessandri by less than 3 percent of the vote.

By the time President Kennedy came to office in 1961, the Chilean political parties were already gearing up for the next presidential election scheduled for 1964. In the 1961 congressional elections, the ruling conservative coalition under President Alessandri suffered serious losses, while the FRAP alliance made substantial gains. The only encouraging development for those who feared a Marxist victory was the steadily increasing strength of the Christian Democratic Party, committed under the leadership of Frei to a left-of-center program of land reform and economic redistribution. The intelligent and liberal Catholic laymen who led the Christian Democrats made a very favorable impression on Kennedy and his closest advisers on Latin America. They shared the Kennedy administration's belief in the goal of democratic social reform under the Alliance for Progress, and, what was more important, they seemed to have the organizational competence necessary to build a political party capable of achieving their objectives. They lacked only adequate financial resources, since the big landowners and industrialists in Chile were not attracted by their liberal program.

In addition, after the disastrous collapse of the Bay of Pigs invasion of Cuba, Kennedy was determined to prevent Castro from succeeding in his attempt to ignite the fires of Marxist revolution throughout Latin America. Intelligence reports kept Kennedy currently informed on the extent of Soviet and Cuban covert support to the FRAP alliance, and they left little doubt that the Russians were engaged in a carefully calculated attempt to bring their chosen instruments to power in Chile through a popular front electoral strategy. So it was that hope for genuine democratic reform and fear of successful Communist manipulation of the electoral process in Chile combined to persuade the Kennedy administration to decide upon a long-term program of covert assistance to the Chilean Christian Democratic Party. Such political funding had to be kept secret to protect the recipients from propaganda attack, and much of the funding was handled through third parties so discreetly that the Christian Democratic leaders were not themselves aware of the true source. The only agency in the U.S. government authorized to distribute secret funds abroad for such political purposes was the CIA. Therefore at the highest policy level, the Kennedy administration directed the Agency to provide covert support to the Christian Democratic Party, and more than $200,000 was authorized and spent for that purpose in 1962.[15]

An understanding of this sequence of events tends to undermine two important elements in the prevailing mythology regarding CIA intervention in Chile. First, as the Church committee Staff Report makes very clear, the Agency was from the beginning a disciplined instrument under the complete control of the President and his principal foreign policy advisers.[16] The Agency did not initiate the policy of covert intervention in Chile but rather acted as an executive agent in carrying out decisions reached at the highest level of the American government, as it was required to do under the National Security Act of 1947. What was done in Chile, for better or for worse, was the responsibility of successive American Presidents—Kennedy, Johnson, and Nixon. The myth that the Agency was rampaging like "a rogue elephant" out of control in the activities that it undertook in Chile does not stand up in the light of the historical record.

Second, the primary purpose of the initial covert political funding in Chile was not to support the reactionary right-wing forces in a struggle against the enlightened advocates of liberal reform. Rather, President Kennedy chose to support a reformist left-of-center party in its confrontation with a radical Marxist coalition which was seeking to exploit the democratic process in order to destroy it. Moreover, the vast preponderance of secret funds spent for political purposes in Chile from 1962 through 1973 was designed to support the left-of-center and moderate parties rather than the reactionary right.[17] Just as in Western Europe in the 1950s, the objective of this covert action was to support those political forces that were committed to the preservation of democratic liberties and to the elimination of the poverty and class inequities on which Communist propaganda fed. Finally, the Kennedy administration was driven by well-founded fears that what had happened in Eastern Europe and in Cuba would be repeated in Chile if the FRAP gained control of the extensive powers of the Chilean presidency. Kennedy rightly feared that Allende would use an electoral victory to try to make an irreversible change in the democratic order. He also viewed with apprehension the consequences for the rest of Latin America if Chilean territory was allowed to become a Soviet and Cuban organizational base for the mounting of revolutionary operations directed against other countries in the hemisphere, as Allende later cooperated in doing.

For all these reasons, the covert political intervention in Chile in 1962 in behalf of the Christian Democrats had very wide support at the senior policy levels in the Kennedy administration, and those of us in the CIA who were involved in implementing this policy also believed in it as fully justified. The only alternative to such covert support seemed to be a policy of passive acquiescence as the Soviets gained their first foothold on the Latin American continent through their heavy subsidies and ideological control of the FRAP. None of these persuasive arguments for Kennedy's initiation of covert political funding in Chile are spelled out clearly in the Church committee's Staff Report, and a rather transparent attempt is made to imply that the Kennedy administration was only marginally involved. Note for example the title of the report: "Covert Action in Chile—1963–1973," as if the covert funding had not begun in 1962. In fact, the unwary and uninformed reader of the report is left with the impression that successive American Presidents meddled in Chilean affairs in a feckless way with no coherent strategy or justifiable objective in mind.

After Lyndon Johnson became President on Kennedy's death, he faced the same problem in Chile that had confronted Kennedy. He decided for the same reasons to continue the Kennedy policy of active covert intervention in behalf of the Christian Democrats in order to maximize their chances of winning the Chilean presidential election in the fall of 1964 and to ensure the defeat of the FRAP. In April of 1964, the CIA was directed to spend $3 million dollars to support the campaign of the Christian Democratic candidate, Eduardo Frei. The electoral picture was simplified by a crucial by-election loss in the spring of 1964 suffered by the governing conservative coalition. The two conservative parties withdrew from their alliance with the Radical Party and threw their support to Frei. In a three-way race between Frei as leader of the Christian Democrats, Allende as the FRAP's candidate, and Julio Duran as leader of the centrist Radical Party, Frei won the election in September with a clear majority of 57 percent of the vote. His platform called for agrarian, tax, and housing reform and "Chileanization" of the American-owned copper mines by the purchase of a majority of the stock. Prior to the election, as the Church committee's Staff Report makes clear, the CIA station chief summarily rejected two attempts by Chilean military officers to secure American support for a coup d'etat in the event of an Allende victory and informed the plotters that the United States was "absolutely opposed to a coup."[18]

With Frei's election assured on a platform that promised "a revolution in liberty" through democratic reform, President Johnson moved to support the new president by appointing Ralph A. Dungan, one of Kennedy's principal advisers, as ambassador to Chile. Thereafter, American support to the ruling Christian Democratic Party was primarily in the form of overt grants and loans, except for a total of approximately $500,000 which the Agency was directed to channel to selected candidates in the congressional elections in 1965 and 1969 to bolster the government's position in the Chamber of Deputies.

Under the Chilean constitution, Frei was not allowed to succeed himself at the end of his six-year term. As the crucial presidential election scheduled for September of 1970 approached, there were significant changes in the Chilean political landscape. Conservatives on the right who had supported Frei in 1964 as preferable to Allende were antagonized by the pace and depth of his land reform, and on the left there were elements in his own party who believed he was not proceeding quickly enough to institute radical social change. As a result of these conflicting pressures, the right-wing Liberal and Conservative parties united to form the National Party and, encouraged by winning more than 20 percent of the vote in the congressional elections of 1969, they later in that year nominated the seventy-three-year-old elder statesman Jorge Alessandri as their presidential candidate. Meanwhile the Christian Democrats were drifting toward the left. A radical faction broke with the party to join the Marxists. In August of 1969, the Christian Democrats nominated as their presidential candidate Radimiro Tomic, who had served briefly as ambassador in Washington and who was clearly identified with the left wing of the party in his demand for faster land redistribution and in favoring negotiations with the Communists.

The Marxists took advantage of this deep division in the opposition by broadening the popular front and changing its name to Unidad Popular or Popular Unity. They welcomed into its ranks the splinter faction that had broken away from the Christian Democrats and, more significant, they won the support of the majority of the Radical Party, which had run a separate candidate in the 1964 presidential election. In the negotiations between the six parties that now made up the popular front, the Communists withdrew their candidate, the poet Pablo Neruda, and threw their decisive support again behind Allende, the Socialist candidate, who became as a result the candidate of the Popular Unity alliance.

This reconfiguration of the Chilean political scene faced the Nixon administration in Washington during the spring of 1970 with a complex dilemma over which it agonized in a series of high-level policy meetings that are described in the Church committee's Staff Report.[19] With the non-Communist opposition evenly split between the conservative Alessandri and the left-leaning Christian Democrat Tomic, and all the polls indicating a very close election, President Nixon decided not to authorize covert funding for either of the non-Communist candidates. Instead, he tried to hedge his bets by directing the CIA to undertake an extensive covert propaganda campaign designed to dramatize for the Chilean electorate the dangers of an Allende victory and the historical consequences of allowing a

Communist-dominated coalition to come to power. As a result, the 40 Committee, the high-level interagency policy group that advised the President on covert action matters and to which the CIA was responsible, authorized the Agency to spend a total of $425,000 during the 1970 presidential campaign to publicize through press, radio, and posters the extent of Communist influence within the popular front and the danger to Chilean democracy of that influence. Nixon tried to avoid fueling a fratricidal rivalry between the two non-Communist parties by denying funds to both of them, while relying on a generalized propaganda effort to cut into the number of those willing to vote for Allende. Obedient to these policy restraints, the Agency in July of 1970 rejected an offer of funds from ITT, which the company wished to have the Agency channel to Alessandri's campaign in order to protect its investments in Chile. Subsequently, ITT officials decided on their own to contribute to Alessandri, and they asked for and received some advice from the Agency on what individuals could be trusted as intermediaries.[20]

Based on this record, it is unarguably clear that from 1962 to the election of September 4, 1970, the purpose of American covert intervention in Chile had been to preserve the democratic constitutional order. When direct political subsidies were employed, they were used to strengthen those democratic elements who were committed to economic and social reform. Covert propaganda was used to alert the population to the danger of the Communist popular front strategy and to counteract the propaganda apparatus that the Soviets and Cubans were secretly subsidizing. The results of the 1970 election caused the Nixon administration to make a radical and fundamental change in this policy. In the three-cornered race for the presidency, Allende received 36.3 percent of the vote, less than he had received in 1964 but enough to give him a plurality. Alessandri received 34.9 percent and Tomic 27.8 percent. Under the Chilean constitution, since no candidate had received a majority of the popular vote, a joint session of the Congress was required to choose between the two front-runners six weeks later on October 24, 1970. According to past practice, the candidate receiving the highest percentage of the votes was usually confirmed as president, and in view of this tradition the general expectation was that Allende would be elected when the Congress met in October.

On hearing the election results, my own first reaction was to think that Chilean democracy would have a difficult and dangerous time surviving Allende's six-year term as president. The superior organization and discipline of the Chilean Communists would give them a dominant influence in the new government, and I did not underestimate the lengths to which Soviets and Cubans would go in attempting to expand their foothold by subsidizing the new government and by using every instrument of power to weaken and eventually destroy the political opposition. But there were some distinctive and uniquely Chilean aspects to the situation that made the outcome appear far less predictable than the Communist takeover in Eastern Europe after World War II. Most significant, the Chilean armed forces were predominantly dedicated to the preservation of the democratic order, and they had not yet been seriously infiltrated by Communist cadres. Moreover, there was no contiguous border with the Soviet Union as there had been in Eastern Europe. The Red Army was far away and Soviet naval forces at that time were limited.

Second, the ultraleft faction in the Socialist Party could be relied upon to challenge the ingenious popular front strategy of the Communists and to antagonize the majority of the population by premature attempts to provoke revolutionary violence. Finally, Allende had barely won by a little more than a third of the vote. The remaining two-thirds were clearly not sympathetic to the Marxist cause. It seemed to me quite possible that, in the reaction to Tomic's defeat, the broad coalition led by Frei and the Christian Democrats could be reconstructed to control a majority of the Congress during Allende's term in office. It could win decisively in the next presidential election, if the United States was prepared to offer consistent and adequate covert support. I think this initial reaction to the election was shared by many of my colleagues in the clandestine service, and we were settling down to the prospect of a long and complicated political struggle when Nixon suddenly made a series of drastic changes in the whole direction of American policy toward Chile.

Having failed in his gamble that a generalized propaganda campaign would be sufficient to stop Allende, Nixon decided that the risk to American interests in the hemisphere of a six-year Allende presidency was so great that anything and everything was justified in attempting to prevent the Chilean Congress from confirming him as president on October 24. In his interview with David Frost, Nixon explained his motivation by recalling a conversation he had prior to the Chilean election: "An Italian businessman came to call on me in the Oval Office and he said, 'If Allende should win the election in Chile, and then you have Castro in Cuba, what you will in effect have in Latin America is a red sandwich and eventually it will all be red.' And that's what we confronted."[21] Driven by this perception, and not wanting to be the first American President to preside over the establishment of a Soviet foothold on the Latin American continent, Nixon abruptly reversed the previous course of American policy. He was not prepared to ride out the threat of an Allende presidency by relying on the strength of Chilean constitutional democracy and on long-term covert support to the democratic opposition. Instead, he called for an all-out effort to prevent Allende's election by the Chilean Congress, even if it meant subverting Chilean democracy in the process.

The results of Nixon's aberrational and hysterical decision have been spelled out in detail in the Church committee report and are in considerable contrast to Nixon's own bland explanation of these events in his memoirs.[22] Nixon's pursuit of this policy proceeded on two levels. The 40 Committee, chaired by Henry Kissinger as Nixon's National Security Adviser, met on September 14 and directed the State Department and the Agency to attempt to persuade the Chilean Congress to abandon previous practice by voting on October 24 for the runner-up, Alessandri, instead of Allende. In order to win over sufficient Christian Democratic votes to make this gambit workable, Alessandri was to agree in advance to resign after being elected and to call for a special election in which Frei would then be eligible to run as the single candidate of the non-Communist parties. This complicated scheme was combined with a decision to bring maximum economic pressure to bear on Chile and to provoke financial panic as an advance warning to the electorate of what would happen if the popular front was allowed to take power. To this end, both the State Department and the CIA were directed to use their contacts in the American business community to secure their cooperation. Because neither Frei nor the majority of the Christian Democrats were prepared to accept this scenario, it never got off the ground, and the $250,000 that had been allocated by the 40 Committee to influence the vote in the Chilean Congress was never spent.

Simultaneously, Nixon proceeded on a second and most secret policy level, which became known as Track II. On September 15, he called in CIA Director Helms and ordered the Agency to mount an all-out, no-holds-barred effort to prevent Allende from taking power, including a military coup if necessary. Also present at this meeting were Henry Kissinger and Attorney General John Mitchell. Helms was told that all the money he needed would be made available and he was specifically ordered by the President not to reveal to the Secretary of State, the American ambassador in Chile, or to anyone outside those directly involved in the Agency, that such a course was being pursued. As the power and authority of the President then existed, Nixon was within his legal rights in issuing such an order. Helms had no choice but to obey or to resign, which he was not prepared to do at so critical a time. However, he did try to point out to Nixon the practical difficulties that lay in the path of a successful military coup. As he explained later in his interview with David Frost, "There wasn't a one of us who thought we had any chance whatever of achieving this objective, and I tried to make that point at this meeting on September the fifteenth. But that was like talking into a gale. I mean, we were to go out and do the best we could, and that was all there was to it."[23]

When Helms returned from the White House, he convened a small meeting in order to convey the President's instructions, and Karamessines and I attended. We were surprised by what we were being ordered to do, since, much as we feared an Allende presidency, the idea of a military overthrow had not occurred to us as a feasible solution. Unlike the situation in some Latin American countries, the Chilean military had an enviable record of devotion to constitutional democracy. There was no evidence that any substantial body of Chilean officers were as yet so convinced of Allende's revolutionary intentions that they would be prepared to intervene to prevent the Chilean Congress from making its own choice. Moreover, as we pointed out, there were practical difficulties. Under previous policy, the CIA station in Santiago had discouraged coup plotting among the military and had deliberately distanced itself from those officers who were inclined to think in such terms. Moreover, the period of time remaining before action had to be taken was so brief that the careful planning required seemed hardly possible. All these objections could not change the reality that the President had made his decision, and we left the meeting resigned to having to carry out a policy that we believed would almost certainly fail. The pride we might have felt at having been among the select few chosen by the President to execute a secret and important mission was more than counterbalanced by our doubts about the wisdom of this course and our fear that an abortive coup might only play into Allende's hands.

After interviewing all Agency officials concerned with trying to implement Nixon's decision to launch a military coup, the Church committee later reached the following conclusion, which I think fairly and accurately represents our reaction to receiving this presidential directive: "On one point the testimony of the CIA officials who were involved in Track II is unanimous: they all said they thought Track II was unlikely to succeed. That view ran from the working levels of the Agency to the top. They all said they felt they were being asked to do the impossible, that the risks and potential costs of the project were too great. At the same time, they felt they had been given an explicit Presidential order, and they tried to execute that order."[24] Once again Nixon had involved the Agency in events that were later to cause serious damage to its reputation but, in contrast to the Watergate affair, in this case there was no legal argument on which to base resistance to his orders. In retrospect, it is possible that we could have forced a reconsideration of this decision by a unanimous act of protest, but the respect for presidential authority ran too deep, and we did not even consider this alternative.

Dutifully following Nixon's instructions, Karamessines established a highly compartmented task force within the Western Hemisphere Division and he dealt regularly with Kissinger and his deputy, General Alexander Haig, in the White House, as the planning went forward to find those in the Chilean military who might be willing to undertake a coup d'etat. He kept me informed of developments and I had access to the cable traffic, but at his request my primary responsibility at this time was to take care of what was going on in the rest of the world, while he concentrated on Chile.

The response from the Chilean military was just about what we expected. The commander-in-chief of the army, General Schneider, was a highly respected officer who advocated strict adherence to the constitution, and his second-in-command, General Prats, shared his views. In fact, the Chilean military's tradition of nonintervention in political affairs turned out to be the major obstacle to Nixon's plan that we had thought it would be. The CIA station in Santiago did, however, make contact with two different groups of military officers who claimed to be prepared to mount a coup, but both groups believed that General Schneider would have to be kidnapped and removed from command if any general revolt was to become possible. Contact with the first group of plotters, led by General Viaux, was broken off on October 15 after Karamessines reported to Kissinger that his plans were too disorganized to have a chance of succeeding. General Viaux, however, proceeded on his own initiative to order the kidnapping of General Schneider on October 22, and in the course of resisting his abductors General Schneider was killed. This shooting resulted in a declaration of martial law and the appointment of General Prats as commander-in-chief. The shock effect of Schneider's death rallied the Chilean military behind the cause of constitutionalism and on October 24 Allende was confirmed as president by the Chilean Congress by a large majority.[25]

According to the subsequent findings of the Church committee, the second group of conspirators with whom the CIA did maintain contact was not involved in General Viaux's attempt to kidnap Schneider nor were weapons provided by the Agency used in that attempt.[26] It was small consolation to us in the Agency to realize that we had not been directly involved in the death of a courageous and honorable officer whose devotion to constitutional order was the cause of the fatal attempt to abduct him. The indirect effect of Nixon's wild scheme to subvert the democratic process in Chile was to solidify military support for Allende's election. This whole unhappy incident stands as a classic example of the misuse of presidential authority and explains the subsequent effort by the U.S. Congress to set limits to the President's power to commit such folly on his sole initiative.

However, after this secret Nixonian aberration, the President returned to a much more rational course in his dealings with the consequences of an Allende regime. In his annual State of the World message in February 1971, Nixon announced a cool but correct diplomatic stance toward Allende, and from that time forward no further attempt was made by Nixon to involve the Agency in any effort to encourage a military coup. In fact, the record shows that from the time of Allende's election, the Agency was specifically enjoined from any action that might be construed as supporting coup plotting, and these orders were carried out. When the Chilean officers finally moved to overthrow Allende in September 1973, they did so on their own initiative and for their own reasons and without consultation or coordination with either the U.S. Embassy or the CIA station in Santiago. Contrary to the generally accepted mythology, the evidence is conclusive that Allende's final downfall was strictly a Chilean affair in which the Agency played no part, although it could be argued that Nixon's month-long attempt to stimulate a coup in 1970 may have made a lasting impression on some of the Chilean officers.[27]

Briefly described, Nixon's policy during the Allende years in dealing with Chile had three different aspects. On the diplomatic front, relations with the new government were formally maintained and the American ambassador in Santiago was not withdrawn. On the economic front, action was taken by the U.S. government to restrict the flow of loans and credits to Chile after efforts failed to obtain fair compensation for the U.S. private firms whose assets in the country were nationalized. To some extent, the Soviets made up for this reduction in American loans by extending credits to Allende valued at approximately $400 million up to June 1972. Since much of this Soviet aid was tied to purchases of Russian equipment, Allende needed hard currency, and was able to renegotiate $800 million in debts to foreign governments and to U.S. banks in order to purchase essential imports.[28] In spite of these offsetting factors, the American credit squeeze had some effect, but most of Allende's mounting economic problems were the direct result of his own domestic policies.

Through very large wage increases to the workers, inflation was deliberately driven up, until it reached the rate of 320 percent in 1973, as a way of forcing private business into bankruptcy and state ownership. Government rationing was the inevitable result, and local committees to supervise the rationing were dominated by the Communists to increase their influence. The nationalization of private industry and the creation of state collectives through the expropriation of agricultural land were pursued without regard to the economic consequences in terms of overstaffing and loss of production. The purpose was not reform but rather to break the independent economic base of the middle class. As Allende's first minister of economy, Pedro Vuskovic, put it shortly after the new government took office, "State control is designed to destroy the economic bases of imperialism and the ruling class by putting an end to the private ownership of the means of production."[29]

On the third level of covert action, the mission assigned to the Agency by the Nixon administration during Allende's rule in Chile from 1970 to 1973 was to support and keep alive the non-Communist political parties and the opposition press and radio stations. The objective was to forge a united opposition that could use its majority voting strength in the Chilean Congress to impede the popular front's drive to force through an irreversible transformation of society. In the long term, the aim was to ensure the survival of a democratic coalition that would have a reasonable chance of winning back the Chilean presidency in the election scheduled for 1976. For this purpose, the Agency was directed to spend a total of approximately $6 million during the 1970–73 period. The majority of the political funding went to the reformist Christian Democratic Party, which once again under Frei's leadership recovered from its electoral defeat. Some funds also went to the support of the conservative National Party and to the encouragement of splinter groups that began to break away from Allende's popular front as the radically Marxist direction of his policy became more evident.

Due to Allende's attempt to silence the opposition press by denial of bank credit, advertising, and newsprint, heavy covert subsidies were required to keep the independent media alive, and the majority of this funding went to the support of *El Mercurio,* Chile's leading newspaper, which as a result managed to survive as an articulate and informed critic of the Allende regime. In effect, this covert action program represented a return to the original purpose of Kennedy's initial intervention and was an attempt to rely on the strength of Chilean democracy and the vitality of the democratic forces as bulwarks against the eventual imposition of a Marxist system. During this stage, there was no covert attempt to "destabilize" the democratic order in Chile, and no funds were authorized for the support of extreme right-wing vigilante groups that sprang up in opposition to the ultraleft guerrilla organizations that Allende allowed to proliferate. Nor was any support authorized for the succession of disruptive strikes by truck drivers and shop owners that contributed to the growing chaos during Allende's last months in power.[30]

However, even the strong Chilean democratic tradition could not survive the growing polarization of the country caused by the rampant inflation, Allende's extralegal measures to force the pace of nationalization, and the mounting violence between right-wing and left-wing extremists. In August 1973, General Prats, who had been consistently loyal to Allende, was forced to resign as commander-in-chief of the armed forces and was replaced by General Pinochet. Naval officers in Valparaiso discovered a plot by left-wing extremists to infiltrate the navy and to provoke a mutiny. Convinced that the discipline of the armed forces was threatened by infiltration, General Pinochet secured the agreement of the army high command to move against the Allende regime. In a carefully planned and highly secret operation, the military coup was launched on September 11, 1973. Allende was killed in the resulting violence and his government overthrown. Pinochet later explained in a press interview how he had managed to preserve secrecy during the planning stage by strictly limiting the number of collaborators and by deliberately excluding U.S. officials from any advance knowledge.[31] His testimony on this point is confirmed by the findings of the Church committee that neither the U.S. Embassy nor the CIA was involved in Allende's final overthrow.

Initially, the Christian Democratic and National Party leaders welcomed the coup as a drastic measure made necessary by the growing anarchy in the country. Their hope that military rule would be only a temporary method of restoring order prior to a return to democratic practice proved to be illusory, as Pinochet proceeded to establish dictatorial control through a right-wing military junta. Indiscriminate and widespread arrests and executions were used to break the organizational structure of the Communist apparatus, and the severe repression practiced by Pinochet against his opposition was distinguished from the police-state methods used by the Communists in Eastern Europe only by being less thorough and less efficient. Under prodding from the Carter administration on human rights issues, Pinochet subsequently released a substantial number of political prisoners and reined in his police agents. On the basis of experience with right-wing dictators in Spain and Portugal, an eventual return to democratic liberty seems far more likely in Chile than in any country where Communist rule has been firmly established.

In all its complexity, this whole episode shows how different reality was from the simplistic black-and-white morality of the prevailing mythology that casts the Agency in the role of having deliberately destroyed Chilean democracy in order to replace it with a military dictatorship. In its reaction to these ambiguous events, the Communist world has been far more realistic than the democratic West in assessing the implications for its own interests and in drawing conclusions affecting its future strategy. After *The New York Times* broke the story of the "destabilization" of Chile, the Communist apparatus throughout the world went into high gear in order to exploit the obvious propaganda benefits by sowing as much doubt as possible between the United States and its Western allies, and by blackening the reputation of the Agency. While making the most of this propaganda windfall, Communist strategists settled down to analyze the lessons to be learned from the failure of Allende's popular front. Boris Ponomarev, a candidate member of the Soviet Politburo, weighed in with the conclusion that in similar circumstances in the future it was crucial "to deprive the old regime of important levers of power" and "to deprive the class enemy of the mass information and propaganda media."[32] Recalling Lenin's warning of the need to smash the old state machine as an essential prerequisite to genuine revolution, M. F. Kudachkin condemned Allende's coalition, the Unidad Popular, for its failure to "take any steps that were at all resolute against Congress and the judiciary."[33]

Even more interesting were the conclusions reached by three leaders of the Chilean Communist Party, writing from exile in the international Communist journal, *World Marxist Review* (January, February and March 1977). All three make it clear that a future left-wing government in Chile would quickly seek to deprive its opponents of all remaining levers of power. Volodia Teitelboim wrote that one of the lessons learned from the Allende experience was that Communists should not let themselves be "Gullivers bound hand and foot by legality." Pointing out that the alignment of the military forces in favor of revolutionary development was crucial, he called for ideological indoctrination in the barracks to destroy the soldiers' "false conception of public duty." Another Chilean Communist exile, Rodrigo Rojas, sharply criticized Allende for allowing his opponents to stage demonstrations and to use the media, the parliament, and the judiciary as means of exerting "psychological pressure" on the armed forces. He condemned Allende for failing to mobilize the "workers' sacred class hatred." The third Chilean Communist, Orlando Millas, called for the foundation of mass organizations, adequately armed and trained, as essential in any future revolutionary situation. Statements such as these indicate how limited the rights of the political opposition would be if a popular front should come to power again in Chile or elsewhere in Latin America.

These conclusions drawn by the Communists from Allende's downfall did not merely remain on paper as theoretical formulations but became the basis for an active strategy of attempting to influence and infiltrate the armed forces in all countries where revolutionary possibilities existed. How quickly the lessons were learned is indicated by the tactics of the Communist Party in Portugal, where under directives from Moscow an astute attempt was made to manipulate the armed forces after the right-wing regime was overthrown in 1974. At the top, genuine ideological conversions of Portuguese officers appear to have been made, as in the case of Vasco Goncalves, while other ranking officers were blackmailed into cooperation by the use of documents stolen by the Communists from the files of Salazar's secret police. On the rank-and-file level, a dissident left-wing organization within the Portuguese Army, called Soldiers United Will Win, was formed, and control of it was seized by the Communists, who used its mass demonstrations as disturbing proof of their influence inside the army. In Portugal, this well-planned attempt to subvert the military finally failed when non-Communist officers managed to assert their authority in November 1975, but the influence of disciplined Communists within the ranks of Portuguese officers serving in Angola played a crucial role in ensuring the establishment of a Marxist regime in Luanda.

Similarly throughout Latin America after Allende's overthrow, intelligence reporting indicated that local Communist parties received detailed instructions from Moscow on how to analyze and exploit the vulnerabilities of the officer corps, including ideological weaknesses and problems of pay and promotion that could lead to exploitable dissatisfactions. Also the provision of sophisticated Soviet weaponry to third world countries created opportunities for ideological indoctrination and agent recruitment among the officers sent to the Soviet Union for training in the new weapons. How thorough and effective this recruitment could be was demonstrated by the successful Communist coups in the spring and summer of 1978 in Afghanistan and South Yemen. The lesson taken to heart by the Soviets and Cubans from Allende's failure was not that they should stop covertly intervening in the future but rather that they should engage in more extensive covert penetration with particular emphasis on the military.

In the United States, exactly the opposite lesson was drawn from the Chilean experience. The reaction to the publicity given Congressman Harrington's revelations, and the subsequent disclosure of Nixon's aberrational Track II, encouraged the belief that covert action of any kind should be far more closely controlled and should be resorted to only in extreme situations when the national security was clearly at stake. To ensure that no future President could behave on his own as Nixon had done, an amendment to the Foreign Assistance Act was passed by the Congress in December 1974.[34] This legislation, known as the Hughes-Ryan Amendment, stipulated that no funds could be expended by the CIA abroad for any covert action purpose "until the President finds that each such operation is important to the national security of the U.S. and reports in a timely fashion, a description and scope of such operation to the appropriate committees of the Congress, including the Committee on Foreign Relations of the U.S. Senate and the Committee on Foreign Affairs of the U.S. House of Representatives."

With the subsequent establishment of the oversight responsibilities of the House and Senate Select Intelligence Committees, plus the continuing jurisdiction of the Armed Services and Appropriations Committees of both Houses, this amendment meant that any covert action had to be reported to eight committees of the Congress, including such staff personnel as are cleared for this purpose. Before a President authorizes any covert action by the CIA, he must now take into account that about two hundred members of the Congress and its staff will have to be promptly informed of the details and he must make a judgment whether essential secrecy has any chance of being preserved under such circumstances. The record so far is not good. Unless the Congress moves to limit the number of committees having jurisdiction in such cases, it is safe to predict that covert funding of attempts to support foreign political leaders under challenge from secretly financed Communist parties and front groups will rarely be risked.

This virtual elimination of the covert action option from the choices available to a President was perhaps the purpose of the Hughes-Ryan Amendment, but so drastic a reaction to the events in Chile hardly seems justified in the face of the clear evidence that the

Soviets have expanded and refined their covert intervention strategy on the basis of the lessons learned in Chile. The understandable revulsion against Nixon's desperate and doomed last-minute attempt to prevent Allende from coming to power concentrated attention on this egregious example of how the covert action capability can be misused, and obscured the fact that under Kennedy and Johnson covert funding in Chile was intelligently employed to provide indispensable assistance to the democratic and reformist political forces in their competition with the heavily subsidized popular front. In the emotional reaction to Nixon's excesses, the Church committee failed to make a careful and realistic assessment of what lessons could be learned from the Chilean experience in contrast to the pragmatic conclusions reached by the Soviets.

In my opinion, such a realistic assessment would conclude that covert political funding makes sense and is most effective when it is part of a long-range and consistent policy designed to strengthen the democratic forces in a society under siege from the Marxist left. Covert political action should not be viewed as a last-minute quick fix or as a desperate alternative to sending in the U.S. Marines. Its effectiveness depends upon a correct analysis of the complex political forces at work in a foreign country. It can succeed only if it is consistently pursued over a period of time, as it was by Kennedy and Johnson in Chile, and is justified only by the extent of the threat posed by the Soviets' covert intervention on the side of their Communist allies. In retrospect, the Nixon administration's first mistake in Chile was its underestimation of the consequences of the split between the non-Communist parties and hence its failure to use its influence early enough to consolidate the non-Communist majority behind a single compromise candidate. Whether such an attempt would have succeeded is questionable, but it should have been made since it was the only way to avoid the dilemma Nixon finally confronted: whether to acquiesce in Allende's coming to power or to destroy Chilean democracy in an effort to defeat him. The generalized propaganda campaign that Nixon finally authorized was no substitute for decisive American backing of a chosen candidate against the united forces of the Marxist left supported by the Soviets. In a sense, Nixon intervened too little and too late before the election and then overreacted irrationally to the trap he had laid for himself.

Whether covert political action, intelligently pursued over a protracted period of time, will again be available to an American President depends upon the ability of the Congress to discipline itself by reducing the number of committees and staff personnel that have to be involved in the decision making. The optimum, in my opinion, would be a single joint House-Senate Committee, served by a professional staff of high quality and limited size, in which was exclusively lodged the jurisdiction for oversight of the intelligence community. Until some such reduction in the numbers of those privy to covert action operations is achieved, essential secrecy will be endangered by continuing leaks, and no President will dare to undertake even the most necessary covert intervention unless there is virtual unanimity in the Congress.

This institutional damage done by Nixon's Track II decision was compounded by the deep wounds inflicted on individual reputations and careers when the decision was subsequently publicized. By weaving a net of peculiar and unique secrecy around his presidential directive to prevent Allende's election, Nixon entangled others in his folly, and created unresolvable dilemmas for men like former CIA Director Richard Helms, who was later forced to choose between his oath to preserve presidentially imposed secrecy and his duty to testify truthfully before congressional committees. In by-passing the 40 Committee and by deliberately keeping the secretary of state, the secretary of defense, and the U.S. ambassador to Chile in the dark, Nixon tried to draw a shroud of permanent secrecy around his highly personal decision to intervene; but in the process he placed a heavy responsibility for maintaining the security of the operation on Helms's shoulders and removed the institutional coordination of 40 Committee review which would have allowed Helms to share this responsibility with others at the top of the foreign policy establishment and to seek their advice.

Shortly after his resignation from the CIA directorship had been forced by Nixon, Helms had to face confirmation hearings before the Senate Foreign Relations Committee on his appointment as U.S. ambassador to Iran. In these hearings in February 1973, and in testimony before the Senate Foreign Relations Subcommittee on Multinational Corporations in March regarding the extent of ITT involvement in Chile, Helms was confronted with as deep and serious a dilemma as any high-ranking government official has recently had to face. Asked in a series of probing questions by the senators whether the CIA had been involved in an effort to prevent Allende's election in 1970, Helms chose to answer evasively, as he later admitted before a judge in pleading *nolo contendere* to the charge that he had "refused and failed to answer material questions" in his two appearances before the committee.[35]

In November 1977, District Court Judge Barrington D. Parker found Helms guilty, suspended the jail sentence, but sentenced him to one year of probation and imposed a fine of $2000. In so doing, he delivered a stern lecture to Helms and castigated his behavior in the following terms: "You considered yourself bound to protect the Agency whose affairs you had administered and to dishonor your solemn oath to tell the truth before the Committee. You now stand before this court in disgrace and shame." Many in the country believed that this harsh judgment was fully justified and that Helms was lucky not to have been sentenced to a jail term.

A fair and objective appraisal of the actual choices available to Helms at the time that he testified before the committee does not in my opinion support the judge's righteous indignation but rather suggests that the Justice Department should never have brought the case against Helms. In the first place, there was a genuine conflict of legal obligations, as Helms's lawyer Edward Bennett Williams argued and which the Justice Department recognized as relevant in entering into a plea bargaining agreement and in urging suspension of the jail sentence. Helms felt bound by the statutory responsibility imposed on the Director of Central Intelligence by the National Security Act of 1947 to protect intelligence sources and methods from unauthorized disclosure. Since at the time he testified he had not been released by the President from his obligation to maintain the secrecy of the covert operations in Chile, he could not testify fully and accurately before the committee without breaking that law. Moreover, Helms also felt bound by the oath that he signed on his departure from the CIA not to divulge, publish, or reveal any classified information to any unauthorized person. Helms put the chairman of the Foreign Relations Committee, Senator William Fulbright, on notice at the beginning of the hearings that he continued to be bound by these prior legal obligations.

In asking him specific questions about covert activity in Chile, the senators knew they were probing into an area which at that time was within the exclusive jurisdiction of the authorized oversight subcommittees of the Senate Armed Services and Appropriations Committees. In fact, at one point during the March 1973 hearing, Senator Symington, who was also a member of one of the oversight committees, complained that detailed questions were being asked that Helms was not authorized to answer before the Senate Foreign Relations Subcommittee.[36] This remonstrance did not stop Senator Frank Church from continuing to ask specific questions regarding covert activity that clearly indicated he did not accept the exclusive jurisdiction of the oversight committees as then constituted. Helms was made the victim of an unresolved jurisdictional fight between Senate committees and tried to thread his way through these mine fields with as few evasions as possible. His dilemma was further sharpened by the fact that he had no authorization from the President even to mention the existence of the Track II strategy to any member of Congress.

Quite aside from these conflicting legal obligations and unresolved jurisdictional questions, Helms was faced with the fact that, at the time he testified before the committee and its subcommittee in February and March of 1973, Allende was still president of Chile and continuing covert support was being supplied by the CIA to the opposition parties. As we have seen, Chile was then in the throes of a desperate struggle as Allende attempted to force through an irreversible change in the basic structure of its society. Any public admission, direct or implied, by Helms that the United States had been involved in clandestinely supporting the democratic opposition would have been exploited by the Communists to smear the Christian Democrats and to justify the imposition of police-state controls. Even more explosive was the hidden time bomb of Track II, which if revealed would certainly have given Allende the excuse he needed to launch an attack on the presence of the U.S. Embassy and to win back the popular support he was losing. In his personal statement to Judge Parker, Helms did not exaggerate when he claimed that fully responsive testimony by him "would have seriously and adversely affected our relations with foreign governments and injured our nation's security. To this day, I believe that full and complete testimony at that time might well have endangered lives."[37]

In the wisdom of hindsight, various options have been suggested that it is claimed would have extricated Helms from his dilemma. None of them bears up under close scrutiny. By refusing to answer any questions on Chile relating to covert activity, he would simply have confirmed that such activity did exist, and Allende's propaganda hounds would have gone baying down that trail. He would also have opened himself to contempt proceedings and ensured dramatic publicity for the whole issue by his public refusal to testify. Since he was no longer a CIA employee, he could not claim the right to testify on these matters exclusively before the duly authorized oversight committees, and if he had tried to assert such a right he could not have testified fully even in that forum because of the restrictions Nixon had placed on Track II. By asking the Senate Foreign Relations Committee hearing on his ambassadorial appointment to go into executive session, he would clearly have confirmed the suspicion that there was something to hide and, again, even in executive session he could not have testified about Track II. An attempt to obtain the protection of a Nixon administration decision to invoke executive privilege would have been equally compromising and could only have been read as a public admission that some kind of covert intervention in Chile had occurred, as would an attempt by Helms to seek protection of the Fifth Amendment.

By the process of elimination, I believe the fair-minded observer is driven to the conclusion that Helms had no choice but to behave as he did. By endangering himself through evasive testimony, he chose the only course that could protect the secrecy imposed by the President and avoid the serious damage that full disclosure at that time would have caused. In a guest column in the *Washington Star* shortly after the sentencing, Eugene McCarthy summed up the dilemma in which Helms was placed by Nixon's Track II. The following paragraph is worth quoting:

> The Chilean operation was unconstitutional or bordering on the unconstitutional. It involved a major change in national policy without constitutional support from the Congress, either explicit through treaty or statutory action, or implicit by knowing acquiescence on the part of the Congress. It was not Helms's responsibility to make these distinctions. Helms properly denied that his agency was participating in efforts to overthrow the Allende government. He could not have taken the Fifth and he could not have refused to answer without prejudicing the secrecy of the action.[38]

If the trap for Helms was set by Nixon in imposing unique secrecy on his Track II decision, it was sprung by William Colby, who succeeded Schlesinger as CIA director. In his memoirs, Colby gives his explanation of the sequence of events and mixture of motivations that led him in April 1974 to reveal the existence of Track II to Congressman Lucien Nedzi (D., Mich.), who was then chairman of the intelligence subcommittee of the House Armed Services Committee. Colby describes how a small group of middle-grade officers in the CIA became convinced that Helms might have committed perjury in his congressional testimony on Chile, and how they persuaded him to submit the whole secret record of Track II to then Acting Attorney General Laurence Silberman in December 1974 for review.[39] After his decision to brief Nedzi on Track II, Colby writes that "I felt good about my conscience and my loyalty to the constitutional role of Congress, but I recognized a dilemma in that I had violated a direct and, when he gave it, legal order of my boss, the President." He praises the middle-grade officers who pressured him into submitting the Track II record to the Justice Department, writing: "And I am glad they did, requiring me to uphold my oath to the Constitution and really demonstrate that a new and American intelligence had been born, not just talked about."

It is probably true that in our open society, and in the aftermath of Watergate, somebody else eventually would have disclosed the facts of Track II if Colby had not started the process that resulted in the full publication of the whole episode in the Church committee report and in the legal proceedings against Helms. I don't doubt that Colby's private conscience was a powerful force nor do I question his loyalty to the Constitution; it is his interpretation of that document that I question. There is nowhere in the Constitution any reference to the role and function of a secret intelligence agency. In the absence of constitutional definition, Colby's responsibilities were clearly defined by statute in the National Security Act of 1947, and under its terms he was responsible to the National Security Council and to the President. Before taking it upon himself to determine what the Constitution required, he was obligated to raise the issue in the National Security Council and to give the President a chance to consider the available options in view of the importance and consequences of the decision.

President Ford might well have decided that there was no choice but to submit the Track II record to the Justice Department for determination as to whether Helms had committed perjury, but the decision was taken out of his hands by Colby's personal decision to brief Nedzi and Silberman. By presuming to be the judge of what the Constitution required and by appealing above the law to the dictates of his private conscience, Colby set a precedent as director of the CIA that was bound to cause widening trouble for the Agency in the future.

Chapter 10

The Family Jewels

JUST AS THE REVERBERATIONS in England from the Chilean revelations were beginning to die down and I was beginning again to enjoy life in London, the long fuse attached to the buried family jewels collected under Schlesinger's directive burned to its end. The first news story by Seymour Hersh exploded under banner headlines in *The New York Times* on December 22, 1974, charging in its first paragraph: "The CIA, directly violating its charter, conducted a massive illegal domestic intelligence operation during the Nixon Administration against the anti-war movement and other dissident groups in the United States, according to well-placed Government sources." The British press picked up the story immediately, and the headlines blazed with allegations that the Agency under Nixon had been used as a domestic Gestapo against those who were protesting American involvement in Vietnam. Although I had never been given access to the full report on the family jewels that Colby had collected, my first reaction was one of astonishment that so misleading a story could be published by a responsible newspaper. I could remember no such "massive illegal" operation directed against domestic dissidents and felt sure that if one had been going on I would have heard about it. I waited confidently for a strong public denial by a top U.S.

201

official but instead, a few days later, I received an additional shock when the news broke that an old friend, James Angleton, had been fired from his job in CIA as chief of the Counterintelligence Staff.

The timing of Angleton's forced resignation had the inevitable effect of seeming to confirm the allegations in the *Times* story and to imply that Angleton had been fired for his part in the affair. For the first time during all the publicity that had washed over the Agency in London, British officials were genuinely concerned by this sequence of events, and began asking me insistent questions in an attempt to understand what was actually going on in Washington. They had worked closely with Angleton over the years in the counterintelligence field in trying to cope with the continuous recruitment of agents by the KGB. Although they differed with him on occasion, they had a high regard for his ability and particularly remembered how helpful he had been to them in the past when they were recovering from the damage done by the KGB penetrations of their own services through Philby and Blake. At a time when elements in the American intelligence community were maintaining that the British were so hopelessly penetrated by the Soviets that liaison with them should be cut to a minimum, Angleton had argued for continuing British-American cooperation on the ground that the British had contained the damage caused by Philby and Blake, and put their house in order by instituting effective security controls. For this past help in a time of trouble, the British were grateful to Angleton, and were naturally concerned as to what effect his public firing might have on counterintelligence efforts against the KGB.

While trying to handle these expressions of official concern as reassuringly as possible, I was suddenly confronted with another revelation in Washington whose repercussions in Britain showed how charged with suspicion the atmosphere had become. The existence of a confidential letter from the CIA to private firms in the United States was revealed in the American press. The letter proposed a research study into the technological advances being made by foreign countries in the field of transportation, and Britain was included on the list.[1] This story led to a flurry of headlines in the London press charging that CIA agents were busily spying on the London subway system. It did not take long to explain to British authorities that the proposed contract called only for technical research to be done within the United States, and that no espionage activity in Britain or anywhere else was involved. However, the incident was enough to stimulate calls in Parliament for an investigation of the CIA presence in England, and a small group of left-wing MPs demanded my removal from the country. Again, it was evident that publicity regarding the Agency could not be confined to the American audience but was beginning to have a corrosive effect abroad.

Fast-breaking events in Washington during January of 1975 made it certain that the storm of publicity swirling around the Agency's controversial role would rise to hurricane force before it could be expected to subside. On January 6, President Ford tried to quiet the protests that *The New York Times'* allegations regarding domestic spying had stimulated. He announced the formation of a special presidential commission headed by Vice President Nelson Rockefeller to conduct a broad inquiry to determine whether any domestic CIA activities had exceeded the Agency's statutory authority and to submit a public report on its findings and recommendations. The conservative character of the membership of the commission led to charges that its report would be a whitewash, and on January 21 the Senate voted to establish its own investigating committee, the Select Committee to Study Governmental Operations with Respect to Intelligence Activities, with Senator Frank Church of Idaho as chairman. Its mandate was much broader than that of the Rockefeller Commission, and it undertook to investigate all the past and current intelligence activities of the United States and to make recommendations for reform. Not to be outdone, the House of Representatives subsequently voted to establish its own Select Committee on Intelligence, with Otis Pike of New York as chairman.

This proliferation of investigating bodies with overlapping jurisdictions, large staffs, and extensive authority to demand access to documents and to compel witnesses to testify raised serious questions of security in the minds of all foreign intelligence officials who had previously cooperated with the CIA in the exchange of information. The British were understandably anxious to have reassurances that the content and sourcing of whatever reports we received from them would be given iron-clad protection against deliberate leakage or inadvertent revelation in the course of the investigation. Theirs was a completely justified concern. The survival of important sources of information could be endangered by a minor slip, and the KGB would be following the course of the investigations with a scavenging eye for just such revealing detail. Therefore, I welcomed a chance to return to Washington in February 1975 for a brief visit to reassure myself on this point, and to find out what substance there was to *The New York Times'* allegations and how they had surfaced. In a conversation with an ex-reporter of *The New York Times* who was serving as an aide to Ambassador Elliot Richardson in London, I had been told that *The New York Times* had decided to run the story under bold headlines only after its accuracy had been confirmed to Seymour Hersh by CIA Director Colby. Such an action seemed incredible to me, but I was anxious to find out what lay behind so disturbing a rumor.

In my meeting with Colby in the spacious director's office in Langley, he was quick to reassure me that every precaution would be taken to protect any sensitive information supplied us by the British and that they could rest assured that their intelligence sources would not be exposed in the course of the investigations. Taking a firm and unyielding stance, Colby subsequently proved his ability to hold the line on the need to protect information received from friendly foreign intelligence services, and throughout the whole period of the investigations I do not believe any foreign liaison source was compromised. Colby needed no encouragement from me to understand the vital national interest that was at stake in protecting the legitimate secrets of our allies, and the congressional committees eventually proved cooperative in agreeing to ground rules that severely limited their access to this type of information.

I then raised with Colby the subject of Angleton's forced resignation. I did not question his right as director to fire Angleton if he was dissatisfied with his performance, as I gathered he was, but I pointed out that the timing could not have been worse. Coming as it did hard on the heels of the Hersh story, it served only to confirm the veracity of the allegations and put the onus for whatever wrongdoing there might have been squarely on Angleton's shoulders. I suggested that if he felt he had to fire Angleton, he should have allowed a decent interval to elapse so as to avoid the direct connection in the public mind between the two events. Agency morale had held up remarkably well under public battering, but this had largely been the result of a sense of institutional loyalty and a conviction that superiors would support their subordinates if they had acted within the proper scope of their authority. Once the belief became widespread that individuals down the line could be sacrificed as scapegoats, it seemed to me that it would become much more difficult to hold the Agency together as a functioning entity in a time of troubles. Colby maintained that he was correct in removing Angleton from his position, but admitted that the Hersh story had received far more publicity than he had expected and that the timing had been unfortunate.

In leaving, I urged Colby to play a more active part in defending the Agency's role and past record, and he explained that his main problem was to maintain his credibility with the Congress and to convince the committees that he was not covering up by holding back information to which they could claim legitimate access. At this meeting, I did not question Colby regarding his role in confirming the Hersh story since I did not wish to raise so serious a matter on the basis of the rumor that I had picked up in London.

Since that time the firing of Angleton and Colby's role in the surfacing of the Hersh story have become something of a cause célèbre, and complicated conspiratorial theories have been woven around the sequence of events. Colby has published his version in his memoirs, and Edward Jay Epstein, among others, has offered his explanation in a widely publicized article in *Commentary*.[2] The chronology of what transpired is not in dispute and both Colby and Epstein agree on the following sequence:[3]

December 17, 1974: Colby informs Angleton that he is relieving him of his two principal duties, his function as chief of the Counterintelligence Staff and his responsibility for liaison with Israeli intelligence. He gives Angleton the option of remaining in the Agency in a consultant capacity or of retiring before the end of the year in order to take advantage of extra retirement benefits that expire on December 31. Angleton argues against this decision, and Colby gives him two days to reconsider.

December 18: Seymour Hersh, a reporter for *The New York Times* who had previously won the Pulitzer Prize for his story on the My-Lai massacre in Vietnam, calls Colby to state that he has an explosive story on illegal domestic CIA activity and asks for an interview. Colby invites him to a meeting in his office in Washington two days later and alerts the White House to potential trouble.

December 20: Colby meets with Hersh and in the interview tries to persuade the reporter that he has an exaggerated and distorted version of events. In trying to put the story in perspective, he admits to past improper domestic surveillance activity but claims that it was not extensive and that it has been terminated.

After the Hersh interview and on the same day, Colby informs Angleton of his conversation with Hersh but insists that he must retire or take the consultant job. Angleton agrees to retire.

December 22: *The New York Times* publishes the Hersh story.

December 23: Angleton's retirement is announced within the Agency and the news quickly leaks to the press.

Although both Colby and Epstein agree on this factual chronology, they put forward widely differing explanations of the motivations that were at work. Colby claims that he did not deliberately leak the family jewels to Hersh but rather tried, by admitting some facts, to convince Hersh that the charge of massive illegal domestic activity was not justified. Colby maintains that some version of the story was bound to be published in any event and that he gave Hersh no material that he did not already have. Colby explains that he trusted Hersh because of his responsible behavior in a previous incident, but admits that in volunteering information he completely failed in his attempt to persuade Hersh to drop his exaggerated allegations.

Epstein, on the other hand, maintains that in admitting to Hersh the accuracy of some of the details in his story, Colby gave the editors of *The New York Times* indispensable and clinching confirmation. They needed this from the highest-placed official source to give them the confidence to run the story on the front page under blazing headlines. My information obtained in London bears out Epstein's supposition that Colby's admissions played a key role in *The New York Times'* editorial decision to give the story maximum prominence. As Epstein puts it in a letter to *Commentary*, "Even in the case of public officials dealing with journalists, it is epistemologically impossible to determine what a journalist actually knows to be true as distinguished from what he merely suspects might be true. Journalistic knowledge is as much a product of confirmation as it is of revelation; in this very real sense, Mr. Colby gave Hersh the story by confirming it."[4]

Moreover, as Colby concedes in his memoirs, at the time of his admissions to Hersh he had not yet submitted his top secret report on the family jewels to President Ford or to Henry Kissinger, and they did not even know then of its existence.[5] In effect, by agreeing to meet with Hersh on December 20 and by confirming essential aspects of his story, Colby made a personal decision to go public with the most sensitive kind of information and again substituted his own judgment for that of the President on a matter deeply affecting the national security. In attempting to explain this extraordinary preemption of the President's prerogatives, Epstein resorts to a dark conspiratorial theory and accuses Colby of having seized upon the opportunity presented by Hersh's investigative reporting as a way of destroying Angleton's reputation and of ensuring that his decision to fire Angleton would not be challenged.

Epstein believes that Colby's bureaucratic purpose was to accomplish Angleton's resignation in order to restructure the Counterintelligence Staff and to make it more responsive to his own conviction that under Angleton's management it had been excessively suspicious of Agency recruitments of Soviet agents. There is no doubt that Colby was convinced, as he explains in his memoirs, that Angleton had a paranoid suspicion that many Soviet defectors and Russians recruited by the Agency were double agents working for the KGB, and he felt this suspicion had become a real obstacle to the improvement of intelligence collection against the Soviet target. Whether he was right or not in this judgment is an open question that will be settled over the passage of time by the performance of agents recruited under Colby's more permissive and optimistic approach to the problem of establishing the reliability of recruitments. However, I find it hard to believe that Colby would deliberately cause such damage to the Agency as his confirmation of the Hersh story entailed simply to achieve this internal bureaucratic objective or to settle a personal score.

More likely, I think, is that Colby was guilty of no more than atrociously bad judgment and appalling naiveté in believing that he could succeed in changing the whole thrust of Hersh's story by confirming those parts of it he knew to be true. He should have known that he had no business meeting with Hersh to confirm any part of his story before the whole problem had been raised with the President and with Kissinger for a considered decision on what strategy to pursue. In his meeting with Angleton on December 20, Colby assured him, according to Angleton's account to Seymour Hersh, that the story should not affect his decision to resign since it will "all blow over in two or three days."[6] Relying on this assurance, Angleton finally decided to resign quietly instead of appealing the decision up the line to the National Security Council and the congressional oversight committees. In my opinion, Colby really believed that he had succeeded in drawing the teeth of the Hersh story when he gave these totally misleading assurances to Angleton, and did not foresee the months of personal anguish for Angleton and disaster for the Agency that were inevitably to follow. Moreover, there is some evidence that both men suffered under the illusion that the fact of Angleton's resignation could be kept secret.

There is one aspect of this strange incident that is difficult to fit into the theory that Colby was very foolish but not a knave. Why, one asks oneself, did not Colby go to Angleton as soon as the *Times* story hit the newsstands on December 22 and ask him to withdraw his resignation for a six-month period? Through this obvious move to protect the Agency, Colby could have avoided the confirmation of the Hersh story that Angleton's simultaneous resignation seemed to provide, and also have spared Angleton his role as scapegoat. Rather than accept Epstein's theory of malevolent intention on Colby's part, I prefer to believe that Colby was motivated on this point by a stubborn determination to go through with a decision once it had been made, and did not have the flexibility of mind to see that a temporary retreat was to the advantage of all concerned, including himself.

The role of the editors of *The New York Times* in this affair deserves some comment. It is true that they had received confirmation from Colby of the accuracy of some of the charges in Hersh's story, but they also had Colby's statement that no "massive illegal" surveillance of American citizens had taken place and his assurance that many of the more lurid details in the story were either false or exaggerated. In the lengthy text of his December 22 article, Hersh makes indirect reference to his conversation with Colby by attributing to "high-ranking American intelligence officials" a warning "against drawing unwarranted conclusions." But this cautionary advice was buried on p. 26, while the opening paragraph on p. 1 attributed to "well-placed Government sources" the damning admission that the Agency had in fact been guilty of "a massive illegal intelligence operation" against the antiwar movement.

Inevitably, it was this lead paragraph and the headlines that went with it that received major replay around the world. It was this flat statement of fact, backed by the reputation for accuracy of *The New York Times,* that convinced large sections of the American public that the CIA had become a domestic Gestapo and stimulated an overwhelming demand for the wide-ranging congressional investigations that were to follow. Whether the editors of *The New York Times* were justified in playing the Hersh story in such a way as to generate among the general public emotional fear of an incipient police state run by the CIA will be long debated. Critics of the *Times* charge that these allegations were either wildly exaggerated or plainly false. The *Times,* they believe, succumbed to a temptation to exploit a sensational story beyond the limits of accuracy in its attempt to rival the *Washington Post* by exposing a public scandal on the scale of Watergate. Defenders of the *Times* maintain that the subsequent record revealed by the congressional investigations more than justified the sensational initial coverage. The fair-minded observer will want to review that official record and decide for himself.

Based on the extensive evidence that is now available, my own view is that the domestic surveillance activity involving antiwar activists conducted by the Agency was neither massive in scope nor clearly illegal at the time that it was undertaken. On the issue of legality, the most conclusive proof is the fact that after the smoke had cleared from the battlefields of the congressional investigations, the Justice Department reviewed all the testimony in an effort to identify criminal behavior and to prosecute those guilty of illegal acts. No such prosecutions were brought against any Agency employee in connection with domestic surveillance. (The Helms case raised entirely different issues, as we have seen.) This refusal to prosecute by the Department of Justice was not motivated by a desire to spare the Agency further embarrassment. In fact, young Department of Justice lawyers were very anxious to prove the impartiality and objectivity of the American system of criminal justice by bringing cases to trial, if any could be found that would stand up in court. In the case of the FBI, the Justice lawyers did find what they considered to be evidence of criminal behavior and as a result three top officials of the bureau were indicted. The assumption must be that CIA officials were not similarly prosecuted because there was insufficient evidence of clearly illegal activity.

The complexity of the factual situation that Hersh as an investigative reporter was trying to unravel is an indication of how difficult it must have been for an outsider to understand what had actually transpired. In trying to make a coherent story out of the leaked descriptions of the family jewels that he was receiving from various sources, Hersh confused and lumped together three separate activities which he construed as a single operational program directed against the antiwar movement.

In the first place, there was the CIA mail-opening project, which involved the secret opening in the United States of first-class letters to and from Communist countries. This project was initiated in 1953 by the Agency as a counterintelligence measure to identify the extent to which the Soviets were using the mails to communicate with their agents in this country and to intercept such communications. In its inception, it obviously had nothing to do with the antiwar movement, which sprang up some fifteen years later. However, the project did continue until its termination in 1973, and in the latter years information from the mail opening that revealed connections between antiwar activists and correspondents in Communist countries was collected and disseminated. Both the Rockefeller Commission and the Church committee found this activity clearly illegal. All the evidence they had collected was submitted to the Department of Justice, which was directed by President Ford "to take whatever prosecutorial action it found warranted."[7]

The Justice Department conducted a much more thorough review of all the available evidence and of the complex legal issues than the Rockefeller Commission or the Church committee had had time for. On January 14, 1977, the department issued its report to the press. As we have seen, the Justice lawyers stated that they would not prosecute any CIA officials for their part in the mail opening because they had concluded that it was unlikely that convictions could be obtained. Citing new evidence obtained from high-ranking officials and the records of the President's Foreign Intelligence Advisory Board, the Justice Department concluded there were persuasive indications that President Eisenhower had known of and approved the initiation of the mail-opening program and that his successors had also been informed of its existence.[8] As the Justice Department's report put it, "In light of such evidence, the Department almost certainly would encounter the gravest difficulties in proving guilt beyond a reasonable doubt."[9] As the law and court interpretations stood at the time the mail opening was conducted, Justice lawyers concluded that such presidential authorization on national security grounds would have been an effective defense for any CIA official brought to trial. However, the Justice Department was also careful to point out that changes in law and court interpretation would make such mail openings unlawful if undertaken today. It is unfortunate but perhaps inevitable that these sober conclusions of the Department of Justice were given nothing approaching the sensational press coverage that the original allegations received. Innocence is much less newsworthy than guilt.

A separate and completely distinct range of activity that Hersh stumbled on in his search for the family jewels was the program undertaken by the CIA Office of Security over the years to protect the Agency against espionage penetrations, leaks of classified information, and physical threats to Agency property. The National Security Act of 1947 placed upon the Director of Central Intelligence the heavy responsibility for "protecting intelligence sources and methods from unauthorized disclosures." In attempting to carry out this legal mandate, successive DCIs authorized continuing security checks within the United States of prospective employees, occasional surveillance of employees or ex-employees suspected of espionage, and, in a few cases, surveillance of American newsmen who were believed to be receiving highly classified information from unidentified sources within the Agency. In the pursuit of this objective, electronic surveillance and surreptitious entry were infrequently employed against individuals in a limited number of incidents, sometimes with the specific authorization of the attorney general and sometimes relying on the broad mandate of the National Security Act.

None of these defensive counterintelligence activities was directed against the antiwar movement until, in 1967, the scale and violence of the protests in the Washington area raised genuine fears of physical assault on Agency facilities and property. A few members of the black community in Washington were recruited by the Office of Security on a part-time basis to attend and report on meetings of black activist groups in order to provide early warning of violent demonstrations against Agency facilities. Coordinated with the Washington Metropolitan Police Department, this defensive activity was terminated in 1968 when the police had developed their own informants and felt competent to provide adequate protection.

As the Church committee was later to point out, "these programs illustrated fundamental weaknesses and contradictions in the statutory definition of CIA authority in the 1947 Act. While the Director of Central Intelligence is charged with responsibility to protect intelligence sources and methods, the CIA is forbidden from exercising law enforcement and police powers and 'internal security functions.' "[10] In view of this basic ambiguity, the Church committee did not condemn this range of activity as unlawful but was critical of the Agency for not having gone to Congress promptly for clarification and for not having consulted the attorney general more frequently for advice. Since that time, new procedures and regulations have drawn a much clearer line as to where the Agency's internal security responsibilities end. In my opinion, the Agency is well out of the business of attempting to identify leaks by conducting surveillance of journalists or to protect its facilities by penetrating private organizations. Under strict new guidelines, the FBI now clearly has exclusive jurisdiction over such domestic counterintelligence activity.

Finally, in his attempt to identify the family jewels, Seymour Hersh uncovered evidence that led him to charge in the second paragraph of his *New York Times* story that the Agency had maintained "intelligence files on at least 10,000 American citizens," adding fuel to the suspicion that the CIA had become a domestic Gestapo. In fact, what Hersh had discovered was one facet of an operational program that was completely distinct and separate in its legal authorization from the mail-opening project and the domestic counterintelligence activity previously described. The history and full details of this program have since been spelled out at length in both the Rockefeller Commission Report[11] and in the report of the Church committee.[12] What they found was that President Johnson and President Nixon had both suspected that the antiwar movement in the United States was receiving guidance and support from Communist groups abroad. Both Presidents brought heavy pressure to bear on CIA Director Helms to discover and document what they suspected to be true. Since the identification of such Communist activity abroad was a legal responsibility of the CIA, Helms had no choice but to respond to presidential directives by attempting to trace whatever connections might exist between American dissidents traveling abroad and foreign Communist parties and front groups.

This program had its inception in the racial disorders of 1967, which led President Johnson to establish in July of that year the National Commission on Civil Disorders (the Kerner Commission) to look into the causes of the riots. The Agency was directed to report to this commission on any foreign connection these disorders might have had. Responding to White House instructions, Helms ordered Karamessines to direct the Counterintelligence Staff to coordinate coverage of possible foreign involvement. At the time, I helped to handle liaison with the Kerner Commission staff, and I remember thinking that it was quite understandable that the President should suspect some Communist involvement in our domestic disorders, since this dramatic evidence of division within American society was being exploited worldwide by Soviet propaganda. However, when we reported that we could find no evidence of foreign funding and control, Lyndon Johnson's reaction was to believe that we lacked adequate sources and to feel that if we dug deep enough we would find proof that his suspicions were justified.[13]

As a result of this continuous pressure from the White House, a Special Operations Group was set up within the Counterintelligence Staff, and it cabled all CIA field stations abroad for any information on Communist connections. The replies were collected and cross-indexed in a central file, which was the beginning of the files that Hersh was later to publicize. In this effort, there was an unavoidable overlap between the domestic jurisdiction of the FBI and the foreign intelligence function of the CIA. Without detailed and specific information on the antiwar groups in the United States, it would have been impossible to alert CIA field stations abroad to the foreign travel of their members and to trace their foreign contacts. A cooperative arrangement was worked out with the bureau whereby such information was exchanged and the files inevitably grew. Without this informational base, the Agency could not have carried out the presidentially assigned task that was clearly within its statutory responsibility for counterintelligence protection abroad.

In July of 1968, the collection program of the Special Operations Group was given a cryptonym in order to limit and control the distribution of cable traffic referring to the foreign activities of domestic dissidents. All reports on this subject were restricted to a single channel and delivered on an "eyes only" basis to the chief of the Special Operations Group. The purpose of these security measures was twofold. The conduct of this operation obviously skirted the edge of involving the Agency in internal security matters and could easily be misrepresented if given publicity. Secondly, there was a commendable determination to protect the reputations of American citizens whose names might turn up in these files. However, the cryptonym chosen for this program from the top of an existing list could not have been more unfortunate in its connotations, and gave a completely misleading impression of the purpose of the operation and its need for secrecy. "Chaos" was the chance cryptonym that resulted, and when later publicized it seemed to confirm the allegation that the objective of the whole program was to harass and spread deliberate confusion among American citizens engaged in exercising their constitutional rights. Both the Church committee and the Rockefeller Commission found no evidence of any use by the CIA of its information for such harassment purposes, although the same cannot be said of the FBI. Nevertheless, "Operation Chaos" became the symbol and proof for many of the danger the CIA posed as the instrument of an incipient police state, and almost any other word would have been preferable as an indicator to control the cable traffic.

On coming to office, Richard Nixon proved to be even more convinced than Lyndon Johnson that Communist money and direction lay behind the domestic antiwar movement, and the failure of the Agency to document these suspicions was taken as proof of inadequate effort and insufficient agent penetrations. Responding to these demands from the White House for improved collection, Helms issued a directive on September 6, 1969, reaffirming the importance of the work of the Special Operations Group and calling for all elements in the Agency to cooperate with it "both in exploiting existing sources and in developing new ones."[14] Helms took care to state in this instruction that he recognized the fine line that had to be respected in this activity in order to avoid overstepping the boundaries of the Agency's legal authority, and he made it clear that he expected operational officers to continue "strictly observing the statutory and de facto proscriptions on Agency domestic involvements."

This directive was not only a response to presidential concern that the Agency's coverage of the foreign connections of the antiwar movement was inadequate, but it was also designed to quiet the doubts and reservations that had arisen within the Agency about the program. In headquarters, there were fears that we were edging dangerously close to forbidden territory, as Colby makes clear in his memoirs.[15] In the field, there was opposition to the waste of time and use of foreign liaison equities on a peripheral target, and growing conviction that no matter how thorough the search it would not be possible to uncover the conclusive evidence of Communist funding and control that Nixon anxiously awaited. Nevertheless, Helms was correct in his judgment that the foreign dimension of domestic dissent was clearly within the Agency's jurisdiction and that there was no choice but to trace down every lead.

I had only a marginal knowledge of the specific activities undertaken by the Special Operations Group within the Counterintelligence Staff in response to Helms's directive to find new sources. The project was highly compartmented and did not come before me for review for security reasons. However, both the Rockefeller Commission and the Church committee subsequently had complete access to the records, and their findings coincide and must be regarded as conclusive in the absence of any new evidence. What they show is that the Special Operations Group from October 1969 to July 1972 recruited twenty-five American citizens who were active in the antiwar movement as agents. They were directed to travel abroad with their left-wing credentials in an attempt to identify Communist funding and control channels. Eighteen of these agents were FBI informants who were referred to the Agency by the bureau and who were prepared to undertake the necessary foreign travel. They were given detailed instructions on what information to look for and were debriefed on their return by the Special Operations Group. Similarly, seven American citizens were recruited independently by the Special Operations Group because of their involvement in the radical left and their willingness to use their established reputations as American activists to gain access abroad to suspected Communist links. The information obtained from these agents was collected in the computerized files of the Special Operations Group and disseminated to the FBI. If the operation had been confined to this activity, there would have been no grounds on which to criticize the

Agency. Under then existing laws and regulations, there was no bar to such recruitment of American citizens for espionage abroad, and it could reasonably be argued that only individuals with a history of association with the antiwar movement could possibly hope to penetrate whatever Communist control and funding channels might exist in foreign countries. In fact, however, as both the Rockefeller Commission and the Church committee point out, three of these recruited agents were instructed by their Agency case officer to travel within the United States and to participate in and report on antiwar demonstrations and planning meetings. This purely domestic espionage activity resulted in the dissemination of intelligence reports to the FBI. In these three cases, the Special Operations Group clearly exceeded its instructions and stepped over the sensitive but fundamental boundary line that Helms attempted to define in his directive.

Helms later testified that he was not aware of these three intrusions into forbidden domestic territory, and certainly I myself had no knowledge of them until I read about them in the reports of the Rockefeller Commission and the Church committee. I do not underestimate the seriousness of this brief and unauthorized adventure into spying on the domestic political activity of American citizens by an Agency that had no legal mandate to engage in such activity. The history of police states indicates that small infringements on the rights of citizens can grow into massive invasions of privacy by huge bureaucratic machines, and the time to protest is when the first such infringement occurs no matter how minor it may appear to be. However, the reader must judge whether these three instances, standing alone as they do, were enough to justify the charge that the CIA conducted "a massive illegal domestic intelligence operation."

Shortly after my return to London from the visit to Washington in early February 1975, the last time bomb hidden among the family jewels exploded. Its effect was made more devastating by the fact that neither I nor 99 percent of all Agency employees had any prior knowledge of its existence. On February 28, on the CBS Evening News, Daniel Schorr stated that President Ford had "reportedly warned associates that if current investigations go too far they could uncover several assassinations of foreign officials involving the CIA." As Colby describes in his memoirs, this allegation was the result of an off-the-record admission by the President in a meeting with editors of *The New York Times* in January. In attempting to justify his selection of the conservative membership of the Rockefeller Commission, Ford cited the need for tight security since otherwise problems "like assassination" might be revealed. When a version of this story was leaked to Schorr, he confronted Colby on February 27 with the President's admission. What happened next has since been described by both Colby and Schorr, and their accounts coincide.[16] Schorr asked Colby, "Has the CIA ever killed anybody in this country?" Colby replied, "Not in this country," and went on to explain that such methods had been banned since 1973. As Colby admits, this evasive reply only confirmed for Schorr the suspicion that assassinations had occurred in foreign countries and compounded the damage caused by Ford's original indiscretion. As Schorr describes his reactions, "It struck me the next day that while I was lacking the names of victims (I still assumed there were some), I nevertheless knew a great deal." On the basis of Colby's confirmation, CBS management gave Schorr a two-minute spot on Walter Cronkite's national news show, which he used to make the charge quoted above.

Once the accusation that an agency of the U.S. government had conducted assassinations abroad was on the public record, a full-scale investigation was inevitable. All the documents and records relating to possible assassination attempts were turned over to the Rockefeller Commission. Unable to complete its investigation within the time frame of its mandate, the commission was directed by the White House to transfer these records to the Church committee. After an exhaustive six-month inquiry, the committee released its findings to the public in November 1975 in the form of an interim report.[17]

The committee's conclusion that the CIA had not actually participated in the successful assassination of any foreign leader was small consolation to the American public or to myself and the vast majority of CIA officers. After finding the Agency not guilty of planning the killing of Diem in Vietnam, of General Schneider in Chile, or of Trujillo in the Dominican Republic, the Church committee produced convincing evidence in the form of operational cable traffic, official memoranda, and personal testimony that proved that CIA officials had planned assassination attempts against Patrice Lumumba in the Congo in 1960 and against Fidel Castro in Cuba between 1960 and 1965. In the case of Lumumba, poisons were shipped from CIA headquarters to the CIA station chief in the Congo with instructions to eliminate the African leader. The plot was never carried out, and the Church committee found no Agency involvement in Lumumba's subsequent death at the hands of tribal opponents.[18] In the case of Castro, a series of Agency plots obviously failed in their purpose, but not before certain CIA officials had committed the monumental folly of attempting to involve the Mafia in the attempt to do away with the Cuban leader.

Knowing the institutional discipline that prevailed within the Agency at that time, and on the basis of my own acquaintance with men like Allen Dulles and Richard Helms, I find it very difficult to believe that these plots were undertaken without presidential knowledge and authorization. Indeed in the Lumumba case, the Church committee reached the conclusion that the evidence was "strong enough to permit a reasonable inference that the plot to assassinate Lumumba was authorized by President Eisenhower."[19] In the Castro case, the committee was more evasive in concluding: "There was insufficient evidence from which the Committee could conclude that Presidents Eisenhower, Kennedy or Johnson, their close advisors, or the Special Group authorized the assassination of Castro."[20] In all my years in the Agency I never heard assassination plotting seriously discussed. It had no part in any of the training courses and played no role in the operational doctrine of the clandestine service. It was one of the things that we accepted as routine in the behavior of the KGB but ruled out for ourselves as beyond the pale for an American intelligence agency. These two cases were unique in the history of the Agency (as the Church committee demonstrated). So drastic a departure from previous practice would not have been undertaken in my opinion unless there had been strong pressure and specific direction from the White House. However, I cannot prove it and can understand why some of the top Agency officials may have been less than forthcoming in their testimony before the Church committee in an effort to protect the presidency.

However, even if there was specific presidential direction in these two cases, I do not myself believe that the Agency leadership should have agreed to carry out such orders. As the Church committee report makes clear, one of the senior CIA operational officers approached to take part in the planning for Lumumba's death flatly refused to participate on moral grounds.[21] His example should have been followed by the Agency hierarchy from top to bottom, and such adamant refusal to become involved in assassination would have quickly discouraged whatever pressures were being brought to bear. This was one issue on which resignation was preferable to disciplined obedience.

Political assassination in time of peace is one weapon that has no place in the American arsenal. It is morally indefensible and goes against the American grain. There are pragmatic reasons as well. In our open society it is impossible to believe that such an act could be kept secret indefinitely by even the most stringent security precautions, and the eventual publicity would more than cancel out whatever temporary tactical advantage the elimination of a political opponent might seem to offer. Moreover, the historical consequences of political assassination are incalculable, and there is no guarantee that the removal of one foreign leader would not result in the succession to power of individuals even more hostile and difficult to cope with. The one satisfaction to be derived from the surfacing of this wretched business is the assurance that future Presidents and Directors of Central Intelligence will never again be tempted to see in political assassination a shortcut to the solution of foreign policy dilemmas. Agency participation in these abortive assassination attempts and the subsequently revealed testing of drugs on unwitting subjects are examples of two activities that merit unreserved condemnation and for which I can find no excuse or adequate explanation.

The reputation of the Agency in Great Britain was not improved by the publication of the Church committee's findings on assassinations, and for a few days the details made lurid reading in the London press. I could only find myself in full agreement with the closing paragraph of a sober editorial on the subject that appeared in *The Times:*

> But American interests do not depend only on nuclear weapons and friendly governments or client states. They depend also on the ability of the United States to convince people that it represents certain values and principles and ways of life that are worth defending. If it uses the same methods as the KGB, it will come to be regarded in the same light. Obviously it cannot

always appear as a knight in shining armour, and moral postur-
ing in the wrong context can sometimes be as damaging as
immorality, but if American power is to survive in the world
Americans must think as much of what they are defending as
of the means of defence.[22]

Even as this publicity began to die down, I was forcibly reminded
just before Christmas 1975 that the unilateral American renuncia-
tion of assassination as a political weapon was no guarantee against
its use by our opponents on the world stage. On Christmas Eve I
received a cable from Washington with the sad news that an old
acquaintance, Richard Welch, the CIA station chief in Greece, had
been assassinated by three unidentified terrorists as he was getting
out of his car in Athens. Welch's former wife and children were living
outside London, and I was instructed to inform them of what had
happened. I reached Welch's son, a Marine lieutenant, by phone and
was relieved to find that I did not have to be the first to deliver the
tragic news. The family had already been informed by others of the
murder, and I could only stammer my condolences and explain to
Welch's son in what high regard we had all held his father.

This untimely death brought home to me how exposed and vulnerable many CIA officers were in trouble spots around the world. The
diplomatic cover arrangements provided by the State Department
were often loosely structured and transparently incapable of withstanding any close scrutiny. The Agency itself had often neglected to
take the time and care necessary to make cover jobs a credible form
of protection. More serious, there were no effective legal sanctions
against the disclosure in the U.S. media of the identities of CIA
officers serving under cover overseas. Now that Welch's murder had
dramatized the dangers involved, I thought that the time was ripe
for reform; and two days after Christmas I sent a cable to Washington
suggesting that the Church committee might address itself in a practical way to these deficiencies by coming up with remedial legislation. Unfortunately, reform has been slow in coming, and at this
writing there still exists no legal penalty for the public revelation of
the identity of CIA officers serving abroad.

My own exposure in friendly London had been taken for granted
from the time of my original assignment because of previous publicity associating me with the Agency. However, after Welch's death,

an event occurred that heightened my fear of the danger of assassination and caused me to take added precautions. A Trotskyist publication in London, *Voice of the People,* carried in its January 1976 issue an interview with Philip Agee, the ex-CIA officer who had earned some notoriety in London by exposing the names of suspected CIA officers in England and in other countries. In this interview, Agee charged that the CIA station in London was working closely with British intelligence against the Irish Republican Army (IRA), and my photograph was prominently featured as the chief of station responsible for these activities. Agee went on to suggest that CIA bases in Dublin and in Belfast were working under my direction, in cooperation with the British, to recruit penetration agents within the ranks of the IRA and to monitor its communications by tapping phones and bugging offices. Agee concluded with the somber warning, "You can be sure that the CIA is at the very least monitoring the scene to determine the strength of the working class movement in Ireland so that when that strength reaches a certain point the decision would be made to intervene to try to weaken it."[23]

These allegations were completely false. There were no CIA bases in Dublin or Belfast and no CIA officers assigned to work there. In Great Britain, the terrorist threat posed by the extremist wing of the IRA was exclusively within the domestic jurisdiction of the British police and security services, and they neither sought nor needed assistance from my office in dealing with this internal problem. But the falsity of the allegations did not make them any less dangerous. The Irish terrorists had demonstrated their capacity to blow up restaurants and pubs and to conduct selective assassinations of British military and security officials. My wife and I had become familiar with the sound of exploding bombs that sometimes shook the windows of our house at night. What Agee had done by publishing false allegations in his interview was to single me out as a prime target for the terrorists. By describing me as a key figure in the security apparatus deployed against them, he gave these ruthless terrorists the motive and reason for seeking my elimination. Instead of living with a vague and generalized fear of terrorist action, I now had to accept the fact that my name must be high on the list of priority targets. My driver and I took even greater precautions in altering the routes we took driving to and from the embassy. But there was no way of changing the reality that I had to leave my house in the morning and return in the evening and that my address had been widely publicized. For a time, I felt very much like a sitting duck, and it was hard for me to forgive Agee, whom I had never met, for using false charges to put me so directly in the gun sights of the terrorists. Fortunately, no terrorist attack was attempted, but certainly he had done his best to provoke one.

Agee's true motivation remains shrouded in some mystery. Resigning from the Agency in 1968 after ten years of service in Latin America, he published his first book in England in early 1975 as a way of avoiding the prior review by the Agency required by his security oath. The book purported to be a diary of his work for the Agency in South America, and in it he described how he gradually came to see the CIA as an instrument of capitalist oppression and to sympathize with Castro's revolutionary Marxism. In order to render the Agency's work ineffective, he identified more than a hundred individuals in the book as CIA employees under cover, and using Britain as a base, he subsequently in press conferences and articles revealed the names of many additional officials whom he claimed were CIA officers serving in American embassies throughout the world. Except for his attempt to provoke the IRA against me, he was only a minor irritant during my stay in London and after a brief flurry of coverage in the responsible press he was for the most part able to promote publicity for his charges only in far left-wing publications with limited circulation.

After my departure from London in July of 1976, the British government must have had reason for thinking that he was something other than a sincere if eccentric idealist. In November of that year, British authorities served notice on Agee that he must leave the country, with the explanation that he "had maintained regular contacts harmful to the security of the United Kingdom with foreign intelligence officers." Agee appealed this decision to a three-man review board. After extensive hearings the expulsion order was reaffirmed, and Agee was forced to leave England in June 1977. Subsequently he sought refuge in France, from which he was also expelled, and then in Holland, which also deported him.

In July of 1976, my official three-year tour of duty in London came to its necessary end. With genuine regret, my wife and I said good-by to many friends and flew back to Washington. Looking back over what I have written about our stay in England, I realize that my concentration on the trials and tribulations that the Agency had to endure during this period gives a quite misleading impression of the tenor of our lives. Only a small proportion of my time was spent in trying to cope with the consequences of the publicity generated in Washington. My normal working day was filled with a busy and productive exchange with British authorities of information dealing with the major events occurring throughout the world. This cooperative sharing of significant intelligence was so obviously to the mutual advantage of both countries that the work retained its fascination for me throughout my stay. Short of being near the top of the government in Washington, I know of no vantage point that offers a wider and at the same time more specifically detailed view of the forces at work behind the scenes on the world stage than the job I was lucky enough to enjoy in London.

In addition to the intrinsic interest of the work itself, there was the attitude of British officials with whom it was my privilege to deal. If they had doubts occasionally whether the Agency would survive as an effective organization, they did not reveal them to me. Because of their fear that the rash of revelations in Washington might endanger their own sensitive sources, I did notice that their source descriptions became less specific and more opaque, but I do not believe they withheld any substantive information that was important to the common defense. They looked on the Agency as on a friend suffering from a severe but temporary illness, and did everything possible to assure me that they expected our recovery to be rapid and complete. Such supportive encouragement made it easy for me to get through even the worst days of disastrous publicity.

In fact, it is difficult for an American who has not served in one of our embassies in Western Europe to realize how deeply these democratic states feel encouraged by our successes and threatened by our failures. At least in my experience, anti-Americanism is only skin deep and confined to a narrow sector of the population. Basically, they see their fate indissolubly bound up with ours and none more so than Great Britain. As the most powerful of the world's democracies, the consistency of our purpose and the strength of our joint defenses are seen by the large majority of the British people as their best hope of preserving political liberty. His country having survived more wars than we have over the centuries, the average Englishman is perhaps more aware than his American counterpart that a secret foreign intelligence service plays an essential role in the capacity of even the most democratic nation to defend itself. I came to understand that the periodic demands for my expulsion by a small group of radical MPs in Parliament were completely unrepresentative of the true sentiments of the large majority. Throughout my stay in England, I was made to feel in my contacts both with officials and with private citizens that my presence was welcome and was seen as a contribution to the close alliance between our two countries.

Chapter 11

The Soviet Challenge

ON OUR RETURN TO WASHINGTON IN July of 1976, we moved back into our small house in Georgetown. I again seriously thought of retiring from the Agency but the new atmosphere in CIA's Langley headquarters changed my mind. George Bush had been appointed by President Ford to succeed Colby as DCI in January, and by the time of my return he had completely dispelled the fears that had been aroused by his former political connections. Having served in the Congress as a Republican representative from Texas and having recently been chairman of the Republican National Committee, he was initially viewed with suspicion as an ambitious politician who might try to use the Agency for partisan purposes. However, he quickly proved by his performance that he was prepared to put politics aside and to devote all his considerable ability and enthusiasm to restoring the morale of an institution that had been battered enough by successive investigations. Instead of reaching outside for defeated Republican candidates to fill key jobs, he chose from within the organization among men who had demonstrated their competence through long careers in intelligence work. He leaned over backward to protect the objectivity and independence of the Agency's estimates and to avoid slanting the results to fit some preconceived notion of what the President wanted to hear.

On the other hand, his close relationship to Ford and the trust that the President obviously had in him gave Bush an access to the White House and an influence in the wider Washington bureaucracy that Colby had never enjoyed. Not only did morale improve as a result, but through Bush the Agency's views carried new weight and influence in the top reaches of the Ford administration. In effect, I found on my return that the working environment at the Agency was far better than I had imagined it to be from my exposed position abroad and I determined to stay on for a period before retiring. Bush and "Hank" Knoche, the newly appointed deputy director, asked me to serve as a special assistant, and gave me as a first assignment the task of reviewing the entire structure of the intelligence community to determine the adequacy of the institutional arrangements for providing strategic warning against an attack on the United States and for handling major international crises. Some preliminary work had already been done by a working group representing all the Agency directorates and I took over the chairmanship from a senior officer who was being assigned overseas.

This was my first opportunity to get a bird's-eye view of the complex interplay between all the departments and agencies that make up the American intelligence community. Our job was to determine whether improvements could be made or gaps existed in the process by which the vast flow of incoming information was reported and analyzed in order to give the President the most important information of all, timely advance warning of impending crisis or military attack. At the same time, due to some dissatisfaction within the Ford administration with the handling of the *Mayaguez* affair, we undertook to look into the machinery for crisis management in order to ensure in the future that intelligence reports and estimates were given due weight by the policymakers at each stage in the unfolding of a major crisis.

As a result, I received an intensive education in many esoteric fields with which I had been before only vaguely familiar. Although I was fully acquainted with the whole process of clandestine collection from human sources, I had never been exposed previously to a detailed explanation of how our most sophisticated surveillance satellite systems worked or what their capabilities and limitations were. I was mightily impressed by the progress that had been made since the first U-2 lumbered through the skies over Russia. I was genuinely astonished at the marvelous ingenuity of the solutions that had emerged from the cooperation between the CIA, the most gifted American scientists, and the private corporations operating on the outermost edge of modern technology. Discoveries and technological breakthroughs in this field had led to the "national technical means of verification" that made possible the first SALT agreements with the Soviets. But they also, and perhaps more significantly, provided some new protection against the sudden and secret deployment of military forces in preparation for impending attack.

In reading the history and Agency-conducted postmortems of past international crises in a search for what might have gone wrong when intelligence failed to provide advance warning, I was struck by one common denominator running through the incidents in which the Agency performed inadequately. From the Soviet invasion of Czechoslovakia in 1968 to the Egyptian-Syrian attack on Israel in 1973, to the secret deployment of Cuban troops in Angola in 1975, there were in each case bits and pieces of information collected in advance that should have alerted the intelligence analysts and policymakers to what was coming. But to find these germs of wheat in the abundant chaff and to understand their significance in time to affect decision making was no easy job in the face of a preponderance of evidence pointing the other way. More important, these intelligence gems usually contradicted the prevailing optimistic assumptions of the policymakers concerning Soviet behavior, and these preconceptions were to some extent shared by the intelligence analysts. There was a persistent tendency to assume that our opponents on the world stage would act in a logical and rational manner, like Western statesmen, and intelligence that went against this prevailing preconception tended in some cases to be discounted. As a cure, some of us in the working group suggested the appointment of a senior worst-case advocate, whose job it would be to sit in on the policy level briefings in time of crisis and to argue his case persistently on the basis of all the available evidence like an official Socratic gadfly.

Another problem was inherent in the nature of the evidence itself. In the early stages of the Soviet effort to emplace nuclear missiles in Cuba in 1962, there were persistent reports from agents and refugees that large missiles were being unloaded, but these reports were consistently discounted by the analysts, except for CIA Director John McCone himself, because so risky a gamble with the peace of the world seemed incredible. Only when the hard and incontrovertible evidence of the U-2 photography settled the issue were the decisions taken to publicize the presence of the missiles and to demand their removal. Clandestine reporting from a human agent operating inside the ranks of the opposition is always subject to critical questioning and attack on the ground that it may be deliberate disinformation or tainted by error and exaggeration. The only cure for this tendency that we could suggest was to propose the closest possible working relationship between the desk chiefs on the analytical side of the Agency and the branch chiefs in the Operations Directorate. In this way, the analysts might learn over time, without being given the identities of agents, to respect the reliability and access of specific sources and to give their reporting due weight in time of crisis. In my opinion, this consideration alone argues strongly for maintaining in one Agency in close proximity the analytical staff and those responsible for clandestine collection. To isolate these functions in separate institutions, as some have advocated, would only make more difficult the day-to-day communication that allows the operator to find out in detail what the policymakers need to know and permits the analyst to gain some confidence in reliable agent reporting.

In trying to evaluate the Agency's strategic warning capability and to detect weaknesses in our protective intelligence armor, I was compelled for the first time in my career to concentrate full-time attention on the whole range of weaponry available to the one nation powerful enough to threaten our survival, the Soviet Union. It was impossible to determine the adequacy of our early warning systems without knowing in detail the specific capabilities and quantities of the armaments against whose use we sought protection. Moreover, the continuing adequacy of our strategic alert mechanisms depended on future trends in the relative strength of American and Soviet armament. We had to concern ourselves not only with the present balance of power, but how it was likely to be shifted by weapons in the early stages of development and testing that might later make sudden surprise attack more possible. As a consequence, I was subjected to a cram course on the whole range of current and projected Soviet armament by the best-informed experts in the intelligence business. And I was given access to the most highly classified yearly estimates by the Agency of the extent and nature of Soviet military strength.

What I discovered in the course of doing my homework was profoundly disturbing. While I was in London I had kept abreast in a general way with the progress the Soviets seemed to be making in military technology, but it was only after a close study of the full panoply of their military preparations that I realized the scale and intensity of their effort. At the time that I was first exposed to this voluminous information, much of it was highly classified, but since then most of the relevant data have been placed in the public domain in the form of published CIA reports, open congressional hearings, or well-informed studies by private interest groups and research organizations. The conclusions that I was forced to reach can now be fully documented from the public record, and it is no longer necessary to imply arcane knowledge of secret intelligence in order to describe the shift that has been taking place in the world balance of power.

After absorbing all the briefings and reading all the material that I could lay my hands on, the first thing that struck me was the consistency of the Soviet military buildup over a prolonged period of time. This was no sudden crash program designed to achieve some immediate result. Rather it represented a coherent decision by the Soviet regime to allocate from their gross national product over fifteen years a far higher proportion of their resources to military defense spending than did the United States. The evidence for this conclusion has now been published in three research papers by the CIA.[1] Admitting some margin for error in view of the deep secrecy surrounding the Soviet defense budget, these CIA studies conclude that Soviet military spending, measured in constant 1970 prices, rose at an average annual rate of 4 to 5 percent from 1967 to 1977. More significant, defense spending during this decade consumed an almost constant share of Soviet GNP, varying between 11 and 13 percent, depending on how defense spending is defined. Defense investment is estimated to have consumed one-third of the final product of all Soviet machine-building and metalworking industry. Between 65 and 75 percent of the males reaching draft age were conscripted into the Soviet armed forces. Defense also claimed a large share of the best Soviet scientific, technical, and managerial talent.

Taking the 1967–77 period as a whole, the cumulative dollar costs of Soviet defense activities were estimated by the CIA as about equal to U.S. outlays for defense. But the trends for the two countries during this decade were entirely different. U.S. defense spending in constant dollars declined continuously from the high point of the Vietnam war in 1968 through 1976, and only began to pick up slightly in 1977. As a consequence of these diverging trends, the dollar costs of Soviet defense were estimated to have equaled U.S. defense spending in 1971 and to have exceeded American outlays by an increasing margin in each year thereafter. By 1977, the estimated costs of Soviet defense exceeded those of the United States by about 40 percent. In 1978, the total Soviet defense expenditure was estimated at approximately $146 billion, which was almost 45 percent higher than the U.S. spending of $102 billion.

With total Soviet defense spending exceeding that of the United States by this significant margin, the estimates showed that the Soviets were by 1977 committing substantially more resources to nearly every broad category of armament and force structure than the United States could afford from its smaller total defense budget. For example, CIA analysts concluded that, over the whole 1967–77 period, the Soviet expenditures for strategic forces, including nuclear weapons and intercontinental delivery systems, were almost two and a half times those of the United States, while in 1977 the estimated margin of Soviet spending for this purpose was three times that of the United States. Only U.S. outlays for bombers were higher than Soviet expenditures for any weapons system every year throughout the decade.

This same trend was also evident in a comparison of U.S. and Soviet spending for general purpose forces, which include ground, tactical air, naval, and airlift and sealift forces. Since 1973, the estimates showed that Soviet expenditure for this category had exceeded comparable U.S. outlays by a margin of 50 percent each year. Even more ominous for the future were the trends in the field of research and development. Whereas U.S. spending on the development of new weapons systems declined steadily over the decade until 1977, the number and increasing complexity of the new weapons continually being tested by the Soviets demonstrated that they were spending significantly larger amounts for this purpose than the United States was. Since these comparative figures were first published by the CIA, they have not been attacked as unduly alarmist or as presenting a worst-case analysis. Rather, informed criticism has charged that the CIA analysts consistently tended to underestimate the growing margin of Soviet superiority in defense spending.

There is a temptation to discount the implications of these divergent trends by arguing that Soviet industry is so inefficient and its scientific knowledge so far behind the West's that higher defense expenditures do not necessarily translate into larger and more effective armaments. However, the one-party Soviet police state has demonstrated over a period of time that it is quite competitive with the United States when it comes to the development and production of advanced military hardware. What it lacks in flexibility and technical expertise, it can make up for through its ability by decree to allocate scarce materials and the best scientific talent to defense industry. After looking at the panoply of new armaments emerging from the Soviet laboratories and testing ranges, my own conclusion was that it would be very unwise for Americans to underestimate the quality of Soviet defense production. We have already paid a high price in the SALT I negotiations for the arrogant and unfounded assumption that we were years ahead of the Soviets in our ability to produce MIRVs (Multiple Independently Targetable Reentry Vehicles).

In trying to fathom the Soviet purpose behind this massive and continuing military buildup, it did not seem to me necessary to reach a worst-case conclusion. I could find no convincing evidence that the Soviets were deliberately planning to launch a full-scale nuclear attack upon the United States, nor was there any indication that their military preparations were designed to reach their zenith at some particular time. A review of Soviet military doctrine, of the speeches of Soviet leaders, and of the intelligence reporting was reassuring on this point. No Soviet official was on record in the last ten years with the argument that nuclear war against the United States was a practical and desirable way of advancing Soviet objectives. There seemed to be a general consensus that such a war would be a disaster for both sides and should be avoided if at all possible.

On the other hand, I could find little evidence to indicate that the Soviets were prepared to rely for their defense on the American concept of "mutually assured destruction." They clearly do not believe that our mutual ability to destroy each other's cities can be depended upon to prevent nuclear war. Having survived twenty million casualties to win the conflict with Hitler's Germany, they do not regard the even higher losses that nuclear war would bring as "unthinkable." In their minds and on the basis of their experience, the best way to deter attack is to be in a position to fight, survive, and win an all-out war. For this reason, American ideas of "nuclear parity" or "strategic sufficiency" have no attraction for them. As we have seen, their military expenditures continued to increase at a steady rate in spite of declining American defense spending. The fact that the Soviets have felt it necessary to maintain some forty divisions on the Chinese border has added to their defense costs, but it was by no means sufficient to explain the widening gap between U.S. and Soviet defense outlays. And many of these divisions could be shifted to the Western front, if relations with China were to improve.

Those, like former Defense Secretary Robert McNamara and others, who hoped that the Soviets would be willing to settle for parity once they achieved it, have been proved wrong in their expectations. Current and projected Soviet defense outlays are clearly aimed at achieving a superior war-fighting capability, not because they plan to attack but because they see in such superiority the most effective deterrent. While not believing nuclear war to be either desirable or inevitable, they believe it is possible. Since deterrence may fail, they are preparing in a practical and determined way to be able to fight and win a future war against the United States and its allies however it may begin and with whatever weapons it may be fought. It seemed to me in the latter half of 1976 and in 1977 that the available evidence left room for no other conclusion, and the official data that have been released to the public since then tend to reinforce that finding.[2]

My responsibility for assessing the adequacy of our strategic warning procedures forced me to concentrate on those aspects of the growing Soviet arsenal that could directly threaten surprise attack on the United States. In reviewing the Soviet order of battle, it was very quickly clear to me that the single most threatening feature was the steady Soviet deployment in increasing numbers of a whole new generation of land-based ICBMs, the SS-17, 18, and 19. By 1976, there was no longer any doubt that the Soviets were proceeding to replace their older missiles with new ones that could carry a much heavier payload to the target. By then, and in fact much earlier, it had become evident that the Soviets had mastered the art of MIRVing their missiles in a much briefer time frame than had been expected. Monitoring of the tests of the new missiles had revealed that each of them carried numerous nuclear warheads and that these warheads could be independently aimed at separate targets with increasing accuracy. Moreover, while our most modern missile, the Minuteman III, carried three warheads with an explosive power of 170 kilotons, the new Soviet missiles not only carried more warheads but they were much bigger. For example, the SS-18, their largest new missile, had proved its ability to deliver on separate targets eight to ten warheads, each with a destructive power of 1 megaton.[3] By more efficient use of fuel and new launching techniques, the Soviets had substantially increased the payload their missiles could deliver and exploited this advantage by increasing the number, size, and accuracy of their warheads.

It did not take much imagination to foresee where this process of replacing old missiles with bigger and more accurate ones would lead. By 1976, the intelligence community and the Department of Defense were increasingly alarmed by the probability that the Soviets would be in a position by the mid-1980s to destroy in a preemptive first strike 90 percent of our land-based ICBMs in their fixed silos, most of our B-52s on the ground and our nuclear submarines in port, and still have in reserve two-thirds of their warheads in order to hold our cities hostage against a retaliatory American second strike launched from our submarines at sea and our bombers on alert. In comparison, if the United States committed all its ICBMs in an assault on the Soviet ICBMs, we could hope to destroy no more than 65 percent of their ICBM silos, because their sites had been hardened to be twice as resistant as ours to attack and because our warheads were smaller than theirs.

In fact, this pessimistic prognosis of Soviet progress has turned out to be excessively optimistic because of the speed with which the Soviets have proceeded to replace their older missiles and the ever increasing accuracy of their big warheads. In 1978, for example, they added one thousand new and more accurate nuclear warheads to their ICBM arsenal.[4] This unexpectedly rapid deployment caused our defense planners to admit that the American ICBM force might become extremely vulnerable even sooner than 1985. As Secretary of Defense Harold Brown cautioned in his Annual Report to Congress in January 1979, "What is in prospect is this: The Soviets will have at least the hypothetical capability, in the *early* to mid-1980s, to destroy a large percentage of our ICBM silos, non-alert bombers and SSBNs (missile submarines) that might be in port; they may also be able to give as much as 10 to 20 percent of their population at least some kind of temporary protection against our retaliation."[5]

In his last phrase, Brown was referring to the massive effort that the Soviets have been making in the civil defense field. Evidence of the size and seriousness of this effort was already beginning to accumulate by the time of my return to Washington, and in 1978 the CIA published an unclassified version of its findings.[6] This report clearly showed that since the late 1960s the Soviets had been engaged in a long-term nationwide program under military control to provide blast shelters for the leadership and essential personnel. In addition, through realistic evacuation planning for the urban population, it was estimated that the Soviets were in a position with two or three days' advance warning to cut their casualties by 50 percent from the well over 100 million they would suffer in a surprise nuclear attack. If they had a week or more to complete their planned urban evacuation, it was estimated they could further reduce their casualties to "the low tens of millions." This extensive ongoing civil defense program was estimated to employ more than 100,000 full-time personnel; to duplicate a similar program in the United States in 1976 would have cost about $2 billion. Again it seemed to me that this massive effort was one more convincing indication that the Soviets were seriously planning to be able to fight a nuclear war and to survive it in a stronger postwar position than their adversaries. They were clearly not prepared to rely on the deterrent effect of "mutually assured destruction" of exposed urban populations.

Space does not permit a detailed description of the whole range of Soviet military preparations that I was exposed to in the course of an attempt to evaluate our strategic warning procedures. Besides, the Soviets have made steady progress in nearly all aspects of offensive and defensive preparation since that time and most of the information necessary to understanding their current posture is contained in the Secretary of Defense's annual reports to Congress. These reports are essential reading for anyone who seeks to comprehend the Soviet military effort and to judge the adequacy of our defensive reactions. Suffice it to say that in whatever direction I turned, I was confronted with evidence of a continuing Soviet improvement in the weight and quality of their armament combined with the maintenance of a standing army nearly double our own in size. In some fields, they were demonstrably ahead, as in the size of their missiles and in their development and successful testing of an orbital antisatellite interceptor with the capacity to destroy many of our surveillance satellites in time of extreme crisis. They were far ahead in their offensive and defensive preparations for chemical warfare. New nerve gases were being deployed in rockets and shells on the Western front in Europe for possible use in a surprise attack that could immobilize the defending forces and make unusable rear air bases and nuclear storage facilities. At great expense, they had sealed their battle tanks for protection against chemical agents and trained and equipped their troops for gas warfare both defensively and offensively, while our own defensive preparations lagged far behind.

In other fields they were catching up fast. They were testing and deploying new MIRVed ballistic missiles for their submarine fleet with greater range, throw weight, and accuracy, adding substantially to the first-strike potential of their land-based missiles. They were steadily improving their strategic warning radars in order to increase the time needed to launch their ICBMs successfully before the missiles could be destroyed by an attempted American first strike. They were building up a blue water navy with increasing capacity to project their power far beyond their borders and to challenge American control of the seas. They maintained and were improving a huge tactical air defense network against the American bomber fleet, consisting of advanced fighter planes and surface-to-air missiles, while American air defenses were sadly neglected. They were developing and testing the new Backfire supersonic bomber, which on a one-way mission could reach most of the United States but which they maintained was a nonstrategic weapon for use on the Eurasian land mass. And they were developing and have now deployed in increasing numbers a mobile intermediate range ballistic missile with three powerful and accurate nuclear warheads, the SS-20, for possible use against the military bases and cities of our NATO allies. Their preponderance in modern tanks and artillery on the NATO front was a cause of increasing concern to our allies, as was the advanced state of readiness in which these forces were kept.

Only in the development of small, highly accurate cruise missiles did the Soviets seem to lag far behind the United States, but the speed with which they had overcome previous technological inferiorities was a warning that this advantage should not be overestimated. I could conclude from this mass of evidence only that the Soviets were methodically and systematically preparing for every conceivable type of warfare. Although their doctrine did not envisage an American first strike as a likely possibility, they were preparing for the contingency that their intelligence might give them advance warning of such a strike and were prepared with their large ICBMs to preempt with a first strike of their own. Their strategic warning radar network was improving their chances of being able to launch their missiles on warning even after the American missiles were in the air, and new cold-launch techniques were reducing the reaction time required. By the hardening of their missile silos and their construction of impregnable underground command centers, they were preparing to ride out a nuclear attack if one should take them by complete surprise, and still be able to direct an effective retaliation. Their steadily improving civil defense structure gave them some hope of being able to survive and continue fighting a war even after the initial nuclear exchange. And on the Western front in Europe, their preponderance in manpower and nonnuclear weaponry, combined with their chemical warfare capability, gave them the option of successfully fighting a conventional war, in which neither side would dare escalate to nuclear exchange.

To me and to many others in the intelligence community and in the Defense Department, the most disturbing feature of the situation we confronted was not so much the existing balance as it stood in the 1976–77 period, but rather the predictable consequence in the future if clearly perceived trends were allowed to continue. By replacing their older missiles with their new generation of bigger and more accurate ICBMs, the Soviets were moving, as we have seen, inexorably to the point where by as early as 1980 they would be able in a first disabling strike to destroy so many of the American ICBMs, bombers on the ground, and submarines in port that the American retaliatory capacity might no longer function as a credible deterrent. If after suffering such losses an American President realized that the Soviets still retained two-thirds of their ICBM warheads for use against our cities, he would have to hesitate before ordering our remaining bombers and submarines to launch their missiles against the Soviet cities. His dilemma would be made even more acute by his knowledge that the Soviet urban population was much better protected by civil defense precautions than were the American city dwellers. With so great a perceived advantage, it seemed to me that the Soviets would have succeeded in shifting the basic fulcrum on which the world balance of power rests, with incalculable consequences for ourselves and our allies.

Both within the government and in the private think tanks, there were some who argued that this prospect was not as bleak as it first appeared. They maintained that the Soviets would be restrained from ever actually using their advantage by fear of the American ability to launch our ICBMs on warning as soon as our radars and surveillance sensors detected a Soviet launch and thereby prevent our missiles from being destroyed on the ground. To me this defensive reaction seemed more a theoretical possibility than a politically realistic alternative. It appeared to me that no American President, given only about twenty minutes' advance warning and no more to rely on than potentially fallible electronic data, would be likely in that time frame to commit our ICBM force. And against what targets would our ICBMs be aimed? A launch against the Soviet cities with their civil defense shelters would only bring down a much more damaging counterstrike on our unprotected urban population, and any American President would hesitate before engaging in so unequal an exchange. Similar considerations applied to the American ability to retaliate with our submarines at sea and bombers in the air after our ICBM force had been destroyed. Again, an American President would have to weigh the damage that could be wreaked on the Soviet cities by our surviving submarines and B-52s against the much higher casualties that the Soviets could inflict with two-thirds of their ICBMs held in reserve and their submarine fleet intact. By preparing actually to fight and survive a nuclear war while we relied on mutually assured destruction, the Soviets were changing the odds to their advantage in any showdown confrontation.

Even more alarming was the fact that in the 1976–77 period no active measures were being taken to prevent our ICBMs from becoming sitting ducks. Since the late 1960s our ICBM force had remained static in numbers, consisting of 54 older Titan missiles with single warheads; 450 Minuteman IIs, also with one warhead on each; and 550 Minuteman IIIs, each carrying three independently targeted warheads. Although some effort had been made to improve the explosive yield and accuracy of our warheads, no attempt had been made to replace these small and aging missiles with new ones capable of matching the thrust and payload capacity of the new generation of Soviet missiles. This situation was made worse by a decision to close down our production line for the manufacture of the Minuteman III missiles, so that a long lead time would be required to resume production. Measures had been taken to make our launching sites more resistant to the blast effects of near misses, but this hardening process had not kept up with the increasing accuracy and explosive power of the new and more numerous Soviet warheads aimed against them. Stuck in their single fixed silos, our obsolete ICBMs were becoming each day more vulnerable to a Soviet preemptive strike and less believable as an effective deterrent to such an attack.

Since the deployment of antiballistic missiles to protect our ICBMs was severely limited by the terms of the ABM treaty we had signed with the Soviets in 1972, the only way to right the balance was to build a bigger and more accurate missile of our own and to find some method of basing it that would not leave it exposed to attack in a single fixed silo. For example, it was technically feasible to place each missile in a field of some twenty widely spaced silos and to move it from one silo to another so that the Soviets would not know its exact location. Called the Multiple Aim Point System (MAPS), this basing mode seemed a practical method of reducing the vulnerability of our ICBM force, and the "racetrack" system was a later refinement of this approach.

Although the urgent need for a larger and more accurate American ICBM no longer confined to a single silo was clearly apparent in 1977 if our capacity to retaliate was to seem credible to the Soviets, hesitation and debate within the Carter administration postponed a decision until funds were finally requested for the construction of a new ICBM in the FY 1980 defense budget. A commitment was also made to reach an early decision on how best to deploy it. But it is estimated that it will take at least six years to deploy the new missile in sufficient numbers to affect the balance. Therefore we now face a dangerous gap in the early 1980s. This will be a time when our 1,054 ICBMs in their fixed silos will be extremely vulnerable. The rapid deployment of cruise missiles in our B-52 bombers will begin to improve the situation somewhat by 1982, since their extreme accuracy makes them effective against even the heavily protected Soviet ICBM silos. But because of their slow speed they may prove vulnerable to improving Soviet air defenses and to being shot down by the ground fire the Soviets could mass around their silos for terminal protection. Moreover, these air-launched cruise missiles would take twelve to thirteen hours to reach their targets, giving the Soviets plenty of warning time in which to launch their threatened ICBMs. Lacking the required explosive power and accuracy, even our newest submarine-launched missiles are not yet effective against hardened Soviet targets.

The conclusion is inescapable that the American ability to retaliate effectively against a Soviet attack on our strategic forces will remain deeply in doubt during the early 1980s. Only by 1987 will the United States, through the mobile deployment of our new MX missile, begin to restore the credibility of the American second strike. By then, also, we may have taken effective measures to repair the dangerous imbalance between our token civil defense system and the massive precautions the Soviets have taken in this field. The five-year gap in our defenses that is now clearly foreseeable may prove a difficult and dangerous time for the American people and our allies. A new SALT agreement, even if ratified, cannot offer any additional protection during this period because the very high upper limit of 820 that it sets on MIRVed Soviet ICBMs allows them to deploy more than enough accurate warheads to destroy our ICBM force and to keep in reserve enough to discourage retaliation.

In surveying the adequacy of our strategic warning procedures, it was brought home to me by the experts that much more was required than simply the deployment of a new ICBM in a multiple basing mode to protect our second-strike capability. We were growing increasingly dependent for strategic warning on a marvelously ingenious satellite surveillance system that was, however, itself becoming dangerously vulnerable to destruction in time of crisis by the new Soviet orbital antisatellite interceptors.[7] The Soviets were moving toward the time when they would be able to blind our satellite sensors in a confrontational crisis and thereby make retaliation less prompt and less effective. We had then no similar interceptor as a counterthreat against their satellites, and the measures necessary to protect our satellites were expensive and slow to be undertaken. And our strategic warning radars were vulnerable to attack by Soviet missiles launched from submarines close to our shores.

It was also obvious to all concerned with this problem that the American capacity to launch a believable second strike depended on the existence of a diversity of heavily protected command and control centers and on a communication system capable of surviving the initial attack. My own visit to one of our most important command centers was not reassuring. It was built to survive the kind of attack the Soviets were capable of launching in the late sixties but was admittedly incapable of withstanding the new bigger and more accurate warheads. Similarly, the arrangements for evacuating the American high command to survivable command posts in periods of extreme crisis left a good deal to be desired. In his annual report to Congress for fiscal year 1980, Defense Secretary Harold Brown focused on these vulnerabilities, and presumably effective steps are now being taken to repair these deficiencies.

After exposure to this cram course in the size and quality of the Soviet military buildup, it was still possible for me to believe that a primary purpose of the Soviet Union's sacrifice of living standards to armament production was defensive. Given their experience in World War II, the leaders in the Kremlin have an understandable tendency to overensure against the possibility of attack, and they may well see their drive for military preponderance as the only sure way of guaranteeing the defense of the homeland. But it is not possible to conclude that this defensive purpose is the only and exclusive explanation of their motives. In their speeches and doctrine, the rulers in the Kremlin display a lively awareness of the advantages to be derived from "a visible preponderance of military power." What we call the balance of power, they call "the correlation of forces," and they do not underestimate what is to be gained by being seen throughout the world as militarily superior to the United States. They see the fulcrum on which the world balance rests as being the comparative relationship between the strategic nuclear forces of the U.S. and the U.S.S.R.

If they had any doubt about this before, it was indelibly etched on their minds by their experience in the Cuban missile crisis of 1962. Having secretly introduced land-based missiles into Cuba, Khrushchev was forced to withdraw them when faced with President Kennedy's ultimatum. He knew that the United States enjoyed superiority in conventional arms in the area and that an American force stood ready in Florida to invade if he did not back down. More important, he realized that he was at a decisive disadvantage if he chose to escalate to nuclear war. He knew that additional American nuclear submarines had put to sea and that American strategic forces were on full alert. Most important, he realized that at that time the United States possessed an overwhelming advantage in nuclear weaponry and that in any nuclear exchange the U.S.S.R. stood to suffer about 100 million casualties and the United States 10 million. Faced with this prospect, Khrushchev backed down, but the lesson was learned. As the final terms of the withdrawal were being hammered out, one of the principal Soviet negotiators, V. Kuznetsov, put their future intentions bluntly to his American counterpart, John J. McCloy. He warned, "We'll live up to this agreement but we'll never be in this position again." The massive buildup of Soviet strategic forces began before the Cuban missile crisis, but that crisis must have hardened their resolve.

Behind major international confrontations between the United States and the Soviet Union stands the shadow of nuclear war, and the outcome of these crises will be determined, as in the case of the Cuban missile crisis, by each side's perception of which one is better prepared to fight and survive such a war with the least damage to its population and industry. The danger of the Soviet strategic superiority that is certain to emerge in the early 1980s is not that the Soviets will seek to gamble everything on one final throw of the nuclear dice. The real danger is that under the umbrella of their strategic strength, the Soviets will be tempted to probe continuously for weak points in Western defenses and to engage in an increasingly aggressive exploitation of targets of opportunity in the continuing struggle for allies, strategic bases, and raw materials, secure in the knowledge that at no point will a strategically inferior United States dare to risk an escalation to nuclear war. The Soviet invasion of Afghanistan in late December of 1979 demonstrates their readiness to use their armies to impose their will on the third world. Their superiority in conventional forces on the Western front is much more real a threat when it can no longer be offset by U.S. nuclear superiority. Similarly, the conventional forces of their Cuban and Vietnamese allies become much more usable under the protecting panoply of Soviet strategic strength. Even before the Soviets began to achieve nuclear parity, their policy was adventuresome enough. Although much inferior to the United States in nuclear strength, Stalin dared risk the blockade of Berlin and the encouragement of the North Korean attack on South Korea. As I watched the strategic balance shifting first toward parity and now toward superiority, the outlines of a new more adventuresome foreign policy by the post-Stalin Soviet leadership began to emerge.

In the following chapters, I try to trace how—at least from my vantage point—the Soviets appear to have reacted to their new self-confidence in their improving strategic position. And I attempt to explain how the Soviet decision-making system and the Soviet intelligence organs actually operate to give them peculiar advantages in the global struggle for power. Some understanding of the Soviet governmental structure, its objectives and instrumentalities, seems to me essential to comprehending the role and relevance of American intelligence. It is for this reason that I first discuss Soviet foreign policy and intelligence capabilities, because so much of what the United States has tried to do in these fields can be understood only as a defensive reaction to the threats posed by Soviet behavior. In this respect, my approach is in direct contrast to the line taken by the Church committee in its report and to the picture presented by many of the recent books on American intelligence. Much of the discussion of CIA activities has taken place in a vacuum that omits coverage of the Soviet challenge. It is time to redress the balance. My hope is that my subsequent discussion of the structure and functioning of the American intelligence community will make more sense once the reader understands that the CIA has had a real and formidable opponent to cope with.

Inevitably, the story of my personal career and experiences plays a decreasing role in the remainder of this book. On the occasions where autobiographical material is relevant I have introduced it, but basically the book now becomes the story of how the Soviet Union has tried to expand its power in the world and of how the American government is organized to confront that challenge. There is inherent drama in this worldwide rivalry and the revealing details of how it is actually waged.

Chapter 12

The New Geopolitical Offensive

THE JOINT SOVIET-CUBAN decision to introduce large numbers of Cuban troops into Angola in 1975 to turn the tide of the civil war there was, in my opinion, the first clear-cut and dramatic demonstration of how the Soviets are likely to react to their improving strategic strength. By that time, American officials were willing to concede that the Soviets had achieved a position of rough parity with the United States in nuclear armament, and the overwhelming American superiority that had played so decisive a role in the resolution of the Cuban missile crisis had disappeared. Sensing that the strategic balance was shifting in their favor and correctly estimating that the trauma of Watergate and the withdrawal from Vietnam had at least temporarily impaired the American ability to react, the Soviets gambled successfully on a bold, aggressive move on the world's chessboard. In an operation spanning three continents and requiring the well-timed orchestration of political assets and conventional military resources that had been built up over many years, the Soviets with their Cuban allies imposed their chosen instrument on the people of

243

Angola as the new government when the Portuguese colonial masters finally withdrew on November 11, 1975.

This Marxist government, based on one of the three black nationalist guerrilla organizations that had been fighting the Portuguese, the Popular Movement for the Liberation of Angola (MPLA), remains in power to this day with the indispensable support of 20,000 Cuban troops. In one strategic stroke, the Soviets, with Castro's help, succeeded in fundamentally changing the balance of power in southern Africa to their advantage. In so doing, they gained effective political influence in a huge slice of the Dark Continent, obtained access to new strategic ports and airfields, and secured a political base from which to operate against the remaining non-Communist countries in Africa. How this geopolitical coup was consummated is worth our scrutiny because it tells us a great deal about the less obvious forms of power and influence that the Soviets are likely to utilize increasingly under the protective cover of their nuclear predominance.

From my vantage point in London from 1973 to 1976, I was in an excellent position to observe the unfolding of this drama. When the Caetano regime, the successor to the Salazar dictatorship, collapsed in Portugal in April of 1974, both the American and British governments became increasingly concerned about the threat posed to NATO by the well-organized Portuguese Communist Party (PCP). As a result, there was suddenly a voluminous exchange of information on developments in a country that had once been regarded as a backwater. From this flow of reporting, it was possible to put together a picture of the strategy that the Portuguese Communists were pursuing with Soviet guidance and assistance beneath the surface of events. As it turned out, the PCP failed in its bid for power inside Portugal largely as the result of its defeat in two national elections, in which it polled at most 14 percent of the vote. After more than forty years of repression under the right-wing dictatorship of Salazar, the Portuguese people were not ready to trade in their newfound freedom for a dictatorship of the left, and a large majority of the vote went to the democratic socialist and centrist parties, which had received encouragement and support from their sister parties in Western Europe. Lacking an adjacent boundary, the Soviets were in no position to threaten military intervention to assist their Portuguese allies and had to accept their electoral defeat. But even in defeat, the PCP played a critical role in the eventual Communist triumph in Angola through its conspiratorial apparat, its infiltration of the Portuguese armed forces in both Portugal and Angola, and through its extensive control and influence over the media in the period up to the abortive coup in November of 1975.

The bloodless military coup in Portugal that overthrew the Caetano regime on April 25, 1974, was not the work of the PCP. It was masterminded by a group of middle-grade younger army officers who had secretly organized themselves in 1973 as the "Movement of the Armed Forces" (MFA). Many of them, like Captain Otelo de Carvalho, had served in the Portuguese colonial army in Africa and had become convinced that the colonial war could not be won. They were influenced by the Marxist rhetoric of some of the African nationalist leaders against whom they fought, particularly Amilcar Cabral, the leader of the insurgent movement in the Portuguese colony of Guinea-Bissau. Cabral was assassinated with the help of the Portuguese secret police in January of 1973, but his writings on the role of the lower-middle class in revolutionary situations were influential among the young Portuguese officers, most of whom came from that class. In addition to a vaguely defined commitment to the need for a social revolution and a belief that Portuguese colonial policy was bankrupt, these officers exploited the army's widespread dissatisfaction with the pay and promotion policies of the Caetano regime. On the night of April 24, the leaders of the MFA assembled a handpicked force of 5,000 men with tanks at the Santaren Military School under the pretense of engaging in maneuvers, and by three o'clock the next morning had occupied the center of Lisbon. There was virtually no resistance.

Although the PCP did not plan the coup that brought down the Caetano regime, the Communists moved quickly and effectively to make the most of the new freedom to organize and to exploit the vacuum left at all levels of government by the collapse of the rightwing dictatorship. During forty-five years of repression under Salazar and Caetano, the Communist leaders had been preparing for this moment of opportunity. Over these years, the Soviets had consistently subsidized the underground cell structure of the party in Portugal, helped arrange the secret exfiltration of leaders for training in the Soviet Union and Eastern Europe, and provided asylum for the more prominent leaders. Alvaro Cunhal, who returned to Portugal immediately after the coup to assume leadership of the PCP, had

spent his years in exile in Moscow and Prague. The strength of the
PCP lay in the hard core of its disciplined and tested leadership.
Many of them had spent years in prison and resisted torture by
Salazar's secret police. Except for the splitting away in the mid-sixties
of an extreme left faction that believed in immediate armed revolt,
the party had remained impressively unified, and in return for Moscow's consistent support it had demonstrated undeviating allegiance
to the policy line laid down by the Soviets. Neither in its underground phase nor in its open existence after the coup did it ever flirt
with the heretical "Euro-Communist" deviations that characterized
the leadership of the Italian and Spanish Communist Parties. It was,
under Cunhal's leadership, consistently loyal to Moscow, an obedient
and disciplined instrument of Soviet policy.

Once again I was struck by the contrast between the long-term and
coherent political strategy of the Soviets in planning for the end of
a right-wing dictatorship and the belated improvisations of the West.
Undeterred by long years of failure and repression under Salazar, the
Soviets had systematically and consistently supported the conspiratorial structure of the PCP so that, when the dictatorship fell,
the Communists were far better organized to seize the levers of
power than their opponents. By contrast, the United States and its
Western European allies had been content for forty years to do
business with Salazar and had almost completely neglected the pleas
of the various democratic opposition groups that had sought support
in the West for their badly organized efforts to gain wider political
freedom. In fact, so deep had been this neglect of the opposition to
the dictatorship that in the early days of the revolution, both American and Western European intelligence had great difficulty in identifying the names and numbers of the players in a revolutionary situation that had been neither anticipated nor planned for. One of the
major reasons for the eventual loss of Angola was this asymmetry
between the consistency of the long-range covert political strategy
of the Soviets and the improvised reactions of the West. It is this
contrast that has led to the observation that the Russians play chess,
while the Americans play poker.

The initial tactical plan of the PCP was brilliantly executed. As I
watched it unfold from my observation post in London, I had to
admire its efficiency, if not its motivation. Under orders that passed
down from the Central Committee of the party through its strict

hierarchy to the smallest disciplined cell, the PCP members moved rapidly to occupy the institutions and offices of the defunct Caetano regime. Within two weeks after the coup in April 1974, more than one hundred sections of the PCP had taken over key positions. The police forces of the discredited ancien régime were in disarray, and there was no authority to stop the Communists. Under the slogan *sanear*—to cleanse—they seized control of the editorial offices of the newspapers that had formerly backed Caetano, the governing boards of the partially state-owned enterprises like the railways, the national airlines, and most important of all, the national radio and television corporation. Their weekly newspaper, *Avante,* previously printed underground in small numbers, suddenly blossomed into a mass publication preaching the rigid party line. They seemed, at first, the only political group in the country that knew exactly what it wanted and how to get it.

Aware of the anti-Communist sentiment of the largely Catholic population, particularly in the northern half of the country, the PCP took over one of the defunct political organs of the Caetano regime, the Democratic Electoral Commission. It placed a radical Catholic professor of economics in charge and renamed it the Portuguese Democratic Movement (MDP). Through its control of this stalking horse, it increased the numbers of secret activists in the national ministries and in the municipal governments throughout the country. Moreover, having secretly infiltrated the state-controlled labor unions that functioned under the Caetano regime, it used this influence after the April coup to establish a single central trade union body, the Intersindical, under Communist control, and used it to inhibit the formation of free trade unions by the democratic socialist and moderate parties.

Reports flowing into London provided some insight into how the formidable political machine of the PCP was organized and subsidized. At the top was a fourteen-member Central Committee under the chairmanship of Cunhal. It met for three hours each week to hear reports from subordinate committees and to adjust tactics to the changing political scene. One regular subcommittee, for example, was vested with responsibility for directing the Communist campaign to infiltrate all elements of the media with trained activists and to assure either Communist control or neutralization of opposing views. The committee supervised the massive distribution of wall posters and handbills that flooded Portugal at this time, and under its direction work stoppages were conducted that harassed and periodically prevented publication of the respected *Republica* newspaper published by the democratic socialists. Another subcommittee had the assignment of allocating cadre strength throughout the labor movement, so as to maximize Communist influence at all levels as new unions sprang into existence to replace the official government unions of the Caetano era. In this subcommittee was also vested the directive authority for the establishment of agricultural cooperatives under Communist control to organize in the name of the landless peasants the takeover of the huge holdings of the big landowners in southern Portugal. There was a separate subcommittee on party organization with responsibility for directing the PCP cells throughout the country, which quickly increased in number to 420. Supplemental to this structure was the party organization of the MDP front group, which had an additional two hundred local cells to maintain control. A budget subcommittee supervised the raising and allocation of funds. At the height of its power, the PCP raised from party dues and contributions more than $100,000 per month within Portugal, which was generously supplemented by about $900,000 per month in secret subsidies received from the Czech Embassy in Lisbon, which acted as a channel for contributions from the Soviet Union and other Eastern European governments.

Most significant for the future of Angola, however, was the special subcommittee of the PCP that was responsible for the recruitment and positioning of agents within the armed forces both in Portugal and in the African colonies. At the top, the Communists had in the person of Colonel Vasco Gonçalves, a former member of the PCP, a consistent ideological sympathizer. A leading member of the Movement of the Armed Forces, he was first appointed prime minister in September of 1974, and he presided over four increasingly Communist-influenced provisional governments until forced from power in August 1975. In this capacity, he played a critical role in the timing and implementation of the Portuguese withdrawal from Angola. In addition to the selective recruitment of genuine ideological converts in key positions, the Communists were able to secure the cooperation in their Angolan plans of certain high-ranking Portuguese officers who had compromised themselves during the previous regime by involvement with Salazar's secret police. Immediately after the April coup, a well-prepared group of Communist activists had taken over police headquarters in Lisbon, and a few days of intensive file search gave them incriminating dossiers on a select number of military officers. These officers lived in constant fear of blackmail, and the Communists used their hold over them to compel cooperation in the execution of the Angolan gambit.

In the lower ranks, a network of Communist cells was built up in the armed forces serving both in Portugal and in Africa. In order to demonstrate the power it had within the army, the PCP utilized mass demonstrations to set thousands of uniformed soldiers marching in disciplined ranks among the civilian crowds; and they clothed additional men in stolen uniforms to make their strength seem even more impressive. Within Portugal itself, this Communist attempt to infiltrate the armed forces backfired in late November 1975; after PCP involvement in an abortive coup, the officer ranks were purged of Communist sympathizers, and career professional soldiers of anti-Communist conviction reasserted their control over the Portuguese armed forces. But it was too late to prevent the transfer of power to the MPLA as the new government in Luanda, the capital of Angola, on November 11, 1975. The Portuguese army was withdrawn, leaving behind substantial stocks of weapons for MPLA forces to use in the continuing civil war.

Moreover, in the period leading up to this precipitate withdrawal, Communist cadres at all levels in the Portuguese units stationed in Angola facilitated the shipment of Soviet and Cuban arms deliveries to the MPLA guerrillas through Luanda and other ports on the African coast. Portuguese air force pilots were even accused of flying reconnaissance missions for the MPLA. By refusing to insist on an orderly transfer of power through a referendum to determine the voting strength of the competing factions, and by their hasty withdrawal timed so as to leave the MPLA in control of Luanda, the Portuguese authorities played directly into the hands of the Soviet strategists. What Communist infiltration of the Portuguese armed forces had failed to achieve in Lisbon was crowned with success in Luanda, and the many years of Soviet support to the conspiratorial structure of the PCP paid off in making a crucial contribution to the establishment of a Marxist revolutionary government in the heart of Africa.

It should also be pointed out that in the other major Portuguese

African colony, Mozambique, there was only one well-organized independence movement, the Mozambique Liberation Front (FRELIMO). Its political orientation was satisfactorily radical from the PCP's point of view, and the Portuguese Communists wholeheartedly supported the granting of independence to this regime on June 25, 1975, creating a radical state on the east coast of Africa on the borders of Rhodesia and South Africa.

If the disciplined PCP was a Soviet bishop on the Angolan chessboard, it seemed to me sitting in London in 1974 that the Soviet king in this game was the MPLA itself, which somehow had to be protected and moved into a position of safety as the recognized government of Angola. After the April coup in Lisbon in 1974, the new Portuguese government announced to a population weary of the long and costly African colonial wars that it intended to liberate the African colonies and to grant them independence. In contrast to the situation in Mozambique, where FRELIMO existed as the only active insurgent movement, the problem in Angola was complicated for the Portuguese by the fact that three distinct independence movements had been fighting the colonial power for years, each with its separate tribal allegiances and each claiming the right to inherit its share of political power in any new independent government. These movements were the Popular Movement for the Liberation of Angola (MPLA), under the leadership of Dr. Agostinho Neto; the National Front for the Liberation of Angola (FNLA), under its founder, Holden Roberto; and the National Union for the Total Independence of Angola (UNITA), under Jonas Savimbi. A brief review of their separate histories is necessary to an understanding of how the civil war evolved.

The MPLA was founded in 1956 on the initiative of the Angolan Communist Party. By 1963, an authoritative Soviet publication was describing the MPLA as "a progressive political party of the Angolan people formed in 1956 with the active participation of illegal workers' circles of Luanda," and stated that it stood "for the establishment of a united front of all patriotic forces in Angola engaged in the national liberation struggle."[1] Agostinho Neto, an African born near Luanda and educated as a doctor in Lisbon, became its president in 1962, after escaping from imprisonment by the Portuguese in 1960. He visited Moscow in the mid-sixties under the auspices of Alvaro Cunhal, who was living there in exile, and became a prominent member of the World Peace Council, a Soviet-controlled front. In August 1968, Neto again visited Moscow and obtained an annual subsidy of about $300,000 for organization and propaganda. In addition, he arranged to have MPLA militants trained in the Soviet Union in the arts of guerrilla war, and for the shipment of limited amounts of arms. Neto was himself a member of the Mbundu tribe, which lives in the region surrounding Luanda. Although the membership of the MPLA included many racially mixed and educated urban dwellers, its main tribal base and popular strength lay in the Mbundu people.

Because of bitter factional clashes inside the MPLA, Moscow reduced its financial assistance in 1972. But in August of 1974, after the coup in Lisbon, the Soviets sent a message of strong support to the Congress of the MPLA meeting in Lusaka, the capital of Zambia, stating that they had always considered the MPLA "as the leading force in the Angolan liberation movements, as the real spokesman of the hopes and will of the Angolan people." Neto had a long session with KGB officials during this Lusaka meeting, and thereafter the Soviets steadily escalated the amount of arms and training they were prepared to provide. The radical regime in the Congo Republic was willing to cooperate as a staging area for Soviet supplies and arms. Training centers and transshipment facilities were established in Brazzaville, the capital of the Congo Republic, and in its port city, Pointe-Noire, so that by October of 1974 the MPLA was receiving increasing amounts of Soviet infantry weapons by air and sea lift via these transshipment points, and Communist Portuguese military officers were facilitating the transfer of these arms to the MPLA forces in Luanda.

As an interesting aside, it is important to note that in addition to the Soviet connection, the MPLA leaders had a long history of cooperation with Castro's Cuban Communists dating back to the mid-sixties. In a unique account of this relationship, the Colombian novelist Gabriel García Márquez has given a version of how Neto first met with Che Guevara when Che was fighting in Africa with the Congo guerrillas in 1965.[2] According to this account, Neto visited Cuba the following year and met with Castro. Arrangements were made for the subsequent training of MPLA cadres in military and technical skills in Cuba, and many of these men now serve in key positions in the Angolan government. As García Márquez boasts at the end of his article, "That fleeting anonymous passage of Che Guevara through

Africa planted a seed that no one could uproot."

The second Angolan insurgent movement, the FNLA, was founded by Holden Roberto in 1954. He was born in 1923, the son of a Christian peasant, and was named after a Protestant American missionary. The FNLA's tribal base was the Bakongo community of about 700,000 people in northern Angola. During the fighting against the Portuguese in 1961, about 400,000 of the Bakongo tribe fled as refugees into the Republic of the Congo (now Zaire), and Roberto thereafter established a secure exile base in Zaire with the approval and support of the Mobutu regime. From forest redoubts inside Angola, and by hit-and-run raids across the Zaire border, Roberto kept up the pressure on the Portuguese colonial forces and succeeded in occupying most of the two northern Angolan districts, forcing out the guerrilla troops of the MPLA and UNITA. Although from 1973 to 1974 the FNLA received some support and training from the Chinese Communists, there were no strong ideological links to Peking, and the FNLA was basically a nationalist movement with heavy reliance on its Bakongo tribal base. The Chinese Communists subsequently withdrew their support.

As the result of a split in the FNLA, the third Angolan insurgency movement, UNITA, was founded in 1966 by Swiss-educated Jonas Savimbi, who had previously been Roberto's chief lieutenant. Savimbi was a member of the largest tribal group in Angola, the Ovimbundu people, more than 2 million of whom lived on the Benguela plateau in southern Angola. For a year, Savimbi made the most of a secure exile base in Zambia in which to train his forces, but after attacks by his guerrillas on the Portuguese-operated Benguela railroad that carried Zambian copper through Angola to the coastal ports, Savimbi's headquarters was ordered out of Zambia. Thereafter, Savimbi directed operations from inside southern Angola and most of his weapons were obtained by successful attacks on Portuguese troops. Although Savimbi visited Mao Tse-tung in Peking in 1964 and received some very limited assistance from the Chinese in his early days, he evolved into an independent nationalist leader with an ideological position close to that of European democratic socialists. All those who met him were impressed by his charismatic personality and his organizing genius. Even John Stockwell, the ex-CIA officer who wrote a generally critical book about the Agency's abortive role in Angola, went out of his way to praise Savimbi's courage and organizational ability.[3] With the largest tribal base of the three nationalist movements, Savimbi in the early seventies not only fought the Portuguese with increasing success but also resisted the armed attempts of the MPLA to encroach on his territory.

While the Soviets and the Communist cadres in the Portuguese armed forces were secretly channeling an increasing flow of weapons to the MPLA in the fall of 1974, the new provisional Portuguese government was attempting to deal in an even-handed way with the three separate Angolan independence movements. The Portuguese authorities insisted on a cease-fire agreement between the three groups as a condition for the holding of negotiations leading to independence, and in October 1974 this armistice was signed. This was followed by the signing of the Alvor agreement in January 1975, which provided for a complex power-sharing arrangement under a transitional government in which the three liberation movements and the Portuguese would jointly participate until full independence was granted on November 11, 1975. Eight thousand men from each of the three movements, and 24,000 Portuguese troops, were to form a national armed force to supervise elections to a constituent assembly to be held within nine months; but there was no provision for enforcing this agreement. Most observers agree that if honest elections had been held, FNLA and UNITA, with their larger tribal constituencies, would have decisively defeated the MPLA.

Reacting to evidence that in December 1974 the Soviets, in addition to making arms shipments, had flown a large number of MPLA officers and NCOs to Russia for military training in the new weapons, the U.S. government took its first tentative step toward covert involvement in the Angolan civil war shortly after the signing of the Alvor agreement. An article by Seymour Hersh in *The New York Times* revealed this covert activity in December 1975.[4] Two versions of the rationale and history of this program have since been written by U.S. officials who participated. One is an article by former Assistant Secretary of State for African Affairs Nathaniel Davis, who explains his reasons for opposing the program.[5] The other is the book by Stockwell, who had served as head of the Agency task force responsible for implementing the activity and who did not submit his book for clearance by the Agency. Both accounts are highly critical of the U.S. involvement for somewhat different reasons. The fact that these revelations have appeared allows me to discuss the American covert role in these events, which would otherwise have had to remain secret.

On January 22, 1975, responding to pleas from President Mobutu of Zaire, who feared the establishment on his border of a Soviet-supported MPLA regime in Angola, President Ford and Henry Kissinger approved a recommendation of the 40 Committee that the CIA be directed to provide Holden Roberto's FNLA with secret funding in the amount of $300,000. This money was specifically earmarked not for arms but for organizational expenses. It was designed as a symbolic act to prove to Mobutu and Roberto that the United States was not prepared to stand aside while the Soviets proceeded unchallenged to arm and train the MPLA as they had been doing. When I heard of this decision in London, it did not seem to me to be an unreasonable or excessive response to the accumulating evidence of growing Soviet military support to the MPLA. In fact, it seemed the least that could be done to preserve the balance between the contending factions on which any hope for the successful implementation of the Alvor agreement rested. However, I do recall wondering how long such a covert CIA program could be kept secret under the new rules that required eight committees of Congress to be notified in an environment of continuing investigatory attack on the Agency. In view of the scale of Soviet military assistance to the MPLA, there was also an obvious question as to whether this limited nonmilitary commitment would be sufficient to right the balance. Certainly, however, the critics are wrong who suggest that this modest step was the initial act of big-power escalation that provoked the Soviets into their subsequent massive involvement. The Soviets had taken the first step back in October 1974, when they began their arms shipments with the help of their Portuguese Communist allies, and it was compounded by their decision in December 1974 to fly MPLA cadres to the Soviet Union for training in the modern weapons that were being introduced.

Some critics of Angolan policy have subsequently claimed that at this point the United States should have "mustered its diplomatic forces" and sought to avoid big-power intervention by seeking conciliation under the auspices of the Organization of African Unity (OAU).[6] Aside from the fact that the OAU was deeply split on East-West ideological lines, there was also the problem that the Soviets were well aware of the numerical weakness of the MPLA, which would have been revealed in any fair election. After forty-eight years of conspiratorial construction of the PCP, and twenty years of careful nurturing of the MPLA, the Soviets were not prepared in a sudden outburst of devotion to the democratic process to allow votes to determine the fate of their chosen instrument of power in Angola.

Another line of criticism suggests that President Ford and Secretary of State Kissinger should have realized that covert action by the CIA was no longer a viable option after Watergate and Vietnam—at least temporarily—and was bound to leak. It is argued that they therefore should have gone openly to the Congress and sought the funds necessary for intervention with a frank exposition of the geopolitical importance of Angola. Such open intervention was not a realistic alternative. Portugal was still legally responsible for Angola, and an open attempt to intervene in its internal affairs not only would have been resisted by the Portuguese government but would have been overwhelmingly condemned in the United Nations.

With the wisdom of hindsight and in view of the eventual termination by the Congress of the covert American attempt to intervene, it is clear that Ford and Kissinger really faced a stark choice. They could either do nothing and hope that the Soviets would eventually become so bogged down in the complexities of African tribal politics that their Angolan triumph would prove more trouble than it was worth. Or, more realistically, they could have taken the evidence of Soviet covert intervention directly to the Kremlin and made it clear that the whole edifice of détente depended on a Soviet decision to desist. Faced with a collapse of the SALT process, the ending of grain shipments, and a cutoff of technology transfers, the Soviets might have been willing to reconsider; and if they were not, at least the American people would have been alerted to the full extent of the danger that they confronted. But in a year preceding an election, neither Ford nor Kissinger was willing to risk the exposure of their popular but fragile policy of détente to such a test. Instead, the appearance of détente was maintained, while we attempted to compete in a covert rivalry in which the Soviets held the high cards because of the pervasive secrecy of their system and the vulnerability to exposure of the CIA covert capability.

From March to July of 1975, the Soviets concentrated their efforts on ensuring the complete ascendancy of the MPLA in the Angolan capital of Luanda and in the surrounding region where the MPLA enjoyed the tribal support of the Mbundu people. Control of Luanda was essential if the MPLA was to dominate the workings of the transitional government set up by the Alvor agreement, utilize the port facilities, and be in a position to proclaim itself as the new independent government of Angola in November. Beginning in March 1975, the Soviets escalated their support of the MPLA forces by providing ever increasing amounts of more sophisticated weaponry through air transport flights into Brazzaville and by Soviet and East German freighters unloading at Pointe-Noire. The Communist cadres in the Portuguese armed forces facilitated the transshipment of these weapons to the MPLA troops in Luanda. At the same time, as one of Castro's chief lieutenants, Carlos Rafael Rodriguez, was later to admit, the Cuban government began infiltrating Cuban military technicians as trainers for the MPLA.[7] By late spring, there were as many as 230 Cuban military advisers in Angola. In the north, with logistical support from Mobutu, the FNLA forces attempted to expand their tribal base against MPLA resistance, and in the south Savimbi's UNITA guerrillas attempted to contain an MPLA drive southward along the coastline.

These continuing clashes between the three independence movements led to a summit meeting in Nakuru on June 16–21 between Neto, Roberto, and Savimbi. It was held under Kenyan auspices, and a last attempt was made to salvage the Alvor settlement. All three parties signed the Nakuru agreement, calling for restoration of the transitional government, an end to violence, the establishment of a single national army, and the holding of elections in October. However, intermittent fighting inside Luanda between the troops of the three movements stationed there under the terms of the agreement culminated on July 9 in all-out civil war. The MPLA, armed with its new weapons, succeeded in driving out the FNLA and UNITA troops and took over what remained of the transitional government. From then until their final triumph, the Soviets never permitted their MPLA allies to lose control of the capital with its symbolic and strategic significance. The Soviet king in the Angolan chess game had been maneuvered into a safe position on the board and was never thereafter successfully challenged.

Reacting to the breakdown of the Alvor and Nakuru agreements and to the clear evidence that the Soviets intended by massive arms shipments to ensure the military victory of their MPLA ally, Ford and Kissinger then made their decision to provide covert military support to FNLA and UNITA, in an attempt to prevent a Communist takeover of the entire territory of Angola. The belief was that these two movements had sufficient numerical strength and popular support, given an adequate supply of weapons, to expand their tribal enclaves in the north and south and thus either defeat the MPLA or force a compromise settlement that would prevent the country from slipping into the Soviet orbit, with all the strategic consequences that were foreseeable. The two neighboring African states that would be most directly threatened by a Soviet-imposed Angolan client regime, Zaire and Zambia, fully supported the concept of a covert program of American military assistance. President Mobutu of Zaire agreed to the use of his territory as a staging base for the shipment of arms to the FNLA, while President Kaundu of Zambia agreed to allow airfields in his country to be used as transshipment points for weapons destined for Savimbi's UNITA guerrillas. As Henry Kissinger was later to testify before Congress, "By mid-July, the military situation radically favored the MPLA." Zaire and Zambia had become "more and more concerned about the implications for their own security" and "turned to the United States for assistance in preventing the Soviet Union and Cuba from imposing a solution in Angola, becoming a dominant influence in south central Africa, and threatening the stability of the area."[8]

In mid-July 1975, President Ford approved a 40 Committee recommendation that the CIA be directed to mount a covert program of military support to FNLA and to UNITA. By the time the program was terminated some six months later, a total of about $32 million had been spent by the CIA in supporting these two independence movements in their battles against the MPLA, approximately half for weapons and the other half for food and transportation.[9] On July 29, the first planeload of arms was on its way from the United States to Zaire. Following the secret briefings held pursuant to the Hughes-Ryan amendment, opposition to this covert involvement in Africa grew in the Senate Foreign Relations Committee, led by Senator Dick Clark (D., Iowa), the chairman of the subcommittee on Africa. When the $32 million authorized had been exhausted, Senators Clark, Alan Cranston, and John Tunney introduced an amendment to the 1976 Defense Appropriations Bill that prohibited the expenditure of Agency funds in Angola except for intelligence purposes. Following the disclosure of the CIA involvement in Angola by Seymour Hersh in *The New York Times,* this Tunney amendment was passed in the Senate on December 19, 1975, by a vote of 54 to 22. On January 27, the House also voted in favor of this restriction by 323 to 99. On February 9, President Ford signed it into law, and CIA covert action in Angola was effectively terminated by the Congress through the exercise of its power over the purse strings. Traumatized by Watergate and Vietnam, the country had no stomach for another undeclared war in a far-off country about which most people knew very little.

In retrospect, it is quite clear that the scale of the abortive American covert intervention in Angola, although substantial, was totally inadequate to cope with the forces that the Soviets were willing to commit to the struggle. On each step up the ladder of escalation, the Soviets were several steps ahead of the United States. Once having made the decision to intervene militarily in the fall of 1974, the Soviets followed their usual practice of ensuring a decisive margin of superiority. Watching from London as the drama unfolded, I could put together a pretty clear picture of the sequence of events, although some crucial episodes remain shrouded in mystery. By the spring of 1976, enough evidence had accumulated from a wide variety of sources to reconstruct a fairly accurate chronology, although both the Soviet and Cuban governments have gone to great lengths to obscure and distort the sequence in which events actually occurred. Throughout, the Soviets were able to derive a critical advantage from being able to mask with secrecy large movements of troops and armaments and to depend upon the secret coordination of disciplined Communist parties. Here, then, as clearly as I could reconstruct it in London, is the story of how the Soviets brought their queen, Castro's Cuban troops, into play on the Angolan chessboard to win a decisive victory and to prepare the way for future successful adventures in Africa.

First, it should be remembered that by 1975 the relationship between the Castro regime in Havana and the Soviets had changed drastically from what it had been a decade earlier when Che Guevara first made his romantic debut as a guerrilla hero in the Congo. After Guevara's career as a modern Robin Hood was ended by his arrest and execution in Bolivia, Castro began his retreat from the guerrilla adventures that had caused so much friction between his guerrilla leaders and the more cautious and pragmatic Latin American Communist parties who took their guidance from Moscow. Massively dependent on the Soviets for economic assistance and military hardware, Castro was compelled to become a much more disciplined member of the international community of Soviet-controlled Communist parties. Symbol and proof of this transformation was the fact that by 1971 the Cuban intelligence service, the DGI, was under close tutelage of the KGB. Cuban intelligence officers were regularly sent in large numbers to the Soviet Union to complete their training, and KGB specialists in Cuba exercised a supervisory role over the planning and execution of Cuban intelligence operations. This change in the Soviet-Cuban relationship was an essential precondition for the role Castro was now to play in Africa.

In July of 1975, even before the first trickle of covert American military support began to reach the fighting fronts in Angola, there was evidence that the MPLA leaders had approached the Soviets with the complaint that their cadres were unable to use effectively or to maintain the ever more sophisticated weaponry that the Soviets were giving them. Fearful of the potentially superior numerical strength of their FNLA and UNITA opponents, they pleaded not only for Soviet military training experts but for a Soviet troop presence to operate the new equipment on the battlefield. The Soviets reportedly explained to their MPLA clients that the introduction of Soviet troops into the Angolan civil war was too dangerous an escalatory move and might well provoke the United States into committing its own forces to the struggle. Instead, they advised the MPLA leadership to seek assistance from the Cubans.

An MPLA mission flew to Havana and met with Castro in early August to argue their urgent need for trained troops. Perhaps fearful of American reaction, Castro was reported to have appeared initially reluctant; but the MPLA leaders pleaded that it was his revolutionary duty to help them as he had previously done in sending Cuban troops to South Yemen and Syria. By mid-August, Castro, for whatever reason, made up his mind to take the risks involved, and the decision was made to proceed with the extensive logistical planning necessary to mount a massive sea and air lift of large numbers of Cuban troops, equipment, and supplies across the Atlantic to Angola. This chronology is consistent with the testimony of Cuban prisoners later taken in the fighting, who claimed they were told in August that their destination was Angola. Also the lead time required for assembly and shipment explains the fact that Cuban troops began disembarking in Angola in late September.

To the best of my knowledge, there is no clear evidence available on the respective roles the Soviet and Cuban leaders played behind the scenes in reaching this momentous decision. Certainly, there had to be very close and continuing coordination between them once the decision was made, because the bulk of the heavy weapons and ammunition that the Cuban troops were to use in Angola had to be flown or shipped from the Soviet Union. The timing of this huge tri-continental logistical operation had to be closely meshed to ensure the simultaneous arrival in Angola of the troops from Cuba and the arms from the U.S.S.R. Perhaps it was a joint decision in which both parties could see mutual advantages, but my own guess is that the Soviets took the initiative in pressuring Castro. The commitment of Cuban forces to the Angolan fighting was so preferable in every way to the exposure of Soviet troops that the Soviets had every reason to urge this solution, while Castro had to reckon with the morale effects of heavy casualties and the possible defeat of his expeditionary force in a distant country whose name and location most Cubans did not even know.

In his version of these events, Gabriel García Márquez gives a distorted and, I believe, inaccurate description of the actual chronology.[10] He claims that the final decision to commit Cuban troops, as distinct from military advisers, was made by the Cuban high command on November 5, 1975, on its own initiative, and that only after the decision was made was the Soviet Union informed. The propaganda effect of this account was threefold. First, it made it appear that Castro had acted independently in responding to the appeal of his revolutionary brothers in the MPLA, and not as a junior partner in the implementation of Soviet geopolitical objectives. Second, it supported the thesis that Cuban troop intervention was a reaction to the invasion of Angola by some 1,500 South African troops that occurred in October. The Cuban intervention would be more palatable in Africa if it appeared to have been a response to the involvement of white South African racists in the struggle, whereas in fact the timing of the arrival of Cuban troops in September proves that the decision was made at least two months before the South Africans intervened. Finally, the Cubans were sensitive to the charge that they intervened covertly in a strictly African civil war, and by claiming that the troops arrived simultaneously with the establishment of the MPLA as the government of Angola on November 11, they could hope it would appear that their forces had only responded to a request for assistance from a legally constituted government. This chronology of Angolan events has been supported by Communist-controlled media and front groups throughout the world and has been influential among sectors of Western opinion that have not taken the trouble to look closely at the facts and the dates.

In one respect, however, the García Márquez version has the ring of authenticity. His explanation of the factors that led Castro to assume that the United States would not forcibly intervene openly to stop this power play is an accurate description of the assessment of American reactions which I think must then have prevailed at the top level of both the Soviet and Cuban governments. García Márquez writes that Washington would think twice about openly intervening because "it had just freed itself from the quagmire of Vietnam and the Watergate scandal. It had a President no one had elected. The CIA was under fire in Congress and low-rated by public opinion. The United States needed to avoid seeming— not only in the eyes of African countries, but especially in the eyes of American blacks—to ally itself with racist South Africa. Beyond all this it was in the midst of an election campaign in its Bicentennial year."[11]

Whatever history may eventually reveal about the respective roles of Moscow and Havana in arriving at this bold decision, it was a brilliant and daring conception that added a whole new and dangerous dimension to the Soviet ability to project Communist power into the third world. By supporting the proxy army of Cuba, the Soviets avoided the direct commitment of their own forces which could so easily alarm the United States and provoke American counteraction. Because of Castro's prominent role in the nonaligned movement, his army enjoyed the reputation of being part of the third world and was not as much feared and resented as would have been the troops of one of the superpowers. Moreover, among the Cuban troops sent to Angola, care was taken to ensure that almost half were black, so that a racial identity appeared to exist that would not have been the case if Soviet troops had been sent. Finally, the Soviets had learned from the expulsion of their 4,000 military advisers from Egypt by Sadat that the presence of large numbers of Soviet personnel provoked bitter resentments. The Cubans assimilated more easily and got on better with the native population.

For Castro, too, there were obvious advantages in the new strategy. The guerrilla adventures of Che Guevara had had romantic appeal, but in each case they had failed in conception and execution. They had lacked the careful calculation of the odds and of the strength of the opposition that the Soviets could offer their Cuban partner through their worldwide intelligence apparatus. Guevara had relied upon a spontaneous mass uprising of the peasantry, which never occurred, whereas joint operations with the Soviets depended on a heavy military preponderance ensured by the provision of large amounts of modern weaponry transported by Soviet planes and ships. By becoming a junior partner in the Soviet geopolitical offensive, Castro lost the freedom of action he had once enjoyed, but he gained indispensable Soviet political and logistical support and a role on the world stage for a vaulting ambition that had never been content to be confined to improving the lot of the Cuban people on one small island.

Once decided upon, the commitment of Cuban troops to the Angolan civil war proceeded with dispatch and utmost secrecy. The arrival of Soviet and Cuban ships and planes in Pointe-Noire and Brazzaville could not be masked from American surveillance, but by unloading troops at night and by strict security discipline during the sea voyage a successful effort was made for some time to conceal the fact that troops as well as weapons and supplies were being transported. Cuban prisoners later captured in the Angolan fighting testified that during the sea voyage they were ordered to stay below decks during daylight hours to prevent their being spotted by American surveillance. Both the Soviets and Cubans wanted to reduce to a minimum the chance of American intervention by making the deployment of Cuban troops a fait accompli by the time the United States discovered what was going on. And they wanted to exploit the shock effect of the sudden appearance of these trained troops on the battlefield.

In spite of sporadic agent reporting that Cuban troops were arriving, the CIA and the American policymakers were slow in facing up to the size of this large-scale intervention. On September 24, Cuban troops were identified disembarking at Pointe-Noire and being transported by trucks into Angola, but it was only later that it was realized that by November 4,000 Cuban combat troops had been deployed. By January 1976 the figure had reached 15,000. By February, the CIA estimated that the combined Soviet-Cuban sea and air lift had transported 38,000 tons of weapons and supplies to Angola at a total cost for the operation of approximately $300 million, ten times the size of the American covert intervention. The armaments included armored cars, T-54 tanks, mass fire rockets, helicopters, and MIG fighter planes. The Soviet intervention dwarfed the scale of the American effort in every respect, and proved once again that when the Soviets determine to commit their military resources they do so decisively and with overwhelming superiority, leaving little to chance.

Before the air bridge from Soviet territory to Brazzaville on Angola's border could be safely used to bring in the large amounts of arms and munitions needed by the Cubans, a secure staging area was required on the African coast of the Mediterranean, where airfields with long runways and refueling facilities could service the large Soviet transport planes; their range when fully loaded was not sufficient to make the trip in one hop. Making a virtue of necessity, the Soviets approached the radical nationalist regime in Algeria for permission to use its airfields. The Algerians drove a hard bargain, demanding in return a $500 million military assistance program not only to equip their own forces but to strengthen the POLISARIO guerrillas, who were beginning their fight against the Moroccan army of King Hassan II for control of the Spanish Sahara. The Soviets agreed, and within a year $96 million worth of equipment had been delivered to the Algerians, including MIG-21s, T-62 tanks, and surface-to-air missiles. In making this deal, the Soviets killed two birds with one stone. They not only gained the indispensable use of staging bases in Algiers for their transport planes, but they strengthened the POLISARIO guerrillas in their struggle for the Sahara, thereby weakening the conservative Moroccan monarchy by forcing it to commit increasing resources to a drawn-out and debilitating conflict. Moreover, the Boumediene regime in Algiers, although not Communist in orientation, was a radical one-party state, whose opposition to Israel and support of the Palestinian guerrillas fitted Soviet strategic objectives in that area.

Another incident in Angola that occurred in the summer of 1975 demonstrates how the commitment of Soviet military strength to one country can carry with it future destabilizing consequences for neighboring states. To understand this episode, it is necessary to follow the bewildering shift of alliances that finally brought the Katangan mercenaries into alliance with the MPLA and the Cuban forces in Angola. Under colonial rule in the Congo (now Zaire), the Belgians had recruited in the rich southern copper mining province of Katanga (now Shaba) a local constabulary from among the predominant Lunda tribe. They were professionally trained and proved to be competent soldiers. They supported Moïse Tshombe in his attempt to establish a secessionist regime in Katanga, but when Tshombe's rebellion failed, these Katangan mercenaries, about 5,000 strong, fled with their families into northern Angola rather than accept the authority of Mobutu's central government.

The Portuguese colonial administration offered asylum to this well-trained professional force on condition that the Katangans would agree to join them in putting down the three nationalist insurgent movements. The Katangans accepted the offer, and for years these black mercenaries fought effectively alongside the Portuguese against the FNLA, MPLA, and UNITA. In the summer of 1975, a group of Portuguese Communist officers and Cuban military advisers met with the leader of the Katangan mercenaries, General Nathaniel Mbumba, at his base in northern Angola. They made him an offer he couldn't refuse. They pointed out that the withdrawal of the Portuguese colonial army was inevitable and argued that the Katangans had better switch and join with the MPLA in fighting against the other two black nationalist movements if they wanted to be on the winning side. The Katangans accepted this proposal but laid down one condition. For their services on the MPLA side in the continuing civil war, they demanded assurances that when the fighting in Angola was over they would be given Communist support in their plans to return to Shaba province and take over their tribal homeland from President Mobutu's regime. The deal was made.[12]

Having been given the promise of future assistance in the achievement of their long-cherished irredentist ambitions, the Katangans were supplied with Soviet weaponry and fought well on the side of the MPLA against FNLA and UNITA. Jonas Savimbi, the UNITA leader, had a healthy respect for the military prowess of the Katangans. As recounted by John Stockwell in his book, Savimbi had no hesitation in rating them as far superior to the MPLA. In a conversation with Stockwell in late August 1975, Savimbi is quoted as saying, "The MPLA is no problem to us. They run away. But in Luso we are fighting the gendarmes from the Katanga. They are very strong and they don't run away."[13] This Katangan gambit played a critical role in helping the MPLA to hold valuable territory and in winning time for the deployment of Cuban troops.

The Cubans stuck by their bargain after the MPLA had been established as the government of Angola, and it was to their interest to do so. They knew that the Katangan mercenaries could count on considerable support among their fellow Lunda tribesmen inside Zaire and that Mobutu's army was poorly trained and disciplined. Loss of the Katangan copper mines would be a devastating blow to Mobutu and could open the way to the installation of a radical regime in the heart of Africa. After the civil war was over, Cuban military technicians joined the Katangan training camps near the border between Angola and Zaire. New young recruits from the Lunda tribe were armed and trained in Soviet weaponry, including mass fire rockets and antitank weapons. In March 1977, about 2,000 well-equipped Katangans marched across the border into Zaire, and the Cubans took pains to mask their supporting role by holding their troops back from involvement in the actual fighting. The invasion would very probably have succeeded if it had not been for the timely intervention of Moroccan troops flown in by the French.

Retreating to Angola, General Mbumba's men were reequipped by the Cubans and given additional training. A year later the Katangans struck again from their base camps in Angola, this time at the Shaba mining town of Kolwezi, by going through Zambian territory to bypass Mobutu's troops defending the border. Transformed by Castro's blessing from mercenaries into progressive revolutionaries, they now called themselves the Congolese National Liberation Front. Again only the last-minute intervention of the French Foreign Legion and Moroccan troops with American logistical support saved Mobutu from defeat. Castro has steadfastly denied any Cuban connection with these two Katangan invasions of Zaire; but this brief history of the Katangan role in the Angolan civil war shows how deeply the Cubans were involved from the beginning, and demonstrates again how the establishment of Communist influence in one country transforms it into a launching base for attacks on adjoining states. The domino theory may be too simplistic an explanation of this phenomenon, but defeat does have consequences, and targets of opportunity will be exploited once a new territorial base has been secured.

Returning to the Angolan civil war, it is quite clear in retrospect that the brief intervention of the South African government in the fighting was an invaluable propaganda windfall for the Soviets and Cubans, and had a devastating impact on the attitudes of many African nations toward the struggle. The South African armed forces did not intervene unilaterally or on their own initiative. They responded to a request from Savimbi, whose UNITA forces in central Angola in September and early October 1975 were hard-pressed on two flanks by the Katangan mercenaries and Cuban-led MPLA troops. Savimbi was under heavy pressure from President Kaunda to open the Benguela railroad by the time of independence on November 11, with the danger that he would lose his staging bases in Zambia if this could not be accomplished. After consulting with non-Communist African leaders including Mobutu, Kaunda, Felix Houphouet-Boigny of the Ivory Coast, and Léopold Senghor of Senegal, Savimbi made his decision to request the assistance of South African troops.[14] The United States was not involved in this decision, and even so severe a critic as Stockwell admits there was no American encouragement, although he claims there was tacit coordination in the subsequent fighting. In response to Savimbi's request, on October 23 the South Africans committed a small covert mobile strike force of about 1,200 men in armored cars, supplied by air, and with this support UNITA forces were able to drive northward until they were within a hundred miles of Luanda on November 11. President Vorster of South Africa obviously hoped to keep this intervention small enough to remain secret. His purpose was to ensure a moderate black independent government in Angola rather than one under Communist control.

Meanwhile, in the north of Angola, Roberto's FNLA forces, strengthened by covert American assistance and accompanied by some units of Mobutu's poorly disciplined Zairian army, drove southward against MPLA resistance until they were almost within sight of

Luanda. But the MPLA still held the capital, and on November 11, as the Portuguese high commissioner departed and the Portuguese troops withdrew, the MPLA declared itself to be the new government as the People's Republic of Angola and was immediately recognized by the Soviets and the Cubans. Thereafter, Soviet and Cuban military assistance could be portrayed as a response to the request of a legitimate government and Luanda's port facilities could be openly used to bring in the mounting wave of arms and munitions. In November, Cuban troops were committed to combat against the FNLA and Zairian army units and, effectively using 122-mm mass rocket fire, scored a series of victories over the less well armed forces of Holden Roberto, driving them back to the Zaire border in disarray.

The tide had turned. On November 22, a story broke in the press revealing the South African troop presence in Angola, and was exploited to the hilt by the Communist propaganda machine to justify the Soviet and Cuban intervention as a defensive reaction to racist South African aggression. At an OAU summit on January 11–12 in Addis Ababa, the African nations split 22–22 on the issue of recognizing the MPLA as the new government, but within a few weeks a large majority of African states had shifted toward recognition. The votes in the American Congress in December and January signaled the end of American intervention, and in the face of these developments the South Africans withdrew their forces in January 1976. Their abortive intervention had been remarkably successful for a brief period in strictly military terms, until they faced the mass fire power of the Cubans, but politically this South African attempt to assist the non-Communist cause was fatal. It appeared to give retrospective legitimacy to the prior Cuban intervention and enabled the Soviets and Cubans to claim that their imposition of a minority Marxist regime on the Angolan people was a black nationalist victory over the hated South African racists.

Abandoned by the South Africans and cut off by the U.S. Congress from any further American assistance, Savimbi fought a disciplined delaying action as he retreated south, giving up one town after another to the advancing Cubans with their tanks and helicopters. But he maintained his UNITA forces largely intact and in a last meeting with a CIA officer on February 1, 1976, he vowed to revert to guerrilla warfare and to defend his tribal homeland by harassing actions launched from the jungle. In mid-February, he wrote a farewell letter of thanks to President Kaunda of Zambia. It is worth quoting in part since it conveys the quality of the man:

> UNITA lost 600 men in the battle for Huambo. The machine of war that Cuba and the Soviet Union have assembled in Angola is beyond the imagination. To prevent the total destruction of our forces we have decided to revert immediately to guerrilla warfare. The friends that have promised to help us did not fulfill their promises and we must face our own fate with courage and determination. . . .
>
> I have always tried to the best of my ability and courage to serve the interest of Angola and Africa. I am not a traitor to Africa and the hard days that we expect ahead will prove to the world that I stand for my principles. In Angola might has made right but I will remain in the bush to cry for justice.[15]

Savimbi has remained as good as his word, and to this day his well-organized UNITA guerrillas have kept the occupying Cuban troops under continuing harassment in southern Angola. The best evidence of UNITA effectiveness is the fact that the Cuban occupation army, with all its planes and tanks, has not yet as of this writing been able to open the Benguela railroad, since UNITA guerrillas are able to destroy bridges as fast as the Cubans repair them. But except for this continuing guerrilla insurgency in southern Angola, the Soviets and Cubans have succeeded in imposing their minority Marxist clients on the Angolan population.

Using the chess analogy, the Angolan operation was a brilliantly executed geopolitical strategic triumph. The Soviets from the beginning correctly assessed the main weakness of their American opponent, the fact that with our will sapped by Watergate and Vietnam we would not be prepared to match the superior forces the Soviets were willing to commit. The Soviet bishop on the board, the Portuguese Communist Party, honed to a disciplined edge by years of clandestine organization, was brought into play early and gave indispensable support to the Soviet king, the MPLA. The power and mobility of the queen, the Cuban expeditionary force, was successfully masked until it was brought into play and then was given decisive effect by the massive infusion of Soviet weaponry timed to coincide with the arrival of the Cuban troops. The Katangan constabulary was a Soviet castle on the board, and by exploiting the irredentist hopes of these nonideological allies, the Soviets brought them into play to win time for the deployment of the Cuban queen. The Algerian gambit worked to perfection to ensure the success of the Soviet airlift. Finally, the fatally flawed intervention of the South Africans was exploited to turn African opinion around and to transform a growing propaganda defeat into a political triumph. In February of 1976, when it was clear that the Angolan game had been won, there must have been a discreet celebration in the Kremlin and an exchange of mutual congratulations among the members of the Politburo, who had taught the poker-playing Americans a lesson in how to play strategic chess. And all of this was accomplished without the Soviet Union's losing the benefits of détente. American grain shipments continued, transfers to the U.S.S.R. of valuable Western technology increased, and the SALT negotiating process had the effect of persuading the Americans to acquiesce passively in the increasing strength of strategic and conventional Soviet weaponry.

Nothing succeeds like success, particularly in the rivalry between nations where perceptions of relative power can be as important as the actualities. Moreover, each new advance on the board opens up a host of opportunities that would not otherwise have been available. So it was with the extension of Soviet influence into Angola, and on my return from London to Washington in the summer of 1976 I watched with mounting apprehension as the Soviets proceeded systematically to exploit the geopolitical possibilities of their newly established territorial base. It did not require access to secret intelligence reporting to understand the broad outlines of the emerging Soviet strategy toward southern Africa. It was solidly based on longstanding Leninist doctrine, and in its tactical implementation it depended on a pragmatic and opportunistic exploitation of the political vulnerability of the minority white regimes that ruled over large black majorities in the countries that lay to the south of Angola's border.

The doctrinal origins of this policy can be traced back to Lenin's conception of the vulnerable dependence of Western European governments on their colonial territories as expressed in the theses of the Second Comintern Congress of 1920. In effect, Lenin argued that "national revolutionary movements" deserved support even though they were not Communist initially in their political orientation, because they could be used to weaken the colonial powers and by infiltration, dependence, and indoctrination could over time be brought around to becoming disciplined Communist parties. As Stalin put it brutally in 1920, "the more developed proletarian West cannot finish off the world bourgeoisie without the support of the peasant East."[16] In this context, the MPLA was seen as a "revolutionary democratic party" in the process of transition toward communism, and the black nationalist movements that had sprung up in opposition to the minority white regimes in southern Africa were similarly seen as susceptible to manipulation and eventual conversion to the true faith.

Even before the victory in Angola was complete, the Soviets spelled out for the world to read what the consequences would be for neighboring states to the south. On June 5, 1975, the official Soviet newspaper, *Pravda,* announced that the collapse of the Portuguese colonial empire had created "a totally new situation in Africa's south where the so-far still enslaved people of Rhodesia and the Republic of South Africa, inspired by the success of neighboring peoples, are rising to battle against colonialism and racism." To make the picture complete, the Soviet delegate to the U.N., Jakov Malik, warned the Security Council on June 6 that South Africa's hold on its colony of South West Africa, now called Namibia, was doomed. In Malik's words, "The tasks of the anticolonial struggle will not be accomplished fully until the people of Namibia become free. This in turn calls for greater pressure to be put on the racist regime in South Africa in order to isolate it as much as possible in the world arena."[17] Nobody in the West could claim that he had not been warned. The United States was put on public notice even before the Angolan fighting ended that the Angolan base, once secured, would be used to topple Ian Smith's white minority regime in Rhodesia, to break South Africa's colonial rule in Namibia, and eventually to undermine the authority of the white minority in South Africa itself.

By the time the Soviets and Cubans had successfully installed their MPLA client in power in Angola, opposed only by the determined harassment of Savimbi's UNITA guerrillas, the black nationalist resistance to Ian Smith's white regime in Rhodesia had evolved in such a way as to make Angola's geographical position a vital factor in any effort to arm and train the black guerrillas fighting against Rhodesia's whites. By the end of 1976, Joshua Nkomo, one of the principal black nationalist Rhodesian leaders, had sought asylum in neighboring Zambia. With the full support of Zambian President Kenneth Kaunda, he established the political base of his movement, the Zimbabwe African People's Union (ZAPU), in the Zambian capital of Lusaka. His guerrillas were armed and trained in camps within Zambia, and from these bases they conducted guerrilla raids across the border into Rhodesia. Although Nkomo had a commanding presence and considerable ability, his popular base inside Rhodesia was fairly narrow since it depended primarily on the support of the Ndebele tribal group, which makes up about 15 percent of the black Rhodesian population.

Neither President Kaunda nor Joshua Nkomo was a committed Marxist. In fact, Kaunda described the Soviet movement of Cuban troops into Angola to replace the Portuguese colonialists as "a plundering tiger with its deadly cubs now coming in through the back door." And Nkomo had a reputation for opportunism and flexibility. However, the small and ill-equipped Zambian army had neither the weapons nor the skills necessary to support the ZAPU guerrillas in their unequal struggle against Ian Smith's disciplined and well-armed Rhodesian troops. Moreover, the training camps established in Zambia were vulnerable to Rhodesian air strikes and commando raids. The Soviets and Cubans were quick to offer a solution, and it was accepted. Training camps for ZAPU forces were established in Angola, where Cuban instructors trained the guerrillas in more sophisticated types of Soviet weaponry. By the early spring of 1977, a logistical supply route for arms and munitions had been set up. To avoid interception by Savimbi's guerrillas, the weapons were airlifted by Cuban pilots to the Angolan town of Luso near the Zambian border, and from there truck convoys delivered the arms and supplies to the ZAPU base camps, inside Zambia, from which the ZAPU guerrillas launched their operations into Rhodesia.

Well aware of the political danger to his own independence of allowing a large number of Soviet and Cuban military advisers into his country, President Kaunda stubbornly tried to control and limit the size of the Soviet and Cuban presence against Castro's argument that they were needed close to the fighting front. On occasion, Kaunda even successfully resisted demands from his own Zambian officers for Cuban-manned antiaircraft batteries to defend against Rhodesian air raids. But in spite of these constraints, there were by

October of 1977 a limited number of Soviet and Cuban officers serving with the approximately 8,000 ZAPU guerrillas based in Zambia. Not the least of Kaunda's worries was his concern that the ill-disciplined guerrillas were beginning to outnumber his own armed forces and to pose a potential threat to the stability of his regime.

For his part, Nkomo became increasingly dependent on Soviet and Cuban support. In addition to military training and supplies, the Soviets covertly provided Nkomo with substantial sums to cover the costs of political organization and propaganda for his movement both inside Rhodesia and internationally. With this assured base of superpower support, Nkomo became increasingly less interested in the possibilities of a peaceful compromise settlement to the Rhodesian struggle and more susceptible to the influence of the Soviets because of his dependence on them. In addition, if past experience is any guide, we can be sure that military training of the ZAPU guerrillas was combined with heavy doses of Marxist indoctrination by the Cuban officers. Similarly, selective recruitment of well-paid agents among these leadership cadres by the KGB and the Cuban intelligence service, the DGI, can be assumed to have been continuous. The Soviets and Cubans exploited their control of Angolan territory to win increasing influence over one of the two main Rhodesian guerrilla movements and thereby gained significant leverage over the final outcome. While the United States and Britain pursued their plan for internationally supervised elections in Rhodesia and rejected the compromise internal settlement reached by Ian Smith and the three internal black leaders, the Soviets placed their money and their arms at the service of Nkomo's ZAPU guerrillas in the belief that as in Angola, superior force on the ground would decide the issue.

The Soviets, however, did not bet all their money on one horse. In addition to ZAPU, there was another large black guerrilla movement active in Rhodesia, the Zimbabwe African National Union (ZANU), and its popular support came from the majority Shona tribal group. In 1976 its leader, Robert Mugabe, was given asylum in neighboring and newly independent Mozambique by President Samora Machel, who had established his radical regime in power after the withdrawal of the Portuguese in 1975. With the support of Machel, Mugabe established base camps for his ZANU guerrillas in Mozambique and quickly expanded guerrilla operations across the border into

Rhodesia. Initially more attracted to the Chinese than to the Soviet brand of communism, Mugabe at first received most of his foreign support from Peking, but the Soviets and Cubans, with their superior resources, gradually replaced the Chinese as his principal source of arms. In October 1977, Machel flew to Havana and arranged for the stationing in Mozambique of some 500 Cuban military advisers, most of whom became engaged in training the ZANU guerrillas in the use of weaponry that was brought in by Soviet freighters at the port of Maputo, the capital of Mozambique.

With their feet firmly planted in both guerrilla camps, the Soviets watched from the sidelines as the leaders of the front-line African states, particularly President Nyerere of Tanzania and President Kaunda of Zambia, tried to weld the two movements into a unified political and military entity. Nkomo and Mugabe were persuaded to become coleaders of a new Patriotic Front, but an attempt to merge their armies in training camps in Mozambique broke down in bitter tribal fighting. As whites fled Rhodesia in increasing numbers, one likely result appeared to be a black civil war between the ethnically divided ZAPU and ZANU guerrilla armies. Having armed both sides, the Soviets could attempt to use their influence to arrange a compromise solution, and if this failed, they had the option of waiting until the final stages of the struggle to commit the Cuban troops from their bases in Angola, thereby determining the outcome and picking the winner. The one thing that Moscow showed no interest in was a peaceful solution through democratic elections held under international supervision. The courageous and successful efforts of the British Conservative government to arrange a cease-fire and to supervise free elections in Rhodesia represented the last chance for a peaceful settlement that would reduce Soviet influence over the outcome. Mugabe's decisive victory in the elections held under British auspices in February 1980 gave his ZANU party a clear majority in the new government of an independent Zimbabwe. Mugabe's initial moderation inspired hopes that his Marxist convictions would be tempered by pragmatism, but there was also the danger that his moderate policies were only temporary and tactical, allowing him time to gain control of the levers of power in the army, the police and the intelligence services. The Soviets could be counted on to push him toward a confrontation with the white minority, and to offer him all-out assistance in the looming struggle against the South African regime.

Meanwhile, the Soviets did not neglect the opportunities that beckoned on Angola's southern border with Namibia. The largest and most influential of the black resistance movements to white South African rule in Namibia was the South-West Africa Peoples' Organization (SWAPO), backed by the U.N. and the Organization of African Unity. The victory in Angola had hardly been consolidated before SWAPO's leader, Sam Nujoma, was invited to Moscow in early 1976, and in an October visit to Havana, he praised Cuba's intervention in Angola and thanked Castro for "practical, material, diplomatic and political support."[18] Although SWAPO's leadership was not by any means entirely Marxist in orientation, some of the leaders, like Nujoma, talked in Marxist terms, and the Soviets and Cubans moved quickly to strengthen their influence and the dependency of SWAPO on them by offering to establish training bases for SWAPO guerrillas on Angolan soil. The offer was accepted, and before long Cuban officers were training SWAPO guerrillas in the use of Soviet arms at Angolan bases from which they launched raids into Namibia against the white South African troops. Whatever the future of mineral-rich Namibia was to be, whether a peaceful transition to independence under U.N. auspices or prolonged guerrilla war, the Soviets and Cubans had rapidly established themselves as the principal benefactors of the leading independence movement, and by combining military training with political indoctrination could expect to enjoy increasing influence over the future political direction of the country. Again Angolan territory provided an indispensable launching base for the outward thrust of Soviet power against another adjoining state.

By the time I left the government and retired from the Agency at the end of 1977, the Soviets seemed to me to be well on their way toward positioning themselves for the final assault on their major geopolitical African objective, South Africa itself. By using the Angolan base to arm, train, and indoctrinate the guerrilla armies, with the indispensable help of Cuban troops, they obviously planned to forge a chain of client states across the northern border of South Africa. The final attack on the last white redoubt could then begin under the popular banner of black majority rule. The Soviets view South Africa as peculiarly vulnerable to a sophisticated combination of internal and external pressures. Uprooted and harshly discriminated against, the black workers in the South African cities and mines are a classic example of an oppressed industrial proletariat. They are seen as highly susceptible over time to Marxist indoctrination and organization.

To exploit this target, the Soviets already have in the South African Communist Party a disciplined instrument under effective Moscow control with an influential minority of Eastern European whites in its leadership. It operates illegally inside South Africa and has a well-organized exile base. It has close ties to the principal anti-apartheid resistance organization, the African National Congress, which operates cadre training bases in Tanzania and is partially supported by Soviet funding. The Soviet objective seems to be to prepare for a protracted struggle by building military and political leadership for the future, while advising against attempts at premature revolt. In effect, the Soviets see South Africa as the Achilles heel of the West. Neither the United States nor any European country can defy world opinion by coming to the aid of the South African whites so long as they practice an oppressive policy of apartheid. Yet the West is heavily dependent on South African supplies of gold, platinum, and other scarce metals. South Africa's strategic position across the oil tanker routes from the Middle East, and its industrial base, make it the richest prize in Africa for the Soviets.

Unless the white South African minority undergoes a profound change of heart and is able to reach a reasonable political and territorial settlement with the large black majority, the future is predictable. A prolonged and bloody racial war will be the likely result, with urban terrorism and guerrilla raids of mounting ferocity stretching ever thinner the capacity of the white South African security forces to contain them. As the principal source of arms, training, and indoctrination for this popular rebellion, the Soviets and Cubans will be in a position to pick up the pieces and to have a dominant influence on whatever regime eventually emerges. This prospect is so bleak over the long run that the United States has everything to gain and little to lose in using what time remains to persuade and influence the white South Africans to move toward a reasonable internal settlement that gives the black majority a stake in the country's defense. Only by real progress toward racial equality can the South African whites escape isolation and eventual defeat. Through genuine reform they can gain the support of the West and of the non-Communist African states. The choice is theirs, and if they fail to make it, the

United States can only watch the tragedy unfold and passively acquiesce in a seismic shift of power to the advantage of the Soviets.

Before my retirement I was to watch from inside the Agency one more daring demonstration of Soviet willingness to project its power far beyond its borders into an area vital to American security. This move owed much in conception and execution to the lessons learned in Angola, and in fact control of Angolan territory and the Cuban troop presence there proved to be an important element in its success. It is very doubtful that the Soviets would have dared to risk the commitment of 20,000 Cuban troops and the delivery of $1 billion worth of arms to Ethiopia in the late fall of 1977, if they had not already tested the effectiveness of such massive intervention in Angola and learned there that the United States was not likely to react.

In October 1977, events in the Horn of Africa had moved to the point where the Soviets were faced with a dangerous and difficult decision. After the downfall of Emperor Haile Selassie in Ethiopia in 1974, they played a cautious waiting game as a savage fratricidal struggle for power took place among the revolutionary officers who took over and ruled Ethiopia through a shadowy Armed Forces Cooperative Committee called the Derg. They announced a drastic program of "Ethiopian Socialism" and proceeded to nationalize banking and industry and to put into effect sweeping land reforms. Large quantities of Marxist literature were widely distributed. The official Soviet media reported enthusiastically on these developments, and growing numbers of Soviet and East European delegations began to arrive. But perhaps because of the inherent confusion and uncertainty of a revolutionary situation from which no clear winner had emerged, the Soviets initially hesitated to back any one element; they seem to have spread their covert funding among a wide variety of individuals and organizations.

The Soviet hand was forced by developments in the latter half of 1976. Colonel Mengistu emerged from the bloody infighting and executions within the Derg as the new Ethiopian strongman. Under a $200 million modernization program for the armed forces agreed to before the revolution, the United States had continued to provide military assistance, and the Mengistu regime bought additional U.S. items with its own funds. A delay in these military shipments was instituted by the United States in late 1976 because of the revolutionary chaos, and Mengistu turned insistently to the Soviets as the only alternative source of major military assistance. In December of 1976, the Soviets made their first military support agreement with Mengistu after Jimmy Carter was elected to the presidency in the United States. By March of the next year, Soviet tanks were arriving in some quantity. Reacting to its concern for human rights and to Mengistu's indiscriminate killing of his political opponents, the Carter administration in mid-April 1977 informed the Mengistu regime that it was closing the large U.S. communications base in Kagnew and cutting down the size of the American Military Advisory Group. In retaliation, Mengistu expelled the entire Military Advisory Group and the USIA section in the United States Embassy, and ordered the embassy staff cut in half. On May 3, Mengistu flew to Moscow for a prolonged official visit and returned with a new agreement for large-scale military assistance from the Soviets.

In making this decision, the Soviets deliberately put at risk their heavy political and economic investment over the years in Somalia, amounting to over $1 billion, their strategic base structure at Berbera, and the 4,500 Soviet personnel who were advising the Somali armed forces down to the battalion level. Through this advisory presence in Somalia, the Soviets must have been aware that Somali President Siad had already committed regular Somali forces to the support of the Somali guerrillas who had invaded the Ogaden region of Ethiopia and were already fighting Mengistu's army. Perhaps the Soviets hoped that by backing both sides in this struggle they could exert sufficient influence to preside over a compromise settlement. In fact, in March Castro had visited all the countries of the Horn and tried to sell the Soviet-preferred solution, a federation of the radical regimes in Ethiopia, Somalia, and South Yemen in which the Eritreans rebelling against Mengistu's rule would be included as autonomous members. Although he was warmly received in all these countries, Castro's mission was a failure, and in May the Soviets, by throwing their support behind a massive military assistance program for Mengistu, signaled their willingness to risk the loss of their alliance with Somalia in return for gaining a new ally in Ethiopia, a country with ten times the population of Somalia and an even more strategic position on the Red Sea opposite oil-rich Saudi Arabia. Perhaps the Soviets speculated that they could later regain their position of influence in Somalia by conspiring to overthrow Siad after he had been defeated in the Ogaden. In this respect, ironically, Soviet expectations were at least initially disappointed, because Siad was able to survive defeat thanks to the efficient police state that the Soviets had taught him to impose.

In spite of the influx of Soviet weaponry, flown to Aden and thence to Addis Ababa, and the increasing number of Soviet and Cuban military advisers and even South Yemeni fighting units, the war in the Ogaden did not go well for Mengistu. In early July, Somali forces succeeded in cutting the Addis Ababa–Djibouti railway. With much of the Ethiopian army tied down in fighting the rebels in Eritrea, whose objective was independence, Mengistu's forces were forced to surrender large sections of the Ogaden to the advancing Somali troops. With tribal rebellions breaking out in other parts of Ethiopia, Mengistu's position was desperate by October, and it was evident that Soviet weaponry and both Soviet and Cuban military advisers were not going to be enough to save his army from defeat. The Soviets faced the loss of their entire position in the Horn, in both Somalia and Ethiopia. In late October, Mengistu flew to Moscow and Havana, and this was followed by a flight to Moscow by Raul Castro, together with the Cuban generals who later directed the Cuban troops in the fighting in Ethiopia. During the course of these visits, the crucial decision was made to commit large numbers of Cuban troops to the war and for a greatly expanded group of Soviet military advisers. President Siad reacted by expelling all Soviet military advisers and closing down all Soviet installations in Somalia on November 13. Soviet General Petrov arrived in Addis Ababa on November 17 to become the senior commander.

In effect, the Soviets applied the lessons of the Angolan gambit to the Ethiopian problem and succeeded in wresting victory from the jaws of defeat by a bold commitment of Cuban troops, artillery, planes, and pilots. The decision was made easier for the Soviets by the fact that the Somalis were clearly the aggressors in their invasion of the Ogaden. The Soviets were able to portray their intervention as a response to a request for assistance from a legitimate government attempting to defend its territory against attack, and the African nations in the OAU tended to accept this explanation in view of their concern for the inviolability of national boundaries. The United States was reduced to bringing diplomatic pressure to bear on the Somalis to withdraw, while announcing a policy of not giving assistance to either side.

While Washington looked on with growing concern and barely concealed frustration, the Soviets mounted a huge airlift of troops, weapons, and supplies, which were immediately committed to the Ogaden front to turn the tide of battle. In the last week of November, a thousand-man Cuban expeditionary force was flown from Havana to the U.S.S.R. and from there to Ethiopia. The Angolan base again proved its utility. With time of the essence, in the first week of December Cuban troops and military specialists were flown by Ethiopian planes from Luanda to Addis Ababa, and they immediately moved into action to rescue Mengistu's beleaguered forces in the Ogaden. The size of the Soviet airlift is indicated by the fact that in the first week of December 1977, eighteen large Soviet transport planes, AN-22s, landed with military cargoes and advisers in Addis Ababa, having overflown Turkey and Iran and using Aden as a staging base. By the end of the year, there were more than 2,000 Cuban combat troops deployed on the fighting front, and the number quickly escalated until the Cuban troop presence exceeded 17,000. As is their usual practice, once having decided to intervene militarily, the Soviets overinsured against the possibility of failure by committing a decisively superior force which quickly rolled back the outgunned Somali forces in the Ogaden. While Cuban troops were not committed to the subsequent fighting against the Eritrean rebels, Soviet and Cuban advisers substantially assisted Mengistu's forces in attempting to crush that rebellion.

At an estimated cost of $1 billion, the Soviets had succeeded once again in a bold military move on the African chessboard. They rescued their Marxist client, the Mengistu regime, from certain defeat and in the process positioned their surrogate Cuban army on the shores of the Red Sea, where it posed a direct threat to the Arabian peninsula with its oil riches that were the lifeblood of the industrial West and of Japan. By a daring switch of alliances, the Soviets had leapfrogged into the Middle East and established their influence in a country of over 30 million, strategically situated to threaten Saudi Arabia and Yemen in the north, the Sudan in the west, and Kenya to the south. The Americans had lost an ally and the Soviets had gained one in an area close to the jugular vein of the industrial world, the narrow seas through which the huge oil tankers passed that fed the factories of the West and of Japan. Officials in the Carter administration who were familiar with Ethiopia took some comfort from the fact that in contrast to colonialized Angola, the Ethiopians had a long and proud history of national independence. The hope was that in time this deeply felt nationalism would assert itself and that Marxist indoctrination would prove to be only skin deep, as the Soviet and Cuban presence came to be increasingly resented. Initially, however, Mengistu threw himself enthusiastically into the role of Marxist liberator, and within a year Rhodesian guerrillas were being flown in Soviet planes into Addis Ababa for training by Ethiopian officers under Cuban supervision. We must face the specter of Mengistu playing the role of a black Castro on the African scene, with his troops being used by the Soviets as another proxy army poised for intervention against new targets of opportunity.

My decision to retire from the Agency at the end of 1977 was the result of a number of factors. After being appointed to succeed George Bush as director of the CIA in the spring of 1977, Admiral Stansfield Turner made it clear that he intended to bring into positions of authority within the Agency men of his own choice and that he would look outside the Agency's professional ranks for many of those he needed as replacements. When I asked him what I might look forward to in my own career, he was generous in his praise of past performance but explained that my prominent and well-publicized association with covert action programs in the past would make it impossible for him to appoint me to any of the top positions. Such an appointment would give "the wrong signal" to the public and imply that covert activity was being given a new lease on life. He regretted that I had become "a victim of the times" and promised me useful work to do until my normal retirement at age sixty. Given the damage done to the Agency's reputation by all the investigations and publicity, I could not quarrel with the Admiral's desire to refurbish its image by bringing in new blood at the top and, after some brief reflection, chose early retirement rather than lingering on for the sake of a larger pension.

In addition, my present publishers, Harper & Row, had been urging me for some time to start work on this book. I saw it as an opportunity to try to set the record straight on a number of historical events and at least to present my own version of what had motivated me during an active life. Perhaps most important was my own mounting concern that the scale and nature of the challenge posed by the Soviet Union was not widely understood by an American public still suffering from the shock of Watergate and Vietnam. If I could make some contribution to a clearer and more realistic American comprehension of the dangers that we faced and the role that a competent intelligence service might play, it seemed to me very much worth the effort and, given the pace of events, the sooner the better.

Another powerful incentive toward early retirement from the Agency was a generous offer from an old friend, Charles Bartlett, a nationally syndicated Washington columnist. We had gone to college together and remained friends over the years. Planning a research project and a book of his own, Bartlett needed some relief from the constant pressure of producing three columns a week and he proposed that I write one column a week under my own name, while he continued to write the other two. Fearing that my pen had become rusty with disuse and my prose corrupted by bureaucratic jargon, I accepted the challenge of facing a large and critical national readership on a weekly basis with trepidation. As soon as I had retired, I began work on a series of sample columns that Bartlett could show the Field Newspaper Syndicate to persuade them to offer my output to the newspapers throughout the country that carried his column. With Bartlett's indispensable guidance, I wrestled with the hard discipline of trying to convey my thoughts lucidly in the brief space of 750 words, which was the maximum length of the column.

Bartlett was a harsh taskmaster in demanding clarity of expression and liveliness of style, and he drummed into me the importance of starting each column with a brief dramatic lead paragraph that would entice the attention of the wayward reader. I was not writing logical briefing memoranda for a captive bureaucratic audience, and he stressed the average reader's acute susceptibility to the MEGLO (my eyes glaze over) syndrome. Jokingly, I reminded him of how Flaubert had torn up every week short story drafts submitted to him for criticism by de Maupassant and only after a year allowed de Maupassant to keep one as sufficiently competent to deserve retention. Thanks to Bartlett's demanding criticism and after many false starts, I managed to produce a few columns that he thought were good enough to use as examples, and the syndicate accepted me as his junior partner and began sending my copy out to the subscribing newspapers every week.

To my delight and relief, most of the papers began to run my column with increasing regularity. At the start, I made it clear that in retiring from the CIA I had severed all connections with the Agency and would call the shots as I saw them if the Agency overstepped its bounds or made mistakes of judgment. In fact, I was among the first to call the Agency to account for its failure to analyze correctly the extent and depth of the opposition to the Shah in Iran.[19] For its part, the Agency dealt with me as it did with other journalists. At my request, the Agency's public affairs office would occasionally arrange unclassified briefings for me as it does for all accredited newspapermen, and I found that my former colleagues were universally closemouthed in refusing to discuss classified matters with me. I owe a debt of gratitude to newspaper editors around the country who were willing to accept at face value my assertion of complete independence from my former employer and to judge my work on its merits. There are few countries in the world where such a change of careers would have been possible, and now that it is my business to search behind the official press releases, I have come to have a healthy respect for the industry and integrity of the large majority of my fellow journalists.

Concentrating primarily on the international scene with which I was familiar, I found there was plenty to write about and no dearth of good sources. On coming to office, President Carter had appointed to key positions in his foreign policy establishment in State, Defense, the NSC, and elsewhere men and women with widely differing views on the role of American power in the world. Many of those who had supported Senator George McGovern in the 1972 campaign jumped on the Carter bandwagon early and were rewarded with key policy positions, particularly at the assistant secretary level in the State Department. They were quite young, and the bitter Vietnam experience had been the watershed event in their lives. The lessons they had drawn from it regarding the limits of American power and the dangers of the "imperial presidency" tended to dominate their thinking and to condition their reactions to the rush of world events.

But the Carter foreign policy establishment also included a minority of those who saw in the judicious exercise of American power the only way of setting some limit to the expansion of Soviet influence, whose growth was so dramatically demonstrated in Angola and Ethiopia. Far from being a monolithic entity, the Carter administration seemed to me to be a complex mix of opposing factions, with the President in his speeches and foreign policy decisions tending first to favor the views of one group and then the other. It was a fertile field for the inquiring columnist, and I was surprised to find how open and eager the competing factions were in trying to seek support for their views in the press. This struggle for the control of American foreign policy over which the President presided was not reassuring to our friends and allies who hoped for a coherent consistency, but it did provide the meat of controversy to hard-working journalists.

Needless to say, I found myself in this continuing debate largely on the side of those who felt that Vietnam was behind us and that it was time to work closely with our allies to shore up the American position and to recognize the reality of the widening geopolitical offensive that the Soviets were waging. During 1978, I tried in a series of columns to identify as they occurred new strategic moves by the Soviets and to assess the longer-range consequences. When a coup occurred in Afghanistan in the spring of 1978 and was quickly followed by Soviet recognition of the successor regime, an ex-U.S. ambassador to that country who was living in retirement in Washington was able to give me the political history of each of the newly announced cabinet members. They had all been members of the Afghan Communist Party and many of them had served on its central committee.

It was clear to me that through penetration of the Afghan armed forces and use of a small minority of disciplined Communists, the Soviets had scored a major breakthrough in a vital region. In a column, I attempted to warn of the eventual consequences for neighboring Iran and Pakistan, while the State Department initially tended to downplay the significance of what had occurred.[20] It was only later that the Carter administration admitted that Soviet diplomatic recognition had been followed up by a large influx of Soviet military advisers and a widespread purge of the leaders of the previous regime. Bound by a treaty of friendship to the Soviet Union, Afghanistan quickly became a full-fledged Soviet satellite whose minority Marxist regime the Soviets seemed determined to keep in power against the rising opposition of the conservative tribes in the countryside. The specter of a pincer movement closing on the Persian Gulf was clear enough, with Ethiopia forming one prong and

Afghanistan the other. At the risk of appearing alarmist, I tried to point this out.

These fears were later realized when, during Christmas week of 1979, the Soviets sent the Red Army crashing into Afghanistan to impose a more pliable puppet as the head of their satellite regime and to crush a mounting Muslim rebellion with which a disintegrating Afghan army was unable to cope. In a column published three days before the invasion, I warned that Soviet troops on the Khyber Pass endangered all southwest Asia and demonstrated the Soviet willingness to risk its troops in active combat beyond the truce lines established in 1945.[21]

I had no wish for the role of Cassandra, but events in South Yemen provided additional evidence that the oil states in the Gulf were the strategic objective of the Soviet advance. In late June 1978, the comparatively moderate president of South Yemen, Salim Robaya Ali, was overthrown and killed in a bloody coup led by a hard-line Communist with a record of rigid loyalty to Moscow, Abdul Fattah Ismail. Press reports indicated that Soviet, Cuban, and East German military advisers played a key role in the episode. It seemed to me significant that the coup occurred at a time when Robaya Ali had withdrawn South Yemen support from the Dhofar rebels who were trying to topple the Sultan of Oman, and just at the moment when he was negotiating with Saudi Arabia for improved relations and economic aid. In fact, signs of moderation on the part of Ali's regime were so encouraging that at the time the coup occurred a State Department mission was on its way to Aden to begin promising negotiations.

By conspiring in Ali's well-timed overthrow, the Soviets not only put a stop to this rapprochement with the West but gained new dominating influence within South Yemen. In my column, I said their objectives were obvious: to consolidate their access to the Aden airfields and harbor facilities for their planes and ships; to reinstitute the previous support to the Dhofar rebellion as a way of installing in Oman a regime favorable to them on the narrow Strait of Hormuz opposite Iran; and to secure a base from which to threaten the unstable conservative regime in the Yemen Arab Republic to the north and thus eventually to destabilize the richest prize of all, Saudi Arabia itself, where more than a million émigré Yemenis performed manual labor. In the light of subsequent events, my closing paragraph did not exaggerate the danger: "The Carter administration is facing a genuine and growing crisis of confidence in an area vital to the prosperity and survival of the West. The administration has procrastinated until it is left with only one alternative: urgent, coherent planning with the allies for a common effort to bolster the protection of these crucial resources."[22]

These fears were given substance by the speed with which the Soviets built up their military presence in South Yemen, including increased shipments of modern weaponry and an influx of advisers. In February 1979, the South Yemen regime launched a three-pronged attack across the border into the Yemen Arab Republic. This time the Carter administration did not attempt to downplay the seriousness of this aggressive move or the extent of the Soviet supporting role. This was a deliberate and well-planned attack, involving in its initial phase a professionally coordinated assault with mass rocket and artillery fire, planes, and Soviet tanks. To me and to other journalists, Carter officials spelled out their belief that so massive and sophisticated an attack could not have been mounted without the full support and backing of the approximately 1,000 Soviet military advisers and hundreds of Cuban and East German technicians that were by then known to be in South Yemen. Reacting to so clear a threat to the Saudi oil fields, the Carter administration announced a crash program of $400 million of military assistance to the Yemen Arab Republic, largely paid for by the Saudis. There was some reasoned and well-justified criticism in Congress that the Yemenis might not be able to absorb and effectively use such a large amount of modern weaponry, but the majority reaction in Congress and in the editorial comment around the country was generally supportive of this first open attempt since Vietnam to draw a line beyond which the expansion of Soviet influence would be deemed to threaten vital American interests. A temporary truce in the fighting was hastily arranged through the mediation efforts of the Arab League, but Yemen continued to be vulnerable due to tribal rivalries fueled by South Yemen infiltration and clandestine arms deliveries.

Meanwhile, during 1978 I tried to follow from outside the government the events in Iran that finally led to the Shah's downfall and to the disintegration of the Iranian army. This development was so obviously to the Soviet advantage in its effect on the balance of power in the region surrounding the Persian Gulf that it was difficult for me to accept the Carter administration's initial assurances that the revolutionary turmoil in Iran was entirely indigenous in its motivation and that the Soviets were not involved. I was quite prepared to accept that the revolution had deep roots in the Islamic religious opposition to the corruption of the Shah's regime and to his overly ambitious attempts to force the pace of modernization. But, if past performance was any guide, it seemed to me very probable that the Soviets were working behind the scenes to fan the flames of revolt and to gain increasing influence within a genuinely popular revolution by the strategic deployment of their disciplined Communist cadres.

These suspicions turned out to be well-founded. After some digging, I was able to get my hands on an English translation of some of the radio broadcasts that were being beamed into Iran in the Farsi and Azerbaijani languages from clandestine transmitters located within the Soviet Union, at Baku near the Iranian border. In my column, I pointed out that for many months this radio, completely under Soviet control, had been beaming highly inflammatory broadcasts into Iran, calling for the Shah's overthrow as a puppet of the United States and demanding the immediate expulsion of all Americans from the country.[23] Calling itself the "National Voice of Iran," this radio purported to be the true voice of the Iranian people and pretended to be broadcasting from inside Iran, referring to the Soviet Union as "our friendly northern neighbor." Even while Premier Brezhnev was solemnly warning President Carter not to intervene and claiming that the U.S.S.R. "maintains traditional neighborly relations with Iran," these powerful broadcasts were calling for a national jihad—holy war—against the Shah and charging that "a joint conspiracy" existed between the palace and U.S. imperialism. At the height of the riots in December 1978, this radio poured fuel on the flames by falsely charging that American officers had ordered the Iranian army to fire on demonstrators and that Americans in helicopters had machine-gunned the unarmed crowds.[24]

I also tried to warn that the underground Communist organization in Iran, the Tudeh Party, had led an illegal existence inside the country for many years, while its exile leadership, funded by Moscow and located in East Berlin, had been consistently obedient to Soviet policy directives. It seemed to me that the demonstrated strength of Communist activists in the organization of the strikes in the Iranian oil fields proved that the growth of this clandestine party might well have been underestimated and that it might play a significant role in the future struggle for control of a revolution that might take years to run its course. Khomeini and the conservative Muslim clergy were not Communists and neither were the liberal intelligentsia who had joined with him in an uneasy alliance to overthrow the Shah, but I warned that in the ensuing political anarchy and economic chaos the disciplined Communists with Moscow's covert support might become formidable contenders for power in the later stages of an ongoing revolution. Anxious to bring to a successful conclusion the protracted negotiations with the Soviets for a SALT II agreement, the Carter administration was slow to admit this evidence of Soviet intervention in Iran's internal affairs and protested only mildly and belatedly when the official Soviet press in mid-December began taking an anti-American line in its comment on Iranian developments.

As events in southeast Asia at the end of 1978 demonstrated, the Soviet geopolitical offensive was not confined to targets in Africa and the Middle East. After the Vietnamese invasion of Cambodia, I tried to point out in another column that the Soviets had given Hanoi a green light for aggression by concluding a formal treaty with the Vietnamese in November, which seemed to promise protection against Chinese retaliation.[25] By shipping military supplies to Hanoi and by fully backing the Vietnamese in the U.N. against charges of aggression, the Soviet purpose was clearly to humiliate Peking and to demonstrate to Washington the weakness of the China card. Even the Communist governments of Yugoslavia and Rumania denounced what they saw as a dangerous extension of the Brezhnev Doctrine, which had been used to justify the Soviet invasion of Czechoslovakia in 1968. Soviet sponsorship of aggression by one Communist regime to overthrow another set a precedent that left them in peril. The brutality of the ousted Pol Pot regime in Cambodia could not mask the fact that the Vietnamese, with Soviet support, were guilty of deliberate armed aggression. China's subsequent punitive expedition into Vietnam was designed to prove to both Hanoi and Moscow that proxy warfare by the U.S.S.R.'s "Asian Cubans" would not be passively tolerated on China's borders.

By the beginning of 1979, I thought it indisputable that the Soviets were engaged in exploiting their improving strategic nuclear strength to put into practice on a global scale the lessons first learned in their successful intervention in Angola. Covert support and direction of disciplined Communist parties, the capability to transport arms quickly over vast distances through a growing fleet of planes and ships, the availability of proxy armies, the training, arming, and indoctrination of guerrilla forces: all these instruments had been brought into play in the orchestration of a geopolitical offensive that was gradually transforming the political map of the world. Western access to allies, scarce raw materials, and strategic geographical positions was increasingly threatened with each new advance. At the end of 1979, the Soviets proved by their brutal invasion of Afghanistan that they were prepared to commit their own armed forces to gain control of third world countries when the more indirect means of aggression failed. Before considering what choices are open to the American people in dealing with this situation, it is instructive to take a brief look at the peculiar advantages that the Soviets derive in this rivalry from the internal structure of the Soviet system and at the state apparatus through which they make and implement decisions in the field of foreign policy.

Chapter 13

The Soviet: Apparat: Government

TRYING TO UNDERSTAND how a secretive, one-party police state like
the Soviet Union actually works, how it reaches its decisions in the
fields of foreign and defense policy and implements them, is a frustrating experience both for academicians in our universities and for
intelligence analysts inside our government. The budgetary and policy decisions affecting Soviet national security are hidden behind a
wall of strictly enforced secrecy. A deliberate and continuous effort
is made to mislead and deceive the outside world. There are no open
congressional hearings in which, as in our country, the executive is
compelled to testify and to answer detailed questions. There are no
Church committee investigations of the KGB in which the organization and decision-making processes of that institution are laid bare.
There is no free press to expose hidden policy failures or clandestine
operational successes. There is no independent judiciary to protect
the rights of individual citizens against the state or to set constitutional limits on the exercise of executive power. Books, newspapers,
and technical journals are rigidly censored to exclude anything and

everything that the regime does not want either its own people or the outside world to know. Most significant, no organized political activity outside the confines of the Soviet Communist Party is permitted to exist, so that no open political opposition can challenge the wisdom of the policy decisions of the ruling elite or expose to public view the mistakes it has made. No free trade unions or independent consumer groups are allowed to organize in order to bring public pressure to bear on the allocation of resources as between the military and civilian sectors. There is no public debate over the issue of guns or butter, and it was only after the defection of a key Soviet official that the CIA was able to estimate correctly the very high proportion of Soviet gross national product going to defense.

Yet despite this pervasive secrecy and deliberate deception, it seemed to me that by the time I left the government a pretty clear picture had emerged of how in broad outline the Communist Party of the Soviet Union (CPSU) under General Secretary Leonid Brezhnev decided and implemented the country's foreign and defense policies. Although personalities and procedures are bound to change under Brezhnev's immediate successor, the main outlines are likely to remain similar unless there is a violent and disruptive struggle for power. Such a succession crisis is always possible in the Soviet Union, since one of its principal weaknesses is the lack of any clear constitutional provision for orderly succession, and gunfire can decide the outcome as it did when Beria was eliminated after Stalin's death. But on the assumption that the practices of the Brezhnev era will still be relevant after his departure, and at the risk of considerable oversimplification in the interests of brevity, here is how it seems to me the machinery of the Soviet state functioned as the Brezhnev era was drawing to its close. This picture is not too different from the general impression of how the Soviet regime operates that most well-informed Americans share, although I think I can add some revealing details.

At the top of the Soviet pyramid of power stands the Politburo, with thirteen full members and nine candidate members. Nominally subordinate to the much larger Central Committee of the CPSU, the Politburo usually functions as the final decision-making body of the Soviet regime, and its decisions are normally ratified by the Central Committee without serious objection or debate. Only on the very rare occasions when the Politburo itself is so deeply split that one faction is prepared to appeal to the Central Committee does that committee function as a court of last resort. During his tenure as general secretary of the CPSU, Brezhnev has chaired the weekly meetings of the Politburo, and by 1973 he had established himself as first among equals. However, unlike Khrushchev, he was careful to respect the collegial nature of the Politburo, and there is evidence that on all important matters he polled its members before coming to a decision.

After 1973, Brezhnev moved to consolidate his controlling influence over foreign and defense policy by becoming chairman of a small executive committee within the Politburo that deals with national security issues. It is called the Defense Council, and one of the earliest of the rare public references to its existence in open Soviet literature appeared in *Krasnya Zvezda* on 7 April 1976. Frighteningly little is known about the workings of this most vital organ of Soviet power, but by the end of 1977 the best-informed guesswork indicated that the Defense Council was composed of the following members:

Leonid Brezhnev	General Secretary of the Party and Chairman of the Defense Council
Dmitri Ustinov	Defense Minister
Andrei Gromyko	Foreign Minister
Aleksei Kosygin	Premier
Yuri Andropov	Chairman of the KGB
Yakov Ryabov	Party Secretary for Defense Affairs
Nikolai Ogarkov	Chief of the General Staff
Leonid Smirnov	Chief of the Military Industrial Commission

As can be seen from the jobs they held, these men were those whom Brezhnev would logically have chosen as members of his national security team, and these eight individuals represented an extraordinary concentration of power over the global activities of the Soviet regime.[1] The decisions of the Defense Council appear to be referred to the full membership of the Politburo for a vote before being finally announced, but to my knowledge there is no evidence of a major decision's being overturned in this wider forum. On matters of a strictly military nature, such as weapons procurement, the

Defense Council is provided staff support by the Main Operations Directorate of the General Staff. When foreign policy issues are involved, the International Department of the Central Committee appears to be responsible for the staff work, and Boris Ponomarev, the influential chief of that department and also a candidate member of the Politburo, has occasionally been asked to join the Defense Council's deliberations on such matters.

Once made and ratified by the full membership of the Politburo, the decisions of the Defense Council have an entirely different character from the decisions reached by the National Security Council, which is the highest policymaking organ in the foreign affairs field in the executive branch of the U.S. government. Politburo directives are binding commands that must be obeyed, and they are carried out down through the whole elaborate hierarchical structure of party and state administrative organs. Under the principle of democratic centralism, debate and questioning are allowed within the secret confines of the party bureaucracy up to the time when the final policy decision is made at the top. After that, it is the duty and obligation of every good party member to carry out the policy decided upon. Only in times of general war does the American democracy come close to the centralized decision-making process that is the normal, every-day, peacetime practice of the Soviet regime.

The concentration of so much power in so few hands has disastrous consequences within the Soviet Union, as I shall point out in my last chapter. But in the kind of worldwide rivalry for arms, allies, bases, and raw materials that the Soviets are now waging, this disciplined and secretive command structure has many obvious advantages. As we have seen, it enables the Politburo to sacrifice living standards to armament production, to pursue secret long-term strategies of political penetration, and to launch sudden offensive operations on the scale of the Afghanistan intervention. The value of our democratic institutions in protecting the freedoms of the individual and the superior efficiency of our domestic consumer economy should not blind us to the fact that the Soviets are very well organized for what they see as an inevitable global competition for power.

What order of priorities do the eight members of the Defense Council bring to their exercise of such vast power and authority? This question has been endlessly debated, and many ingenious theories have been spun around the speculation that there is within the Kremlin a deep division between hawks and doves. There is no denying that tactical disagreements have existed in the past and will continue in the future. But contrary to the widespread belief that basic Soviet policy intentions present an enigma, it seems to me clear that the members of the Defense Council and the wider Politburo are remarkably united in their vision of the future and are fully in agreement on a basic set of strategic priorities. The record of their actions, the Leninist doctrine in which they profess to believe, the testimony of defectors who have had access to high-level policy discussions, all combine to depict a clear order of fundamental priorities. Here are the primary policy goals in the descending order of importance in which I think the Soviet rulers place them. These priorities can change with time and circumstance, but as of this writing I am convinced that they are entirely consistent with actual Soviet behavior.

Priority No. 1

The defense and strengthening of the "socialist system." First priority is assigned by the Politburo to the maintenance in power of the CPSU inside the Soviet Union itself, and to the maintenance under effective Soviet influence of the foreign Communist parties that have seized power abroad. Other considerations are consistently sacrificed to what they conceive to be necessary to defend these ruling Communist parties against the threat of internal dissidence or external attack. At home and within the Warsaw Pact, the overriding importance of this priority explains their determination to achieve a safe margin of military superiority over any possible combination of opponents, even at considerable sacrifice of their own living standards. Similarly, their fear of the dissident movement is very real both within their country and in Eastern Europe, and the brutal ferocity with which they have been willing to suppress the human rights activists is an indication of the priority they attach to preventing any kind of organized political activity outside the Communist Party, even at high cost to their external reputation and other foreign policy goals. It should be remembered that the first priority of the KGB and the satellite intelligence services is not foreign espionage or subversion but rather the detection and suppression of internal dissidents and active opponents of the regime.

Under this priority also comes their compelling need to have in power on their borders Communist parties that owe their first allegiance to Moscow. The invasions of Hungary in 1956, of Czechoslovakia in 1968, and of Afghanistan in 1979 show the lengths to which they will go to achieve this objective. They have treated as a matter of the highest priority the independence of action in foreign policy demonstrated by Ceausescu's Communist regime in Rumania. The Soviets have bitterly resented Ceausescu's flirtation with Communist China and have suspected the Rumanians of leaking military secrets from the Warsaw Pact to China. Long-standing cooperation between the Rumanian intelligence service and the KGB has been broken off. But for all his defiance of Moscow on foreign affairs issues, Ceausescu has continued to run a harsh one-party police state within the country, and he has not experimented with Dubcek's liberalizing reforms that finally brought Soviet troops into Prague. Given this fact and Rumania's isolated geographic position, the Soviets have so far been willing to tolerate Rumania's heretical foreign policy in the belief that economic and political pressures will eventually bring the country back into line.

High on the list of Soviet priority concerns has been the future of Yugoslavia after Tito's death. The Soviets fear the extent to which Tito allowed Communist control, discipline, and ideology to atrophy. By discreet offers of assistance from the KGB to the Yugoslav security service, they think they can with patience and persistence bring the Yugoslav party back under control. There is a very real possibility that Yugoslavia may not be able to survive as a unified Marxist state and may degenerate into civil war between nationalities, some of which will seek help from Washington and some from Moscow. The Soviets do not discount the danger that Yugoslavia might then become the fuse for World War III that it was for World War I.

To an extent that most Americans would find surprising, the Soviets are concerned about the stability of the regime aligned to them that rules in Mongolia. They see as essential to their defense the need for preserving in power a friendly regime in this buffer state on the long Chinese border, and they realize that the gross disparity between Soviet and Mongolian living standards is a vulnerability that the Chinese are likely to exploit through propaganda and infiltration. They seem determined to improve Mongolian living standards at whatever cost in order to ensure stability in this vital area. Similarly, they reproach themselves for their past crude mishandling of relations with the Albanian Communist Party and seem to believe that Albania can be persuaded to rejoin the Warsaw Pact, now that an open break between Albania and Peking has occurred. They are prepared to work toward reconciliation with patience and persistence, with the strategic end in view of establishing naval basing rights on the Albanian coast.

The Soviet attitude toward North Korea is one of grudging respect for the iron work discipline imposed by Kim Il Sung and for his refusal to accept Khrushchev's advice to modify his cult of personality. But they resent his attempt to balance between China and the Soviet Union and to play them off against each other. They seem genuinely worried by the North Korean tendency to portray the great powers, the U.S.S.R. and the U.S., as having common interests that set them apart from and in conflict with the interests of the impoverished third world. They clearly see a threat to their ideological conception of a world divided into bourgeois capitalist and socialist states in any theory that identifies them with the United States as a rich developed nation in competition and conflict with the poorer overpopulated and underdeveloped countries.

In Communist Cuba, the Soviets are well satisfied with the trend of relations with Castro that culminated in the assertion of total KGB control over the Cuban intelligence service in 1970. As we have seen, Cuban economic dependence on Moscow and a large role for Castro in Soviet strategy in the third world have ended Castro's romantic involvement in half-baked guerrilla adventures, and the Soviets seem quite prepared to pay the huge subsidies annually required to keep Cuba afloat in return for the proxy use of the Cuban army.

In Indochina, the Soviets see a continuing struggle for influence with the Chinese and were prepared to sign a treaty with Vietnam in November 1978 and to support the Vietnamese attack on Cambodia as a way of consolidating their influence with the Vietnamese Communists.

In their attitude toward the inevitable stresses and strains that develop in their relations with satellite Communist regimes, the Soviets can on occasion be quite philosophical and speak of themselves as a father who has carefully brought up his children only to find that some are rebellious. But there can be no doubt about the highest level of priority they attach to maintaining these satellites within their orbit and to winning back through patient persuasion and covert operational activity those few who have strayed from the fold.

Priority No. 2

The strengthening of ties with new governments and with revolutionary progressive movements. Under the heading of this second broad priority come all the policies and initiatives that were so dramatically demonstrated in action in the case of the Angolan intervention. As proved by the crucial role played by the Portuguese Communist Party in the Angolan operation, the Politburo is well aware of and exploits to the hilt the operational potential of the many nonruling Communist parties outside the Soviet-dominated bloc, which owe primary allegiance to Moscow as members of coalition governments, as legal opposition parties, or as illegal underground movements. In addition to being one of the two most powerful nations on the world stage the Soviet Union is also the first country in which a Communist party seized state power; and the Soviet Politburo claims by historical right the leadership of the world Communist movement.

Among ruling Communist parties, China's and a few others dispute this claim, and among nonruling parties a few such as the Italian and Spanish parties have successfully asserted some internal independence of action while continuing to support most Soviet foreign policy positions. But the large majority of nonruling Communist parties in the world today owe their primary loyalty to Moscow. The Chinese have been notably unsuccessful in trying to organize strong Maoist splinter parties and have virtually given up the effort. In my opinion, it is quite wrong to leap from the fact that world communism is no longer Stalin's monolithic entity to the conclusion that unity has been shattered into so many diverse and competing elements as to pose no continuing threat. Predominant influence over a large sector of the world Communist movement, and the Soviet determination to fund, train, and guide nonruling Communist parties, add a unique dimension to the capacity of the Soviet Union to extend its power in ways not available to even the most expansionist nation-state of the past. The Politburo exploits to the full the special advantages that flow from a position of leadership over a supranational ideology and organizational structure in pursuing its geopolitical offensive, which as an objective is second in priority only to the defense of the home base and to the preservation in power of its satellite regimes.

The eventual establishment in power of disciplined Communist parties in all nations is the long-term Leninist goal of Soviet foreign policy, but the Politburo realistically recognizes that in most of the countries of the third world, local Communist parties are as yet too weak and disorganized to have any chance in the immediate future of exercising governmental authority. In these situations, therefore, the Soviets pursue a dual strategy. While patiently and persistently training and clandestinely subsidizing local Communist cadres for the future, the Politburo simultaneously pursues an opportunistic and pragmatic policy of attempting to expand Soviet influence over the newly independent and nationalistic regimes that came to power in the wake of the collapse of Western colonial rule.[2] Where vestiges of colonialism remain, as in southern Africa, we have seen how the Soviets have tried to gain a controlling influence over the guerrilla movements.

In addition to massive infusions of propaganda, the deployment of their international front organizations, and the use of proxy armies, the Soviets in recent years have come increasingly to rely on military assistance programs as a primary method of increasing the dependence on them of third world governments. In 1976, the Politburo approved new agreements for approximately $2.34 billion in military assistance and delivered $2.5 billion in arms, in contrast to a total provision of economic aid that amounted only to $900 million.[3] In subsequent years, this priority emphasis on military assistance has continued for obvious reasons. In 1977, annual Soviet arms deliveries reached $3.5 billion, and annual sales were more than $4 billion in that year.[4] By selling arms or extending credits for their purchase, the Soviets kill many birds with one stone. Where direct sales are possible, as in the case of Libya and Iraq, the Soviets receive badly needed hard currency in exchange for surplus arms. Most important, military officers and technicians from the receiving country have to be sent to the Soviet Union for training in the use of the new equipment; and while they are there, they are subjected to political indoctrination and to selective recruitment as long-term paid agents by the KGB or Soviet military intelligence, the GRU. Frequently, Soviet military advisers and trainers are accepted by the receiving country as instructors in the use and maintenance of sophisticated weaponry. Some of them also function as collectors of intelligence, as political indoctrinators, and as recruiters of deep-cover agents. Finally, the increasing dependence of the receiving country on the Soviet Union for the supply of spare parts to keep its military force in operation means that the cost of a diplomatic break with the Soviets becomes virtually prohibitive.

There is some risk for the Soviets in this selective proliferation of military assistance programs. The cases of Egypt and the Sudan are often cited as examples of how small independent nations can break the chains of dependency forged by heavy reliance on Soviet weaponry. But the Soviets are clearly willing to risk occasional setbacks in view of the increasing influence they gain in the large majority of cases, and they have learned from the Egyptian experience to avoid too large an infusion of Soviet personnel, preferring now to minimize their physical presence by relying on Cuban and Eastern European technicians. Through the successful coup in South Yemen in 1978, they have also demonstrated that indoctrination and penetration of the officer corps of recipient countries in the course of training programs can provide the crucial ingredient in bringing full-fledged Marxist regimes to power much sooner than would otherwise be possible.

In their internal policy discussions, the Soviet leaders stress the vital dependence of the West on the oil supplies of the Middle East and their determination to take advantage of the U.S. commitment to the survival of the state of Israel as a vulnerability that can be exploited throughout the Arab world. In the opposition of the Arab states such as Iraq and Libya to any peaceful compromise solution of the problem, and in the determination of the Palestinians to regain their lost lands, the Politburo sees a unique opportunity to extend Soviet influence into a region that would otherwise be closed to it by the nature of the antagonism between the Muslim faith and Marxist doctrine. The existence of the state of Israel, heavily armed for its defense by American weapons, serves to justify and make acceptable to the Arabs the billions of dollars of Soviet arms sales to Libya, Iraq, and Syria and the dependency and influence that these sales engender. Although the Soviets probably do not actively seek a new Arab-Israeli war because of the high risk of direct confrontation with the United States, they opposed the Camp David settlement between Egypt and Israel and prefer to keep the dispute simmering. An eventual peace in the area under American auspices would remove the issue that justifies their pervasive presence. On the chance that peace might possibly be achieved and a Palestinian state established on the West Bank, they not only have supported the Palestine Liberation Organization but have secretly exfiltrated for training in the Soviet Union a select group of Palestinian administrators, in the hope of exercising a major influence in such a state if it ever comes into existence. The Soviet role in relation to the various Palestinian terrorist groups has been ambiguous. While publicly deploring terrorism, they have masked their own involvement by channeling training and arms supplies to the terrorists through the East Germans and the Cubans. For example, Naif Hawatmah, the leader of the most Marxist-oriented of the Palestinian guerrilla groups, the PDFLP, visited Havana in early 1977 and received assurances of arms and training from Castro.

In the execution of this opportunistic policy toward the Arab world, the Soviets have occasionally had to face a conflict between the short-term immediate interests of their own state and the short-term interests of local Communist parties under their control. The Soviets have tended to resolve the dilemma by sacrificing the welfare and frequently the lives of their local Communist allies in favor of the Soviet state interest. They continued to support Nasser during his rule in Egypt in spite of his harsh suppression of the Egyptian Communist Party. The Lebanese Communist Party bitterly objected to continuing Soviet military support of the Syrians in the summer of 1976, and more recently the Soviets did not halt their arms supplies to Iraq despite the summary execution of a large group of Iraqi Communist leaders. The Soviet explanation to local Communist parties in this situation is that what benefits the Soviet Union will in the long run benefit them, and that as good disciplined Communists they must accept the temporary hardships.

Priority No. 3

The policy of peaceful coexistence, détente, and international trade. By the clear evidence of their actions, the members of the Politburo view the whole range of policies that have come to be associated with the term détente as of tertiary importance, in comparison with the two primary objectives of maintaining Communist regimes in power and of extending their influence into the outside world. Good relations with the United States have always been sacrificed to the higher necessity of preserving governing Communist parties by harsh repression and armed invasion, as in Eastern Europe and Afghanistan. As Brezhnev pointed out in answer to Kissinger's protest on Angola, there is nothing in the definition or practice of détente that can be permitted to prevent the Soviet Union from carrying out its higher obligation to support "progressive" movements in their struggle against imperialism. In effect, I believe the Soviet leaders look upon détente, the SALT negotiating process, and the expansion of international trade as temporarily expedient tactics, designed to win time and opportunity for the successful achievement of Priorities No. 1 and No. 2.

The need for such expediency is forced upon them by an objective reality to which they have had to adjust. They accept the fact that the United States is at present so well armed in modern weaponry that nuclear war is not a rational way of advancing their primary objectives, although they continue to prepare for it as a possibility. They also are acutely aware of the American superiority in scientific technology, and they often discuss among themselves the importance of closing the technology gap. Given their current technological inferiority, they fear an all-out arms race in which, with the full commitment of its resources, the United States might establish a commanding lead. Therefore, they have been prepared to negotiate for agreed limits on strategic weaponry in the belief that they can thereby constrain to some extent the application of American technology to new weapons. At the same time, through hard bargaining on the terms of the SALT agreements and by building up their strategic arsenal to the outermost limits of what is allowable, they have succeeded in improving their relative strategic position.

Whether they actually counted on the fact that the SALT negotiating process would in itself also tend to lull the American public into passive acceptance of growing Soviet superiority in conventional forces is open to question. But they have been the beneficiaries of this result.

The Politburo's perception of the technology gap is also the main reason for the Soviet interest in the relaxation of tensions that led—until the invasion of Afghanistan—to a much increased flow of Western credits and technology to the U.S.S.R. When the U.S. Congress passed the 1974 Trade Act with a provision that Soviet relaxation of emigration curbs was required in order to make them eligible for nondiscriminating tariffs and export credits, the Kremlin simply turned to Western Europe and Japan for much of the technology and credits that it needed. Contrary to Henry Kissinger's hope that this increased involvement in international trade would improve the Soviets' behavior by entangling them in a web of mutual dependency, the Politburo has in fact employed Western credits and technology transfers to avoid having to undertake basic economic reforms that might otherwise have required relaxation of their internal political controls. Imports of American grain derived from the efficient use of farm machinery have been used to compensate for the disastrous consequences of their inefficient system of collectivized agriculture and to postpone indefinitely the day when they have to grant a dangerous degree of economic independence to their farmers.

They have also been spared the necessity of diverting major resources from the defense sector. By playing one Western nation off against another, they have purchased intact entirely new technologies, including equipment and know-how, that have helped them in the development of new weapons.[5] The only political price they have had to pay in return for these advantages is the exercise of some restraint in their avoidance of overt pressure on exposed Western nerves in such sensitive areas as West Berlin.

However, even the most sanguine members of the Politburo would admit that some formidable obstacles remain before the road ahead is clear toward a world composed largely of Communist regimes loyal to Moscow, with the United States and a few other Western democracies reduced to impotent isolation. One of their prime concerns is the People's Republic of China. They view the

Chinese Communist leaders as xenophobic nationalists who are convinced of their superiority as inheritors of "the Middle Kingdom" and who look down on the rest of the world as barbarians. Moscow believes that Peking is determined to join in a temporary military alliance with the United States as the distant great power in order to create a counterweight against the U.S.S.R. as the nearby great power. The Kremlin genuinely fears that the Chinese leaders will attempt to stir up trouble between the U.S.S.R. and the U.S. and deliberately foment a war between them that would leave an undamaged China triumphant on the world stage. The Soviet leadership resents and does not quite know how to cope with the way the Chinese exploit their own weakness by propagating the concept that they are leaders of an impoverished third world aligned against the two rich superpowers. The Soviets are convinced that the Chinese do not really expect a Soviet attack, but are deliberately inculcating the fear of such an assault as a way of unifying their own population. The Kremlin may have entertained some slight hope that a reconciliation with China was possible immediately after Mao's death, but it now expects a ten-year period of tension and sees no hope of improved relations until an entirely new Chinese leadership emerges. In the meanwhile, the Soviets intend to maintain their more than forty divisions on the frontier with China, and are adamantly opposed to any concessions in the disputes over the location of their common border. An eventual rapprochement between the two Communist giants is always a possibility; but if the attitude of the Soviet leadership toward their quarrel with China is any indication, that possibility remains remote.

Another major obstacle that the Soviet leaders see standing in the way of the steady advance of their influence in the world is that body of opinion in the United States they accuse of being opposed to peaceful coexistence, détente, and disarmament. They identify this opposition as being composed of three distinct groups; the military-industrial complex, the American labor movement, and the "Zionists." In the first group, they place all those in the United States who call for increased American defense expenditures. In their propaganda, they describe those who try to alert the American public to the danger of increasing Soviet military strength as "cold war warriors," and they profess to believe and perhaps do believe that these opponents are motivated either by a fanatical and irrational anticom-

munism or by a selfish thirst for the profits to be made from armament production. Not included in this military-industrial complex
are those prominent American businessmen who are committed to
exporting high technology to Russia. In official Soviet propaganda,
these men are praised by the Soviet leadership for their realism and
common sense; but the real attitude of the Politburo toward them is
best exemplified in Lenin's exchange with Karl Radek that Aleksandr
Solzhenitsyn described in his speech on June 30, 1975, to the AFL-
CIO. In commenting on Soviet economic difficulties at a party meeting in Moscow, Lenin described the eagerness of Western businessmen to sell capital equipment to the Soviets and remarked, "When
things go very hard for us, we will give a rope to the bourgeoisie and
the bourgeoisie will hang itself." When Radek asked, "Where are we
going to get enough rope to hang the whole bourgeoisie?" Lenin
replied, "They'll supply us with it."

The second group opposed to their policies, the American labor
movement, is a cause of particular concern and frustration to the
Soviet leadership. Whereas in France and Italy a large sector of the
labor movement is under the influence of Communist-controlled
labor federations and tends to support Soviet foreign policy objectives while opposing defensive military preparations, the reverse is
true in the United States. The AFL-CIO, under the leadership of the
late George Meany, has consistently opposed the advance of Soviet
influence and has supported a strong American military posture. This
vocal opposition to its purposes on the part of an industrial proletariat
that should theoretically be on its side is particularly galling to the
Politburo, and the Soviet leaders do not underestimate the effect of
this opposition by American unionized labor, both in the United
States and on foreign trade unions. Finally, the third group identified
by the Politburo as having a major negative influence on American
policy toward the Soviet Union is composed of American Jewish
organizations, or "Zionists," which the Soviets hold responsible for
blocking the extension of credits and the removal of tariff barriers in
order to obtain freer emigration for Soviet Jews.

What the Politburo fears most is that these three groups, working
together, will be able to organize American opinion behind an expanded military budget and a much more active defense in the third
world of American interests. In their discussions with the Communist
leaders of Eastern Europe and of Cuba, the Soviet leadership has

cautioned against the danger of prematurely awakening the American giant, and they genuinely fear the impact of American technological superiority and economic efficiency not only on the arms race but on the competition for allies in the underdeveloped world through economic assistance programs. Until the invasion of Afghanistan, the Politburo exercised some restraint in the pursuit of its geopolitical offensive. Awareness of the latent strength of the opposition to Soviet expansionism within the American body politic, combined with respect for what American technology could achieve if once aroused, accounts for whatever restraint is still evident in Kremlin policy.

Finally, the third and most serious obstacle to the achievement of Soviet objectives in the world, more troubling to the Politburo than the enmity of China or the danger of an aroused American opinion, is the threat to their system that they see posed by the dissident movement both within their country and in Eastern Europe. As a self-perpetuating and privileged elite ruling over a one-party police state that allows no organized political opposition, the members of the Soviet Politburo were profoundly disturbed by the unanticipated internal reaction to the Helsinki Declaration signed in 1975 by the Communist European states and the Western powers. Brezhnev and his colleagues had seen the approval of this document as a way of making permanent the consolidation of their rule in Eastern Europe, and of removing any remaining challenge to their authority in this area. Initially, they were well satisfied with the results. They saw in the American acceptance of the Declaration an admission by the United States in the name of détente that Communist rule in the region was now accepted internationally as legitimate, and that the Yalta promise of free elections was a dead letter.

What the Soviet leaders did not foresee was the successful exploitation by a wide variety of democratic dissidents in the Soviet Union itself, in Poland, in Czechoslovakia, and even in East Germany of the general commitment stated in the Helsinki Declaration to a freer movement of people and ideas and to improvement in the human rights of citizens. Language that the Soviets had thought was so general as to be meaningless and so clearly unenforceable as to pose no threat was infused with life by Yuri Orlov and his courageous friends in Russia and in Eastern Europe. They presented a growing challenge through the organization of independent groups to monitor and report to the outside world on the failure to implement this promise of wider freedom. More significant, the dissident movements in Russia and Eastern Europe tended to reinforce each other, and there even seemed to be informal cooperation between them. Spontaneously, monitoring groups modeled on Orlov's group in Moscow began to spring up in Armenia, in the Ukraine, in Georgia, and elsewhere. Orlov seemed to the Politburo on the verge of committing the cardinal sin in the Leninist bible. Under the banner of Helsinki, he appeared to be organizing the beginnings of a political opposition, and the protests against Soviet repression of human rights came not only from intellectuals but from large ethnic nationalities demanding the teaching of their native languages; from Protestant, Catholic, and Orthodox religious groups protesting the suppression of religious freedom; and from Jews and Pentacostalites demanding the right to emigrate.[6]

When President Carter in his first few months in office added the weight of the American presidency to the support of an international human rights campaign and singled out individual Soviet dissidents for praise and recognition, the Soviets were much more profoundly concerned than even their violent official propaganda reaction would lead one to suspect. In the beginning of 1977, the Politburo was not only worried by the campaign of the human rights activists but disturbed by wider threats to public order. Food shortages in the major cities led to fears of possible riots in Leningrad. In Moscow, a bomb explosion in the subway system was taken seriously as an act of political protest, and Brezhnev himself had to intervene to settle an unauthorized work stoppage. The reaction of the Politburo to these pressures was predictable. Instead of attempting to deal with the real internal causes of this unrest, it issued a draconian decree in May 1977. The growth of dissent within the country was blamed on a grand conspiracy of external forces, including imperialists (Americans), Maoists, and Zionists. Active dissidents were identified as "hirelings of imperialists." These external forces were accused of instilling bourgeois views among the young and immature through foreign propaganda and encouraging antisocialist, nationalist, and religious sentiments.

The decree called for a tightening up across the board of the repressive machinery of the Soviet state.[7] Intensified security procedures for the protection of classified information were promulgated and more severe censorship was instituted over overt publications. Increased security controls over the storage and transportation of weapons and explosives were put into effect. Tighter controls over access to printing and duplicating machinery were called for to stem the flow of *samizdat,* the unauthorized material secretly copied and disseminated by internal dissidents. The Politburo demanded that all leadership cadres of the Communist Party intensify political vigilance and indoctrination. New restrictions were added to reduce the number of Soviet citizens allowed to travel abroad and to limit their contacts with foreigners inside the Soviet Union. In order to avoid embarrassment during the Belgrade Conference convened to review the implementation of the Helsinki Declaration, the trials of leading dissidents were postponed, but when the conference was over, the Soviets brought Yuri Orlov, Anatoly Shcharansky, and Alexander Ginzburg to semipublic trial. The long and brutally harsh sentences imposed were designed to demonstrate to would-be dissidents that widespread protests in the West and even the expressed concern of the American President could not protect them from the prompt retribution of the Soviet state.

In my last chapter, I explore at greater length the origins and future possibilities of the dissident movement inside the Soviet Union and in Eastern Europe. It is sufficient to make the point here that the Politburo is acutely aware of the broad and diversified discontent that exists beneath the orderly surface of Soviet life. Its reaction has been ruthlessly to suppress with police harassment and judicial sentences any overt manifestation of this simmering dissatisfaction. Moreover, the leading dissidents like Andrei Sakharov believe that one of the compelling motives for the expansionary thrust of the Soviet regime into the outside world is the attempt to demonstrate to its own people that the Communist system is in fact the wave of the future and to overwhelm with the clamor and chauvinistic appeal of foreign triumphs the deep domestic discontent. One of the leading dissidents who escaped into exile, Andrei Amalrik, put it succinctly and in my opinion correctly when he warned, "The Soviet Union needs to maintain the pressures outside its borders, to score successes however illusory, in order to keep the lid on at home."[8]

With this perception in mind of how the Politburo views its foreign policy priorities and the major obstacles that lie in the way of its ambitions, the Soviet decision-making process under Brezhnev's regime deserves a closer look. Under the Politburo and its inner Defense Council stand the vast machinery of the CPSU and the governmental structure of the state, continuously functioning to feed intelligence and policy recommendations up through the hierarchy and then implementing the command decisions taken at the top. An unclassified chart prepared in the CIA gives a simplified picture of how the upward flow of information and policy advice appears to function (see Figure 1). This chart fails to describe the key importance to the formulation and execution of Soviet foreign policy of the various Central Committee departments that staff the party Secretariat and whose chiefs report directly to the Politburo and the Defense Council. Of the approximately twenty departments, three are particularly concerned with foreign policy: the International Department, the Bloc Department, and the Administrative Organs Department. Staffed with highly trained and competent party functionaries, these departments play a critically important role in shaping and refining the policy options that are presented to the Politburo at its weekly meetings.

For many years the International Department has been headed by the influential Boris Ponomarev, who, in addition to being a secretary of the Central Committee, is also a candidate member of the Politburo.[9] In addition to formulating policy for all the nonruling Communist parties, this department has responsibility for policy advice toward the United States, Western Europe, Japan, and the third world. Under the Politburo's direction, it is the authoritative source of policy guidance for the whole battery of Communist international front organizations, and for national revolutionary movements and guerrilla groups. This department is likely to have had the final responsibility for the presentation to the Defense Council of the Angolan operation in all its complexity and coordinated detail, accompanied by military and intelligence annexes spelling out the respective roles of the Soviet and Cuban military forces and the KGB and DGI. The top staff members of the International Department travel abroad frequently under varying forms of official cover, and are sometimes assigned for long periods to a Soviet embassy to handle critically sensitive matters, much to the annoyance of local Soviet ambassadors.

In reporting to the Politburo, this department not only presents

Figure 1

INFORMATION FLOW FOR FOREIGN POLICY DECISIONS

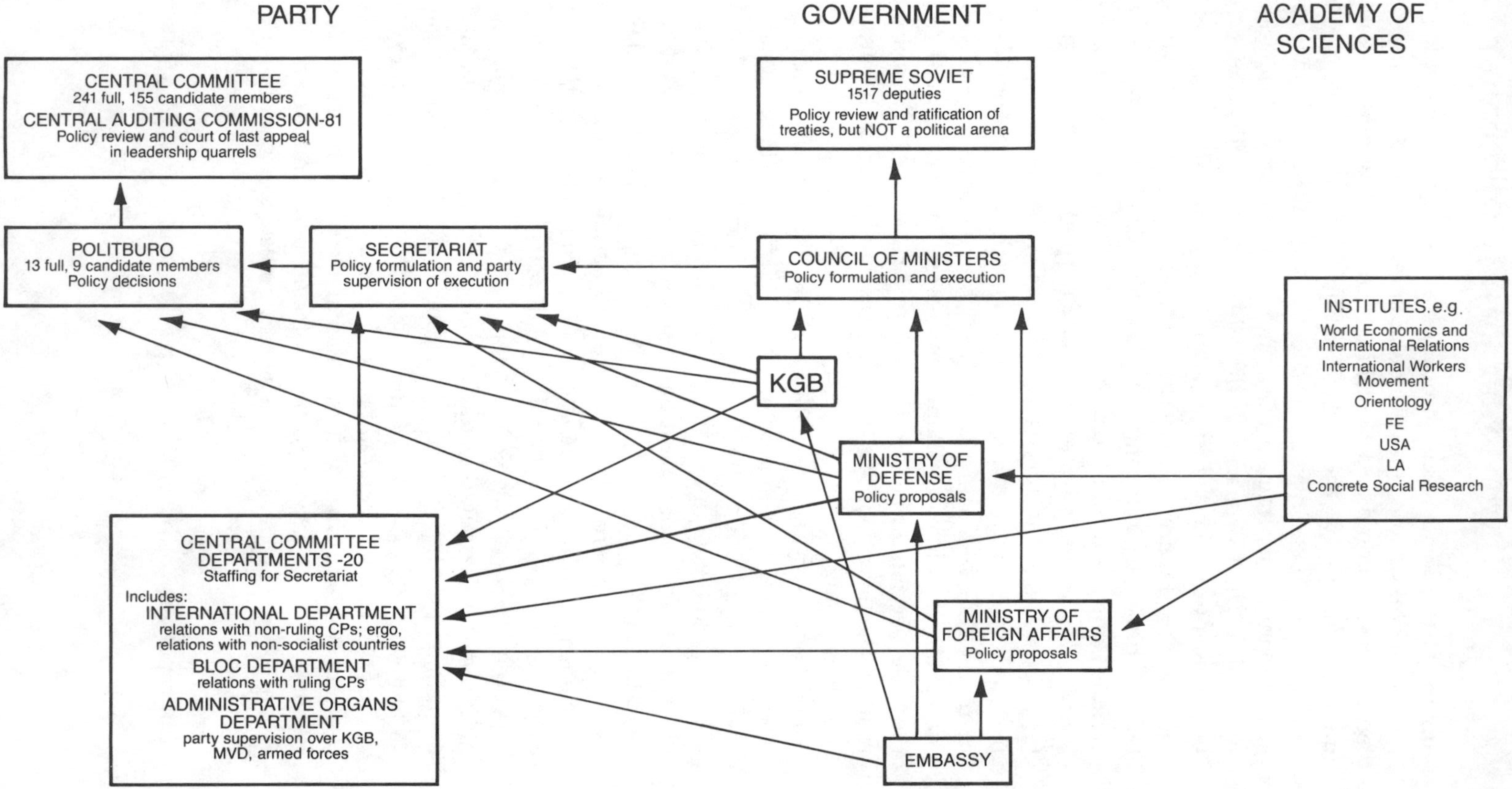

PARTY

GOVERNMENT

ACADEMY OF SCIENCES

INSTITUTES, e.g.
World Economics and
International Relations
International Workers
Movement
Orientology
FE
USA
LA
Concrete Social Research

CENTRAL COMMITTEE
241 full, 155 candidate members
CENTRAL AUDITING COMMISSION-81
Policy review and court of last appeal
in leadership quarrels

SUPREME SOVIET
1517 deputies
Policy review and ratification of
treaties, but NOT a political arena

COUNCIL OF MINISTERS
Policy formulation and execution

MINISTRY OF DEFENSE
Policy proposals

MINISTRY OF FOREIGN AFFAIRS
Policy proposals

EMBASSY

KGB

SECRETARIAT
Policy formulation and party
supervision of execution

CENTRAL COMMITTEE DEPARTMENTS -20
Staffing for Secretariat

Includes:
INTERNATIONAL DEPARTMENT
relations with non-ruling CPs; ergo,
relations with non-socialist countries
BLOC DEPARTMENT
relations with ruling CPs
ADMINISTRATIVE ORGANS DEPARTMENT
party supervision over KGB,
MVD, armed forces

POLITBURO
13 full, 9 candidate members
Policy decisions

the intelligence assessment of a given situation but also proposes the policy recommendation on how to deal with it; and it also appears to have authority for supervising the execution of large-scale covert action operations. Unlike the usual practice in most democratic countries, the responsibility for intelligence evaluation and for foreign policy formulation are not separated in this system, but are combined in the powerful International Department. Most important, this department seems to be in charge of the covert funding, training, and guidance given to nonruling Communist parties, although the KGB, the Eastern European intelligence services, or a foreign Communist party may actually handle the secret transfer of funds. Below the Politburo, the International Department appears to be the most powerful and decisive element in policymaking within its very wide area of geographical and functional responsibility. It is the general staff of the Soviet geopolitical offensive.

The second department of the Central Committee that plays a vital role in the Soviet decision-making process in the foreign affairs field is the Bloc Department, also called the Department for Liaison with Communist Workers' Parties in the Socialist Countries. Konstantin Rusakov is the current chief of this department, and he is responsible for recommending to the Politburo policy initiatives affecting not only the Eastern European satellites but also the ruling Asian Communist parties, China, Albania, and Yugoslavia. He and Ponomarev apparently work together closely when a problem arises in which their responsibilities overlap, as in the case of preparing for international Communist meetings in which both ruling and nonruling parties are represented.

Through the Administrative Organs Department, the Politburo maintains its control over the personnel structure of the Soviet national security apparatus. This department is responsible to the Politburo for reviewing and recommending all senior appointments and promotions in the Soviet armed forces, in the militia, the judiciary, the procuracy, and the KGB.[10] Through this essential cog in the party machinery, Brezhnev and his colleagues have been able to ensure the loyalty of the elite party members by a finely tuned system of rewards and punishments that determines whether an individual's career rises or falls. Since one's position in the hierarchy determines the extent of one's access to the good things in life—cars, dachas, imported goods—the recommendations of this department can make the difference between success and failure for the aspiring Soviet bureaucrat. When the general secretary of the party is in firm command, as Brezhnev has been since 1973, the Administrative Organs Department is an indispensable and powerful instrument for keeping the army and the secret police under the dominating control of the party.

Advisory to the International and Bloc Departments, as Figure 1 indicates, are the geographical and functional institutes that are located within the Academy of Sciences. These are the closest approximations to the privately funded think tanks that flourish on the American scene, but they have covert operational and intelligence roles that are specifically denied to the American institutions. For dealing with the United States, the most important of these research centers is the Institute on the United States and Canada, under the direction of the peripatetic Georgy Arbatov. With a competent professional staff of more than a hundred, this institute concentrates its research attention on current political, economic, and cultural developments within American society. It serves as a high-level debriefing center for visiting American dignitaries and academic experts, whose views and insights into the American political scene are carefully elicited and disseminated within the hierarchy. It performs a subtle propaganda function in peddling to these visitors a sophisticated explanation of the current Politburo foreign policy line, and its top staff members often travel to the United States to perform a similar function when they participate in academic conferences and exchange programs. There is good reason for believing that its staff is permeated with highly trained KGB officers who use the excellent cover of the institute to assess and to attempt to recruit as agents influential Americans that they meet in the course of these contacts. This institute has a reputation within the ruling elite for being more objective and factually accurate than the official Soviet media, and its studies and reports are given a strictly limited circulation among the top policymakers. On occasion, this body has contributed draft texts to Brezhnev for the preparation of those of his speeches directed at the American audience. It is also regularly tasked by the International Department for research papers and analysis of prospective American reactions to proposed policy initiatives. It would be surprising if it had not been asked for a cold-eyed, strictly objective assessment of what the American reaction might be to the deployment of Cuban troops in Angola before the final decision was taken.

Another of the research centers in the Academy of Sciences that plays an important role in foreign policy formulation is the Institute of World Economics and International Relations. Its director in 1977 was N. V. Inozentsev, and it concentrates on Western Europe, Japan, and the third world. With a large staff of about 560 professionals, it has in addition to its research responsibility propaganda and intelligence functions similar to those exercised by Arbatov's group.

The Ministry of Foreign Affairs, a branch of the Soviet governmental structure, is clearly subordinate in its foreign policymaking role to the party organs, the Politburo and the International Department. Andrei Gromyko as foreign minister long enjoyed a special relationship with Brezhnev, and his elevation to full membership in the Politburo was a visible symbol of Brezhnev's success in establishing preeminence. Since the days of Stalin and Khrushchev, the Foreign Ministry has had to become increasingly involved in the negotiation of complex technical issues, and an attempt has been made to improve the quality of the Soviet diplomatic service through the recruitment and training of more competent people. However, one of its primary missions remains that of providing diplomatic cover for a very large number of KGB officers assigned abroad; and in some countries the Soviet diplomatic presence is almost a hollow shell designed to hide the number of KGB operatives.

Chapter 14

The Soviet Apparat: KGB

THE KGB—THE COMMITTEE OF STATE SECURITY—plays an important role in the formulation and execution of Soviet foreign policy. But before considering that role, it is worth stressing that its primary responsibility is to ensure the security of the CPSU against any direct or indirect threat to the party's total control over the Soviet population. In its dual internal and external functions, and in the unlimited scope of its police authority under the direction of the Politburo, it bears no resemblance to any institution in the American government, although it is often compared to the CIA since both organizations engage in foreign espionage. The nearest one can come to an American analogy would be to imagine that the FBI and the CIA had been fused into a single organization with full control over all state and municipal police organizations. Imagine that this monster is directly responsible to the chief executive and subject neither to restraint by Congress or the courts, nor to criticism by the press. Its secret agents would permeate every cranny of American life and its dossiers on every citizen would control each person's access to education, jobs, and housing. A description of how the KGB functions in its suppression of internal political dissent is covered in the last chapter; and I confine myself here to a brief description of its foreign policy functions, since John Barron in his book *KGB* has given an extensive and reasonably accurate picture of its headquarters structure.[1] Then by exploring how a typical KGB station actually operates inside a Soviet embassy in a foreign country, I hope to be able to give the reader a realistic sense of what American intelligence confronts in its work abroad.

The KGB assumed its present name in 1954, although of course under other names its organizational lineage can be traced directly back to Lenin's establishment of a secret police apparatus to consolidate the Communist Party's triumph in the Revolution. The KGB's current chief is its chairman, Yuri V. Andropov, who is also a full member of the Politburo and of the Defense Council. Like the Ministry of Foreign Affairs, the KGB currently appears to be under firm party control by the relevant departments of the Central Committee, including review by the Administrative Organs Department of its assignment and promotion of personnel. The International Department exercises oversight over the KGB's conduct of large-scale covert action operations. My own estimate is that the KGB's present strength is about 400,000, which includes the large force assigned to guard duty on the borders and the smaller group of personnel working under cover abroad.

In the headquarters structure of the KGB in Moscow, the operating component that plays the most significant role in the formulation and execution of Soviet foreign policy is the First Chief Directorate. It is responsible for conducting espionage abroad for the collection of clandestine intelligence. It has the duty of running counterintelligence operations designed to identify and neutralize the penetration of Soviet embassies and official installations by hostile intelligence services, and in this connection it is responsible for ensuring the loyalty of all Soviets stationed abroad. It has broad responsibilities in the mounting of covert action operations and is assigned the important function of training, monitoring, and controlling the intelligence and security services of the Communist regimes in Eastern Europe, Asia, and Cuba. This First Directorate, with more of its personnel assigned abroad than in the Soviet Union, has by itself greater numerical strength than the entire CIA, yet publicity concerning the

CIA would suggest the opposite to the world.

If we add together the number of KGB officers assigned abroad and the much smaller number of Soviet military intelligence officers overseas, these intelligence personnel occupy on the average 30 percent of the official positions in Soviet embassies worldwide; but in some strategic underdeveloped countries this figure can go as high as 70 percent. The KGB does not confine itself to the use of diplomatic cover to disguise the extent of its overseas presence. Every form of Soviet overseas activity is exploited for cover purposes, including TASS, Soviet banks and trading corporations, Soviet-owned business companies, students and academics on exchange programs, scientific delegations, etc. In addition, the KGB fills a large number of the slots allocated to the Soviet Union in the United Nations, so the permanent staffs of the U.N. headquarters in New York and of the U.N. specialized agencies in Geneva and Paris are heavily loaded with KGB officers who use their U.N. status as a flexible cover for their agent recruitment and covert action operations.

The intelligence reports and assessments flowing into the Moscow headquarters of the First Chief Directorate are disseminated to the International and Bloc Departments of the Central Committee, to the Soviet General Staff, to the Ministry of Foreign Affairs, and to the specialized institutes in the Academy of Sciences. As both chairman of the KGB and full member of the Politburo and its inner Defense Council, Andropov seems to have the option of holding extremely sensitive intelligence reports for dissemination by himself at the highest level. His dual role gives him enormous potential influence over policymaking through his ability to control the level and extent of dissemination.

The Second Chief Directorate of the KGB, also located in its Moscow headquarters, has a significant influence on Soviet foreign policy because of the nature of its operations and the intelligence reports and covert action opportunities that flow from them. This directorate has the responsibility within the country for the recruitment of agents for intelligence purposes or political action from among all foreigners stationed in the country, either on permanent assignment as diplomats, journalists, or businessmen, or traveling as tourists or members of visiting delegations, or being trained in the universities and military schools. The Soviets prefer to make the final recruitment pitch to a potential foreign agent under the completely controlled circumstances that the unlimited police authority of the KGB provides in the Soviet Union. Similarly, sexual entrapment and other forms of blackmail can be more safely conducted within the controlled confines of their own country, and massive physical and electronic surveillance capabilities give the Second Directorate a surrounding environment of total access to the conversations, telephone calls, and correspondence of the selected target.

An equally important function of this directorate is to provide counterintelligence protection to the regime by identifying and neutralizing all hostile foreign intelligence efforts to recruit Soviet citizens and to communicate with them if once recruited. The task of disrupting and destroying all activities within the country of Soviet émigré organizations also falls to this directorate. Any Western operation designed to maintain contact with a recruited agent inside the Soviet Union has to take account of and cope successfully with the formidable size, efficiency, and unlimited authority of the Second Chief Directorate. How it is organized into geographical and functional departments to carry out these offensive intelligence collection and defensive counterintelligence responsibilities is adequately described in John Barron's book.[2]

With this background on the two chief directorates in the KGB's Moscow headquarters that have a major impact on Soviet foreign policy, the best way of describing how the machinery actually functions is to depict in detail the inner workings of a typical KGB Residence in a medium-sized Western European country. The picture that emerges is as authentic and accurate as my memory and experience permit. I have tried to keep to what is known, to avoid speculation and exaggeration, and to acknowledge areas of ignorance where they exist. Figure 2 is my effort to convey the organizational structure and functional division of responsibility within such a KGB Residence, and it is a useful point of reference in trying to understand how the KGB operates abroad.

The resident is usually the highest-ranking KGB official in a Soviet Embassy and is in charge of all KGB personnel under whatever forms of cover they may be serving. He is responsible directly to KGB headquarters in Moscow, which KGB officers refer to as "the Center." He has full authority over his staff and conducts liaison with the Soviet ambassador and with the chief of the Soviet military intelligence (GRU) unit in the embassy. He is also responsible for maintain-

Figure 2

ORGANIZATIONAL STRUCTURE OF A TYPICAL KGB RESIDENCE

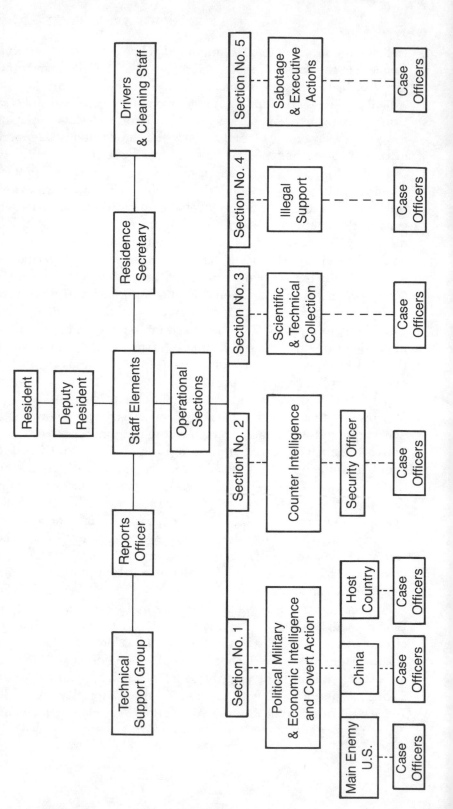

ing liaison with the chiefs of the Eastern European and Cuban intelligence services functioning under diplomatic cover in their respective embassies, and for providing them with policy guidance and
advice, except in the case of Rumanian intelligence, whose ties to the
KGB appear to me to have been broken. Typically, he reads and
releases all cable and dispatch traffic addressed to the Center and
reviews all plans for secret meetings with agents prior to implementation. He also is normally the only one who knows the true identity
of all agents operating in the country, except for such deep-cover
"illegals" as may be run directly from the Center in Moscow. Depending on the size of the residence, the deputy resident may also
serve as the chief of one of the five main operational sections.

The Technical Support Group serves the operational sections as a
staff element, and provides the trained technicians and advanced
equipment required to conduct all forms of electronic and photographic surveillance. If the problem is to place a miniaturized microphone in the residence of the American ambassador, it is this support
group that provides the technicians to do the job. They can be quite
imaginative, as in the case of one American ambassador who found
that a microphone had been planted in the heel of his shoe, which
continued to transmit from his office and his home whenever he was
wearing that pair of shoes; even guarded conversations conducted in
the open air of his garden could be recorded. Telephone taps and
photographic coverage are specialties of this staff element, which
also has the defensive responsibility for ensuring that no hostile intelligence service succeeds in making an audio penetration of official
Soviet installations. Periodically, visiting technical experts arrive
from Moscow to brief this group on the latest developments in new
equipment and on the most recently discovered evidence of successful hostile penetrations. In this peculiar and secretive corner of U.S.-
Soviet rivalry, the two countries are in fact engaged in an intense and
costly competition for the most advanced forms of both offensive and
defensive equipment, and the ingenuity and technical competence
of the KGB are not to be underrated.

The reports officer is another staff element, and helps to prepare
the intelligence information obtained from agents in final form for
submission to the Center. His slot is a luxury the smaller residences
cannot afford; there the operations officers have to do the final editing. The residence secretary is responsible for the secure vault area

and for the maintenance and security of the files kept there. In this area, which resembles a bank vault, all classified intelligence reports have to be prepared, and documents cannot be taken out of this area by KGB case officers. The chauffeurs who drive the KGB cars and the cleaning staff are all security-cleared Soviet citizens. Knowing from their own successes how easy it is to bribe local employees in these jobs, the KGB takes no chances, unlike the Americans, who for economy reasons employ local people for these tasks.

The chief of Operational Section No. 1, and the KGB case officers under his command, are responsible for collecting political, military, and economic intelligence through the recruitment of secret agents who have some form of access to the information required by the Center. This section is normally divided into three subsections, according to the identity of its priority targets. The first and most heavily staffed is called the Main Enemy subsection, since its agent recruitment effort is directed against all American citizens and foreigners who could conceivably have or gain access to classified U.S. information. Throughout KGB directives and literature, the United States is regularly referred to as "the main enemy," as if to remind its operatives continuously of the overriding priority attached to the recruitment of well-placed American sources. The target population includes the entire official American presence in the country, visiting officials from Washington, trade and cultural delegations, and the domestic servants or hotel personnel who might gain access to classified documents carelessly handled. Experience indicates that every conceivable form of inducement is used, from strictly financial to ideological persuasion, from sexual entrapment to blackmail. Over the years, successful recruitments have been made at all levels, but the daily bread-and-butter business of the KGB is to concentrate on American personnel at the lower end of the pay scale. Financial inducements can be attractive to code clerks and military communicators who take no part in policy level discussions but do have daily access to the flow of sensitive cable traffic to and from Washington.

Once an American source is recruited, or a foreigner with good access to such a source, extraordinary precautions are taken to protect the relationship against discovery by hostile surveillance. Face-to-face meetings between the KGB case officer and his new agent are kept to an absolute minimum, and such secret meetings are meticulously planned in advance, with approval required from the resident himself. A chart is kept within this section of all safe sites that have been used to meet agents, from dark, abandoned city streets to distant country inns. Maximum use is made of dead drops such as a hole in a particular tree in a park where instructions are left and the reply is subsequently recovered. Another device is the car toss, which involves encasing the message in a carefully camouflaged container which is thrown out at a prearranged location. The KGB has developed "brush meetings"—where identical briefcases or envelopes are quickly exchanged in a brief encounter on a crowded city street— to a high art. Finally, the most advanced technology has been applied to the costly development of the most sophisticated agent communications: where, for example, a car radio has hidden within it a sending and receiving device that can transmit thousands of words in a brief spurt of masked electronic data.

As might be expected from the tensions that exist between the Soviet Union and China, the second subunit of this operational section in countries where the Chinese Communists are represented is targeted against Chinese officials and foreigners who have any form of access to them. Agent penetration of Maoist splinter political groups in the host country where they exist is a favorite KGB method of gaining access to the extraordinarily reclusive Chinese target, both for information on their local political strategy and for purposes of deliberate disruption.

The third subunit of this section is directed against the host country in which the KGB Residence is located. If the country is an ally of the United States, agent recruitments within the official establishment, at all levels, can be a useful window into joint intelligence, military, and economic planning with the United States and into shared development of new weapons systems. A classical example of KGB success in this field was the early recruitment of Kim Philby in his Oxford days and the careful management of his career until he became a high-ranking officer in British intelligence.

KGB instructions and directives frequently refer to a category of agents known as trusted persons—people who are ideologically motivated. These are secret members of the local Communist party, or individuals whose Marxist convictions have developed to the point where they believe secret cooperation with the Soviet Union is a higher obligation than loyalty to their own country. These trusted persons are not paid agents; but they are handled with even greater care and secrecy than the ordinary agent, since they often function at high policy levels and are not only sources of excellent intelligence on the host country's intentions but also function as agents of influence with the capacity to affect covertly the national decision-making process.

This third subsection also seems to be responsible for the day-to-day liaison with the leaders of the local Communist party, if they happen to be loyal to Moscow and if the party functions illegally within the country. This relationship between the KGB Residence and an illegal but disciplined local Communist party appears to be closely supervised by the International Department in Moscow and, although the evidence is ambiguous, the secret transfer of funds to such an illegal party seems to require the approval of the International Department as to purpose and amount, although the actual clandestine transaction may be handled by KGB case officers. When a disciplined illegal Communist party gains legal status and functions openly within a country, the KGB appears to lose its liaison function and policy guidance is taken over directly by the International Department, although covert funding may continue to be handled by KGB operatives. In situations where very large, continuing subsidies are involved, as has often been the case in Italy, the financial and cover requirements exceed the capacity of the KGB, and elaborate financial institutions are erected to mask the transfer of such large amounts. The most thorough and detailed description of how such large-scale covert political funding has actually worked in Italy first appeared in public print in an article in the *New Republic* by Claire Sterling and Michael Ledeen.[3]

Intelligence collection objectives and political action purposes are inextricably fused in this funding of local Communist parties. For example, in a large African country in 1975, the International Department approved the grant of approximately $200,000 to the local Communist party for organizational and propaganda expenses; but the grant was made conditional upon the local party leaders' ability to fulfill very specific requirements for intelligence on the local government's military and political intentions, and on the party's willingness to accept detailed policy guidance in its political strategy. In this case, a representative of the International Department was sent from Moscow to the Soviet Embassy, where he personally handled the negotiations with the local Communist leaders rather than leaving them to the KGB Residence. Specific examples such as this strengthen the case for believing that the KGB is clearly subordinate to the International Department in its relations with local Communist parties and acts more as a disciplined executive agent rather than as an initiator of policy in this field.

In addition to the conduct of official liaison with the leadership of illegal Communist parties, the KGB also has the sensitive responsibility of recruiting singleton deep-cover agents within both legal and illegal Communist parties, and this function appears to be performed by the host country element of Operational Section No.1. The purpose of such recruitment is to convert a few influential local Communist party members into secret and completely controlled Soviet agents who can both report to the KGB on factional tendencies within the local party and exercise effective influence in support of Soviet policy directives. It is clear that the decision to effect such a penetration of a local party is regarded as a high-level policy matter and requires approval by the International Department in Moscow. The number and identity of such KGB agents seeded throughout the world Communist movement is one of the KGB's most closely guarded secrets, and local party members are known to speculate among themselves as to who among them may be in this special category.

This network of controlled high-level penetrations has a peculiarly important role when factional splits occur within a local party, or when there is organized resistance to Moscow's directive authority, as in the case of some of the European Communist parties. When Moscow becomes so dissatisfied with the independence of action asserted by a local Communist party that the serious decision is made to split the party in order to create a separate faction loyal to Moscow, these deep-cover penetration agents function as both sources of information and as agents of influence in accomplishing the split. In March of 1977, for example, Moscow moved to split the local Swedish party known as the Swedish Left Party of Communists. A new organizational entity calling itself the Swedish Communist Workers Party owing its first allegiance to Moscow was created under the chairmanship of Rolf Hagel, and all loyal European Communist parties were directed to send representatives to its congress on November 11–13, 1977, to demonstrate broad support. In the management of such a complex maneuver, KGB penetration agents play a critical role, and the threat of such splitting tactics is the Kremlin's ultimate weapon in dealing with recalcitrant Communist parties in democratic countries.

In third world countries where active revolutionary movements, guerrilla organizations, or terrorist groups exist, there is a strict division of functional responsibility between the International Department, the KGB, and Soviet military intelligence (GRU). The International Department has final authority for approving the selection of individuals from these groups for training in the Soviet Union; and during their residence in the Soviet Union they are identified by pseudonyms, with their real names kept in a central file in the International Department. The First Operational Section of the KGB Residence appears to have the responsibility of proposing candidates to the International Department. Once approved, the trainees are secretly exfiltrated to the Soviet Union by the KGB under false documentation; and after their training is completed they are reinfiltrated back into their native countries to put their new paramilitary skills to use as controlled agents inside their indigenous revolutionary organizations. While in the Soviet Union, these selected trainees are assigned under alias to special training camps operated by the GRU, where they are instructed by GRU experts in everything from weapons familiarization to the techniques of bank robbery and guerrilla tactics. By its input into this continuous training cycle, the local KGB Residence ensures itself access to an agent cadre of well-trained and competent guerrilla leaders whose advanced skills can gain them a position of influence within whatever revolutionary movement they may be assigned to. In view of the existence of this training cycle, Soviet protestations that they are not involved in the wide variety of guerrilla and terrorist organizations operating in Latin America and elsewhere must be taken with a large grain of salt. In recent times, the countries whose citizens under alias were receiving paramilitary training included many in Latin America and Africa.

Another major responsibility of the typical KGB Residence is the monitoring and coordination of the operations of the East European and Cuban intelligence services within the host country. As we have seen, the resident himself conducts the liaison with the local chiefs of these services; but there are also numerous working-level contacts between the operational officers under cover in the different embassies. As a Czech intelligence officer—Ladislav Bittman, who defected after the Soviet invasion of his country in 1968—has described, these satellite intelligence services are under the effective control of the KGB.[4] The KGB resident has access to the identity of their agents, and their most significant reporting is translated into Russian for direct transmission to Moscow. Intelligence operations are jointly planned, and Bittman correctly described the KGB's supervisory role when he stated, "No important decision is made without them." In fact there is some resentment within these services against the tendency of the KGB to take over and run for itself the most promising agents that they develop.

Directive authority by the KGB resident over the work of the Polish, Czech, Hungarian, Bulgarian, and Cuban intelligence sections functioning in their respective embassies very considerably extends the reach of the KGB, and provides it with a much larger number of trained case officers under diplomatic cover to handle locally recruited agents than would be available from its own resources.[5] For example, when the British government expelled 105 Soviet intelligence officers in 1971, the satellite services, particularly Polish intelligence, stood ready to supply case officers to handle agents who would otherwise have lost their ability to communicate. There also appears to be some division of labor in instances where a satellite service may enjoy peculiar advantages. The East German intelligence service has apparently been given wide discretion to exploit its easy access to the West German population, and the proliferation of thousands of spies in West Germany, at all levels, seems to be primarily the work of the East German service, although the KGB maintains its right to monitor and to receive the most significant results. Recruitment of unilateral Soviet agents within the satellite services is a KGB responsibility, but prior authorization by the International Department seems to be required.

As indicated in Figure 2, the Second Operational Section has responsibility for the performance of the KGB Residence's counterintelligence functions. Its first priority is to ensure that no hostile intelligence service succeeds in recruiting agents among the official Soviet population in the host country. The security officer in this section recruits secret informants within the ranks of the Soviet diplomatic and military personnel in the embassy to report on their private lives and drinking habits, for which he is usually cordially disliked. On a more sophisticated level, this section also handles deep-cover, paid KGB agents who have been infiltrated into the diplomatic and military services over a period of years in order to observe and report on morale and evidence of disloyal attitudes toward the regime. Some of these agents are "coopted," in the sense that they are not paid but are willing to cooperate with the KGB in reporting on their fellow employees in return for discreet KGB assistance in advancing their careers, in obtaining higher education for their children, and in gaining access to scarce housing. Evidence of such discreet cooperation with the KGB is always a plus factor in a Soviet official's dossier when he comes up for promotion or reassignment.

If, as a result of these precautions, a Soviet official is identified who has been approached by a hostile intelligence service, an initial decision is made as to whether to "double" him, by having him appear to accept an offer to work for the foreign service, when in fact he continues to take orders from the KGB, passing on to the hostile service only that information which the KGB authorizes for transmittal in order to whet the appetite of the foreign government. Through these carefully planned double-agent operations, the Counterintelligence Section not only expands its knowledge of the personnel and operating procedures of hostile services, but also ties up their personnel in an unproductive waste of time and effort that leaves them less opportunity for concentration on genuinely vulnerable targets.

In addition to these defensive responsibilities, the Counterintelligence Section is responsible for penetrating the host government's intelligence services, while the highest priority is assigned to identifying and, if possible, recruiting American intelligence officers or those who have useful access to them. An attempt is made in this section to maintain a current roster of all CIA personnel serving under cover in the American embassy, and to construct an organizational chart of the CIA station with all duties of its personnel identified. From this target list, selection is made of those who have some attribute that might make them vulnerable to recruitment, and every year throughout the world CIA officers serving overseas are subjected to a considerable number of recruitment pitches by the KGB, often involving very large financial inducements.

Another specific and high-priority target of this section is any organized group of Soviet émigrés. Perhaps because of the important conspiratorial role that émigrés played in the successful Communist seizure of power in Russia, the KGB is paranoid in its fear of what émigrés may be up to in trying to stir up trouble inside Russia, and an inordinate amount of case-officer time seems to be spent on trying to penetrate and discredit émigré organizations of both Russians and East Europeans. It is against this target that the KGB is most likely to use the ultimate weapon of assassination. The fatal stabbing with a poisoned umbrella of a Bulgarian émigré in a London street in the fall of 1978 is only one recent example.

Disinformation activity is another specialized function of the Counterintelligence Section. It can vary all the way from the placement in the press by a local agent of a story identifying an American embassy official as a CIA employee to participation in an orchestrated worldwide campaign based on a series of ingenious forgeries of official U.S. documents. A good example of the latter type of activity is described by Bittman in his book. Under the supervision of the KGB, the Czech intelligence service surfaced in the press throughout Latin America forged letters and documents purporting to prove that after President Kennedy's death U.S. Latin American policy had moved into a repressive phase, directed at severe economic exploitation and CIA-sponsored right-wing coups. In spite of official U.S. denials of the authenticity of these forged documents, the campaign had considerable impact and wide replay in the left-wing press.[6] I remember an ingenious forgery by the KGB of what purported to be the penultimate draft of a British cabinet policy paper setting forth British policy toward the labor movement in Africa. It was subtly designed to incite fears of British neocolonialism among newly independent African trade unions, and even attempted to create tensions between the British and American governments. This forgery was done so expertly that the two British Foreign Office defectors in Moscow, Burgess and McLean, were suspected of having had a hand in its drafting, and only scientific tests finally proved its falsity. Official British denials never caught up with the damage that it caused. A useful study of more recent Soviet forgeries was issued by the House Intelligence Committee in 1979, and American newspaper editors could be more alert than they are to this poisonous stream of forgery that is continuously being injected into the free press worldwide.[7]

Operational Section No. 3, as its name implies, is staffed with technically trained intelligence officers whose task is to collect intelligence on the advanced technology of the West. As much of this information as possible is acquired openly by the Soviet government through strategic purchases of critical technologies from the United States, Western Europe, and Japan. American corporations have engaged in a potentially suicidal competition to sell the Soviets entire technologies, including "turn-key" plants accompanied by manufacturing know-how and training programs. Many of these advanced manufacturing processes, particularly in the computer and electronics fields, are quickly adaptable to a wide variety of military uses. By importing these most modern Western techniques from abroad, the Soviets spare themselves the expense of conducting their own research and development programs in these fields, and are able to concentrate their research talent on the secret development of new weapons systems.[8] And a great deal of information is published in Western technical and scientific journals that would never see the light of day in the Soviet Union. Nevertheless, a small but critical amount of Western technological know-how relating to weapons development and technical intelligence collection devices is still kept hidden from the Soviets, either by top-secret security classification or by the denial of export licenses. It is against this very high priority target that the specially trained KGB case officers in the Third Operational Section are deployed. What the Soviets cannot buy from the West to close the technology gap, they attempt to steal through persistent espionage, often with startling success.

The extent of the threat posed by this KGB commitment to industrial espionage was dramatized in two fairly recent cases. Only after their conviction and sentencing to long prison terms for espionage in the spring of 1977 did two young Americans, Andrew Lee and Christopher Boyce, acknowledge the full range of the damage they had done, as revealed by *The New York Times* in April 1979.[9] In this post-trial confession, they admitted that between April 1975 and December 1976 they had sold to KGB case officers in Mexico and Vienna, for more than $80,000, technical information about several secret CIA satellite reconnaissance systems that the Soviets had not even known existed. Boyce worked as a low-paid clerk for a Californian aerospace firm, TRW Systems Group; but his job was in the code room in which top-secret messages were exchanged with CIA headquarters in Washington. Thousands of these classified documents, in clear text, were sold to the KGB. They gave the Soviets indispensable new information on how these satellite systems worked, making it easier for them to devise countermeasures with resulting damage both to the American ability to monitor compliance with SALT restrictions and to keep track of new Soviet weapons developments not covered by the treaty. Compounding these losses, William Kampiles, a young former CIA employee, was discovered in 1978 to have sold for $3,100 to KGB case officers in Greece the technical manual describing the most advanced CIA satellite surveillance system.[10] With these two triumphs of KGB technical intelligence collection now on the public record, it is possible to speculate about what other successes may have been achieved.

The title of Operational Section No. 4 is somewhat misleading. It does not actually handle illegals except in extreme emergencies. An "illegal" in KGB parlance is a singleton agent dispatched from Moscow with a completely constructed false identity. He takes up residence and works in a foreign country, documented from birth certificate to passport as if he were a native-born citizen, and equipped with a carefully crafted life history that can withstand close questioning. His identity is not known to the local KGB resident, and instructions as to how to contact him are apparently provided only when there is an emergency. He communicates directly with Moscow by coded shortwave radio and is used to handle only those recruited agents who are so important that all contacts with Soviet officials must be avoided in order to prevent suspicion. Colonel Rudolf Abel in his photography shop in Brooklyn was an example of such an illegal. This section concentrates on collecting identification documents and any material that might be useful to Moscow in constructing such false identities in the future.

The Fifth Operational Section engages in establishing an agent network that is held in reserve for the execution of sabotage operations in the event of war. The collection of detailed plans on critically vulnerable military and industrial installations is a primary function of this section, and it also has responsibility for carrying out assassination assignments on the rare occasions when this form of political warfare is authorized by the Center in Moscow. In view of the very close relationship between the KGB and the Bulgarian intelligence service, it is a reasonable guess that the assassination of the Bulgarian émigré in London in 1978 was conducted under the close supervision of this section; and the sophisticated nature of the device lodged in the tip of the umbrella to inject the rare poison also argues for a technical contribution from the KGB, if it did not in fact conduct the operation itself. It was from this Fifth Operational Section that a KGB officer defected to British intelligence in London in 1971, and his testimony played a critical role in identifying the 105 Soviet intelligence officers who were subsequently expelled from Britain. Since his defection, there has been some evidence that organizational changes have been made in the structure of KGB Residences including the distribution of the Fifth Section's functions among the other four.

On the basis of abundant testimony from KGB defectors over the years, it is possible to make some useful generalizations about the morale and motivation of the KGB case officers who do the pick-and-shovel work for the resident and his operational section chiefs. In the field of intelligence collection, KGB case officers are evaluated by the Center on the basis of the quantity and quality of the reports they extract from their individual agents. In order to impress the Center, the numbers game is played assiduously and a single long report is often broken down into separate reports in order to give the impression of increased activity and to add to the monthly total reported to headquarters. In order to improve the prospects for career advancement, KGB officers returning to Moscow for consultations often carry with them expensive gifts of scarce Western luxury products, which are judiciously distributed among their superiors in the Center as a form of discreet bribery.

Although the International Department of the Central Committee holds a close rein over major covert action subsidies to local Communist parties and front groups, the separate residences seem to have a substantial covert action contingency fund and wide discretion under International Department policy guidelines to attack covert action targets of opportunity as they arise. Little is known about the approval and review process in the use of these operational funds, but the KGB case officers do not appear to be divided into intelligence and covert action cadres as is the practice in the West. A KGB case officer who is running an elected member of a Western government's parliament for intelligence collection purposes does not hesitate to give him additional funds if such assistance is needed to help him in a propaganda campaign against the deployment of the neutron bomb. Similarly, a newspaper editor who is subsidized primarily as a covert action agent to influence the editorial content of his paper is also exploited for intelligence collection purposes if he has access to highly placed sources. The distinction between intelligence collection and covert action does not seem to exist in KGB practice, and agents are used interchangeably, for both purposes, in advancing toward broad Soviet objectives.

As we have seen, KGB officers are assigned a wide variety of covers within a Soviet embassy, including diplomatic, TASS, Novosti, trade missions and the like. They do their cover jobs in the embassy offices in which these components are located, and often complain that they are not sufficiently trained for the jobs to perform them in a credibly competent way. They also complain that their true identities are frequently widely known within the embassy. They are easily identified because of the late working hours that are necessitated by the frequency of night meetings with agents. They also can be identified by the special privileges they enjoy, although there is less complaint on this score. For example, KGB officers are exempt from attendance at the frequent lengthy ideological lectures given by the chief embassy representative of the CPSU, which all other embassy personnel must attend. This privilege is particularly resented by Soviet military intelligence officers, who have to attend these party meetings even though they must also conduct frequent night meetings with agents.

A persistent source of low morale among KGB officers serving abroad, which has sometimes led to defections, is discontent with the slow pace of career advancement and a general belief that promotion is based more on whom you know in the Center than on what you have done. Another contributing factor to the substantial number of KGB defections is exposure to the realities of life in the West, and the fact that the high living standards and political freedoms enjoyed in Western society bear so little resemblance to the dismal propaganda version of bourgeois life with which Soviet citizens are indoctrinated.

To complete the picture of the Soviet intelligence presence in their embassies abroad, a final word should be said about Soviet military intelligence. In Moscow, the Chief Intelligence Directorate (GRU) of the Soviet armed forces reports to the chief of the General Staff in the Ministry of Defense. GRU officers are recruited and trained, and serve as military officers with military ranks. GRU head-quarters is divided into geographical sectors and its primary function is to collect strategic intelligence on the United States, China, NATO, and Japan. Through secret agent operations and a massive network of intercept stations designed to eavesdrop on hostile communications of all kinds, it attempts to collect intelligence on the military intentions, order of battle, the sophistocated weapons systems, and military research and development programs of principal potential adversaries. It conducts liaison with the military intelligence services of the Eastern European satellites and Cuba. As we have seen, it operates guerrilla warfare training programs within the Soviet Union for individuals from national liberation movements. GRU personnel, in much smaller numbers than the KGB, serve abroad under cover as military attachés and members of various military-related missions.

The typical GRU Residence in an embassy is much smaller than its KGB counterpart, and its primary responsibility is to recruit agents within the host country's military forces and defense-related institutions. The GRU also operates the antennae that can often be seen on the roofs of Soviet embassies, and through this extensive intercept capability it has often scored substantial successes because of the general laxity of security maintained in the West in open telephone calls. It was only through the defection of a GRU officer in Brussels in 1973 that NATO learned of the close monitoring by the GRU of radio-telephone links between NATO headquarters and its subordinate commands, with the resulting leakage of large amounts of classified information because of poor security discipline.

The relationship between the GRU and KGB residents in an embassy is often tense. The GRU is under the obligation to clear all agent recruitment attempts with the KGB in advance in order to prevent competing approaches to the same individual, but the KGB does not seem to have the same responsibility toward the GRU. In addition, GRU officers deeply resent the security overview that the KGB maintains over their private lives and the intrusive activity of KGB informants. In comparison with the KGB, the GRU has a narrowly defined mission of collecting military intelligence. Although GRU officers usually have a limited general education, they are competently trained in their specialties, have high morale, and pose a major additional problem for Western counterintelligence services.

Chapter 15

American Foreign Policy—The Need for a New Consensus

In a sense, the content of the four preceding chapters is an intelligence assessment of the role of Soviet power around the world. In defining Soviet priority objectives and describing the military, political, and intelligence instrumentalities that the Soviets use to achieve their purpose, I have tried to give as accurate and objective a picture of the nature of the Soviet challenge as the available evidence permits. If this evaluation is accepted as reasonably close to reality, then certain consequences follow for American foreign policy and for the kind of American intelligence system needed to sustain it. Since even the best intelligence on the intentions and capabilities of other nations cannot rescue a basically misconceived and incoherent strategy from failure, it makes sense first to describe in broad terms what foreign policy response to the Soviet challenge seems required of the United States. In subsequent chapters, the role of American intelligence in helping to implement that policy will be more clearly understandable.

If Soviet strategy and tactics are as I have described them, then the first thing that strikes one is how dangerously unrealistic were some of the foreign policy prescriptions that flourished in the wake of the Vietnam experience. One popular school of thought read the lessons of Vietnam and Watergate to mean that we should severely restrict our overseas commitments, withdraw our troops from exposed positions, limit our defense expenditures to that which is required to discourage nuclear attack, and reduce our intelligence collection to technical surveillance of the Soviet strategic capability. Once we had given up the role of "world policeman" and "the imperial presidency," the belief was that we could then safely shift resources from the defense and intelligence budgets to the improvement of our environment and the reconstruction of our blighted cities, while at the same time winning reliable friends abroad by grants of economic aid with no strings attached. The sometimes unstated assumption behind this line of argument was that we could not presume to intervene in the affairs of other nations until we had reformed ourselves. The hope was that the construction of a more egalitarian, more democratic, and more generally prosperous America would make this country into an attractive model, exerting real influence in the world through the power of its example.

This line of thought was basically similar to that put forward by the idealistic wing of the America First movement before World War II, when Hitler had already begun his march through Europe. The pursuit of such a policy would open up to the Soviets the opportunity to organize the rest of the world against us, and I have tried to show that they have the ideological motive and the bureaucratic machinery to make the most of such an opportunity. While not consciously choosing isolation, we would have isolation thrust upon us.

Under such a policy, as American troops withdrew from Europe, the Western democracies would have no choice but to come to terms one by one with the superior power and presence of the Warsaw Pact forces. The best they could hope for would be a process of Finlandization, whereby they were permitted to maintain their internal democracy at the cost of their right to oppose or criticize the dictates of Soviet foreign policy. Such tendencies toward independence and liberalization as do exist among European Communist parties would be strangled, and the hopes of the dissident movement within the Soviet Union and Eastern Europe would be blighted. New Angolas and Afghanistans would multiply across the face of the third world, and Japan would be forced into accommodation or desperate rearmament as South Korea fell. By a process of gradual political and economic asphyxiation, the United States would be denied access to oil, markets, and essential minerals, ending up as a besieged, impoverished garrison state with its democratic allies subverted and its only remaining defense its retaliatory nuclear capacity. The consequence of any prolonged withdrawal by the United States from its responsibilities as the only democratic superpower was so demonstrably disastrous that this course of action has already lost its appeal for most of the American public. The time is ripe for the construction of a new consensus.

The fact that for the foreseeable future the United States is the only nation in the world with sufficient resources to compete effectively with the Soviet Union in terms of military power limits our freedom of choice. If we do not maintain a rough equivalence with the Soviets in the military field, no other nation is now equipped to do so. In the absence of our countervailing presence, all other nations outside the Soviet bloc become vulnerable. We did not deliberately choose the role of being one of the world's two superpowers and we are uncomfortable with it. But there is no escape. Once reconciled to this reality, the broad outlines of what must be our defense posture and foreign policy can be defined in terms that are acceptable to liberals and conservatives, to Republicans and Democrats. There is wide room for debate on specific budget figures and on tactical implementation, but once most Americans accept the reality of growing Soviet military strength and understand the motivation behind it, they can agree in general terms on what needs doing.

The indispensable first requirement for the conduct of an effective American foreign policy is the maintenance of a U.S. defense establishment large enough to convince the Soviets that they cannot achieve a decisive superiority in either strategic or conventional forces. We can and should seek to economize where possible by reducing costly interservice rivalry in the procurement of new weapons systems and in the more efficient use of manpower; but our overall strength must be kept at a level consistent with what the Soviets are doing in the present and planning for the future. American defense spending cannot be decided in the abstract but must depend on the most accurate possible annual estimate of the size and nature of Soviet military expenditures. Overestimation by intelligence analysts of Soviet resource commitments can lead to an unnecessary and costly intensification of the arms race, while underestimation leads to dangerous vulnerability.

Because of the impact of Vietnam and of overly optimistic assumptions in the past that the Soviets would be willing to settle for strategic parity once they achieved it, we have a great deal of catching up to do. The more recent polls seem to indicate that the American public is increasingly aware of this need, and President Carter moved belatedly to abandon his unwise campaign promises of deep defense cuts and toward the beginning of an effort to restore the balance. Much more remains to be done and the burden will continue to be a heavy one. However, it weighs more heavily on the Soviets than on us, because their defense expenditures must be squeezed out of a GNP substantially less than ours. To the extent that Americans demonstrate steadily and quietly our determination to maintain our side of the military equation, we preserve the balance of forces on which peace depends and reduce the chances of miscalculation and adventurism.

The cost of an unrestricted armaments competition is so high, and the diversion of scarce resources from human needs so serious, that no opportunity to limit this rivalry can be overlooked. The development of high-altitude surveillance satellites during the last decade by both the United States and the Soviets created such an opportunity. All previous schemes for arms limitation had foundered on the rock of Soviet refusal to permit any effective international inspection within their borders. The surveillance satellite provided for the first time an extraterritorial means of inspection that could at least be relied upon to identify the location of ICBM silos, and the number of bombers, submarines, and warships under construction. On the basis of this technological breakthrough, the SALT I interim agreement and the anti-ballistic missile treaty were signed by the United States and the Soviet Union in 1972. So long as the closed nature of their one-party police state causes the Soviet leaders to reject the intrusion of international random on-site inspection, new arms limitation agreements will continue to have to be confined to the control of only those weapons whose numbers and characteristics can be accurately identified by "spies in the sky." The competition for all forms of military power that cannot be so identified will continue unchecked, and the march of miniaturized technology, as in the case of the cruise missile, threatens to make verification by satellite surveillance increasingly less relevant and less reliable.

Moreover, experience with the limitations set in SALT I taught Americans a grim lesson in the advantages that a secretive totalitarian state enjoys over an open, democratic society in the negotiation and implementation of arms control agreements. These lessons have been explicitly spelled out in a number of studies.[1] The Soviets in the SALT I negotiations succeeded in winning crucial advantages by hard bargaining and by the deliberate concealment of the fact that new types of ICBMs were ready for testing. In this way, they protected their right to deploy a whole new generation of missiles that allowed them to catch up with and surpass the Americans in the weight of nuclear payload they could accurately aim against hostile targets. In the ABM treaty, they effectively succeeded in preventing the Americans from exploiting our technological advantage in this field, and used the time to catch up with American know-how. In my opinion, the Soviet interest in arms limitation has been primarily motivated by their fear of American technological superiority and by their belief that arms control agreements can be used to constrain the application of this advantage to weapons development. They proved right in this calculation during the course of the SALT I agreement, since during this period the United States remained content with its aging and increasingly vulnerable Minuteman missiles.

However, the most serious lesson taught by the SALT I experience is the fact that the Soviets will invariably build up their weapons systems to the outermost numerical and qualitative limits allowed by any agreement. In contrast, the elected American Congress is continuously under pressure to respect the popular demand for larger domestic expenditures. There is also a continuing American tendency to take a more optimistic view of the SALT negotiating process than the facts warrant and to believe that it must inevitably lead to reduced armaments, decreased tension, and more détente. I do not mean to suggest that fully verifiable upper limits set on strategic weaponry must work to the disadvantage of the United States. My point is that in all such agreements, the United States and its allies must match the Soviet commitment to build up to the outer limits of what is allowed. Only in this way can the balance of power be maintained and arms limitation be prevented from becoming a device to lull the American public into a passive acceptance of a dangerous inferiority. Eventually, a more democratic and open society may develop in the Soviet Union that will permit the free access and on-site inspection that genuine disarmament requires; but until that day comes there will be strict limits on what arms control agreements with the secretive Soviet state can accomplish.

The second basic priority of American foreign policy is the maintenance in good repair of our NATO alliance with the industrialized democratic nations of Western Europe and Canada. We need them and they need us. We are not only the one nation that can compete militarily with the Soviets, but we are also the strongest of the democratic states. Assured by our treaty commitments of the protection of our nuclear retaliatory capacity, our NATO allies can join with us in maintaining enough conventional military strength to defend against the buildup of the Warsaw Pact forces. Behind this bulwark, the democratic countries of Western Europe can hope to survive and prosper with their freedoms intact. Again belatedly, the Carter administration moved in 1978 to recognize that the steady increase in the quality and quantity of conventional Warsaw Pact forces, combined with the deployment of the intermediate range Soviet mobile SS-20 missile and the Backfire bomber, posed a mounting threat to NATO. Together with our allies, an effort is being made to close the gap; but much remains to be done. The traditional reluctance of democratically elected parliaments to make adequate provision for defense until it is too late can be overcome on both sides of the Atlantic by bold political leadership that is prepared to spell out in unambiguous terms the extent of the threat, and to rally public support for the sacrifices that have to be made. The Europeans should realize that their willingness to shoulder their proportionate share of the burden is essential to the steadiness of support in the U.S. Congress for NATO expenditures.

The commitment to the American side of the skilled manpower, industrial base, and armed forces of Western Europe has consequences beyond our own self-interest. The deeper and more lasting bonds of a shared belief in individual freedoms and democratic institutions unite us in a common endeavor that is more than a mere marriage of convenience. The continuing strength and attractive power of the democratic faith has been demonstrated by the progress made toward free institutions in Spain and Portugal after their right-wing dictatorships fell, in spite of the aggressive and well-organized threat of Communist minorities. The lip service to parliamentary democracy by the Italian and Spanish Communist parties is the homage that vice pays to virtue, and is itself an admission of the wide popular commitment to free institutions.

The economic burden of maintaining the NATO alliance in sufficient strength to counterbalance the Warsaw Pact weighs heavily both on our European allies and on ourselves. The negotiations in Vienna for Mutual and Balanced Force Reduction (MBFR) have been an attempt to work out with the Soviets and their Eastern European allies agreed-upon limits on the size of the opposing forces, based on a common ceiling. One must hope that this effort will eventually succeed, because the productive resources of both sides can be put to better use than the competitive proliferation of armored divisions. However, anyone familiar with the slow pace of the Vienna talks and the inherent difficulty of verifying accurately the number of troops withdrawn will remain skeptical. In the meanwhile, any reduction of the American troop strength in Europe that is not verifiably balanced by reductions on the Soviet side is dangerous. Such a unilateral withdrawal from the main defense line of our most vital alliance would inevitably be construed by both friends and opponents as a weakening of American political will, and would invite new Soviet pressures.

The third basic priority of American foreign policy is the maintenance of our alliances with the democratic nations in the Western Pacific and the preservation of the independence of non-Communist Asian countries. In this area, there is very little room left for reduction of American commitments. Given our withdrawal from Indochina and the imposition there of Communist rule, Japan, Australia, and New Zealand look to us for reassurances that we will stand by our treaty commitments. After making an ill-advised campaign promise to pull back American troops from South Korea, President Carter learned how destabilizing a premature withdrawal could be. A reduction of American military support to the South Korean regime has to be approached with extreme caution in view of the massive buildup, with Soviet assistance, of the North Korean armed forces. The xenophobic Communist dictator of North Korea, Kim Il Sung, proved in the Korean War that he is capable of wildly misreading American intentions, and the impact on Japan of a Communist victory in South Korea would have serious consequences. Moreover, the South Korean regime is likely to make more progress toward democratic freedoms when it feels itself secure in the presence of American military support than when it believes it is in the process of being abandoned to the tender mercies of the doctrinaire dictatorship in the North.

The task of protecting our Pacific allies against Soviet-supported expansion would have proved beyond the capacity of even the most determined and resourceful American effort if it had not been for the split that developed between the Communist regimes of China and the Soviet Union. One need only imagine what the position of all the independent nations on the perimeter of China would be if the Sino-Soviet Communist alliance had lasted. The United States, Japan, and the smaller Asian nations are the fortunate beneficiaries of the divisions that arose between Peking and Moscow. Whatever the proximate cause of the continuing rivalry between the two Communist giants, there is good reason for believing that the differences between them lie deep. There are vast lands beyond the present northern and western borders of China, seized and colonized by the Russians under the czar, to whose loss the Chinese are not reconciled. Their more immediate territorial quarrel arises from the Chinese claim that the Soviets are illegally occupying certain islands in the Manchurian rivers that lie on their side of the main channel. The Soviets find it impossible to compromise because of the strategic location of the disputed territory, and because of their fear that any territorial concession will simply whet China's appetite for more.

Behind the varied and bitterly argued ideological disputes, there is the unresolved question of which regime can claim the right to lead the world Communist movement and to provide the authoritative interpretation of the doctrine handed down from Marx and Lenin. Moscow and Peking are the divided capitals of a secular religion, and differ as profoundly as did the Catholic and Protestant princes during Europe's religious wars as to which is the legitimate custodian of the true faith. There are deep cultural and racial antagonisms rooted in the violent past. The steady buildup of more than forty Soviet divisions on the Chinese border, backed by increasing numbers of rockets and planes armed with nuclear weapons, dramatizes the extent of the mistrust and feeds the mutual fears. Limited as our knowledge is of the play of political forces behind the bamboo curtain in Peking, we would be well advised to watch carefully for any sign of rapprochement with Moscow; but my own guess is that we can count for a long time to come on continuing rivalry and conflict between the two most powerful Communist states.

Once the fact of this seismic division became apparent to the outside world, President Nixon and subsequently President Carter were wise to move to take advantage of the new relationship. Now that American forces have been withdrawn from Indochina, the Chinese Communists clearly see that the main threat to them is the growth of Soviet power, whether it be exercised in terms of armored divisions on their northern border or projected against their southern flank by the Soviet alliance with Hanoi. Their perception of this strategic threat has converted the Peking leaders into true believers in the NATO alliance, and they have actively encouraged Japan and the Philippines to strengthen their ties with the United States and to improve their defenses. As Vice-Premier Deng Xiaoping persistently warned during his first American visit, the Chinese leadership fears that the West is not sufficiently alive to the Soviet threat, and is too hesitant and indecisive in reacting to Soviet support of aggressive moves by their Cuban proxies.

The decision of the Carter administration to terminate the defense treaty with Taiwan at the end of 1978, and to break diplomatic relations in order to normalize relations with Peking, was a risk worth taking. The Peking regime showed its hunger for diplomatic recognition by proceeding in the face of a declared American intention to continue selling defensive arms to Taiwan. Facing threats on two fronts, Peking is not likely to risk the loss of badly needed American technology and credits by opening a third front against Taiwan. A written pledge by Peking not to use force against Taiwan was never in the cards, since that would have acknowledged lack of sovereignty over a province of China. Moreover, the Chinese Nationalists themselves ruled out the recognition of the island as an independent republic by stubbornly insisting on their claim to represent all China. The real choice lay between proceeding with diplomatic recognition to help consolidate pragmatic Chinese policy, or indefinite delay, at the risk of losing the strategic and economic advantages of the new relationship. There is a reasonable hope that Taiwan can look forward to a protracted period of economic growth, bolstered by the purchase of American arms. A reversion to dogmatic Maoism on the mainland is always possible, endangering the safety of Taiwan. But in the event of such a reversal, there would be time to consider a new defense arrangement with that beleaguered island.

Taken together with the ratification in October 1978 of the new peace and friendship treaty between Japan and China, the normalization of relations with Peking opened up new diplomatic vistas for the United States. Although a crucial clause in the joint communiqué announcing normalization warned Moscow that both the United States and China are opposed to efforts by any other country to "seek hegemony in the Asia-Pacific region," there is no need at present to join in an open military alliance with China against the Soviet Union. This is what Peking wants, and Moscow may yet succeed in provoking what it fears most by actions such as its invasion of Afghanistan. The United States has the opportunity to take advantage of the rivalry between China and the U.S.S.R. In this process, there may be ways of creating new persuasive incentives for improved Soviet behavior. In coordination with its NATO allies and with Japan, the United States can decide what types of technology or weaponry to sell to China and can make the flow dependent on Soviet performance. The Soviets, for example, may be more interested in removing their MIG-23s from Cuba when they realize that modern fighter planes can be sold to China.

In the long run, the greatest danger in the Chinese connection is that the American government will lean too heavily on it as a counterweight to Soviet power. Weakened by the disruption of the Cultural Revolution, China is for the time being a tractable giant, urgently dependent on Western technology and credits. It will take years for Chinese society to build the educational base needed to absorb modern technology. However, as China's power grows, Chinese leaders will use it to play off Moscow against Washington. In a game of triangular diplomacy that involves two Communist nations, the United States cannot be sure that it can control the outcome. In Asia, the link with Peking is a tactical necessity on which most Americans can agree, but it is no substitute for a continued reliance on the military strength of this country and its democratic allies.

In the Middle East, the Soviets see their interests best served by a prolongation of the long-simmering conflict between Arabs and

Israelis, with all the opportunities for exploitation that this situation presents. In direct contrast, the American interest lies in the earliest possible resolution of this ancient quarrel. The primary objective of American foreign policy in this region is easy to define but infinitely difficult to achieve. It is nothing less than a comprehensive and peaceful settlement that leaves Israel living within defined borders made secure by the fact that they are recognized and accepted as final by its Arab neighbors and by the Palestinians. It is a consummation devoutly to be wished because without it there will certainly be a spiraling arms race, recurrent and more destructive wars, threats to the oil supply that is the lifeblood of the West, and the ever present danger of a direct confrontation between the Soviet Union and the United States.

Whether the Camp David agreement between Israel and Egypt proves to be a stepping-stone toward a wider settlement that involves the Palestinians and the moderate Arabs remains uncertain as this book is written. President Carter, in his eagerness to nail down an agreement between President Sadat and Prime Minister Begin, failed to get clear commitments from Israel on the question of Palestinian autonomy on the West Bank and on the issue of Arab rights in East Jerusalem. The danger is that Israeli intransigence on these basic questions could make it impossible for the moderate Palestinians and Arabs to join Egypt in the negotiating process, and the net result of Camp David might yet turn out to be a polarization of the Arab world that leaves Sadat completely isolated and increasingly vulnerable. A great deal will depend on political developments within the democratic state of Israel, and on the ability of moderate Israeli leaders to make in their own long-term interest the additional compromises that may be necessary. In spite of all the obstacles, mutual suspicions, and conflicting historical claims, the United States has no choice but to continue to use its influence in the effort to achieve a settlement, because the alternative is so predictably catastrophic. In the years ahead, American foreign policy will face few tasks more demanding and urgent than a peaceful agreement in this area, and we may have to offer U.S. military guarantees to ensure it beyond what we have yet been willing to consider. Increasing American dependency on oil supplies from this region further dramatizes the urgent need for a peaceful resolution, and demonstrates the necessity of reducing that dependency by strict conservation and the development of other forms of energy as rapidly as possible.

There is not space here to try to define all the complex policy dilemmas that the United States will face in the next few years in attempting to deal with the problems of what has come to be known as the third world. The countries falling into this loosely defined category profess varieties of neutrality and nonalignment in the rivalry between the Soviet Union and the United States. Most of them are in the earlier stages of economic development. One thing is certain. Their problems will not go away nor will benign neglect diminish them. Some of the poorest of these nations, like Bangladesh, are already so heavily burdened with escalating population growth that it is difficult to see how they can escape the Malthusian vise. Others at the higher end of the scale are well on their way to productive self-development. In fact, the disparities between the societies that have been lumped together under the third world umbrella are so great that it is more accurate to talk in descending order of a third, a fourth, and a fifth world, as some economists have done.

With good reason, we Americans are less certain now of our ability to cure the ills of these less developed nations than we were when President Truman announced his Point Four program of technical assistance or when President Kennedy established the Peace Corps and declared the Alliance for Progress. We have learned the hard way that "development has to come, in overwhelming degree, from within, not from without."[2] In addition, overpopulation in some places is increasing so rapidly that it could devour without appreciable improvement in living standards even the most massive commitment of American resources. Recognition of these realities can help to relieve the unwarranted guilt complex with which many Americans approach the poverty that is so widespread beyond our shores. However, if any generality is applicable to so complex and intractable a situation, it is fair to say that a decent concern for our fellow human beings, and a realistic self-interest in our own survival on a shrinking planet, continue to require that we do much more than we have been doing to help improve the lot of more than half of mankind. Stronger support for effective birth control programs, increased transfers of capital and technology on favorable terms through both national and international lending agencies, and a reduction of our trade barriers against third world products are all practical measures that intelligent liberals and conservatives can agree on as urgent priorities of any American foreign policy that looks beyond the immediate horizon.

While there is a prevalent American tendency to view the third world as one vast hospital ward to whose patients it is our duty to minister, the Soviets take a quite different view, as their record demonstrates. They see the social malaise of the lesser developed countries not as a disease to be cured but as an opportunity to exploit in the conduct of their geopolitical offensive. They are quite selective in their approach to this promising political terrain. The statistics of their recent military and economic assistance programs and the evidence that has surfaced of their covert political interventions reveal a tendency to concentrate on countries that have a special strategic significance, because of either their political alignment, their advantageous geographical location, or their possession of scarce raw materials and minerals. The Soviets have made minimal financial contributions to the work of the international agencies and lending institutions that have been constructed to minister to third world needs, and they have virtually absented themselves from the dialogue between the industrialized Northern nations and the underdeveloped countries in the South. They prefer to engage in strictly bilateral aid programs, where the maximum political concessions can be obtained from the strings attached. They justify their abstention from the international efforts of the industrial West to assist the lesser developed countries on the ground that these endeavors are doomed attempts to treat the symptoms, whereas the disease is the capitalist bourgeois system itself which can be cured only by successful revolutionary action.

It is the Soviet geopolitical offensive into the third world that makes it so dangerous to accept the advice of George Kennan and others who advocate the reduction of American commitments to some indispensable minimum. In Kennan's view, this minimum should be confined to "the preservation of the political independence and military security of Western Europe, of Japan, and—with the single reservation that it should not involve the dispatch and commitment of American armed forces—of Israel."[3] This prescription for a withdrawal to an inner defense line solves the dilemmas of American foreign policy in the third world by asserting that we have no vital interest there worth defending. It assumes that in drastically shortening the lines we are prepared to defend, we might thereby safely be able to reduce our military establishment. In fact, we and our few remaining allies would have to spend a great deal more as the Soviets exploited the opportunity systematically to organize the large majority of the earth's population and resources against us.

Moreover, bitter experience has proved that the attempt to limit American responsibilities by publicly declaring that certain countries lie outside our protective perimeter invites aggression against those excluded.[4] The North Korean attack against South Korea in June 1950 was a direct response to the public American declaration that South Korea was not included inside our defense line. Faced with the hard fact that a North Korean victory would destabilize the American alliance with Japan, the United States was compelled to fight a costly war to reestablish a defense line that might well never have been breached if American policy declarations had not confused our opponents as to the real nature of our intentions.

Just as the size of the American military budget cannot be decided in the abstract but must depend on accurate estimates of Soviet defense spending, so American commitments in the third world cannot be limited by drawing in advance arbitrary defense perimeters but must depend on a careful calculation of the extent to which a Soviet threat to a particular country can shift the world balance of power dangerously against us. Once it is determined that the threat posed by Soviet intervention could seriously upset the world balance, there is the further difficult judgment to be made as to whether local political conditions and surrounding circumstances permit successful American intervention to restore stability. Determining factors will include the relative balance of military power in the crisis area, the extent of economic leverage available to the United States, and the amount of political influence that can be brought to bear. The world balance of power is now so finely drawn that it is difficult to identify the country whose absorption into the Soviet orbit would not have serious consequences; but even in these circumstances the local conditions may be such that it is wiser to accept a tactical retreat rather than risk a confrontation that we are bound to lose. The decision of the Carter administration not to intervene on the side of the Somalis in their war against Ethiopia in the Ogaden represented an example of such restraint dictated by an accurate assessment of the local balance of forces. However, too many tactical retreats in third world confrontations with the Soviets can add up to a general rout, and lead to the widespread perception of growing American impotence. Then allies begin to slide toward neutrality, and neutrals start to dicker for the best terms they can get. Given the outward thrust of Soviet power, the United States cannot escape active involvement in the complex struggle for influence throughout the third world. Neither condemnations of the imperial presidency nor the abstract definition of limited defense perimeters will help us to deal with the many difficult and ambiguous choices that we will inevitably have to face.

In this many-faceted rivalry the United States in alliance with Western Europe enjoys significant advantages, provided the overall military balance with the Soviet Union is restored. In the field of trade, Western consumer products and technology are consistently of a higher quality than those available from the Soviet bloc, and given a free choice, the less developed countries tend to buy from the West rather than from the East. Similarly, Western weapons systems are generally preferred for their greater effectiveness by third world buyers. The system of competitive private enterprise has outperformed the Soviet economic model as an engine for rapidly raising living standards in countries where it has been given an opportunity, such as Singapore, Taiwan, and South Korea. In contrast to the one-party Communist police states, democratic institutions retain their appeal in nations as poverty-stricken as India; and American respect for individual human rights commands a wider base of popular support than the totalitarian practices of Moscow. The existence of a free press in the West, with its influence as a purveyor of news throughout the third world, is a powerful antidote to the massive Soviet propaganda apparatus; and American popular culture in the form of music and films has a pervasive influence.

Offsetting these economic and cultural advantages that the West enjoys are the organizational weapons that we have seen the Soviets deploy. Covert intervention through long-term secret subsidies to disciplined Communist parties and front groups, manipulation of large-scale military assistance programs for political effect, the use of the proxy armies of their satellites, and direct Soviet intervention all combine to present a threat to the independence of third world nations to which the United States has not found an adequate answer. In attempting to deal with these cruder forms of Soviet intervention, the American government will probably be compelled to rebuild its own covert action capability, and once again to use the CIA as a means of providing timely and discreet assistance to indigenous political forces that are prepared to stand up to the Soviet-controlled and subsidized apparatus. As in the past, the success of such efforts to contain massive Soviet intervention will depend on the ability to maintain secrecy and on the quality of the political judgment exercised in the choice of leadership groups deserving of support. A few more serious reverses to American interests in the Middle East and Africa as the result of Soviet intervention should be enough to persuade the President and the Congress that the struggle within nations can be as decisive as the rivalry between them. So long as the Soviets remain committed to continuing massive intervention, the policy of nonintervention in the internal affairs of other countries is a declaration of unilateral political disarmament by the United States.

Chapter 16

The Role of "Finished" Intelligence

THE BROAD OBJECTIVES of American foreign policy outlined in the previous chapter may come in time to enjoy the support of a large majority of the American people, as improved understanding of Soviet purpose and methods builds the basis for a new consensus. Whether these objectives can in fact be achieved, in whole or in part, will depend upon a host of day-to-day tactical decisions made by our government in its dealings with allies and adversaries. The outcome will be vitally affected by the ability of a democratically elected Congress to allocate sufficient resources to foreign policy and defense needs in the face of competing demands for more consumer goods and larger social welfare programs. The timeliness and relevance of these decisions will in turn depend not only on the wise judgment of the President and of the congressional leaders, but also on the availability to them of current and accurate intelligence on the capabilities, activities, and intentions of foreign governments. There is a role for inspired innovation in the conduct of diplomacy, but most of the time foreign policy decisions are no better than the informa-

347

tion on which they are based. What this information consists of is the subject of this chapter.

One of the basic missions assigned to the CIA by the National Security Act of 1947, under which it was established, was to ensure that the President and his principal advisers on the National Security Council (NSC) were provided promptly with intelligence from all sources on any threat to the national security. The lesson of the surprise attack on Pearl Harbor had been learned. In the days leading up to that disaster, bits and pieces of vital information had been flowing into various government agencies which, if collated and looked at in their entirety, would have given a clear warning of impending attack. The lack of a central point of coordination and communication deficiencies resulted in a failure to read the warning signals in time, and the blazing hulks of the American battleships at their moorings in Pearl Harbor spelled out the message that in the modern era, the United States could not afford again in time of peace to be without a centralized intelligence system to provide strategic warning.

In the heat of current controversies, it is sometimes forgotten why the Congress established the CIA in 1947 as a new and independent federal agency and gave it the responsibility for producing foreign intelligence. By deciding to create a separate agency, with its own budget, reporting directly to the President and the NSC, the Congress tried to ensure that the CIA's assessments would be as objective and disinterested as possible. Because they were independent of both the State Department and the military services, the Director of Central Intelligence and his staff were to be freed from the temptation to bend intelligence assessments to fit preconceived policy assumptions or to serve parochial budgetary priorities. In order to make sure that no item of possible national intelligence interest could be deliberately withheld, language was included in the act that gave the CIA access to all relevant foreign information collected by other departments and agencies.[1]

Even in the early days, the flow of raw reports and data from overseas was so voluminous that a large staff of expert analysts had to be assembled who could review, compare, and cross-check. The product of their analysis of the raw information is called "finished intelligence" and represents a judgment on what is significant and should be taken into account when making policy decisions. Since

1947, the flow of raw information from abroad has turned into an avalanche, and highly specialized analytical staffs have been built up to refine this mass of material into a form sufficiently succinct to be usable by policymakers. Complex procedures and bureaucratic machinery have been established to ensure coordination between the various agencies that collect and produce foreign intelligence.

The CIA may be the most publicized U.S. foreign intelligence agency, but it is by no means the only one. Within the Department of Defense, there is the Defense Intelligence Agency, with responsibility for the reporting of our military attachés overseas and for producing finished intelligence on defense-related matters for the Secretary of Defense and the Joint Chiefs of Staff. Also within the Defense Department is the National Security Agency, which is responsible for monitoring the airwaves for all that can be learned from foreign communications and electronic signals, whether encoded or in the clear. The army, navy, and air force maintain separate intelligence establishments to produce tactical military information. Finally, the Defense Department is responsible for funding orbiting satellite systems that have in recent years increased the flow of information on Soviet weapons systems.

Within the Department of State, the Bureau of Intelligence and Research reviews the diplomatic reporting from our embassies overseas and provides finished intelligence to the Secretary of State. The Federal Bureau of Investigation, in the Department of Justice, contributes significantly from its agent reports and liaison relationships with foreign internal security services. The Energy and Treasury Departments have intelligence components concerned with foreign intelligence in their specialized fields, and the Drug Enforcement Administration is involved through its efforts to trace and interdict the supply lines through which illegal drugs enter the country. All these agencies make up what has come to be known as the Intelligence Community, as graphically represented in Figure 3. The most recent public document that defines the interrelationships and coordinating mechanisms between these agencies, the CIA, and the National Security Council is Executive Order 12036, issued by President Carter on January 26, 1978. It is required reading for those who want an understanding in specific detail of the present structure of the intelligence community. The organization of the Agency under this executive order is portrayed in Figure 4. This executive order is

Figure 3

THE INTELLIGENCE COMMUNITY

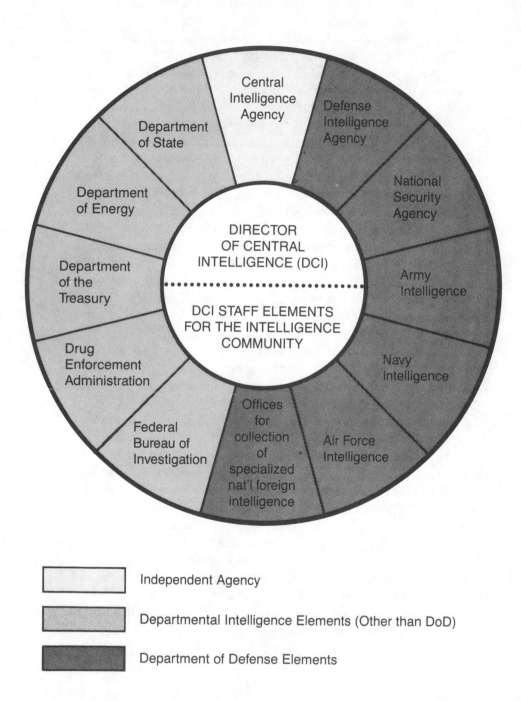

Central Intelligence Agency

Defense Intelligence Agency

Department of State

National Security Agency

Department of Energy

DIRECTOR OF CENTRAL INTELLIGENCE (DCI)

Department of the Treasury

Army Intelligence

DCI STAFF ELEMENTS FOR THE INTELLIGENCE COMMUNITY

Drug Enforcement Administration

Navy Intelligence

Offices for collection of specialized nat'l foreign intelligence

Federal Bureau of Investigation

Air Force Intelligence

Independent Agency

Departmental Intelligence Elements (Other than DoD)

Department of Defense Elements

Figure 4

ORGANIZATION UNDER NEW EXECUTIVE ORDER

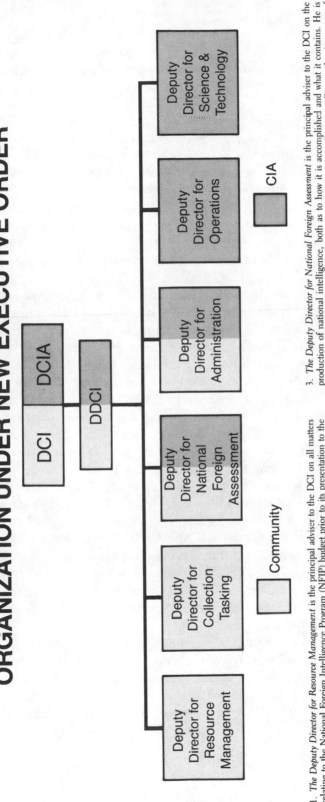

1. *The Deputy Director for Resource Management* is the principal adviser to the DCI on all matters relating to the National Foreign Intelligence Program (NFIP) budget prior to its presentation to the President and Congress. He will ensure the DCI has full access to relevant information and will conduct audits and evaluations as necessary. He will also assist the DCI in arriving at budget recommendations and will oversee the execution of the budget once it is approved.

2. *The Deputy Director for Collection Tasking* is the principal adviser to the DCI on all collection efforts within the Intelligence Community. He is responsible for assigning, through the National Intelligence Tasking Center, (NITC), which he heads, intelligence collection objectives and tasks to all intelligence elements of the Intelligence Community. He establishes priorities for tasking national intelligence collection systems in response to the production priorities set by the National Foreign Assessment Center. Through the NITC, he ensures dissemination of the information collected.

3. *The Deputy Director for National Foreign Assessment* is the principal adviser to the DCI on the production of national intelligence, both as to how it is accomplished and what it contains. He is responsible for organizing national efforts to assess and evaluate foreign intelligence data in support of national intelligence objectives as established by the National Security Council. He is the Director of the National Foreign Assessment Center and oversees the production of that Center. He also monitors product quality and evaluates product responsiveness.

4. *The Deputy Director for Administration* is responsible for supporting administratively those Intelligence Community components under the jurisdiction of the DCI as well as performing other tasks as assigned. He will continue to serve all his assigned functions as the Deputy Director for Administration of the CIA.

5. *The Deputy Director for Operations* and the *Deputy Director for Science and Technology* will continue to serve all their presently assigned functions for the Central Intelligence Agency.

expected to be supplanted by the new legal charter for the intelligence community, on which the Congress is working in a prolonged effort to reach agreement on legislation to replace the National Security Act of 1947.

The finished intelligence produced by the CIA for foreign policy decision makers has been packaged in various forms over the years, and has been adjusted to the working habits of successive Presidents. At present, the most important publications that appear on a daily basis are two in number. The first is the President's Daily Brief, known in the trade as PDB. It is written under the supervision of the deputy director for National Foreign Assessment in the National Foreign Assessment Center, as shown in Figure 5. In this center in Washington are concentrated CIA's analysts and estimators who produce the bulk of the Agency's finished intelligence. The distribution of the PDB is limited to the President and a very restricted number of his principal advisers, since it contains information from the most sensitive sources available to the entire intelligence community. It is designed to be read in ten or fifteen minutes by the President at the beginning of each working day. It does not attempt to recapitulate what the news media have reported in the last twenty-four-hour period, but rather to summarize the significance of what secret sources have reported that bears on current world developments. Successive Presidents have found it a useful and objective executive summary. In the hands of the director of the CIA, it is a powerful instrument for focusing the attention of the President on potential crisis areas and for alerting him to situations that may require rapid policy adjustment. Occasionally, when fresh intelligence sheds new light on a complex problem, an annex is attached to the PDB to give the President more extensive background for the decisions he has to make. In the newspaper world, a limited number of reporters produce copy for millions of readers, whereas in this case an army of analysts labor to produce a document for one man and his small circle of top advisers; and its timeliness and accuracy can affect decisions that shape our lives.

The second current intelligence publication of the CIA is the National Intelligence Daily. Also produced in the National Foreign Assessment Center, it is distributed on a daily basis to about two hundred top-level foreign policy officials in Washington, and cabled to a limited number of key U.S. ambassadors and CIA station chiefs serv-

Figure 5

NATIONAL FOREIGN ASSESSMENT CENTER

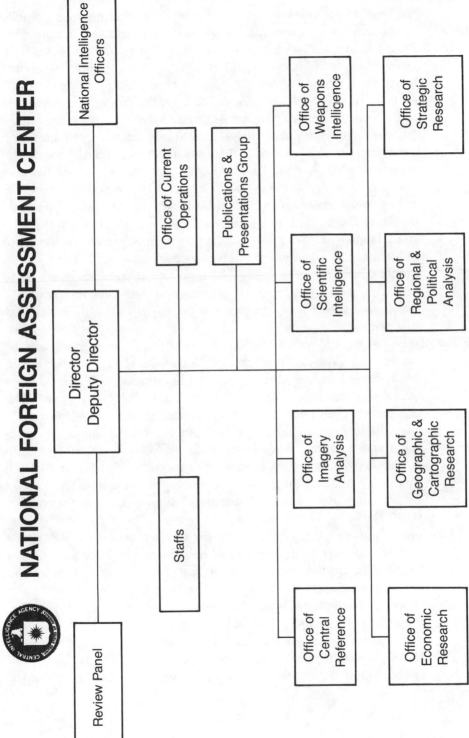

ing overseas. Specific items are coordinated with member agencies of the intelligence community when time permits. It is somewhat longer than the PDB, but serves the same purpose for a larger audience. For security reasons, it does not contain some of the extremely sensitive information that is carried by the PDB.

In addition to these two regular daily publications, the specialized staffs in the National Foreign Assessment Center, as shown in Figure 5, produce a wide range of studies and assessments each month on every conceivable subject that might affect U.S. relations with the outside world. They vary in subject matter from analysis of the economic effects of Chinese population trends to predictions of the size of the Soviet grain harvest. Studies of the future trends in world oil production have their impact on national energy policy, while analysis of the growth of organizations involved in international terrorism influences the allocation of funds to airport security. Political assessments of the future stability of friendly governments can lead to timely measures of support or, where the assessment is wrong, as it was in the case of Iran, can result in failure to adjust in time to new situations.

In the last few years, the CIA has made it a policy to release the products of some of this research in declassified form, and the resulting coverage in the press has given the general public a basis for evaluating the product on which their tax dollars are spent. The quality obviously depends not only on the accuracy of the raw intelligence fed into the analytic process but also on the intelligent judgment and breadth of knowledge of the individual analyst. Generalizations are difficult to make on such a vast and varied research effort; but my own general impression during my last year with the Agency in 1977 was that the overall quality of the performance was good, particularly in the economic and scientific fields, though political analysis of developments in the third world tended to suffer from a lack of concentrated talent, area knowledge, and language competence. Also there is no doubt that in the aftermath of Watergate and the congressional investigations, there was a falling off in the Agency's ability to recruit into its pool of analysts the top of the class from the best graduate schools. The inherent challenge of the work, and its direct bearing on this country's ability to survive and prosper in an uncertain world, should over time repair this situation and make up for the fact that the work of many intelligence analysts is so heavily classified that they cannot receive public recognition for their achievements. By the selective hiring of academic experts on a consultant basis, and by contracting out some of the research to universities willing to cooperate, the research managers in the Agency have been able to tap the specialized knowledge and talent that lies outside the government in the American academic world.

In addition to the daily publications and the monthly flow of assessments of current developments, the finished intelligence produced by the CIA includes the National Intelligence Estimates. As their name implies, these documents attempt to project into the future existing military, political, and economic trends, and to estimate for policymakers contingencies that require prompt action if the American position in the world is not to be seriously challenged at some later date when it will be too late to take remedial measures. As we have seen, the most important of these National Estimates is the annual review of projected Soviet military spending and weapons development. This estimate becomes the base line against which is measured the sufficiency of our own military posture, and it therefore directly influences the size of the U.S. defense budget and the amount of taxes individual Americans must pay. Under current procedures, these estimates are prepared by a team representing the interested components of the intelligence community under the supervision of a National Intelligence officer located in the National Foreign Assessment Center. The final document is reviewed by the National Foreign Intelligence Board, on which sit the chiefs of all the member agencies of the intelligence community, and is then submitted to the National Security Council and the President by the CIA director. Where the coordination process cannot reach agreement, the dissenting agencies have the right to submit their reservations, so that real issues in dispute are not hidden under a cloak of deliberate ambiguity or bland generalization.

The National Intelligence Estimate is perhaps the most severe test of the ability of the intelligence analyst because he must go beyond the current data and attempt to peer into the cloudy future to predict how the Soviet Union and other nations are likely to behave. Obviously such estimative judgments offer wide scope for error. However, decisions have to be made on the basis of all the evidence available—and the best informed guesswork—in order to meet budgetary deadlines. Knowing how difficult this estimative task is, I hesitate to criticize the Agency's professional estimators, but on one basic issue I think they are vulnerable. In the late sixties and early seventies they leaned over backward to avoid worst-case assumptions about Soviet military intentions, and as a result tended to underestimate the scale and pace of the Soviet buildup.[2] The fervent hope that the Soviets might be willing to settle for parity may have influenced their judgment and delayed for too long the realization that American restraint in the deployment of strategic weaponry could not be relied on to slow the steady advance of Soviet military strength.

In addition to the regularly scheduled annual estimates of key factors in the world balance of power, the President or members of the National Security Council can call for Special National Intelligence Estimates (SNIEs) when some unforeseen development requires a new look at all the possible consequences. The National Intelligence officer for the geographical or functional area affected then pulls together a team of experts from the intelligence community, and produces on a crash basis a coordinated estimate that takes into account every scrap of relevant information. The policymakers facing up to the decisions that have to be made at least have the reassurance of knowing that the number of unknowns in the equation they must solve has been reduced to the bare minimum, and that no intelligence-gathering resource has been neglected in presenting the dimensions of the problem.

Crisis warning presents a special kind of challenge to the intelligence analysts and provides a dramatic and unambiguous test both of their competence and of the adequacy of the evidence available to them. International crises can erupt suddenly or develop slowly. There is obvious need for as much advance warning as possible, to allow policymakers time to defuse the threat, or to take precautions to deal with it if it proves unavoidable. When a particular crisis builds slowly over an extended period, the form of finished intelligence used to report it is usually the President's Daily Brief and the National Intelligence Daily. Frequent updatings of the developing crisis situation in these publications serve to alert the President and his advisers and to keep them currently informed. If intelligence indicates that a sudden and unexpected crisis is imminent, the director of CIA may decide to issue an Alert Memorandum to the top policymakers which puts them on notice that they may have to take emergency action, and incidentally makes it a matter of record that the Agency did in fact sound the alarm in advance. In the postmortems that inevitably follow any major international crisis, both policymakers and congressional committees often tend to place the blame for error on "intelligence failures," and the Agency has learned from experience that it is wise to have on the record unambiguous proof of its foresight, if such is available.

Once a crisis has been recognized as serious and unavoidable, it is the business of the CIA director to mobilize the intelligence community to provide prompt and accurate assessments of the capabilities and intentions of all foreign governments involved, and of what their reactions are likely to be to the actions our own government is considering. A specialized form of finished intelligence called the National Intelligence Situation Report is issued by the DCI at frequent intervals during a major crisis to keep the policy level advised of fast-breaking developments. It is prepared by a community task force, usually under the direction of a senior CIA analyst. Through this coordination, an attempt is made to put in the hands of the crisis managers a single authoritative report that summarizes all important developments in the latest reporting period and to prevent the White House from being swamped with separate, redundant, and sometimes conflicting reports from the individual intelligence agencies.

What does the record show on the CIA's performance in providing advance warning on major crises? As noted, I had occasion to look into this subject at some depth during my last year with the Agency. In my opinion, the performance record is mixed. It is neither as bad as the House Select Committee on Intelligence reported in findings that were leaked to *The Village Voice,* nor as good as supporters of the Agency would like it to be.[3] In addition to the reasons already described for the failures that have occurred, one additional point is worth making here. In the Iranian crisis in 1978, there was a clear failure to anticipate the depth of the opposition to the Shah and to give sufficient advance warning to allow time for any kind of remedial action. The U. S. government was literally overtaken by events and found itself with very little knowledge of the various opposition movements that coalesced to force the Shah's downfall. During the spring and summer of 1978, as the demonstrations mounted in intensity, the daily publications of the CIA, according to White House staffers, tended to play down the seriousness of the deteriorating situation; and one CIA assessment was sent to the White House in August that confidently predicted that the Shah would succeed in bringing the dissatisfaction under control. The State Department reporting from Iran appears to have been equally in error.

There are two considerations that explain, although they do not excuse, this lack of perception. The first is the damage that has been done over the last few years to the morale of the CIA operations officers whose job it is to recruit human agents under difficult and dangerous circumstances. Many of them have been identified publicly by Philip Agee and his friends, and therefore no longer enjoy the advantage of secure cover. The drumfire of congressional investigation and press criticism has also taken its toll, and there is an understandable tendency to keep one's head down and not to take risks. The second explanation is the fact that the U.S. monitoring sites in Iran were judged to be so essential to intelligence coverage of Soviet missile testing that contact with the Shah's political opposition was avoided in order to maintain good relations with him. For fear that the Shah might close down the monitoring bases, the CIA station seems to have relied primarily on Iranian authorities for information concerning opposition strength and motivation. This self-imposed restriction prevented the station from recruiting agents within the different segments of the opposition, and cut the station off from the best and most reliable source of information on the forces behind the gathering political unrest. As the perceptive reporting of the French newspaper *Le Monde* indicated in the summer of 1978, it was not necessary to have access to secret agents to understand what was happening, but it would have helped. Similar restrictions on CIA recruiting exist in some other third world countries, and have been accepted by the U.S. government as binding in order to avoid potential damage to valued relationships. The danger of such self-denying ordinances was dramatized in Iran, and the hope is that such restrictions have been reconsidered and relaxed.

Before leaving the subject of finished intelligence, I should add that not all information reaching the top policymaking level has been summarized and edited by an intervening layer of analysts. A particular report from a well-placed and reliable secret agent may be considered so significant that it is sent in its entirety to the President and his advisers. A set of photographs from a surveillance satellite that may be especially revealing will receive similar handling, as in the case of the Cuban missile crisis. The CIA analysts tend to object to this exposure of the policymakers to the raw data because they rightly see themselves as the guardians of objectivity, but on occasion there is no better way of bringing home the true nature of an impending emergency.

Also a final word is in order about the relationship between the policymaker and the intelligence analysts. They do not in real life inhabit separate compartments, communicating only through formal written requirements and the submission of bulky documents in reply. They talk to each other. They have lunch together and inevitably they influence each other. This complex relationship has been described best by Thomas L. Hughes, a former director of Intelligence and Research in the Department of State.[4] The policymaker seeks out and praises the intelligence analyst whose product tends to support the policy line he is urging. The excessively ambitious intelligence officer may tend to downplay the significance of information that calls into question a prevailing policy. All these complex pressures reached their dramatic height during the years of the war in Vietnam. It is no solution to attempt to ensure the objectivity of the analyst by isolating him in a world apart, because he would then quickly lose touch with what the policymaker needs to know in specific and realistic detail. We must accept that the framers of policy and the producers of intelligence will go on mutually influencing each other, and trust that their sense of professional integrity will keep the dialogue honest. The most important procedural safeguard is the fact that the CIA is an independent agency, reporting directly to the President and the responsible congressional committees.

Chapter 17

The Collectors

IT HAS BECOME a fashionable truism to state that 90 percent of what the policymaker needs to know to make intelligent policy decisions is in the public domain. It is, in fact, true that academic experts and serious foreign correspondents can reach a generally accurate understanding of major events by a careful reading of open sources, including the world press, foreign broadcasts, monthly periodicals, and the large number of technical, scientific, military, and economic journals and reports. In recognition of the importance of this publicly available information, the CIA has for years maintained the Foreign Broadcast Information Service (FBIS). Acting as a service of common concern for all government agencies having an interest in foreign affairs, the FBIS translates into English and summarizes on a daily basis everything of significance that has appeared in the radio and TV broadcasts and major press outlets of nations throughout the world. Under a long-standing cooperative arrangement with the British Broadcasting Corporation (BBC), there is an agreed division of labor between the BBC and FBIS under which regional responsibility for monitoring and translating foreign broadcasts is allocated and the resulting coverage exchanged on a daily basis.[1]

The output of this monitoring and translation service is available

to the general public on payment of a reasonable fee. Journalists and
academicians value it highly, as do analysts within the Agency. The
FBIS also keeps track of what is said by the many clandestine and
semiclandestine radios that the Soviets maintain, and which broadcast from the Soviet Union and Eastern Europe into neighboring
countries in their native languages in support of local Communist
parties and front groups. The content of these Soviet-controlled
broadcasts, for which Moscow denies responsibility, can often provide indicators of Soviet policy intentions. For example, the "National Voice of Iran," broadcasting from Baku inside the U.S.S.R.,
pretended to be the voice of the internal opposition to the Shah. The
inflammatory demands of this radio for the Shah's overthrow in the
summer of 1978 contrasted with the comparative restraint of the
official Soviet media at that time, and were a more accurate reflection
of Soviet strategy, contributing to the rising unrest.

Another service of common concern that the CIA performs for the
intelligence community is the maintenance of the Domestic Collection Division. This unit has established completely overt CIA offices
in major cities throughout the United States, and by looking up the
number in the phone book private American citizens can voluntarily
report whatever they think may be of interest as the result of their
travels abroad. These offices are primarily debriefing centers for the
collection of unclassified information from the large number of
Americans who travel abroad on business or pleasure, and their
volunteered observations often provide helpful and sometimes
unique insights.

Indispensable as is this continuous flow of worldwide public information, it can go only so far toward revealing what is really going on
and what is actually going to happen next. It does in fact comprise
approximately 90 percent of what we need to know, but the missing
10 percent is crucial. Taken by itself, the vast mass of open source
information is as useless as an uncompleted bridge that takes us not
quite across a river when it comes to some of the things we need to
know most. However, by sifting and analyzing this freely available
information, it is possible to narrow down and define what is of
importance that is being kept from us, and that we have to try to
collect by the expensive, time-consuming, and sometimes dangerous
methods of secret intelligence operations. Under President Carter's
reorganization of the intelligence community, the NSC Policy Re-

view Committee establishes the general requirements and priorities for secret foreign intelligence collection as seen by the policymakers. An interagency organization under the DCI, the National Intelligence Tasking Center, then has the job of translating these requirements into specific objectives for each collecting agency, defining what items of missing information they are required to spend their resources in attempting to collect. This center is responsible for preventing unnecessary duplication and for ensuring that efforts are not wasted in trying to collect through the tortuous means of espionage what can clearly be read between the lines of openly available material.

At the top of the list of what we most need to know, and what no open source can tell us, is "survival intelligence," which consists of the military capabilities and intentions of our possible adversaries. Because at present the Soviet Union alone among nations has the capacity to deliver a potentially fatal blow against American territory and that of our NATO allies, the highest priority is assigned to collecting accurate and current information on Soviet intentions, and on the capabilities and state of readiness of Soviet and Warsaw Pact armed forces. Since its inception, the Soviet regime has gone to enormous lengths to protect the secrecy of its military planning and dispositions. Soviet scientists engaged in defense-related research cannot leave the country to attend scientific conferences abroad until they have been separated from such work for at least five years, although special waivers are sometimes possible. Most published material in the defense field is highly classified, and there are no leaks in the state-controlled press. Much that is openly available in the United States in the published records of congressional hearings, in trade journals like *Aviation Week*, and in the leaks that well-connected columnists exploit, remains a closely guarded state secret in the Soviet Union, and the penalties for disclosure are harsh and immediate. This difference between the open American society and the closed Soviet state forces the American taxpayers to pay billions to finance the collection of the kind of information in the Soviet Union that is freely available to the Soviet Embassy in Washington.

For years, the analysts in the CIA and the Department of Defense had to depend for their annual estimates of Soviet military strength on a thin trickle of raw intelligence data. By monitoring atomic explosions inside Russia, they attempted to keep abreast of Soviet nuclear progress; and the photographs taken of the military equipment the Soviets chose to display at their annual May Day parades were a prime source of information. Educated guesswork had to be relied on to decipher the reality behind the deliberately misleading Soviet defense budget figures, and only occasionally were well-placed human agents like Colonel Penkovsky able to throw revealing light into the dark recesses of Soviet military planning. This fog of secrecy began to lift with the advent of the U-2 plane, pioneered by the CIA and capable of taking high-resolution photographs while flying over the U.S.S.R. above the reach of antiaircraft batteries. Fortunately, not long after the Soviets demonstrated their capacity to shoot down the U-2, the new photographic surveillance satellites were launched into orbit to supply the analysts in the CIA's National Photographic Interpretation Center with increasingly accurate and timely photographic coverage of the missiles, ships, submarine pens, planes, and armored divisions that go to make up the Soviet order of battle.

Taken together with improved methods of collecting signals and communication intelligence, and of monitoring the telemetry used in Soviet missile testing, this technological breakthrough deluged the analysts producing finished intelligence with a flood of revealing raw data on the current Soviet offensive and defensive capability and on the testing of new weapons systems. By reducing the margin of error, these expensive collection systems have paid for themselves many times over. Originally designed to break through the curtain of Soviet secrecy to give our defense planners the information they needed, they also became the key to breaking the deadlock in the arms control negotiations by providing extraterritorial means of verifying the limits set on some forms of strategic weaponry. We owe this satellite surveillance capability primarily to the imagination and ingenuity of the experts working in the intelligence community. In the course of the SALT debate on the adequacy of the American verification procedures, so many specific details about how these surveillance mechanisms work have been made public that there is no need to describe once again the interlocking array of orbiting satellites, planes, ships, and monitoring bases that now keep continuous watch on the Soviet military posture.

Marvelously ingenious and hugely productive as this technological revolution in the field of intelligence has been, there are strict limits on what it can accomplish even when it comes to survival intelligence. In fact, the pace of innovation in the development of modern weaponry, and the extent to which the Soviets have reduced the commanding American technological lead and in some fields overtaken us, mean that human agents reporting from within the Soviet system are more needed than ever before. Contrary to the testimony of former high-ranking CIA officials like Herbert Scoville, "spies in the sky" do not reduce the need for spies on the ground, and the surveillance satellite is no substitute for the reliable secret agent reporting from inside the Soviet decision-making apparatus.[2] The two sources of information, technical surveillance and human reporting, are both essential, and they reinforce and complement each other. The authenticity of an agent's report that a secret weapons testing facility is located at a given location can be checked by focusing the satellite's camera on the identified installation, and photographic confirmation can strengthen confidence in the agent's bona fides by proving that he is providing reliable information. Conversely, photographic coverage often identifies mysterious installations for whose purpose the analysts have no adequate explanation. In these cases, a well-placed agent can be directed to discover the nature of the secret activity and, if he is successful, clear up the mystery.

The most authoritative definition of the limits of satellite surveillance and the growing need for more and better human sources was contained in the final report to President Ford of the President's Foreign Intelligence Advisory Board (PFIAB) in December 1976. Established by President Eisenhower as an independent body of distinguished private citizens, with a small staff, the PFIAB had for years the responsibility of reporting periodically to the President on the performance, progress, and problems of the intelligence community, until it was abolished by President Carter. Its membership included such distinguished scientists as Nobel physicist Edward Teller, William Baker of Bell Laboratories, and Edwin H. Land of the Polaroid Corporation. Although many of us in the Agency sometimes resented the amount of time we had to spend in reporting to this distinguished group, it did give the President an independent and objective window on the secret world of intelligence; and it gave the Agency crucial support in fighting for the increased budget needed to improve the American satellite surveillance capability. The

PFIAB's swan song was its 1976 report to President Ford; and its summary of the case for increased emphasis on the recruitment of human sources bears repetition.

First, the PFIAB pointed out that Soviet scientific progress across the whole spectrum of modern military technology had been so rapid that the United States could no longer count on the comfortable cushion of time that its technological lead had given it in earlier years. In those days, American technical superiority ensured that any new Soviet weapons system could be promptly identified for what it was and that countermeasures could be developed quickly. Now, the PFIAB warned, the United States was moving into an era when the Soviets' scientific progress gave them the potential to score devastating technological breakthroughs that might suddenly confront the United States with entirely new weapons systems that we would have great difficulty in initially identifying, and in devising effective defenses against. The PFIAB warned that we could no longer count on photographic coverage to recognize such radically new weapons systems in the early stages of testing and deployment.

In addition, there are the inherent limitations of any system that relies for its effectiveness on what has already been deployed under the open skies. The lead time for the development of a new weapons system to the point where it is actually deployed for testing has been estimated to average ten years. In the case of a decisive breakthrough in military technology, this means that if we relied on satellite surveillance exclusively we might discover the existence of a new weapon too late to conduct the time-consuming research to match it or to devise countermeasures. The wall of secrecy surrounding Soviet military research makes this danger particularly acute, and strengthens the case for recruiting human sources inside the Soviet defense establishment. For example, the testing of an antisatellite orbital interceptor by the Soviets came as an unpleasant surprise to American defense planners whose dreams of such a weapon were only on the drawing board, and massive Soviet expenditures on laser and particle beam research have unknown but ominous implications for the future vulnerability of our ICBMs.

Second, the PFIAB made the point that understanding and anticipating Soviet intentions becomes ever more important as the Soviets move beyond parity toward strategic superiority. The danger of the use of conventional forces in either open or covert interventions becomes greater as the Soviets feel increasingly secure under the umbrella of their nuclear strength, and again the importance of having human sources that can provide advance warning increases. We have seen in the secret deployment of Cuban troops into Angola how crucial was the Soviet ability to mask their intentions until substantial numbers had been successfully landed. The PFIAB also noted that the growth of international terrorism and the proliferation of nuclear materials present security problems that the most accurate satellite photography cannot cope with. Only human beings reporting from inside can provide the advance warning that is the first line of defense against terrorist incidents, or the secret diversion of nuclear materials to bomb production by nations or terrorist organizations.

Finally, the PFIAB advised that the Soviets were using increasingly sophisticated concealment and deception techniques to frustrate the effectiveness of satellite photography; and these techniques have been further refined as the result of successful Soviet espionage operations. In the Kampiles and Boyce-Lee cases, the Soviets obtained the detailed information that they had previously lacked on the workings of the most advanced American surveillance systems, and they have put it to good use in their camouflage and deception program.[3] Also, the miniaturization of weaponry resulting from the march of technology promises to make satellite surveillance increasingly ineffective in identifying the types and numbers of new weapons that are already deployed, such as the cruise missile. And it should not be forgotten that the successful testing of the Soviet antisatellite orbital interceptor means that the Soviets are achieving the capability to knock out the whole panoply of circling American surveillance satellites in a time of extreme crisis and confrontation.[4] These limitations and vulnerabilities of surveillance satellites do not detract from the value of these systems; but they do demonstrate that they cannot be relied on exclusively for survival intelligence and that the ancient art of espionage has an even larger role to play than previously in providing strategic warning.

Aside from the collection of survival intelligence concerning possible military threats to national security, espionage operations provide critically important information to the analysts who produce finished intelligence on a very wide range of issues that affect our diplomatic strategy, our international trade policy, and our political relations with the nations of the third world. For example, one subject that the Soviets go to great lengths to conceal is the true nature of their long-term intentions toward Western Communist parties. Do the recent protestations of belief in democratic liberties issued by the Italian and Spanish parties represent a genuine conversion, or are they deceptive tactics designed to facilitate their entrance into Western European governments in order to weaken NATO from within? Agent penetrations of Communist parties outside the Soviet bloc can throw revealing light on internal policy disputes, and on Soviet intentions contained in the secret directives they receive from Moscow. Similarly, many radical third world nations like Libya, while not Communist, maintain one-party police states that are capable of preparing behind a wall of secrecy sudden interventions that can deeply affect American interests. In fact, very few of the newly independent states that emerged from the colonial era have managed to establish open societies and functioning democratic institutions. Coups have to be anticipated, and official propaganda gives no advance warning of sudden shifts in policy. Neither the daily avalanche of openly available media reporting nor the thousands of photographs delivered by orbiting satellites can provide reliable answers to hundreds of questions of purpose and intent with which both policymakers and analysts have to wrestle on a daily basis.

To attempt to close this gap in our knowledge, the CIA was authorized under the National Security Act of 1947 to collect foreign intelligence through the recruitment of human sources. By subsequent executive order and National Security Council directives, the Agency was given the major role in the conduct of espionage operations abroad, and the confidential funds to finance them. In effect, President Truman and the Congress decided that Stalin's closed totalitarian regime, its expanding satellite empire in Eastern Europe, and its conspiratorial apparatus of Communist parties abroad, presented a threat sufficient to justify a major commitment of funds and trained people to espionage operations, something the United States had not previously done in times of peace. Forced prominently onto the world stage by the magnitude of its World War II victory, and facing a determined opponent, the United States had no choice but to compete in the field of espionage as great powers had always done. Isolation was no longer possible, nor the innocence and ignorance that went with it.

The amount of misinformation that has been published on the subject of American espionage is so extensive that it is not surprising that the average citizen is confused and wonders whether there isn't a better way to spend his tax dollar. First, there are the novelists and movie script writers. A small number of these have written serious work that is realistic in detail and searching in its exploration of human motivation. But most of this spy fiction conjures up an overly dramatic and pseudo-sophisticated world, where suspense, intrigue, violence, and sex are commingled in plots that make up in variety for what they lack in realism. Then there are the disaffected ex-employees of the Agency, who portray a bloated and incompetent bureaucracy. Finally, there is the Soviet propaganda machine, which has made the CIA its favorite target in an orchestrated campaign of continuing vilification.

Any attempt to disentangle the truth from this web of fiction and propaganda faces one obvious obstacle. There is no way of setting forth the most convincing evidence for the American public so that it can judge for itself. To identify individual agents is to ensure their arrest and possible execution. To describe the nature and quality of the intelligence they have produced is to provide revealing clues and to endanger their future effectiveness. There is no information more closely guarded and more severely compartmented within the CIA than the true identity of its foreign agents. To allegations that the Agency has been completely incapable of penetrating the wall of Soviet secrecy, the officials of the CIA have no choice but to respond with a stubborn "no comment," while hoping that the American public will understand that they are in no position to defend themselves.

The best assurance American citizens can have that their tax dollars spent on foreign agent operations are not being squandered in romantic adventures of the James Bond variety lies in the independent oversight of such operations, conducted both within the executive branch and by the Congress. The Office of Management and Budget has a special section that is cleared for all information it requires, and is in a position to compare costs with results in its annual budget submissions to the President. The Intelligence Committees of the House and Senate have similar freedom of access, and now delve deeply in the exercise of their oversight authority. It is fair to state that the conclusion of this review process has been to find that on balance the human collection operations of the Agency have been competently and imaginatively managed; and the Congress has continued to demonstrate its confidence by voting the funds required. Which is not to say that anyone is satisfied. There is always more that the policymakers would like to know to simplify the decision-making process. There are and probably will continue to be dangerous gaps in our knowledge. Even the best agents do not live forever. Some retire, some seek asylum in the United States after long service, and a few are executed.

However, if it is not possible with specifics to prove the value of espionage operations, the process of human collection can at least be demystified by giving a realistic explanation of how it works. The primary responsibility for American foreign intelligence collection from human sources overseas, and for the counterintelligence operations needed to protect them, is vested in one of the main CIA directorates, called the Directorate for Operations. As noted earlier, when I was for six years the assistant deputy director of this component, its official title was the Directorate for Plans, and CIA personnel assigned to this unit were commonly referred to as members of "the clandestine service." Its basic organizational structure and functions have not been much affected by the change of name except for some rearrangement of staff responsibilities. The deputy director for Operations and his associate deputy director preside over a headquarters component in Washington that is composed of the separate geographical area divisions responsible for the main regions of the world: the Soviet bloc, Western Europe, Latin America, etc. Each area division chief is in turn responsible both for the management of the country desks, or branches as they are called, in his divisional headquarters in Washington, and for the CIA stations located overseas under official cover in the various U.S. Embassies in the foreign countries within his geographical region. Each station chief is in turn responsible for all CIA personnel assigned to the country in which he is located. The line of command is clear and direct, from the deputy director for Operations to the area division chief to the station chief; and the intelligence reporting flows back up this line in the form of a continuing stream of cables that receive dissemination in CIA's Langley headquarters to the analysts throughout the intelligence community who produce the finished intelligence that goes to the policymakers.

The Agency officers serving under cover in the stations overseas are known as case officers. Under the supervision of the station chief, they are America's front-line troops in the continuing effort to extract from human sources the information that the policymakers require but which cannot be obtained from either the media, communications intercepts, or satellite surveillance. They are both the main competitors with the much larger KGB and its satellite services and, individually, the principal and most important targets of KGB recruitment and harassment. These case officers are not in most instances spies themselves, but their job is to recruit and protect foreign agents who do have access to the required information. In countries that are close allies of the United States, these officers work cooperatively with the host government's intelligence and security services. Within the Soviet bloc their every move is watched, their telephones tapped, and their apartments bugged. In addition to their primary duties, most of them have to work at other jobs within the embassy in order to make their cover credible.

They can receive no public credit for their achievements and even when they receive awards within the Agency their citations are deliberately vague and uninformative. When they retire early in their mid-fifties, which is the practice in the clandestine service, they have little to show prospective employers to demonstrate their competence, and in recent years a clandestine career in the Agency has not been an easily salable commodity on the job market. In spite of these drawbacks, I continued to be impressed up to the time of my own retirement by the quality and ability of the young men and women seeking this kind of intelligence career, and by the generally impressive competence of the personnel serving in the clandestine service. An awareness of the high stakes involved in this peculiar and unique area of our competition with the Soviets perhaps explains the seriousness of purpose and dedication that I found to be widespread.

What then about the motivation of the foreigners who agree to provide secret information to CIA case officers at considerable risk? Among the prevailing misconceptions is the belief that foreign agents working for the United States are primarily motivated by greed, and that the more valuable the information they produce the more money they are paid. In reality, the reasons that persuade foreign citizens to cooperate with American intelligence are infinitely various and range across the whole spectrum of human motivation. Admittedly, some of them are prompted only by financial considerations, but the information they produce is often of marginal value, since they are seldom in positions of authority. The most productive agents are frequently those for whom financial reward is a secondary consideration, and who are primarily moved by far more complex ambitions, resentments, and beliefs. For example, there are those like Oleg Penkovsky who come to the conviction that the Communist system is a growing threat to the survival of human freedom, and believe that they must warn the West of the danger and give it the information it needs to defend itself.[5]

There are others inside the Soviet bureaucracy who are dissatisfied with the progress of their own careers, and who so resent the privileges and favoritism of the elite that they are prepared to act against it. There are still others who have personal reasons for seeking revenge against some arbitrary act of regime injustice from which they or their close relatives have suffered. There are even those who have lost all belief in the official ideology and have become so profoundly bored by the pervasive propaganda that they are prepared to assert their own individuality by an adventurous act of defiance against the entire system. Service abroad by Soviet diplomats and KGB officers tends to expose them more than the ordinary Soviet citizen to the wide gap between propaganda and reality, and the new generation of Soviet officials tends to lack the depth of revolutionary conviction that protected their fathers against disillusionment.

Then, there are many in Eastern Europe who are true believers in the cause of national independence for their countries and who bitterly resent Soviet domination. Some of these are ready, at great personal risk, to carry their opposition to the point of cooperation with the United States in the hope that they can hasten the day when the foreign yoke is removed. Within the U.S.S.R. itself, there are minority ethnic groups with their own ancient national traditions and cultural heritage. Some of them see themselves as victims of an internal colonialism ruled over by the dominant Great Russians, who control the state machinery and access to the best jobs. This suppressed resentment can find expression in a decision to act against the privileged Russian elite. In the far reaches of the third world, there are determined men who have helped their countries win their independence from Western colonial rule. They see Soviet intervention in their internal affairs as threatening a new colonialism, which they are prepared to resist by providing the United States with information on the extent and nature of clandestine Soviet operations. High-minded belief in the cause of human liberty, patriotic nationalism, a personal search for revenge, sheer adventurism, avarice—all these motives and more, from the lowest to the highest, are to be found among those who daily risk their lives by cooperating with American intelligence. Modern espionage is far removed from the caricature of the slinking spy in a trench coat with his hand out for payment.

Another widely held misconception is the belief that the typical CIA officer overseas leads an exotic existence and is himself engaged in penetrating the secrets of the opposition by assuming false identities and disguises and by seducing the beautiful mistresses of high-ranking officials. Reality is far different, as can be demonstrated by following the recruitment and management of an individual agent. Whether he volunteers his services as a "walk-in," as many of the most productive agents have done, or whether his willingness to cooperate results from a long period of careful assessment and cultivation, the first step after he has agreed to supply secret information is to determine whether the offer is genuine. As previously noted, the KGB makes extensive use of double agents to identify American methods of operation, to divert attention from more promising targets, and to plant deliberately misleading information.

In the long run, the true test of an agent's reliability is the accuracy and significance of the secret information that he is able to produce when checked against observable events and collateral evidence. For this reason, a newly recruited agent is always handled with skepticism, and his reporting is disseminated to the analysts only with the warning that the source is new and untested. In the short run, there are, however, ways of reducing the level of uncertainty. A lie-detector test in the hands of an expert operator can be a formidable obstacle for even the best-trained double agent, and the refusal to take such a test sharply reduces confidence in the reliability of any newly recruited agent. Also the computerized central biographic files maintained in CIA headquarters, and painstakingly built up over more than a quarter of a century, are a critical factor in determining the bona fides of new informants. Easily retrievable in these records are the case histories and identities of all the double agents, intelligence fabricators, and accomplished charlatans who have attempted to sell their spurious wares in the past. Accurate and extensive biographic records maintained over a period of many years are the indispensable institutional memory of any competent intelligence service. Without such records, the Agency would be at the mercy of hostile intelligence services in the same way that a man suffering from amnesia is easy prey for the first confidence man who comes along.

The Counterintelligence Staff in the headquarters of the Directorate for Operations in Washington has a vital role to play in the long process of determining the bona fides of a new agent. Against the operating division's natural tendency to want to believe it has recruited a valid source, the CI Staff must maintain its professional skepticism in researching and testing every aspect of the new agent's version of his motivation and career. For many years, a good friend of mine, James Angleton, served as chief of the CI Staff until his retirement was forced by Colby. His respect for the competence of the KGB and his encyclopedic knowledge of the history of their complex double agent operations sometimes led him to persist too long in questioning the validity of sources, but his ingrained skepticism served as a useful antidote to the occasional overoptimism of the case officers in the field. His major contribution was to build a structure of close cooperation between the United States and our Western allies in the counterintelligence field such that even the most sensitive information of high-level KGB penetrations could be promptly exchanged and quickly acted upon to roll up newly discovered KGB networks. And it is to his credit and partly due to his watchfulness that during his long tenure, no proven case of successful KGB penetration of the career staff of the clandestine service occurred, in stark contrast to the unhappy experience of most West European services.

Once an agent has demonstrated his reliable access to valuable information, the problem is how to protect him and continue the flow of intelligence against the threat posed by the counterintelligence organs of the KGB. If he is reassigned to his own country behind the Iron Curtain, the problem of secure communication becomes much more acute but his access to significant information may increase. He may in fact find himself able to provide advance warning of some surprise strategic thrust, and the ability to communicate this perishable information quickly may be vital. Suffice it to say that thorough advance planning and meticulous attention to the minutest detail are the qualities required of a CIA case officer dealing with this kind of case. James Bond would be lost in this real world.

Hostile counterintelligence is not the only threat to a successful agent operation. Ironically, the more valuable and timely the information produced, the more difficult it becomes to protect the source within our government. The true identity of an agent is invariably protected by the use of a pseudonym, by deliberately opaque source description, and by limiting to a very few individuals those who know his real name and position. The names of those CIA officers who have to be informed of his true identity in order to conduct and evaluate the operation are maintained on a "bigot list," so that they can be closely questioned in preparing the damage report that is mandatory in the event of subsequent arrest or exposure. But the important information the agent produces has to be accurately conveyed to analysts and policymakers, and it will inevitably find its way into highly classified publications like the President's Daily Brief. If there is then a leak to the press, it becomes obvious to hostile counterintelligence that they have been penetrated. The specific details of the information leaked enable the KGB to concentrate their counterintelligence effort on those who have had access to this information and help them to identify a narrowing list of suspects.

Very damaging leaks of this kind have in the past occurred in the American press, with the resulting destruction of irreplaceable sources. The heaviest responsibility for such betrayal rests on the government official who chooses to leak the classified information to his favorite reporter or columnist; and FBI investigations to determine the identity of the guilty party are rarely productive. Although there are strict limits set on the number of copies made of highly classified documents, the photocopy machine is a standing temptation, and such proliferation is not only difficult to prevent but creates a bewildering number of possible suspects. The existence of this problem, however, does suggest that some self-restraint and caution is required of newspaper editors. Some editors maintain that, when leaks occur, they are free to decide what classified material to publish, because they are as competent to judge what may affect the national security as any government official. In fact they are in no position to make this judgment. They do not know what revealing clues to agent identification may be contained in the material they publish. If the leaked information was obtained from a friendly foreign intelligence service, not only is their agent endangered but the whole productive liaison arrangement with an allied government may be damaged and the United States may permanently lose access to a wide range of valuable intelligence. Even the most friendly foreign government is not going to continue providing reports to American intelligence from its most sensitive agents if it has to fear that these reports will eventually make headlines in American newspapers.

There is a strong case to be made for the argument that many official documents are overclassified within our government and that the "Top Secret" stamp has been irresponsibly abused. The remedy lies in improving and refining the classification process, and some progress has been made along these lines. On the other hand, it is not too much to hope that the size and seriousness of this problem may cause an increasing number of responsible editors to hesitate before rushing into print with a scoop based on unauthorized access to highly classified documents. Lives and survival intelligence may be at stake. Often enough, a quick check by an editor will indicate that he can use most of the leaked information with only the change of a few words to protect the agent.

From my own experience, I know that the newspaper business in Washington is so competitive, and the pressure for scoops so great, that the exercise of such self-discipline in the national interest is asking a great deal of editors who may turn down a story on these grounds only to find it blazoned in the headlines of a competitor the next day. Nonetheless, such self-restraint is far preferable to the imposition of new restrictive legislation on the freedom of the press, and the problem is sufficiently serious to deserve the attention of the professional groups that represent the media. After all, the freedom of the press, like all our other liberties, depends in the last analysis on the survival of the U.S. government with its constitutional order; and in the nuclear age that survival can in turn depend on the protection of irreplaceable intelligence sources.

Distinct from the recruited agent who remains in place and continues to report from within his government, there is another important human source of vital secret information, the defector. This is the individual who decides to escape from his own government and to seek physical asylum abroad. Over the last twenty-five years, there have been many Soviet defectors, and most of them have sought refuge in the United States, bringing with them invaluable information. Some of them have been scientists who have been able to report in detail on the status of secret weapons research in their field of specialization. Some have been pilots who have been able to escape with their planes, as in the case of the Soviet officer Belenko, who succeeded in landing in Japan with his advanced interceptor, the MIG-25. Some have been high-ranking intelligence officials of the KGB and the GRU, who have been able to give us a current picture of the structure of these organizations and the identities of individual Soviet agents working under cover both in this country and in Western Europe. Some have failed in their attempt to escape, as in the case of the majority of the officers and crew of the Soviet destroyer in the Baltic Sea who seized control of their ship and tried to sail to a Swedish port in November 1975. They were forcibly intercepted by Soviet planes and ships and taken in tow to a Russian port. Eighty-four of them were later publicly announced by the Soviet regime to have been executed, presumably as a lesson to other Soviet naval crews that might be harboring similar thoughts of escape.

Actually, very few of those who seek political asylum in the United States are treated as defectors. Within the U.S. government, the term "defector" has a specific and narrowly defined meaning. An individual becomes a defector under our laws and regulations when his bona fides have been established and he has demonstrated his possession of significant secret information. If the defection occurs in a foreign country, the final decision is made by the DCI on the basis of a recommendation submitted by the defector committee in the U.S. Embassy. It is not a decision that is taken lightly, since once an individual has been given defector status he is usually brought to the United States promptly and normal immigration procedures are waived by the attorney general. The CIA becomes responsible for his debriefing and for his resettlement in this country, usually under a false identity to protect him from the long arm of the KGB. The value of the intelligence he can produce must be assessed as very substantial to justify this special treatment, since in effect the Agency becomes responsible for the safety and welfare of a defector for the rest of his life. Redefection is always a possibility, and the Soviets will go to enormous lengths to pressure a defector to return in order to discourage others who may be thinking of taking so drastic a step. It remains American policy to allow a defector to return to his own country if he freely chooses to do so. Individuals who seek political asylum from a U.S. Embassy abroad, and who do not have access to high-level intelligence, are treated as refugees and must go through a time-consuming process of visa application.

Occasionally in the past, Soviet, Eastern European, and Chinese defectors have sought physical asylum within American embassies located in countries whose policy is to avoid offending the Communist regimes by refusing to allow the would-be defector to make good his escape to the United States. In such situations, the problem becomes one of secretly exfiltrating the defector before the local government becomes aware of his existence, or of disguising him so that he escapes detection on leaving the embassy or at border checkpoints. The secret exfiltration of defectors has become a highly developed and imaginative art, and it is in this process that the real world of espionage comes closest to resembling the dramatic incidents that crowd the pages of the typical spy novel. I remember a case where the local government knew that a defector had sought asylum in our embassy and had set a twenty-four-hour watch to prevent his escape. The CIA station chief established a pattern of weekend picnics for embassy personnel in the countryside near the border of a neighboring and more friendly country. Eventually disguised as one of the embassy secretaries, complete with blond wig, the defector was taken to the picnic area and was safely transported across the border. In another case, a three-day journey on elephant back through dense jungle was part of the escape route.

The danger that a Soviet defector may in fact be a double agent is real; and disagreements about a defector's authenticity have on occasion deeply split the intelligence community, as in the case of Yuri Nosenko.[6] Again, the only conclusive proof of bona fides is the demonstration over time that what the defector says turns out to be true and so damaging to Soviet interests that they could not have deliberately authorized the passage of such information to make him or her appear credible. For example, surveillance can be used to follow those the defector has identified as Soviet agents, and they can be arrested in the act of meeting with their KGB case officers. Over the years, there is no doubt that the accumulated testimony of defectors has added very substantially to our knowledge of how the Soviet system works in its most secret recesses, and thrown revealing light on Soviet plans and intentions.

However, the most crucial contribution that defectors have made is in the field of counterintelligence, where the objective is to discover and neutralize hostile intelligence penetrations of our own government and of our allies. The primary responsibility for counterintelligence protection inside the United States rests with the FBI, whereas, as we have seen, counterintelligence operations abroad are under the jurisdiction of the CIA. A description of how a typical defector case is handled demonstrates that very close cooperation between the two agencies is required. When a KGB officer defects abroad and is successfully exfiltrated into the U.S. by the CIA, the first priority is to interrogate him in depth on all that he may know concerning KGB intelligence operations inside the United States. The FBI normally takes the lead in this phase of the debriefing. The defector's memory is searched for what he may know or suspect concerning the identities and duties of all KGB and GRU officers serving under diplomatic or other forms of cover in this country, the names of KGB illegals such as Colonel Abel, and most important, the identities of American citizens who have been recruited as reporting agents in place.

Because of the very strict compartmentation of information regarding agent identities practiced within the KGB, the defector may frequently not be able to identify individual agents by name, but he can often recall bits and pieces of information that indicate that a penetration must exist within a particularly sensitive government department or weapons research facility. Or he may have seen a series of secret reports that could only have come from a penetration of a policy-level office of our government. It is then the FBI's job to undertake the time-consuming research and interviewing required to narrow down the field of possible suspects, to conduct the required physical surveillance, and eventually—if all goes well—to catch the suspected agent in the act of transmitting classified information to his KGB case officer. If the KGB officer enjoys diplomatic immunity, he is declared persona non grata and must leave the country, while his American agent is brought to trial.

The next priority in the interrogation of a KGB defector is to determine the extent of his knowledge regarding penetrations of the governments and armed forces of our NATO allies. Fortunately, as the result of close cooperation in intelligence work during World War II and our mutual dependence on the NATO alliance, the CIA maintains fruitful liaison relationships with the intelligence and security services of most of the Western European governments. As the interrogation of a KGB defector proceeds, the clues that emerge are transmitted rapidly and with utmost secrecy to the European services affected. Speed is of the essence, since once a defection is known to have occurred, Moscow moves quickly to limit the damage by withdrawing agents and restricting operations. Over the years, the interrogation of KGB and GRU defectors, and expeditious cooperation between the CIA and the intelligence services of Western Europe, have led to breaking up many of the Soviet spy networks. When the arrests of indigenous agents and evictions of KGB case officers posing as diplomats occur, there is usually a brief spate of publicity that reveals little of the exhaustive detective work that makes such arrests possible. There is, however, no room for complacency in the field of counterintelligence, so long as the West retains secrets that the Soviets wish to know. The KGB continues to expand its aggressive recruitment apparatus, and the task of keeping up with the proliferation of Soviet agents resembles the labor of Hercules trying to clean out the Augean stables. For American intelligence, the only safe assumption is that we have been or will be penetrated; and the strict internal discipline of compartmentation in the handling of sensitive information on a need-to-know basis must continue to be practiced in order to limit the possible damage that a penetration can cause.

It is not only in the field of counterintelligence and in the handling of defectors that there is good cooperation between the CIA and the intelligence services of our NATO allies. Although they vary considerably in size and competence, most of these services have demonstrated their ability to collect significant intelligence through their own secret agent operations. Long-standing liaison agreements make possible a mutual exchange of sensitive agent reports, although the identity of the agent is usually not revealed. More restricted liaison agreements in the intelligence field exist with many countries outside NATO. There is no doubt that the flow of secret information from such cooperation has added very substantially to the sum total of our knowledge of what is going on in the world. In countries where such liaison arrangements exist, it is one of the primary responsibilities of the CIA station chief to keep the relationship in good repair and to ensure an equitable balance in the exchange of intelligence.

A comparatively new phenomenon, international terrorism, has increased the importance of effective liaison between the CIA and friendly foreign intelligence services. The murder of members of the Israeli Olympic team in 1972, and the kidnapping of the OPEC oil ministers in Vienna in 1975, are only the most dramatic examples of the ability of terrorist groups to operate across national borders in producing terrorist spectaculars. The march of technology has opened up new opportunities to the terrorist by creating concentrated and more vulnerable targets, such as the commercial airliner and the nuclear power station. Newly developed weapons such as the shoulder-fired antiaircraft rocket and improved explosives have increased the terrorist's striking power. In the future looms the threat of nuclear weapons in the hands of terrorists. Finally, the satellite transmission of instant TV news programs has created a worldwide audience for terrorist events and vastly increased the dramatic impact of violent attacks designed to publicize a political cause. Modern terrorism is global theater, and the terrorists have learned to manipulate the media to their advantage.

In the long run, some of the conflicts that the terrorists exploit are amenable to diplomatic negotiation and peaceful settlement. The creation of an autonomous Palestinian entity on the West Bank and in Gaza might, for example, reduce the appeal of the Palestinian extremists and their ability to recruit young fanatics to their cause. However, nothing less than the apocalyptic transformation of the world would satisfy the anarchists of the Japanese Red Army and the remnants of the Baader-Meinhof gang. Not only are many of the terrorists' demands unappeasable, but the widening gulf between the living standards of the rich and poor nations can become a breeding ground for new terrorist formations. Despite the best efforts to remove the underlying causes, the world is going to have to live with a certain level of international terrorism for a long time to come, and the problem is how to contain it within tolerable limits without sacrificing basic freedoms. An efficient police state, whether of the left or of the right, has comparatively little difficulty in containing terrorism, but that repressive order is maintained at too high a price in human liberty.

A strong case can be made for a policy of more effective diplomatic and economic pressure against those national governments that lend aid and comfort to the terrorists, and for strengthening the international conventions that provide for the trial or extradition of known terrorists.[7] But it is only realistic to recognize that some of the worst offenders, like Libya, are also oil-producing states, which the oil-importing nations are reluctant to confront. In the Abu Daoud affair, the French and West German governments were reluctant to bring to trial one of the known planners of the Munich massacre when pressure was brought to bear for his release. Airport security can be improved; but in the last analysis the most effective means of controlling international terrorism and of reducing the number of incidents is the prompt exploitation of accurate, secret intelligence to abort the terrorists' plans and to protect the intended victims.

One of the high-priority targets today of both the CIA and friendly intelligence services is the penetration of the terrorist organizations now functioning on the world stage. To the extent that reporting sources can be successfully recruited within the terrorist leadership, it becomes possible to learn in advance the identity and location of the intended victims, the false documentation of the hit team, and the secret channels through which the weapons are to be made available. By rapid exchange of information with allied security services, the members of the hit team can be arrested at the border, the weapons can be defused or confiscated before they are used, and the prospective victims alerted in time.

This is a difficult, dangerous, and often frustrating business. On my return from London in 1976 to CIA headquarters, I was assigned as one of my principal duties the task of coordinating and improving the intelligence effort against the international terrorist target; and I quickly came to realize how elusive, suicidal, and ingenious the terrorist can be. The main terrorist organizations are highly disciplined and practice strict need-to-know compartmentation. Even the members of the hit team often do not know up to the last few hours the location and identity of their assigned targets. But progress is being made; and there are a number of American diplomats, hundreds of airline passengers, and a few foreign political leaders who are alive today because there was timely advance warning as the result of effective coordination between the CIA and allied security services. So long as fanatics continue to conspire to kill for political effect and to hold hostages for ransom to finance their operations, just so long will good intelligence combined with effective liaison remain the first line of defense. A peculiarly sensitive dimension of this effort is the attempt to discover and frustrate clandestine diversion of weapons grade uranium to bomb production, by either the major terrorist organizations or the radical states supporting them, such as Libya. Here again, as in the verification role of the American surveillance satellites, the efficient conduct of intelligence operations turns out to be indispensable to the preservation of a peaceful world order.

Another intelligence target that has assumed increasing importance is the international drug traffic. Overhead photography can be useful in spotting the poppy fields but it takes human sources inside the drug-smuggling organizations to identify the secret channels through which the illicit drugs move into the American market. The domestic responsibility for prevention and arrest belongs to the Drug Enforcement Administration, but the CIA cooperates closely with it by supplying leads derived both from individual foreign agents and from liaison services. Contrary to the allegations that the Agency was participating in the drug traffic during the Vietnam war in order to finance its covert operations, the CIA has in fact made a significant intelligence contribution to the suppression and control of this threat to the health and welfare of the American public, as testimony before the responsible congressional committees has indicated.

Finally, a word should be said about what remains of CIA's covert action capability. As we have seen, by direction of the President and the NSC, the CIA was ordered to engage in a very wide range of covert activity during the fifties and sixties; and within the Agency the responsibility for the conduct of these operations has been lodged in the same Directorate for Operations that is responsible for foreign espionage. The geographical area divisions in this directorate and their overseas CIA stations, with the help of specialized supporting staffs, carried out whatever covert action projects were approved at the NSC level, in addition to their intelligence collection, counterintelligence, and liaison functions. Whether it was a covert political support operation, as in the case of the clandestine assistance given to the democratic parties in Chile in 1964, or the secret provision of arms as in the Angolan civil war, the line of command was from the President down to the deputy director for Operations, to the area division chief, and finally to the station chief, who was in turn responsible for reporting back up the line on the expenditure of funds and the progress of the operation.

Any attempt to split off this covert action function from the Operations Directorate and to establish it under some separate organizational structure would only result in a costly duplication of effort, and set the stage for damaging rivalry between competing clandestine bureaucracies, as both the early British and American experiences with such arrangements indicated during and after World War II. Also, intelligence collection and covert action are not distinct watertight compartments sealed off from each other. A well-placed intelligence agent can often bring useful political influence to bear, and a covert action agent inside a political movement is sometimes in the best position to provide significant intelligence on future intentions. Admittedly the desire to ensure the success of a particular covert action operation can be allowed to skew the intelligence reporting; but the remedy lies in insisting on the integrity of the reporting process rather than in the creation of rival bureaucracies.

As of this writing, the CIA's covert action capability remains intact on paper. The Directorate for Operations retains the mandate and the staff structure for the conduct of covert action operations. In spite of the criticism of the wisdom and morality of a number of past covert action programs, neither the President by executive order nor the Congress by legislation has been willing to prohibit the future use of this foreign policy option. The Carter administration has required a higher level of approval and more frequent review within the executive branch, and the Congress under the Hughes-Ryan Amendment has specifically authorized covert activity provided the President "finds that each such operation is important to the national security of the U.S." and that appropriate congressional committees are informed.[8] In theory, then, there is nothing to prevent the President from ordering the CIA to extend covert support to a democratic political movement competing for power in some third world country with a heavily Soviet-subsidized Communist opposition. In fact, however, it is highly unlikely under present circumstances that any such action would be attempted, for the good and sufficient reason that neither in the Agency nor in the White House is there any confidence that the necessary secrecy of the operation could be protected.

As we have noted, the effect of the Hughes-Ryan amendment

passed in 1974 in reaction to President Nixon's intervention in Chile has been to require eight congressional committees to be promptly informed whenever the President approves the use of funds for a covert action operation. In the course of notification, it has been estimated that over two hundred congressmen and congressional staff assistants might become knowledgeable. The first controversial covert action program submitted to the committees under this law was President Ford's program for covert military intervention in the Angolan civil war. It did not take long for the inevitable leak to the press to occur, and the effect was traumatic on both the White House and the intelligence community. Secrecy in the conduct of covert action operations is essential to success, and damage caused by publicity can be so great that it is far better not to engage in such activity if security cannot be maintained. A covert action of any size and significance is bound to be controversial, and among so large a body of congressmen there is likely to be one opposed to the project who will succumb to the temptation to exercise his private veto by a discreet leak to the press.

No President in his right mind would approve a secret operation of any scale under such notification requirements, and the CIA has been understandably reluctant to accept the responsibility for new covert action programs in the knowledge that it will be the target of attack when leaks occur. The inevitable result has been that only a few insignificant and uncontroversial covert action projects have been approved under the Carter administration. The CIA's trained manpower and expertise in this field have been allowed to atrophy. The Soviet covert political offensive into the precincts of the third world has gone uncontested by any countervailing American ability to lend discreet support to friends and potential allies. It was recognition of this self-imposed impotence that led Henry Kissinger to state in early 1979: "We have practically deprived ourselves of covert capabilities." He went on to warn, correctly in my view, "This is especially dangerous in areas where there is a huge grey area between military intervention and normal diplomatic processes."[9]

A good example of the type of situation in which an intelligently conducted covert action program might have had a decisive and beneficial effect existed in Nicaragua in January of 1979. Responding to President Carter's human rights campaign, a broad coalition of Nicaraguan moderates, including businessmen, non-Communist labor leaders, and the Catholic Church, had organized a series of strikes and demonstrations to protest the dictatorial rule of President Anastasio Somoza and to demand his replacement by a democratic regime. Under OAS auspices, the United States joined in mounting a mediation effort which proposed a plebiscite under international supervision to give the Nicaraguan people a chance by peaceful vote to decide whether Somoza should depart. Encouraged by his conservative supporters in the U.S. Congress, Somoza refused to agree to a plebiscite in the knowledge that he could not control the voting machinery and that the vote was likely to go against him. The Carter administration passively accepted Somoza's defiance, and in the ensuing months of mounting civil war the country became polarized between Somoza's National Guard and the Sandinista guerrillas, who were receiving substantial covert assistance from Castro in the form of arms and training.

As a result, when Somoza was finally forced to abdicate in July, the Sandinistas were in a strong position to influence the successor regime, while the moderate democratic opposition had been decimated and disorganized by the months of civil war. A timely decision in January to lend discreet financial assistance to these moderates, and to encourage dissident elements within the National Guard to break with Somoza, might well have forced Somoza to accept a plebiscite and would have avoided the radicalization of the country that Castro was able to exploit. In their refusal to accept the results of a peaceful ballot, the Sandinistas would have isolated themselves as an extremist minority and would no longer have been able to rally popular support against the deposed dictator. The long-term consequences of this missed opportunity may prove serious indeed in the form of increased Cuban influence throughout Central America. It is a dramatic example of how costly the absence of a covert action capability can be in a situation where the Soviets and their allies are prepared to intervene covertly and decisively.

If the United States is to recover the ability to take covert action selectively and intelligently in support of its foreign policy objectives, the Hughes-Ryan amendment will have to be repealed and the oversight of such operations confined to the Senate and House Intelligence Committees. They have a good reputation for security, and the President in notifying them of a proposed covert action project could have reasonable confidence that in the event of majority support the secret would be kept. There is some resistance to such a change among the other committees, and a natural tendency to be jealous of their jurisdiction. And there are some members of Congress who are deeply convinced that the United States has neither the moral right nor the political acumen to engage in any form of covert activity. They see in the Hughes-Ryan Amendment an effective bar to such action and support it for that reason. However, within both the Congress and the executive branch there is a growing body of opinion that covert action is a needed instrument of policy in coping with Soviet intervention; and the repeal of Hughes-Ryan is likely to become more popular as more serious losses of American influence serve to persuade a reluctant Congress. Perhaps by the time this book is published the change will already have been made.

In public lectures and private conversations around the country, I am often asked in worried tones about the present condition of the CIA. The hostility and suspicion generated by Vietnam and Watergate seem to have died down, and an increasing number of people appear to be genuinely concerned with whether the Agency as an institution has survived the congressional investigations and media criticism with sufficient competence and morale to do its job. In reply, I have had to point out that I retired at the end of 1977, and since that time have had no access to the flow of finished intelligence, to the improvements that have been made in satellite surveillance, or to the performance record in the recruitment of new agents. In addition, during my last months in Washington with the Agency I did not have a chance to work closely with Carter's newly appointed director, Admiral Stansfield Turner. Therefore much of my information is secondhand and comes from old acquaintances still working at the Agency, from members of the congressional oversight committees, and from Carter administration appointees in the foreign policy field.

For what it is worth, my own impression is that as an institution the CIA has survived its time of troubles but not without some lasting damage. At the working level, morale seems to have held up reasonably well in the face of public buffeting, but the recruitment of highly qualified younger people has been negatively affected by the bad publicity. The legislation originally submitted in the Senate to replace the National Security Act of 1947 with a new legal charter for the intelligence community was full of restrictions and limitations that would have made intelligence collection cumbersome and difficult in many respects.[10] However, in the course of review by both the Carter administration and the Senate Intelligence Committee, some of the most objectionable and least workable provisions have been modified. My expectation is that when a bill is finally reported out of the Senate Intelligence Committee, it will be one under which the intelligence community can function effectively. Close congressional oversight, rather than a host of legal restrictions, will remain the best protection of the rights of individual American citizens.

There is, however, a broad and deep consensus throughout the intelligence community that what the Central Intelligence Agency needs most is continuity of competent, civilian, nonpolitical leadership at the top. On coming to office, President Carter missed the opportunity to respond to that deeply felt need. As the fourth Director of Central Intelligence in four years, George Bush in the last year of the Ford administration had demonstrated his ability to subordinate his partisan past as a Republican politician to the national security interests of the country as a whole. He had won the loyal support of the CIA's professional staff and enjoyed the confidence of both Democrats and Republicans in the congressional oversight committees. He made clear to Carter that he was ready to put aside political ambition, and was anxious to stay on for another year to provide needed continuity and to give the new President a chance to select an experienced successor from among men who had proven their ability to handle the responsibilities of high office. In addition, a decision to keep Bush on for an interim period would have preserved intact the long tradition that the CIA directorship was not a political plum to be traded with each change of administration.

In retrospect, Carter would have been well advised to accept Bush's generous offer and to have taken the time necessary to pick a nonpartisan and competent civilian successor. Instead, against the advice of his most experienced foreign policy advisers, Carter put forward the name of Theodore Sorensen as his nominee for DCI. Primarily known as a former speechwriter for President Kennedy, and without any broad previous administrative experience or intelligence background, Sorensen ran into predictable trouble in his confirmation hearing before the Senate and had to withdraw. Having created the dilemma for himself of having to come up with a quick-fix solution, Carter reached into the ranks of the military to select his Annapolis classmate Admiral Stansfield Turner, in the face of considerable evidence over the years that career military men had not distinguished themselves in the sensitive role of DCI. Over time, wide agreement emerged in Carter's National Security Council staff, in the congressional oversight committees, and throughout the intelligence community that the choice of Turner was not a wise one.

Although patriotic and hard-working, Turner somehow managed to offend his cabinet colleagues on the National Security Council to the point where they looked forward to his replacement, and the professional career officers of the Agency were so antagonized by his managerial style that they became outspoken in their criticism. I have real sympathy for any man who takes on the very demanding and difficult job of trying to direct American foreign intelligence in our pluralistic and free society, and I have no way of knowing how justified all the criticisms were of Turner's performance. But by the summer of 1980, a clear consensus had emerged in Washington that Turner should be replaced even at the cost of further loss of continuity. It is vitally important that Turner's eventual successor should be a civilian of proven administrative ability, devoted in a nonpartisan way to the highest national interest, and equipped with a broad and sophisticated knowledge of world affairs. The American people and the men and women in the CIA deserve no less in the years of crisis that lie ahead.

Chapter 18

A Hope for the Future

THE MOST PERSUASIVE voices that have been raised in these last few years to warn the American people that they must maintain their defenses and strengthen their alliances against the thrust of Soviet expansionism have come not from within the United States but from the Soviet Union itself. Aleksandr Solzhenitsyn, Andrei Sakharov, Andrei Amalrik, Vladimir Bukovsky, and the many other courageous and determined leaders of the Soviet dissident movement have from their differing perspectives joined in trying to alert the West to the dangers posed by a secretive regime that brooks no internal opposition, controls its people's access to every type of information, builds up its nuclear and conventional weaponry beyond any rational defensive need, and extends its system into the third world through proxy armies, direct aggression, and massive covert interventions. These dissidents have pleaded for extreme vigilance on the part of the United States in the conduct of arms control negotiations, and warned against any agreements that rest on mutual trust rather than on reliable means of verification. They have cautioned that détente can become a trap for the unwary, in which the Soviets gain tangible benefits such as Western credits, grain, and technology, while increasing internal repression and giving in return only verbal assurances that serve to dull the perception of danger.

These eloquent advocates of democratic reform and human rights within the Soviet Union and Eastern Europe fear that the United States and its allies will prematurely weaken in their resolve to maintain the world balance of power, and allow the Soviet regime as presently constituted a position of increasing dominance and incremental advance across the dividing line that still separates the Communist from the non-Communist world. Their deep concern is that such an increase in Soviet power relative to the West, combined with the establishment of new Marxist regimes in the third world subject to Soviet influence, will lend weight and credibility within their country to the regime's contention that its ideology and system are the wave of the future. Their fear is that the courageous voices of dissent and democratic reform inside the Soviet Union will be drowned out by the march of Soviet foreign policy successes, and that an unnecessary retreat by the West will lend a spurious legitimacy to the Soviet claim that the worldwide advance of communism is determined by history.

From inside the Soviet Union, the towering figure of the nuclear physicist and human rights advocate Andrei Sakharov has put these concerns in general terms. He has warned, "Political leaders and all people in the West must know that any display of weakness or inconsistency will have the most painful effect on the fate of many people —including the dissidents in the USSR and the Eastern European countries who are now taking the brunt of repression."[1] Even from his internal exile under house arrest in the closed city of Gorky, Sakharov has continued to try to convey his urgent warnings to the West.

Having fled into exile in the West, the Soviet author Andrei Amalrik has given a more specific definition in psychological terms of this danger: "An aggressive foreign policy (which may take various forms) has a certain symbolic significance—it is a sign of strength and vitality. A victory abroad tends to nullify domestic fiascos. Thus, the recent Soviet penetration of Angola, through the clever use of Cuban troops, helped to vitiate the results of the catastrophic harvest and to retain Brezhnev in power. If Brezhnev had not been able to point to his success in Angola, the harvest might well have led to grave dissatisfaction among the people and possibly to his downfall. . . . This is an ancient phenomenon, this sense of profound satisfaction, this national gratification over the fact that the government has again demonstrated its strength."[2]

Discouraged as they sometimes are by signs of vacillation and disunity in the West, the leaders of the Soviet dissident movement remain profoundly committed to the hope that a nonbelligerent but steady and resourceful defense by the United States and its alliance partners of their relative power and geographical position will allow time and opportunity for the glacially slow process of change to take place within the Soviet Union. In effect, they are pleading with the American people to support a defense and foreign policy that confines the Soviet regime within its present borders, in order to allow time for them to achieve the changes they believe would make the Soviet state safer for the world to live with. They see a direct connection between the establishment of a more open society in the U.S.S.R. and the possibility of a peaceful world order. Sakharov drew the connection most clearly in the following quotation:

> The most important consequence of a "closed" society is the complete lack of democratic control over the activities of the authorities, of the ruling party and government clique—both in the area of domestic policy, economy, environmental protection and social problems and in the area of foreign policy. The latter is especially dangerous and intolerable if you remember that the problem is one of a finger which is lying on the button of universal thermonuclear war. The problem of the "closed" society is closely intertwined with the issue of citizens' civil and political rights; it is almost identical to it. It is precisely for this reason that the issue of human rights is not only a moral but also a paramount practical issue for international trust and security.[3]

The dissidents promise no quick and sudden transformation of Soviet society. As the result of bitter personal experience, most of them have given up the hope they once held that the current leadership in the Kremlin can be persuaded by logic and argument to change its collective mind. Although they differ among themselves on tactics and strategy, they have come increasingly to the conviction that some measures of structural democratic reform and institutional protection of individual human rights are essential prerequisites to the improvement of the conditions of life within the Soviet

Union and to the possibilities of peace and disarmament in the world. Some of these dissidents have been forced into exile, as was Solzhenitsyn's fate. Others, like Amalrik, have chosen to emigrate to the West in order to publish and to speak freely. Still others, like Yuri Orlov, have been silenced by long prison terms, while many languish in psychiatric hospitals. But their ranks are continually renewed by new recruits to their cause and they are united in their demand for a more open society.

The American people have a tremendous stake in the outcome of their struggle. Insofar as the dissidents succeed, they make it possible for us to hope and to plan for an end to the arms race and to look forward to a more peaceful world. If they did not exist and there was no liberalizing ferment of change within Soviet society, we would have to face the prospect of an unending military and geopolitical competition with the bureaucratic party elite that now rules the Soviet state. If such a rivalry is sufficiently prolonged, it must inevitably come to have corrosive effects on our own free institutions.

However, because the spark of political dissent has been lit in the Soviet Union and flames more brightly in Poland does not mean that it will continue to burn. Not only does much depend on the ability of the United States to deny the present regime the foreign triumphs that sustain it, but much also depends on our ability to understand and assess realistically the strength of the dissident movement and the enormous obstacles it faces in bringing about any substantial reform. Finally, on the basis of considerable experience, we can also reach some conclusions as to how best to support the dissident cause through governmental and private actions, while at the same time avoiding those foolish provocations that can only lead to more extreme repression.

The watershed event in the growth of the modern dissident movement in the Soviet Union was the trial of Andrei Sinyavsky and Yuli Daniel, in Moscow in February 1966, for the crime of publishing work critical of the regime in foreign magazines without official permission. The harsh sentences handed down, seven and five years of hard labor, were meant as a signal by the new Brezhnev regime that with Khrushchev's ouster in 1964, the brief thaw in cultural repression that accompanied Khrushchev's "de-Stalinization" campaign was coming to an end. Instead of passively accepting this reimposition of cultural orthodoxy, a small group of young intellectuals in

Moscow dared to protest openly; and thus began the broadening cycle of repression and protest that has gathered momentum and has spread far beyond the original group of young cultural activists. In 1967, Vladimir Bukovsky was sentenced in a closed trial to three years of prison camp for the crime of cooperating with Alexander Ginzburg in the compilation of a White Book documenting the travesty of justice of the Sinyavsky-Daniel trial. In October 1967, Pavel Litvinov, the grandson of the late Soviet commissar of foreign affairs, directly challenged the regime by openly distributing to the foreign press the text of Bukovsky's indomitable final statement before his sentencing. The regime reacted by sentencing Ginzburg and three associates in January 1968 to long prison terms in an obviously rigged judicial proceeding. A wave of protest followed, in the form of hundreds of letters from Soviet citizens to newspapers abroad and to foreign Communist parties denouncing the return to Stalinist methods.

From this youthful defiance of the regime by a small group of Moscow literati, the dissident movement has flowed like a widening river, checked periodically by extreme repression but gathering each time depth and breadth for further protest from new sources of dissent that flow like feeder streams into the main river. The earlier stages of the movement have been well summarized by Abraham Brumberg in a key article.[4] In a previous chapter I described how Yuri Orlov and his courageous friends in Eastern Europe managed to transform the ambiguous promise of wider freedoms contained in the Helsinki Declaration into an incipient political opposition embracing a very wide range of demands for compliance by the regime with the international obligations it had undertaken at Helsinki. There is not space here to describe all the varied strands of protest and dissent that are woven together in the dissident movement as it now exists in the Soviet Union and Eastern Europe, but a few of the highlights can be touched on.

First, the movement has been distinguished from the outset not so much by its numerical strength as by the extraordinary quality of its leadership; and it is this which has earned it such respect in the outside world and created such deep reverberations within the Soviet Union. One may differ with Solzhenitsyn's concept of the role the Orthodox Russian Church should play in a post-Marxist Russia, but his soaring talent as a novelist and historian has almost single-handedly transformed the views held by many Western intellectuals concerning the origins and development of the Soviet dictatorship. No left-leaning student or worker in the West can ever be the same again after reading *The Gulag Archipelago*, and its impact on the Parisian intellectual elite must be mirrored in the effect it is having on the Moscow and Leningrad intelligentsia, where in underground editions it continues to circulate at very high prices. Solzhenitsyn has written the true history of his times, and no future account can ignore the massive accumulation of evidence that he has so dramatically presented as an indictment of the Soviet police state. Similarly, Sakharov's genius as a scientist is matched by the cool lucidity with which he persisted in pleading the cause of wider democratic freedom in the face of all the regime's threats and eventual internal exile. The will and bravery of a Bukovsky and an Orlov are typical of the heroic determination that most of the leading dissidents have shown under every type of persecution. Rarely have the leaders of a political movement demonstrated such a unique combination of talent and civic courage.

However, if brilliant scientists and prominent writers played a crucial role in the early stages of the dissident movement, it is important to recognize that the movement has developed a much broader popular base. As Amalrik has pointed out, the active involvement of scientists like Sakharov, Orlov, and many others is explained by the fact they are by profession accustomed to subjecting facile generalizations to empirical verification, and are most acutely aware of the chasm between the actual performance of the system and its official mythology.[5] In a different way, the creative writer has a direct professional stake in a more open Soviet society, since the pervasive censorship condemns him to silence and stifles originality. For these reasons, scientists and creative writers have been in the vanguard of the dissident movement, and their worldwide reputations have made it peculiarly difficult and costly for the regime to suppress them. But their vocal protests are only the tip of the iceberg.

It is also misleading to think of the dissident movement as being composed largely of Russian Jews demanding the right to emigrate to Israel. This impression has been deliberately fostered by the Soviet regime in its selection of Jewish dissidents for prosecution in some of the most widely publicized trials, as in the case of Anatoly

Shcharansky. In this way, the regime attempts to play on the latent anti-Semitism in Russian society and to imply that a disloyal allegiance to a foreign government on the part of a small minority is the primary motive for dissident activity. In reality, the "refusenik" movement of Russian Jews seeking to emigrate to Israel did not cooperate with other dissidents at first, in the belief that the would-be émigrés stood a better chance of receiving permission from the authorities to leave if they steered clear of general criticism of the regime. It was after the signing of the Helsinki Declaration, with its implied promise of freer emigration, that the refuseniks solidly identified themselves with the broader demand for human rights and cooperated with Orlov's Moscow Helsinki Group.[6]

The best evidence of the growing depth, breadth, and variety of dissent within Russia is contained in the proliferation of documents known as *samizdat*. Literally translated, the term means "self-publishing house." All written material published in the Soviet Union is subject to approval by the State Committee for the Press, and this censorship system is enforced by legally prohibiting to any private group or individual the possession or transfer of printing presses or any other technical means of duplication such as photocopiers or photocopy machines. Typewriters are available in limited numbers for conventional usages. All other forms of duplication require police permission. Therefore, anyone wishing to evade the censor must type his manuscript in as many copies as possible and then distribute the original copies secretly in the hope that they will be retyped again and again until the final extent of dissemination approximates that of printed works for sale in bookstores. The whole process is described as *samizdat*, and someone who engages in the illegal production or dissemination of this typed material is referred to as a *samizdatchik*.

Other similar terms to describe how Soviet dissidents have learned to use modern technology to evade the censor have come into common usage. Thus, forbidden works in the Russian language that have been secretly exfiltrated and then reimported from abroad are known as *tamizdat*, from the Russian word *tam*, meaning "over there." *Radizdat* is used to describe typed transcriptions of foreign radio broadcasts, and *magnitizdat* is used to refer to tape recordings of such broadcasts.[7] The successful exfiltration to the West of a single *samizdat* document through a foreign diplomat or journalist can now lead to its replay back into the Soviet Union by foreign radios, and to the taping of such broadcasts for further replay, until a mass audience of many millions is reached in a way that was impossible during Stalin's hermetic rule.

Since the Sinyavsky-Daniel trial in 1966, this underground literature has thrived on repression; and in spite of severe reprisals against individuals who participate in the production and dissemination of *samizdat*, it has flourished and grown over the years. The most complete collection of *samizdat* material undoubtedly reposes in the files of the KGB in Moscow, but of the thousands of *samizdat* documents that have reached the West, the fullest collection is the *Samizdat* Archive maintained by the Research Department of Radio Free Europe–Radio Liberty in Munich, Germany. Arranged roughly in chronological order of arrival, this is the record of what independent Soviet citizens have been saying to each other beyond the reach of official censorship and have been able to smuggle successfully to the West. In addition, the U.S. Congress, after the signing of the Helsinki Declaration, established the Commission on Security and Cooperation in Europe to monitor compliance with the agreement. Known as the Helsinki Commission and composed of representatives from the House, the Senate, and the executive branch, this commission, with its professional staff, has become a magnet for the flow of *samizdat;* its files now make available to scholars and journalists a growing collection of the more recent underground literature from both the Soviet Union and Eastern Europe.

Of all the *samizdat* documents, perhaps the single most impressive proof of the depth and variety of dissent within Russia is a bi-monthly journal, *A Chronicle of Current Events,* now widely available in English translation.[8] Its first issue appeared in 1968 with coverage of the statements of the young activists protesting the trial of Sinyavsky and Daniel. Since then, it has regularly been reaching the West in typewritten copies, except for intermittent periods during which KGB repression temporarily forced its suspension. Founded by the poet Natalya Gorbanevskaya with a group of friends, it took as its motto Article 19 of the Universal Declaration of Human Rights, which was signed by the Soviet Union, and states:

> Everyone has the right to freedom of opinion and expression; this right includes freedom to hold opinions without interfer-

ence and to seek, receive and impart information and ideas through any media and regardless of frontiers.

If there were an international Pulitzer Prize, this journal would deserve it. It is the sober and scrupulously accurate account of what has happened to all those groups and individuals who for more than a decade have tried to assert the right to freedom of expression. In spite of the arrest or exile of more than one hundred of its editors and correspondents, it has remained calmly factual and does not engage in anti-Soviet polemics. As the *Times Literary Supplement* pointed out in its review of the first forty-five issues of the *Chronicle*, it "has maintained an astonishing level of accuracy."[9] Only once has the KGB made a serious effort in a Soviet court to prove that it published "slanderous anti-Soviet fabrications" and that attempt was so embarrassingly unsuccessful that it has never been repeated—although despite the absence of proof, the editor then on trial, Sergei Kovalyov, a biologist, was given a ten-year sentence.

Focusing first on the trials of young cultural activists in Moscow and Leningrad, the *Chronicle* went on to record the conditions in the labor camps to which they were sent, and then covered extensively the evidence that false accusations of insanity were being used against dissidents in order to confine them to psychiatric hospitals as a way of avoiding the publicity of open trials. The *Chronicle* has covered the long struggle of the Crimean Tatars to regain their homeland from which they were forcibly evicted by Stalin, and awakened Russians for the first time to the cause of the Meskhetian people, who were similarly exiled from their ancestral lands in southern Georgia. In 1969, the *Chronicle* gave extensive coverage to a series of trials of Ukrainian democratic nationalists who continue to agitate for the right to learn and teach Ukrainian language and history; and these dissidents, with a broad popular following in the Ukraine, have gone on to found their own *samizdat* journal, modeled on the objective tone and factual accuracy of the *Chronicle*. Similarly, the *Chronicle* began to give increasing coverage to the emerging Jewish emigration movement and to reprint summaries of its *samizdat* publications.

In the period between 1970 and 1972, the *Chronicle* recorded a series of arrests and trials of nationalists demanding wider cultural

autonomy in Armenia, Estonia, Latvia, and Lithuania, and in Lithuania this protest developed into a mass movement strengthened by
its historical association with a Roman Catholic Church that increasingly opposed religious persecution. By 1973–74, editors of the
Chronicle had established accurate reporting sources among the
democratic nationalists in Georgia, who were protesting the regime's
suppression of their national culture. Also by this time, representatives of the approximately 2 million people of German extraction had
made contact with the *Chronicle,* and profiting from the example of
the Jewish emigration movement, they sought publicity for their
demand for freedom to emigrate by sending their petitions to the
editors of the *Chronicle.*

In response to foreign broadcasts quoting *samizdat* material first
published in the *Chronicle,* Russian religious groups demanding
freedom of worship next made contact with the editors. As a result,
a mass of new material appeared in the *Chronicle* documenting the
extent of the regime's religious persecution of individuals and whole
congregations. The first contacts were made by Russian Orthodox
and were followed in chronological order by Baptists, Catholics, Bud-
dhists, Georgian Orthodox, Pentecostalists, and Adventists. The
many millions of religious believers in the Soviet Union were beginning to find their voice, and to broaden the popular base of dissent
far beyond the limited literary circle in Moscow where the movement had its beginning.

After the signing of the Helsinki Declaration in 1975, the *Chronicle* recorded in detail the rise and savage repression of the movement led by Yuri Orlov to establish publicly identified Helsinki
groups to monitor Soviet compliance with the terms of the Declaration. Monitoring groups sprang up not only in Moscow but in the
Ukraine, Lithuania, Georgia, and Armenia. The *Chronicle* published
the long record of the regime's failure to implement the Helsinki
accords assembled by these watchdog committees, and recorded the
arrests and trials of the courageous individuals who dared publicly to
associate themselves with this effort to make the regime apply in
practice what it had legally undertaken to do by signing the Helsinki
agreement. The *Chronicle* has also regularly carried detailed reports
on the clashes with the authorities of writers and artists who have
sought to challenge the official censorship, and of workers who have
protested the repressive role of the official trade unions and de-

manded free labor unions to protect their rights and redress their grievances.

By publishing secret laws and KGB directives, the *Chronicle* has unmasked the machinery of repression, and its regular annotated bibliography of all *samizdat* known by it to be in circulation has provided indispensable documentation of the growing depth and breadth of the dissident movement. By abstaining from the advocacy of a particular political program and by confining itself to a general allegiance to the right to freedom of expression, the *Chronicle* has become the main clearinghouse and information center for all the varied tendencies within the democratic opposition. Through its wide readership in the Soviet Union, its significant influence upon opinion in Eastern Europe and in the West, and the reverberations it has set echoing through the mass Soviet audience that listens to foreign broadcasts, it has functioned as a sounding board and incipient civil liberties union, providing unity and coherence through the weight of its prestige and unblemished reputation for accuracy. In the words of one scholar, "The *Chronicle,* one might say, broke the enchanted circle which until then had condemned every Soviet dissident to be a voice crying in the desert."[10]

The achievement represented by the *Chronicle* is all the more remarkable when one considers the circumstances under which this *samizdat* journal and others like it have to be written and distributed. Recent Soviet émigrés who have participated in the dissemination of *samizdat* in the Moscow area have described the nature and extent of KGB harassment. The first method of KGB control is widespread and effective telephone tap coverage. The dissidents have learned to recognize that all the main telephone exchanges are tapped, but that coverage is not continuous over twenty-four-hour periods. Second, audio penetration by the KGB of apartments known to be occupied by dissidents is pervasive, through the secret emplacement of microphones in the walls and by "hot-miking" the telephones with a miniaturized device that transforms the telephone into a microphone capable of picking up conversations in the room when the receiver is on the hook. Mail is regularly opened by the KGB, and although care is taken to disguise this fact, the giveaway is the delay of three or four days that suspected dissidents encounter in receiving letters addressed to them. Finally, physical surveillance by teams of KGB plainclothes agents is employed to follow suspects when they leave their apartments.

On the basis of this extensive coverage, KGB counteraction proceeds from early warning to administrative harassment to police hooliganism. When an individual is first suspected by the KGB of receiving or disseminating *samizdat* material, the first step is usually a visit by a KGB officer to the suspect's home or office. The approach is initially low key, and the warning notice is conveyed in a tone that assumes the suspect does not know the seriousness of his offense. He is assured that he need only give up his activity to preserve a clean bill of political health and avoid a negative report in his KGB file. The most persuasive argument used by the KGB in this early stage against participation in dissident activity is the contention that the suspect is unknowingly cooperating with external enemies and foreign intelligence services who are accused of secretly funding the dissidents. Active dissidents are excoriated as "hirelings of the imperialists." This appeal to native patriotism is orchestrated in party seminars throughout the country, and it has a real impact on Great Russians, although it is apparently much less persuasive with national minority groups.

If the suspect persists, a second and more threatening "conversation" with a KGB officer takes place in which the price of continued forbidden activity is spelled out. The suspect is threatened with loss of his job or, if he is in a university, loss of student status and denial of his right to take examinations for his degree. He is warned that he may be evicted from his apartment, lose the right to live in the Moscow area, be denied permanently the chance to travel abroad; and the jobs of his dependents and close relatives are also threatened. If these warnings go unheeded, the suspect may find his apartment ransacked, and physical assault by KGB men disguised as street toughs is not unusual. The final stage of this harassment may be confinement in a psychiatric hospital under debilitating drug treatment or—if the dissident enjoys a world reputation as a writer or scientist—the final act may be forced expatriation, as in the case of Solzhenitsyn. It is important to realize that none of this administrative repression requires any legal finding of guilt in a court of law, that this whole range of punishment is within the competence of the KGB to administer, and that there is no effective legal recourse.

In spite of this continuous harassment, recent émigrés estimate that a floating population of about two hundred dissidents in the Moscow area and many more in the rest of the country continue to engage in the production and distribution of *samizdat*. Beyond this hard core, there appear to be more than two thousand active sympathizers in Moscow who are willing to help by supplying "neutral" apartments and other types of support. Then there is the much larger circle in Moscow and other cities of scientists, writers, bureaucrats, and students who eagerly seek out and read the dissident literature but who refrain from active participation because of fear of KGB reprisals. Finally, there is the large mass audience which listens regularly to the replay of *samizdat* material on the foreign radios broadcasting into the Soviet Union, both in Russian and, in the case of Radio Liberty, in the national minority languages. Short of a full-scale reversion to Stalinist terror, there is little the KGB can do about this large passive group that exists on the periphery of the dissident movement but whose sympathy and interest sustain the morale of the active dissidents.

In addition to administrative harassment by the KGB, the Soviet regime has at its disposal the weapon of judicial repression as a means of discouraging dissident activity. It is used more selectively and as a last resort. The high visibility of an open political trial such as that of Yuri Orlov has the advantage of eliminating the dissident from the scene for the duration of his long sentence. It serves as a warning to all that certain types of dissidence will not be tolerated and defines such behavior in legal terms as seditious. But there are disadvantages. The very fact of a public trial calls attention to the cause the dissident supports, and in the course of the presentation of the case against him, the regime has to acknowledge the extent of oppositional activity. Inevitably, *samizdat* versions of the in-camera court proceedings surface and generate a whole new wave of protest, as in the case of Sinyavsky and Daniel. By openly trying a prominent dissident, the regime risks transforming him into a martyr and giving him a public forum from which to defend his cause before the court of world opinion. For these reasons, the Soviet regime has vacillated in its resort to open trials, and has frequently experimented with "closed" trials held in out-of-the-way places, where the draconian sentence is announced for its deterrent effect on the general population but the court proceedings are kept secret.[11]

In dealing with the deep-rooted and growing dissent within their country, the Soviet leaders face a profound and unresolvable dilemma. Perceiving that the reforms introduced by Khrushchev were having a potentially destabilizing effect on the basic structure of the Communist one-party state, Brezhnev and his cohorts have attempted to stabilize a partially reformed post-Stalin dispensation. In so doing, they have been unable and unwilling to remove the basic cause of the dissent, which is their repression of civic, cultural, and religious freedom. In spite of the massive growth of Soviet military power, the moral authority of the regime leaks away. Elections that provide no real choice cannot confer legitimacy on the rulers in the Kremlin, and the official ideology which once commanded the allegiance of the revolutionary cadres can claim few true believers among the younger generation. The Kremlin has had to resort to a barely disguised appeal to xenophobic Russian nationalism; but this has limited response among the non-Russian national minority groups that now make up almost half the population, and it conflicts with the supranational pretensions of the ideology. Having learned to fear the double-bladed ax of Stalin's terror, which ended by decimating the leadership of the Communist Party itself, the Kremlin tries to keep the dissent within bounds without resorting to Stalin's most extreme methods, which if ruthlessly applied could destroy the dissident movement in the holocaust of a new concentration camp universe. But the administrative punishment of the KGB, and the periodic judicial repression of public trials, have the effect of transforming loyal critics of the regime into active dissidents, as the development of Sakharov's political thinking from 1968 to the present time dramatically demonstrates. Nothing can be more surely designed to stimulate determined opposition among men of courage and integrity than the demeaning attempts at intimidation that are the standard weapons of the KGB. As a consequence, after each new wave of ineffective repression, a new group of dissidents arises, more numerous and better organized than the one before and with a wider base of popular support.

This basic dilemma facing the Kremlin is made more acute by the interlocking relationship that exists between the dissident movement within the country and the even more active and better organized dissident movements that have sprung up in Poland and Czechoslovakia. They feed on each other and they influence each other. In contrast to the dissidents in the Soviet Union, Eastern Europe's dissidents have the powerful force of nationalism on their side, and in Poland the discreet but immensely influential support of the Roman Catholic Church. The interaction between events in the Soviet Union and in Eastern Europe can be traced back to the Sinyavsky-Daniel trial in 1966; and the leaders of the democratic movements in Poland and Czechoslovakia are very well aware of the fact that their eventual hope of liberalization depends on the ultimate success of the Soviet dissidents. In Czechoslovakia, the protests of the Moscow intelligentsia against the Sinyavsky trial were carried throughout the country by foreign radios; and these helped to fuel the first of the Dubcek reforms, which in turn encouraged the dissidents in the Soviet Union, who were then further politicized by the Soviet use of force to extinguish the Prague Spring. Orlov's establishment of Helsinki monitoring groups had an immediate echo in the formation of the Charter '77 movement in Czechoslovakia. In Poland, the Workers' Defense Committees established to protect the rights of workers arrested in the price riots of 1976 have blossomed into a political underground that is almost an alternative government, complete with its own printing presses and "flying university." A beleaguered Polish Communist regime, desperately dependent on a disciplined work force to meet its mounting economic problems, now faces a unified opposition that includes the major segments of Polish society: the Church, the students, the intelligentsia, and the workers. The election of a charismatic and politically astute Polish Pope has only sharpened Moscow's dilemma. The flowering of the democratic opposition in Poland encourages by its example the growth of dissent in the Soviet Union, but Soviet pressure on the Polish Communists to crack down could easily lead to mass revolt. The Soviet leaders could intervene with tanks to suppress a popular rebellion once again, but only at the cost of dangerously adding to the strength of their own internal dissidents.

In addition, evidence accumulates that the Soviet leaders face some very difficult economic choices in the decade of the eighties as the result of a confluence of unfavorable trends. A predictable drop in production in the Western Siberian oil fields means that the Soviet bloc will probably become a net importer of oil by 1982, losing as a consequence the hard currency they now earn from exported oil, and being forced instead to commit their foreign reserves to bidding against the West for scarce oil supplies. Shortfalls in coal and nuclear power production mean that there can be no quick solution in the substitution of other types of fuel. Meanwhile, adverse demographic trends foreshadow a decline in the increase in the working-age population from 2.3 million in 1978 to 300,000 per year in the mid-eighties. Because the growth of Soviet investment is slowing and productivity remains low, these shortages of energy and labor will inevitably generate sharp, competing pressures inside the Soviet bureaucracy.[12] To maintain the present high rate of military spending, the Soviet leaders may well be forced to reduce consumption levels. Rising economic discontent will add a powerful new argument to the dissidents' case against the present regime.

How the Soviet leaders will react to the deepening and many-faceted political and economic dilemmas that they have created for themselves is unpredictable; and their reaction will depend to some extent on whether the United States and its allies allow them to compensate for internal failure by external success. The Russian people are remarkably long-suffering, patient and slow to move against established authority. There are no signs yet that the basic stability of the regime is threatened, and no firm evidence of the close-working alliance between the intelligentsia and the workers that makes the opposition in Poland such a clear and present danger to party control. The party and military elite have much to gain from the continuation of a system that guarantees them so much arbitrary power and special economic privilege. By coopting into their ranks the most able and ambitious of the younger generation, they can hope to keep the vast bureaucracy moving with the momentum of its own weight, driven by the force of careerist ambition, and held together by the fear of KGB reprisals.

But if a united West bars the door to continued expansion abroad, the mounting internal pressures are likely to face the Soviet leadership with radical and difficult choices. They can either choose the road of liberalization advocated by the democratic dissidents, and at some real loss of their own power permit a more open society that allows cultural diversity and decentralized decision making. Or they can choose to impose an even more brutal dictatorship based on a fierce Slavophile nationalism. As Amalrik has warned, "A central role in this development would probably be played by the Armed Forces, helped by and allied with the extreme right-wing dissidents."[13] There is in fact in the dissident literature evidence of the existence

of a group of extreme Russian nationalists. The *samizdat* journal
Veche, named after the old Russian popular assembly and edited by
Vladimir Osipov, was an example of this unique trend in the other-
wise predominantly liberal and democratic dissident movement.[14]

Is there anything that the West, and particularly the United States,
can do to help the democratic dissidents beyond standing firmly and
consistently against the outward expansionary thrust of the present
Soviet regime? On this point, the dissidents themselves are in the
best position to judge. They are unanimous in their conviction that
President Carter's initial emphasis on human rights and his public
criticism of violations by the Soviets were very much to their net
advantage. Although the world attention generated by Carter's
stand did not protect individual dissidents like Orlov from prison
sentences, the publicity given to their cause both inside and outside
the Soviet Union far outweighed in their minds the temporary effect
of a new wave of repression. They clearly hope for nonprovocative
but steady public support from the American administration for the
human rights of Soviet and Eastern European dissidents. As one of
them advised, the United States "must not let itself be swayed either
by the current reactions of the Soviet regime or by the discomfiture
and alarm of its West European allies, or indeed by public opinion,
which fails to understand that the Soviet regime is not going to
change its policies, mildly or drastically, overnight."[15] If anything,
the Soviet dissidents are critical of Carter for not having been more
consistently outspoken on this theme.

A second tangible form of assistance from the West for which the
dissidents are unanimously grateful and on which they will rely heavily in the future is Russian and minority language broadcasting by
Western radios. The central role of foreign broadcasting in breaking
the Soviet monopoly control of information has been described in an
earlier chapter, and it does not need reemphasis here. The U.S.
Congress needs to be more generous in its provision of funds both to
the Voice of America and to the now merged Radio Free Europe and
Radio Liberty Committee, and these additional funds will truly be
bread upon the waters. Then there are the protests of private American individuals and organizations against particularly egregious acts
of repression by the Soviet authorities. The organized boycott by a
large body of American scientists of international conferences scheduled to be held in Moscow, in protest against the harsh sentencing

of Yuri Orlov, was particularly effective in bringing home to Soviet scientists the isolation forced upon them by the regime's policies. Similarly, the international protests of psychiatric associations in the West against the use of false accusations of insanity as a punitive weapon raised the price for the regime of such methods. Direct forms of pressure, such as the Jackson amendment to the 1974 Trade Act making most-favored-nation status dependent on a freer Soviet emigration policy, have been criticized as damaging to détente; but it is interesting to note that the Soviets have in fact increased the flow of Jewish emigration while protesting that they would never give in to such pressures.

There is also the crucial role of the American media. Objective and in-depth Western reporting on the dissident movement and the measures used to repress it is highly valued by the dissidents, and American journalists in the Soviet Union have played a courageous part both in documenting the history of the movement and in exfiltrating key *samizdat* material. It is most important that American newspaper publishers refuse to give in to regime pressures designed to force them to restrict the scope and activity of their correspondents by threatening to close down their Moscow bureaus. American academicians must be more careful than a few of them have been to avoid downplaying defects of the regime in their scholarly work because of their fear of losing their right to visit the Soviet Union in the future. There is a subtle form of blackmail involved here, in which the visiting American scholar is made to feel that the renewal of his visa and his future access to primary sources are dependent on his willingness to mute direct or implied criticism of the regime.

Finally, there is the sensitive question of what role, if any, American intelligence should play in relation to the dissident movement. Clearly, it is a primary responsibility of CIA's analysts dealing with Soviet affairs to follow dissident developments closely, and to reach an accurate evaluation of the strengths and weaknesses of the democratic opposition. The flood of *samizdat* now regularly reaching the West provides the primary source material for understanding the different trends within the dissident movement, and the testimony of active dissidents who have escaped to the West has added a wealth of additional detail. Within the Soviet Union, however, the leading dissidents have kept themselves scrupulously clear of any connection with foreign intelligence agencies in order to deny to the regime the

ability to prove its allegations that they are "hirelings of the imperialists." There is also the practical consideration that the proliferation
by the KGB of double-agent provocations makes it extraordinarily
dangerous for dissidents to have any contact with those who purport
to be in touch with Western intelligence. Similarly, any attempt by
American intelligence to channel funds secretly to the dissident
movement would be quickly discovered because of close KGB surveillance, and would give the Soviet regime a propaganda bonanza
in its effort to convince the Soviet public that all dissidents are working for hostile intelligence services. The dissidents are running their
own show, and although there have been attempts by KGB double
agents to prove involvement with foreign intelligence, no dissident
leader has been found to have such connections. The best thing that
American intelligence can do is to watch the progress of the dissidents from a distance with careful and sympathetic attention.

Whether or not the attempt of the dissident movement to liberal-
ize Soviet society eventually succeeds, the United States has no alternative in dealing with the current regime in the Kremlin but to
preserve the military balance, maintain our alliance systems in good
repair, and prevent further slippage of third world countries into the
Soviet orbit. An effective and well-managed American intelligence
organization is indispensable in the pursuit of this policy. In the
immediate future, the best we can hope for in our relations with the
Soviet state is a condition of competitive coexistence. "Détente" was
always a misleading word to describe this relationship, since it implies a real relaxation of tensions and the possibility of genuine rapprochement. As Henry Kissinger is now among the first to point out,
his earlier hopes that the Soviets would be willing to settle for military parity have not been borne out by events, and his expectation
that Soviet behavior could be modified by entangling them in a web
of mutual economic dependency has proved illusory. What remains
of détente is the realistic necessity of agreeing on those matters
where there is a genuine identity of interest arising out of the fact
that coexistence for both sides on this planet is preferable to the
mutual destruction of nuclear war.

Such matters are few in number but important. Both sides have an
interest in setting limits to the arms race, insofar as external means
of verification permit reliable monitoring of an equitable agreement.

Second, both nations share a concern over the proliferation of nuclear weapons and have a mutual interest in restricting the spread of atomic bomb technology to countries that have not yet acquired this capacity. It is to the advantage of both to reach agreement on procedural arrangements, such as the hot line between Washington and Moscow, that limit the danger of nuclear war by accident or miscalculation. Finally, trade agreements can be mutually beneficial provided they are carefully negotiated so as not to be more to the advantage of one side than the other. So long as the closed Soviet state persists in its present form, we can realistically expect no more than this from a condition of competitive coexistence and must be prepared to resist a predictable and continuing attempt by the Soviets to upset the military balance and to score geopolitical advances in the third world.

It so happens that the firm defense posture and active foreign policy that are essential to our national survival are identical to the policies urged upon us by the advocates of liberalization within the Soviet Union as essential to the success of their efforts. We cannot predict the outcome of their continuing internal struggle to create a more open society, but it will be long and difficult. It will be decided by forces in the Soviet Union over which we have little influence. It is essential that we be quick to recognize any substantial reform when it occurs and make clear in advance that we are prepared to negotiate far-reaching disarmament agreements with a Soviet government that permits freedom of access to information, freedom to travel and to emigrate, and freedom from arbitrary arrest and imprisonment. Under such liberalized conditions, random on-site international inspection would be feasible and the risks of agreed reductions of both strategic and conventional weaponry much reduced.

If and when the advocates of democratic reform within the Soviet Union succeed, we can look forward also to the day when the repressed Eastern European peoples are allowed to choose their own political leadership freely. The differing schools of democratic dissident opinion in the Soviet Union are unanimous in their conviction that the Soviet imposition by force of Communist rule in Eastern Europe must come to an end, and the democratic opposition in that region would move quickly to take over, once the threat of the Soviet army is withdrawn. Many forms of international cooperation about which now we can only dream would then become possible to make this a safer and more prosperous world. Once again the construction of a world legal order to replace the anarchy of competing nation-states would appear on the agenda of farsighted and practical statesmen, and what seemed briefly possible after World War II would have a second chance.

Appendix

CENTRAL INTELLIGENCE AGENCY
WASHINGTON, D.C. 20505

OFFICE OF THE DIRECTOR

9 May 1973

MEMORANDUM FOR ALL CIA EMPLOYEES

1. Recent press reports outline in detail certain alleged CIA activities with respect to Mr. Howard Hunt and other parties. The presently known facts behind these stories are those stated in the attached draft of a statement I will be making to the Senate Committee on Appropriations on 9 May. As can be seen, the Agency provided limited assistance in response to a request by senior officials. The Agency has cooperated with and made available to the appropriate law enforcement bodies information about these activities and will continue to do so.

2. All CIA employees should understand my attitude on this type of issue. I shall do everything in my power to confine CIA activities to those which fall within a strict interpretation of its legislative charter. I take this position because I am determined that the law shall be respected and because this is the best way to foster the legitimate and necessary contributions we in CIA can make to the national security of the United States.

3. I am taking several actions to implement this objective:

I have ordered all senior operating officials of this Agency to report to me immediately on any activities now going on, or that have gone on in the past, which might be construed to be outside the legislative charter of this Agency.

I hereby direct every person presently employed by CIA to report to me on any such activities of which he has knowledge. I invite all ex-employees to do the same. Anyone who has such information should call my secretary (extension 6363) and say that he wishes to talk to me about "activities outside CIA's charter."

4. To ensure that Agency activities are proper in the future, I hereby promulgate the following standing order for all CIA employees:

Any CIA employee who believes that he has received instructions which in any way appear inconsistent with the CIA legislative charter shall inform the Director of Central Intelligence immediately.

/signed/

James R. Schlesinger
Director

Notes

CHAPTER 2: Waves of Darkness

1. Cord Meyer, "Waves of Darkness," in *"The Secret Sharer" and Other Great Stories,* ed. Abraham H. Lass and Norma L. Tasman (New York: New American Library, 1969), pp. 11–30.

CHAPTER 3: Peacemaking

1. Allen Weinstein, *Perjury: The Hiss-Chambers Case* (New York: Knopf, 1978).
2. Cord Meyer, "A Service Man Looks at the Peace," *Atlantic Monthly* (September 1945), pp. 43–48.
3. Henry L. Stimson and McGeorge Bundy, *On Active Service in Peace and War* (New York: Harper, 1948), p. 636.
4. See *New York Times,* 16 June 1946, p. 26, for a report on this convention.

CHAPTER 4: Secret Trial

1. U. S. Congress, Senate Select Committee to Study Governmental Operations with Respect to Intelligence Activities, *Supplementary Detailed Staff Reports on Foreign and Military Intelligence, Book IV,* 94th Congress, 2d sess., Report No. 94-755, Final Report, pp. 31–32.
2. See Senate, Final Report, *Book I,* p. 154.
3. See Senate, Final Report, *Book IV,* p. 38. The Directorate for Plans was established in August 1952 as an organizational entity that included in one clandestine service the functions of secret intelligence collection, counterintelligence, and covert action.
4. CIA Personnel Regulation No. 20-730, 27 May 1953.
5. Allen Weinstein, *Perjury: The Hiss-Chambers Case* (New York: Knopf, 1978).
6. See U.S. Supreme Court, *Greene* v. *McElroy,* 360 U.S. 474, 1959.

CHAPTER 5: Cold War

1. *National Security Council Directive 5412* (15 March 1954).
2. Marcus Raskin, "A Short Account of International Student Politics and the Cold War with Particular Reference to the NSA, CIA, etc.," *Ramparts* (March 1967), pp. 29–39.
3. U.S. Congress, Senate Select Committee to Study Governmental Operations with Respect to Intelligence Activities, *Supplementary Detailed Staff Reports on Foreign and Military Intelligence, Book I,* 94th Congress, 2d sess., Report No. 94-755, Final Report, p. 184.
4. *New York Times,* 15 February 1967, p. 19.
5. *New York Times,* 11 August 1964, p. 6.
6. *New York Times,* 22 February 1967, p. 17.
7. *ADA World,* September–October 1968, p. 23.
8. *New York Times,* 23 February 1967, p. 25.
9. Congressional Record, 16 February 1967, p. 3517.
10. *New York Times,* 30 March 1967, p. 30.
11. *New York Times Magazine,* January 1973.

12. *Sunday Times*, London, 15 June 1975.
13. Alex Mitchell, *Village Voice*, 28 April 1975, pp. 6–7.
14. See Senate, Final Report, *Book I*, p. 186.
15. Letter to President Johnson, 24 March 1967, released as the Katzenbach Committee Report, 29 March 1967.
16. See Senate, Final Report, *Book I*, p. 187.
17. Ibid.
18. Ibid, p. 188.
19. Georgi Dimitrov, "Speech at Seventh World Congress of the Communist International" (2 August 1935).
20. Philip Selznick, *The Organizational Weapon* (Santa Monica, Calif.: Rand Corp., 1952), pp. 113–170.
21. See Senate, Final Report, *Book I*, p. 184.

CHAPTER 6: The Radios

1. *Washington Post*, 24 January 1971, p. A–2.
2. Robert T. Holt, *Radio Free Europe* (Minneapolis: University of Minnesota Press, 1958), p. 10.
3. Allan A. Michie, *Voices Through the Iron Curtain* (New York: Dodd, Mead, 1963), p. 13.
4. *Washington Post*, 3 April 1972, p. A–17.
5. Michie, *Voices*, pp. 277–85.
6. Telegram from Nagy to the Secretary General of the United Nations, 1 November 1956. United Nations Document A/3251, 1 November 1956.
7. Michie, *Voices*, p. 249.
8. Ibid., p. 266.
9. Pavel Tigrid, *Why Dubcek Fell* (London: MacDonald, 1971), pp. 99–102.
10. Facts on File. *Yearbook 1971*, Vol. XXXI, p. 386.
11. *Washington Post*, 25 May 1971, p. A–3.
12. PL 92-94, 30 March 1972.
13. PL 93-129, approved 19 October 1973.
14. Abraham Brumberg, "A Conversation with Andrei Amalrik," *Encounter* (June 1977).

CHAPTER 8: The Agency Under Fire

1. David Frost's interview°with former CIA Director Richard Helms, May 22, 1978, transcribed in full by the North American Reporting service for the National Broadcasting Company.

2. William Colby, *Honorable Men* (New York: Simon and Schuster, 1978), pp. 320–21.

3. H. R. Haldeman, *The Ends of Power* (New York: New York Times Books, 1978), p. 34.

4. Ibid., p. 160.

5. "Animals in the Forest," *Time* (11 February 1974), p. 26.

6. See Rockefeller Commission Report, June 1975, pp. 194–95.

7. U.S. Congress, Senate Select Committee to Study Governmental Operations with Respect to Intelligence Activities, *Supplementary Detailed Staff Reports on Foreign and Military Intelligence, Book I,* 94th Congress, 2d sess., Report No. 94-755, Final Report, p. 608.

8. Vernon A. Walters, *Silent Missions* (New York: Doubleday, 1978), pp. 592–95.

9. Frost interview with Helms, pp. 29–30.

10. Walters, *Silent Missions,* p. 624.

11. *New York Times,* 22 December 1972, p. 1.

12. Colby, pp. 327–35.

13. Walters, *Silent Missions,* p. 604.

14. Colby, p. 332.

15. U.S. Congress, Report of the Special Subcommittee on Intelligence of the House Committee on Armed Services, 93d Cong., 1st sess., 23 October 1973, p. 22.

16. "Memorandum to All CIA Employees," 9 May 1973, signed by James R. Schlesinger, Director.

17. Colby, pp. 340, 345.

18. Ibid., pp. 334–35.

19. Department of Justice, Press Release, AG 202-739-2028, 14 January 1977.

20. Ibid., p. 3.

21. Ibid., p. 10.

22. Colby, pp. 345, 349.

CHAPTER 9: London Assignment: Coping with Watergate and Chile

1. *The Times,* London, 18 January 1974, p. 1.
2. Ibid.
3. *International Herald Tribune,* 30 January 1974.
4. *The Times,* London, 25 January 1974.
5. *Daily Telegraph,* 25 January 1974.
6. *Guardian,* 23 January 1974.
7. *New Statesman,* 25 January 1974.
8. *Guardian,* 14 January 1974. Article by Simon Winchester.
9. *New York Times,* 7 September 1974, pp. 1, 26.
10. "Covert Action in Chile 1963–73." Staff Report of the Select Committee, 94th Cong., 1st sess., Washington, D.C.: U.S. Government Printing Office, 1975.
11. U.S. Congress, Senate Select Committee to Study Governmental Operations with Respect to Intelligence Activities, *Supplementary Detailed Staff Reports on Foreign and Military Intelligence, Book I,* 94th Congress, 2d sess., Report No. 94-755, Final Report, pp. 575–85.
12. Regis Debray, *Conversations with Allende* (NLB, Carlisle Street, London W1, 1971), p. 119.
13. *El Mercurio,* Santiago, 23 August 1973.
14. Senate, Final Report, *Book I,* p. 579.
15. Staff Report, "Covert Action in Chile," pp. 14–15.
16. Ibid., p. 52.
17. Ibid., pp. 57–62.
18. Ibid., pp. 16–17.
19. Ibid., pp. 42–43.
20. Ibid., p. 21.
21. *Washington Post,* 26 May 1977, p. A–12.
22. Richard Nixon, *Memoirs* (New York: Grosset and Dunlap, 1978), pp. 489–90.
23. David Frost's interview with former CIA Director Richard Helms, May 22, 1978, transcribed in full by the North American Reporting service for the National Broadcasting Company, p. 109.

24. U.S. Congress, Senate Select Committee to Study Governmental Operations, *Alleged Assassination Plots Involving Foreign Leaders,* 94th Cong., 1st sess., Report No. 94-465, 20 November 1975, p. 222.

25. Ibid., p. 245.

26. Ibid., pp. 243–244.

27. Staff Report, "Covert Action in Chile," p. 28.

28. Ibid., p. 32.

29. Alain Labrousse, *L'Expérience chilienne* (Paris: Senil, 1972), p. 262.

30. Staff Report, "Covert Action in Chile," p. 31.

31. *International Herald Tribune,* 1 December 1975.

32. *World Marxist Review,* No. 6, June 1974.

33. *Questions of Soviet Communist Party History,* No. 5, 1974.

34. Foreign Assistance Act of 1971, Section 662, as amended, December 1974.

35. U.S. District Court of the District of Columbia, *U.S.A.* v. *Helms,* Criminal No. 77-650, 4 November 1977.

36. "CIA and Activities of ITT," 6 March 1973, Senate Committee on Foreign Relations Report of Proceedings, p. 28.

37. "Personal Statement of Richard Helms," submitted to Judge Parker on 1 November 1977, p. 3.

38. "I say Helms was right to hold back," Eugene D. McCarthy, *Washington Star,* 13 November 1977.

39. William Colby, *Honorable Men* (New York: Simon and Schuster, 1978), pp. 379–87.

CHAPTER 10: The Family Jewels

1. *Financial Times,* London, 10 January 1975.

2. Edward Jay Epstein, "The War Within the CIA," *Commentary* (August 1978), pp. 35–39. See also exchange of letters between Colby and Epstein, *Commentary* (October 1978), p. 4.

3. William Colby, *Honorable Men* (New York: Simon and Schuster, 1978), pp. 387–97.

4. Epstein letter, *Commentary* (October 1978), p. 4.

5. Colby, p. 394.

6. "The Angleton Story," *New York Times Magazine* (25 June 1978), p. 73.
7. Press release by the Department of Justice, January 14, 1977, p. 1.
8. Ibid., p. 11.
9. Ibid., p. 47.
10. U.S. Congress, Senate Select Committee to Study Governmental Operations with Respect to Intelligence Activities, *Intelligence Activities and the Rights of Americans, Book II,* 94th Congress, 2d sess., Report No. 94-755, Final Report, p. 103.
11. Report to the President by the Commission on CIA Activities Within the United States, June 1975, pp. 130–50.
12. Senate, Final Report, *Book II,* pp. 99–102.
13. Rockefeller Commission Report, p. 132.
14. Ibid., p. 136.
15. Colby, p. 316.
16. Ibid., pp. 409–10; article by Dan Schorr, *Palm Beach Post-Times* (27 November 1977), p. D–4.
17. U.S. Congress, Senate, *Alleged Assassination Plots,* 94th Cong., 1st sess., Report No. 94-465, 20 November 1975.
18. Ibid., pp. 19, 256.
19. Ibid., p. 263.
20. Ibid.
21. Ibid., pp. 37–40.
22. *The Times,* 25 November 1975.
23. *Voice of the People,* London, Vol. 4, No. 5, January 1976.

CHAPTER 11: The Soviet Challenge

1. "A Dollar's Cost Comparison of Soviet and U.S. Defense Activities," SR 78-10002, January 1978.
   "Estimated Soviet Defense Spending: Trends and Prospects," SR 78-10121, June 1978.
   "A Dollar Cost Comparison of Soviet and U.S. Defense Activities, 1968–78," SR 79-10004, January 1979.
2. "Department of Defense, Annual Report, Fiscal Year 1980," Harold Brown, Secretary of Defense, 25 January 1979, pp. 80–81.

3. "Is America Becoming Number 2?" Committee on the Present Danger, Washington, D.C. Table 3, p. 7.
4. "Department of Defense, Annual Report, FY 1980," p. 68.
5. Ibid., p. 80.
6. "Soviet Civil Defense," Director of Central Intelligence, NI 78-10003, 1 July 1978.
7. Press Conference by Secretary of Defense Harold Brown, *Washington Post*, 5 October 1977, p. A-2.

CHAPTER 12: The New Geopolitical Offensive

1. *International Affairs*, Moscow, No. 3, 1963, pp. 116-17.
2. Gabriel García Márquez, "Cuba in Africa," *Washington Post*, 12 January 1977, p. A-12.
3. John Stockwell, *In Search of Enemies* (New York: W. W. Norton, 1978), pp. 138-56.
4. Seymour Hersh, *New York Times*, 19 December 1975, pp. 1, 14.
5. Nathaniel Davis, "The Angola Decision of 1975," *Foreign Affairs* (Fall 1978), pp. 109-24.
6. John A. Marcum, "Lessons of Angola," *Foreign Affairs*, Vol. 54 (April 1976), pp. 407-25.
7. *New York Times*, 10 January 1976, p. 24.
8. Senate, Committee on Foreign Affairs, Testimony of the Secretary of State before the Subcommittee on Africa, 94th Cong., 2d. sess., 29 January 1976.
9. Stockwell, pp. 206-7.
10. Gabriel García Márquez, *Washington Post*, 10 January 1977, p. 14; 12 January 1977, p. 12.
11. Gabriel García Márquez, *Washington Post*, 12 January 1977, p. 12.
12. Cord Meyer, "Cubans Trying to Keep Pledge to Katangans," *The Oregonian*, 9 June 1978.
13. Stockwell, p. 151.
14. Ibid., p. 186.
15. Ibid. pp. 235-36.
16. Charles B. MacLaine, *Soviet Strategies in Southeast Asia* (Princeton, N. J.: Princeton University Press, 1966), p. 24.
17. Radio Moscow, *TASS* in English, 6 June 1975.

18. London *Daily Telegraph*, 4 October 1976.
19. Cord Meyer, "Set for a Showdown on the CIA Charter," *Richmond Times-Dispatch*, 17 November 1978.
20. Cord Meyer, "Shock Waves in Asia," *Chicago Sun-Times*, 6 May 1978, p. 28.
21. Cord Meyer, "The Soviet War Against Afghan Self-Rule," *Washington Star*, 24 December 1979.
22. Cord Meyer, "Soviet Vise Closes on Persian Gulf Oil," *New Orleans Times-Picayune*, 1 July 1978.
23. Cord Meyer, "Soviet Intervention in Iran Crisis Rises," *New Orleans Times-Picayune*, 12 January 1979.
24. Cord Meyer, "The Kremlin's Work in Iran," *Washington Star*, 10 February 1979.
25. Cord Meyer, "Proxy Blitzkrieg in Southeast Asia," *Richmond Times-Dispatch*, 19 January 1979.

CHAPTER 13: The Soviet Apparat: Government

1. "The Strategic Intentions of the Soviet Union," *Report of the Institute for the Study of Conflict, London*, March 1978, p. 15.
2. U.S. Congress, House Committee on International Relations, *The Soviet Union in the Third World*, 95th Cong., 2d sess., 8 May 1977.
3. Central Intelligence Agency, *Communist Aid to the Less Developed Countries of the Free World, 1976*, ER 77-10296, August 1977.
4. Central Intelligence Agency, *Arms Flows to LDCs*, ER 78-10494U, November 1978, p. ii.
5. Mark E. Miller, "The Role of Western Technology in Soviet Strategy," *ORBIS*, Vol. 22, No. 3 (Fall 1978), pp. 539–68.
6. *London Financial Times*, 18 January 1977.
7. Cord Meyer, "Kremlin's Fears Harden Outlook," *New Orleans Times-Picayune*, 16 June 1978.
8. Andrei Amalrik, "A Conversation with Andrei Amalrik," *Encounter* (June 1977), p. 36.
9. "Strategic Intentions of the Soviet Union," p. 13.
10. Ibid., p. 14.

CHAPTER 14: The Soviet Apparat: KGB

1. John Barron, *KGB* (New York: Reader's Digest Press, 1974), pp. 70–90.
2. Ibid., pp. 80–85.
3. Claire Sterling and Michael Ledeen, "Italy's Russian Sugar Daddies," *New Republic* (3 April 1976), pp. 16–21.
4. Ladislav Bittman, *The Deception Game* (Syracuse University Research Corporation, 1972), p. 5.
5. Ibid., pp. 123–66.
6. Ibid., pp. 100–106.
7. House Intelligence Committee, *The Forgery Offensive*, February 1979.
8. Carl Gershman, "Selling Them the Rope," *Commentary*, Vol. 67, No. 4 (April 1979), p. 45.
9. *New York Times*, 27 April 1979, p. 1; Robert Lindsey, *The Falcon and the Snowman* (New York: Simon and Schuster, 1979).
10. Cord Meyer, "CIA Must Explain Kampiles Breach," *Baltimore Evening Sun*, 5 September 1978, p. 11.

CHAPTER 15: American Foreign Policy—The Need for a New Consensus

1. David S. Sullivan, "The Legacy of SALT I," *Strategic Review* (Winter 1978).
2. George F. Kennan, *The Cloud of Danger* (Boston: Atlantic–Little, Brown, 1977), p. 40.
3. Ibid., p. 229.
4. Edward N. Luttwak, "The Strange Case of George F. Kennan," *Commentary* (November 1977), p. 30.

CHAPTER 16: The Role of "Finished" Intelligence

1. Ray S. Cline, *Secrets, Spies and Scholars* (Washington, D.C.: Acropolis Books Ltd., 1976), pp. 89–97.
2. William T. Lee, "Understanding the Soviet Military Threat—How CIA Estimates Went Astray," National Strategy Informa-

tion Center, Inc., New York. Agenda Paper No. 6, 1977.

3. "The CIA Report the President Doesn't Want You to Read," *Village Voice*. A 24-page special supplement, 16 February 1976.

4. Thomas L. Hughes, "The Fate of Facts in a World of Men," *Foreign Policy Association Headline Series*, No. 233, December 1976.

CHAPTER 17: The Collectors

1. Ray S. Cline, *Secrets, Spies and Scholars* (Washington, D.C.: Acropolis Books Ltd., 1976), p. 12.

2. Herbert Scoville, Jr., "Is Espionage Necessary for Our Security?" *Foreign Affairs*, Vol. 54, No. 3 (April 1976), pp. 482–95.

3. Robert Lindsey, *The Falcon and the Snowman* (New York: Simon and Schuster, 1979).

4. Nicholas Daniloff, "How We Spy on the Russians," *Washington Post Magazine* (9 December 1979), pp. 33–34.

5. Harry Rositzke, *CIA's Secret Operations* (New York: Reader's Digest Press, 1977), pp. 69–71.

6. Edward Jay Epstein, *Legend: The Secret World of Lee Harvey Oswald* (New York: Reader's Digest Press, 1978).

7. Robert Kupperman and Darrel Trent, *Terrorism* (Hoover Institution, Stanford University, 1979), pp. 140–60.

8. Section 662 of the Foreign Assistance Act of 1961, as amended in December 1974.

9. Henry Kissinger, *The Economist*, London (10 February 1979), p. 32.

10. U.S. Congress, S. 2525, 95th Congress, 2d session, 9 February 1978.

CHAPTER 18: A Hope for the Future

1. Andrei Sakharov, *Alarm and Hope* (New York: Khronika Press, 1977).

2. Abraham Brumberg, "A Conversation with Andrei Amalrik," *Encounter* (June 1977), p. 35.

3. Sakharov, *Alarm and Hope.*

4. Abraham Brumberg, "Dissent in Russia," *Foreign Affairs* (July 1974), pp. 781–98.
5. See also Valentin Turchin, "Scientists Among Soviet Dissidents," *Survey*, Vol. 23, No. 4, p. 86.
6. Ludmilla Alexeyeva, "The Human Rights Movement in the USSR," *Survey*, Vol. 23, No. 4, pp. 77–78.
7. F. J. M. Feldbrugge, *Samizdat and Political Dissent in the Soviet Union* (Leyden: A. W. Sijthoff, 1975), p. 4.
8. *A Chronicle of Current Events*, Numbers 1–45, Amnesty International (distributed by Routledge Journals, London), 1978.
9. Peter Reddaway, "Notes from Underground," *Times Literary Supplement* (London, 16 June 1978).
10. F. J. M. Feldbrugge, *Samizdat*, p. 107.
11. Robert Sharlet, "Dissent and Repression in the Soviet Union and East Europe," *International Journal* (Fall 1978).
12. DCI Testimony before the Subcommittee on Priorities and Economy in Government of the Joint Economic Committee, Congress of the U.S., 96th Congress, 26 June 1979.
13. Abraham Brumberg, "A Conversation with Andrei Amalrik," p. 36.
14. F. J. M. Feldbrugge, *Samizdat*, p. 51.
15. Abraham Brumberg, "A Conversation with Andrei Amalrik," p. 39.

Index

answ mailed 9·20·84

The Directors
cordially request your company
at the Seventh Anniversary Dinner of
The Pumpkin Papers Irregulars

with an address by
William J. Casey
Director, Central Intelligence Agency

to be held at

The International Club
1800 K Street N.W., Washington D.C.
on Wednesday, October 31st, 1984

6:30 PM   No-Host Cocktails
7:30 PM   Dinner

RSVP by October 24th to Joseph B. Durra,
400 Pacific Ave., San Francisco, CA 94133
(Tel. 415-398-4420)